UNDERGROUND
FROM DEADBEAT TO DEAN

Underground
from Deadbeat to Dean
A Memoir

Peter McDonald

LIBRARY JUICE PRESS
SACRAMENTO, CA

Copyright 2021

Published in 2022 by Library Juice Press

Library Juice Press
PO Box 188784
Sacramento, CA 95822

http://libraryjuicepress.com/

This book is printed on acid-free paper.

Note to catalogers: We ask that you not use the Library of Congress' CIP record for this book, which you might find in WorldCat. It contains an erroneous subject heading (Peter McDonald is not Hispanic), and the LoC has not responded to our multiple communications requesting a correction. This is frustrating, so we are keeping our eyes open for an alternative to the CIP program. If you represent an institution that would be interested in receiving our books and creating original catalog records for them, we would like to discuss ideas with you. Thank you for your attention. We hope you enjoy reading about Peter McDonald's remarkable life...

Contents

Preface	1
Chapter 1 - Childhood	5
Chapter 2 - Like Life Without Parole	47
Chapter 3 - Adulthood	77
Chapter 4 - Mixcoatl—The Cloud Serpent Is Angry	119
Chapter 5 - Dudley Do-Right to the Rescue	175
Chapter 6 - You Call This a Career?	213
Chapter 7 - Like the Golden Toad—Sit and Do Nothing	239
Chapter 8 - Real Career Daze	277
Chapter 9 - Westward with the Joads	371
Chapter 10 - The Grief of the World	397
Index	439

Preface

The night I pulled Iggy Pop's head out of the toilet, I knew beyond certainty there had to be a better way to make a living than running punk clubs for a pittance. Iggy had arrived drunk at the Club Vogue in Seattle at about 10pm, with a girl I fancied on his arm. He was clearly inebriated. I let him and his date in for free. That was a mistake. He barged through the crowd, tried to leap onto to the stage during another band's set, lunged to grab the lead singer's microphone, but managed only to careen back into the mosh pit where all the other two-bit wankers were too drunk to catch him. Thud. I literally dragged the sad lunk like a sack of potatoes into the men's room. It stank of pee and cooked heroin spoons, as I heaved the rock icon into a stall to wretch his guts out. The gash on Mr. Pop's forehead bled like a stuck pig. This was remotely interesting as a lifestyle, how? I literally asked myself that as I stood there glumly, the band on stage still thundering a punk anthem despite the ruckus.

Thud indeed. Because that is what my life felt like then. I was thirty-four years old, living hand-to-mouth in a night world of kinky sexual identities, too many drugs, rock prima donnas, and ear-splitting power chords. On a good night, I skimmed $100 to take home. Some nights I could hardly pay the bands. My father kept at me to go to library school. "Make something of yourself," he said. But even as I tired of being an indigent rock promoter, the idea of a staid career, in librarianship of all things, filled me with a sense of bleak panic.

Thirty-four years later, I confessed to my publisher when we discussed the book deal over lunch, that I wasn't sure I'd ever actually read a memoir. I have avoided the popular sort of tell-all memoir all my life. One Merriam-Webster definition of a memoir says it is "an essay on a learned subject." I like to think that, over thirty hard-fought years to becoming a library dean at a large university, I managed somehow to learn a thing or two. In the truest sense, this is perhaps not a memoir, as it spans the better part of a lifetime. Yet it isn't an autobiography, either. What I've aimed to achieve is a narrative that strings together sagas of my undomesticated life to show how what may pass for the content of my character was formed in a patchwork of strange and wonderful experiences. From a childhood in the languid tropics, to LSD with Eric Clapton, to draft dodging up in Canada, to living the hermit's life in Alaska, then years of being a marginal rock promoter drinking with Sid Vicious, to finally landing in library school, each leap was a formative if quirky choice. That last leap culminated in an academic deanship for ten years. In writing these tales of hijinks and hacking it, it is clear that I dedicated half of my life to being an outcast bohemian, which in practical terms makes little financial sense. I suppose if through artistry or antics you manage to commit yourself single-mindedly to becoming famous as a bohemian, think of Keith Richards or the Kardashians, it may somehow work, but for the rest of us it's a wild spiral down to penury. I never much cared for being famous anyway, as it seems like such a bothersome burden.

I recently came across a passage by Carl Jung which seemed as close to a guiding principle for this book as I've found. In his wonderful "memoir," *Memories, Dreams, Reflections* (Pantheon, 1963), he writes in his prologue: "Thus it is that I have now undertaken...to tell my personal myth. I can only make direct statements, only 'tell stories.' Whether or not the stories are 'true' is not the problem. The only question is whether what I tell is *my* fable, *my* truth."

Sounds about right. I have tried to write the facts as I remember them in this narrative, but sadly, like the night with Iggy in the toilet stall, all the people I contacted who were there that night have their own off-kilter Rashomon-like take on what went down. Which story is the correct one? In the end, all I can write is my own memories of events even if they're half-cocked in a haze of forgetfulness. Where the Rashomon-effect of multiple viewpoints intrudes, I trust my own judgment to tell *my* truth, even as I may share the differing memories. Here and there I pop in a relevant poem of mine. And I have tried to keep policy wonky exegesis of the library profession and its internal politics to a minimum. I want to thank my publisher Rory Litwin for putting his trust in this book. Thanks to my sister Carey, and friends Bob Navarro and Paul Pierce for reading drafts. Thanks to Randy Zamorski for the design of the front cover, grafting the revolutionary accoutrements of jazzman Thelonious Monk's radical 1968 album *Underground* onto the staid 1904 print of Johannes Brahms. Thanks to my sister Carey again, and my brother David, for helping to jog my memories of our zany, utterly unorthodox childhoods in the tropics. Not least, thanks to my long-chafing wife Joy for her forbearance as I vanished for weeks to write. And finally, to all those wonderful people, famous to infamous, and every wonderful friend between, I give thanks to all who helped bring this memoir to life—with three bows and much gratitude. Abrazos fuertes, dear readers.

Chapter 1

Childhood

Venezuela and Brazil

The first thing I remembered that day, as I awoke from surgery in a Rio de Janeiro hospital, was the fabulous array of lizards wandering around the walls of my little room. They seemed so magical, these fine wyverns in their colorful suits of bumpy armor. It was as if they had come to my bedside to play, chasing each other around like miniature dragons, eyes bulging with astonishment at their good fortune. They made me forget I had just recently gone under the knife.

    I was barely four years old at the time. Like a seashell sinking beneath the waves, I slipped back into anesthesia-induced torpor, dreaming of shining castles where magicians summoned ethereal beasts. Vaguely I became aware that a kind nurse had entered to check on me, giving me a gentle shake. I looked up, blinking, into her smiling face.

    "Então, como está o nosso pequeno menino corajoso?" she inquired in Portuguese, with that lilting Brazilian inflection, to ask after the brave little boy in her charge.

    I must have nodded that I was fine, but I felt for the first time that my groin was burning. Somehow, at the tender age of four, I had strained at something and gotten a hernia, the stitches from which now ached under the covers. Soon after, my lovely mother came in to see me and sat on my bed. The lizards, meanwhile, paid these grownups no more heed than they had me. If there is still magic on our plundered planet, then it was contained in these bright dragons.

My next memory was that it was evening. Sundown comes early in the tropics, with a languid rhythm of regularity. All at once I became aware of a strange noise in the quiet gloaming. I was a child alone in a dark hospital, and something unseen was rattling the glass doors to the small porch outside my little room. Remote as that day is to my memory, I can conjure it still.

I was abruptly taken aback. For there, as if summoned from a dark dream, was an enormous cane toad (*Rhinella marina*) trying to escape into the more spacious hospital by buffeting its way against the glass that kept him at bay. I sat up, suddenly realizing with horror that the entire floor of the little porch, with its mossy concrete railing from which a fine fern grew out of a crack, seemed to be writhing with these annoyed reptiles, jumping about discontentedly and carrying on with buffoonish insistence. To a wide-eyed four-year-old, they seemed enormous but also quite mesmerizing. Once I was aware that I was safe from their incursion, I was entranced.

Years later I came to realize that cane toads could be used as a reasonably reliable pregnancy test for women. You inject a woman's urine into the lymph sac of a male cane toad. If the poor chap then pees out spermatozoa into its squeezed urine stream, the woman is considered pregnant. In 1956 Brazil, this was doubtless a common, and perhaps the only, test for pregnancy available that was remotely affordable to peasant mothers. Such were the wonders of being born and raised to the age of six in the tropics.

My actual birth place was Caracas, Venezuela, which seems to give the nabobs of American empire such apoplexy today. For my older brother, it was Trinidad; my younger sister, the blonde girl from Ipanema, was born to the tropical samba of Rio de Janeiro. For all of us kids, the sensuous, primitive, ever-colorful languor of the tropics was in the truest sense the cradle of our budding souls; it permeated our lives. Mine was truly a marvelous childhood of wonder, with each lizard a dragon in a centaur's world, each colorful parrot a messenger from the sky gods. In that time of trips beneath white parasols in tow with our black Bahamian cook to the open-street markets in the square, returning with her as she balanced an enormous basket atop her head laden with fruits and vegetables, I believe sheer fecundity filled my little world of imagination, set afire with dreams of jaguars in the jungle. And that jungle always beckoned. There is something in that strange wall of impenetrable vegetation that arouses in a young boy's imagination so many magical things to be fascinated about; it's as if some sort of cartoon florescence of flowering life will simply pop right out of your head for bursting. There were mountains contained in discovering an anthill beneath the banana tree, and chips of color in the flowering trees that broke off and became butterflies. There was always the hope that some wild jaguar would pad out of the forest paths in a fine sable coat just for my own childish benefit. I tore about our tropical garden with scuffed knees when I was still just getting my legs. It seemed to my little mind that all I had to do was scratch in the dirt with a stick, and suddenly, as if I'd drawn a magical symbol of conjuration, a capuchin would appear on our roof, doubtless escaped from a neighbor's yard. Or down would flutter a bluestripe butterfly (*Doxocopa laurentia*) on its very own magic carpet, colored sable-blue in the sunlight and ever so beautiful.

All manner of creepy-crawly things came home in jars when my dad returned from the cane fields and banana plantations. Centipedes as long as mustard-yellow hotdogs with too many legs. Horned myrmidons masked as black beetles. Huge banana tarantulas nimble enough to catch little birds. What's not to like when you're five? It hardly mattered that one day it might be a big black oily scorpion on the slats of the bunk bed above my head, or a flock of noisy macaws in their bright cerulean feathers mobbing a mango tree outside the shutters. Many houses in 1950s Rio didn't have panes of glass for windows. There were monkeys in the trees, jaguars in our imaginations, and jungle insects that sang us to sleep each night. Not long after the trip to the hospital to fix my hernia, I even managed to fall out of a second-story window onto the unforgiving driveway below, on a dare from my brother. I shattered my right leg, so back to the lizards and toads I went, with my battered appendage upraised in a cast.

Brazil was a diurnal surround sound of katydid song, cicadas, frugivore birds, howling monkeys, and ever-flapping flocks of colorful birds that indelibly imprinted the wonder of nature onto my budding mind. Everywhere one looked, the world seemed to be putting forth into bloom bougainvilleas, jacaranda, torch ginger, and palm fruit. And the smells! Rich, hot, just becoming over-ripe fruity smells, such memories of Rio that can be conjured in an instant when I take into my hand today a goiaba fruit or a guava—or the oddball jabuticaba from the Brazilian grape tree, an oddity which grows off the tree's branches like big droplets of sap. The trees encircling our yard were ancient, slow-growing, and immense.

I recall one blustery day in Rio (I was probably five at the time), when we heard that penguins had come ashore on the beach at the end of our street. We immediately begged my mother to let us go see them. The beach was the famous Ipanema of leggy girl fame that faces the southern Atlantic, where the archipelago of the Cagarras Islands, clearly visible from shore, blocks the full onslaught of the landward waves. Most days, my brother and I, and even our younger sister, were free to plunge into the waves and not be threatened by the undertow of huge southern swells. In fact, I believe we could all swim before we could even toddle much beyond a crawl. My brother assures me that we never did get to see the penguins even though we dashed down the street to the nearby beach. My memory is that we did see the little chaps, but fervent is a child's imagination. The penguins seemed as alive, in any case, as the little mermaids I had conjured from the children's books my mother read to us at bedtime. Whatever the truth of it, we are now certain it was Magellanic penguins (*Spheniscus magellanicus*) that came ashore that day, doubtless disoriented but at the same time quite fearless, with that loopy penguin waddle.

So, why were we raised in the tropics? Well, the truth of it is insects. Let me explain. My father was an agronomist who had studied insects through his college years, first at Drexel University, then as a tropical entomologist at the Imperial College of Tropical Agriculture (ICTA) in Trinidad. Dad escaped to this island paradise in part, I am sure, to stanch from his memory the horrors of the freezing forests of the Ardennes during the last great battle of World War II. Half his men had been cut down in unforgiving snowdrifts at the Battle of the Bulge, becoming blocks of ice in contorted poses of death. He was himself badly wounded by shrapnel from a mortar, and was almost two years in recovery. Always a charmer, Dad was egalitarian, funny, and without any affect whatsoever. He had grown up in Lansdowne, PA, a bedroom suburb of Philadelphia near the Main Line rail station. His father, my grandfather Edward D. McDonald Sr., was a Shakespearean scholar teaching first at Temple University and then at Drexel Institute of Technology as chair of the English Department, taking the train every morning for thirty-plus years to the campus in West Philadelphia. Grandfather in the end made his literary name by becoming one of the preeminent American research champions of the litigated and beleaguered D.H. Lawrence, whom he later befriended in a decades-long correspondence. Lawrence, in any case, was but one in a long list of other early 20th-century authors whom grandfather wrote about and came to know.

My mother, nee Ellen Robertson, though born a southerner in Richmond, Virginia (doubtless of blueblood slave-owning stock, with a great-grandfather who sat on the state supreme court), essentially grew up an orphan in the north. She met my father in 1947, when he hitched a ride with her and her then beau from Albany to New York City. I guess she switched her amorous allegiance on that trip, for they were soon an item in post-war New York. My mother had had a troubled childhood, and there was a deep melancholia evident in her soul. It was brought on, no doubt, from her lonely childhood, as she was shunted through formative years of disappointments and loneliness, though she never complained. Her own mother had abandoned her at the age of seven in the early years of the Great Depression, not showing up in Mom's life again until sixty years later, blind and infirm in Miami, an old crone past her centenary year. Mom's distant father ignored her, remarrying the classic evil stepmother. He died of pneumonia when Mom was just fifteen. My mother always made it known, without really outright lying, that she had "lost" her mother as a child, and then her father in her formative years. From as early as I can remember, I accepted the story that I had no grandparents on my maternal side. As I'll share later, none of this was true.

I will say this about my parents: they were fierce, lifelong Democrats, liberal to a fault, well-read intellectuals in *The New Yorker* magazine mode. Both seemed to have adventurous spirits; why else the many years raising their children in so many tropical locales? Married in Brooklyn in 1948, by 1949 my father and his new wife had moved to Trinidad. My mother took up a post as a line editor with the prestigious journal *Tropical Agriculture*. In any event, it was in Trinidad that they began their decades-long lives as American ex-pats. Upon finishing his studies at ICTA, my father was promptly offered a job with Shell Oil's Chemical Division, working on tropical crop pest management, first in Trinidad, then Venezuela, and on to Rio de Janeiro and the Brazilian sugar cane fields. Then, after a hiatus in England, there was a move to Mexico City when Dad was appointed Director for Central America operations; he finally retired from Shell in early 1971.

These environments made for a pretty exciting childhood for a kid with scarce a worry in the world. The point in sharing these daily buffetings by the quirks of nature at such a young age, these improbable encounters and cartoonish critters that abound in the tropics, is that such visions have forever made me feel a deep affinity with wild places, brought home vividly in the conjurations of a child's mind. The same is true for my brother, an avian biologist, and my sister, a psychologist, as well. The deepest contentment, the most at peace with the world that I ever feel, is when awakening alone, in the middle of absolutely nowhere, under the morning stars. This is precisely why, from time to time, I have sought that solitude in the wildest places on earth for long stretches of time. One such solitude lasted sixty-two days, with not another human being in sight. But I get ahead of myself. When I was barely six, my brother seven and my sister just two, we finally left the tropical breezes and languid days of Rio for foreboding England, wherever that was, in 1958.

I was too young to remember our family moving from my birthplace in Caracas to Rio de Janeiro when I was two. But I was old enough to recall with verve the exciting kerfuffle of packing up to move our family from Brazil to some faraway land of enchantment called the British Isles at the smart young age of six. This strange land was apparently all the way across the great Atlantic Ocean, which I only knew as the sheltered bay of Ipanema. But it did seem, in any case, to be a very long long way away. Truthfully, I doubt I knew a thing about the actual size of the planet at that time.

My parent's lives had been hectic until then, with all the constant moving and child-rearing in strange climes, so my schooling had been rather spotty. A budding scholar I was not, at least not in kindergarten. I suppose in some ways the raucous Rio carnival, which came around every February in late summer, was certainly in itself a learning experience, a riot of blaring noise, drunken laughter, perfume sprays, confetti, half-clad celebrants in endless parades wild with glittering costumes and always too much alcohol. The first few years we lived in Rio, the joyous mayhem of carnival terrified me. But by the time I was four, I was a "big boy" at last, able to join in with my own squeaky whistles and whoops.

The sights, sounds, and smells indelibly marked my young being with a sense that, counter to life's normal routines, there was this wild exuberance of abandon which all the grownups somehow, anyhow thoroughly approved of. Permission to misbehave was granted citywide. I took that lesson to heart for the rest of my life.

Not So Merry Olde England

The journey across the globe to England was taken first on an interminable Starliner trip on Braniff Airlines, a sleek airship of 1950s air travel, to almost every city in South America on our way north to the United States, and then across the Atlantic by steamship. I particularly recall the long leg from Rio to Lima, Peru. I believe we were on a sleeper plane, with bunk beds of all things. My brother and I had the top bunk in the plane, my mother and sister Carey were below. I recall that as we crossed the forbidding Andes to Lima, I looked out the window at the moon bright as a burnished penny in the black velveteen of the night sky, as smoking volcanoes gleamed white in the moonlight below. I went to sleep to the hum of powerful engines. From Bogotá we headed over the Caribbean, on up the southeastern seaboard of the United States, till at last we reached the runway of Idlewild Airport in New York City, now JFK

Once in the US we over-wintered in Philadelphia, staying with my grandparents in their modest house in Lansdowne on the Main Line. One miraculous morn came the gifted astonishment of the holiday season: we awoke at our grandparent's home to the marvel of falling snow. The world was washed clean with white powder. It was the first time any of us kids had ever seen this cold, fluffy stuff: real snow. Trust me, for a six-year-old from the tropics, this cold blanket of whiteness was a wonder of enticement. There were snowmen to build, snow forts to man, and the obligatory snowball fights.

When we finally set sail for England from the Hudson docks, it was aboard the magnificent British ocean liner the Queen Mary, on to Southampton. The RMS Queen Mary was every inch an ocean liner of adventure for a six-year-old. To still believe in magic and mythical sea monsters, and also be untethered by irksome parental oversight, I was able at every whim to tear about this huge castle at sea like a pretend Blackbeard pirate. My, oh, my, it was heaven indeed and the sight of dolphins skimming in our wake was a true astonishment, as were the flying fish.

Southampton, though! Good grief, what a dreary, low-slung port of call, with clouds heavy over gray quays in dreary Olde England. In 1958-59, the British Isles, even after thirteen years of peace since the armistice, were still pulling themselves out of the mayhem of the Luftwaffe bombing, unexploded bombs and all. While America basked in the booming fifties, poor England was still struggling to find its footing. And it was raining in Southampton, of course. In the tropics, the rains come often enough, but there was a precise rhythm to the downpours, not only with a rainy season and a dry one, but during the Amazonian monsoons, the rains literally poured down punctually at about three o'clock each day, lasting no more than an hour. Tropical sunlight sandwiched the downpour. Yet the British failed in punctuality with regards to their own inclement weather. Rains, dull dreary pitter-patter rains, cold wet icky rains, slanting sleety rains, torrential downpour rains, rain and rain and more rain, all came days on end, all soggy and puddle yucky. Spots of sun would briefly rend the sky, then inevitably the leaden skies returned again. To this end, we were soon presented with a footwear called Wellington boots, black boats that one had to haul upon one's feet like surly tubes of rubber, and then slosh about in the puddles. Barefoot in the tropics, wellies in England; a child adapts quickly enough.

England beckoned my father, who had been recalled from the honey-warm tropics to London to go to work at the main Shell offices overlooking the Thames. The office complex was an enormous, Stalinesque concrete hulk on the south riverbank, in plain view of Parliament across the river. I believe it has since been torn down and replaced with the north wing of St. Thomas Hospital. Many diehard Brits felt the concrete heap of these headquarters forever tarnished the charm of the river that T.S. Eliot had called a "strong brown god—sullen, untamed, and intractable." An "ugly monstrosity" is how the *London Times* put it, and indeed the whole complex was monstrous. This was my first inkling, when I visited the edifices not long after our arrival, that the wealth and power of capital was essentially a dreadful sort of implacable malevolence: hulking, brutal, obdurate. The curlicues of Big Ben and the quaint Houses of Parliament, only a bridge hop away, seemed somehow whimsical by contrast.

We moved to a rather posh house called Highclere in the Wentworth Estates, which boasted one of the finest golf courses in England. Some may recall that Shell Oil made a name for itself in the 1960s with a very popular television series called "Shell's Wonderful World of Golf." Given that my father was now rising into Shell's upper management, finding a nice rental home, largely paid for by the company, at Wentworth Golfing Estates must have made some sort of 1960s business logic. I will say this about my wonderful father: he was ever the iconoclast. Wounded as an Army Captain at the Battle of the Bulge, he was therefore a man who you'd think would hold a lifelong grudge against the Germans. He nevertheless raised eyebrows of approbation pretty much everywhere in the posh, cloistered world of Wentworth by going out and buying as our first family car in the UK a spanking new VW Bug, fresh off the first lot from Munich. Dad seemed by temperament to revel in thumbing his nose at the British upper-class conformity that he was thrust into.

My own entry into WWII was rather less dangerous than my father's, but for a seven-year-old, it was rather gallant and exciting all the same: we found General Eisenhower's underground WWII headquarters one summer day. Little did anyone above ground know, but buried secretively beneath the manicured lawns of the Wentworth Golf Course was a vast warren of rooms built for Churchill soon after the Blitz began. It had then become a protected command post for Eisenhower when he rose to command the Allied forces in 1942. Old friends from Brazil were visiting my parents at the time and they had two wonderful daughters our age, Vickie and Frederica, whom we knew well. Together with my sister in tow, we were scuffling about some bracken fens some distance from our home when we came upon a narrow, dark, overgrown stairway leading down like Orpheus' benighted muse into the stygian underground below. The stairs down into the underworld were all overgrown with ivy and stinging nettles. We managed to pry open the heavy metal doors whose locks had rusted away in the dreary days of endless rain. Like tomb raiders, we entered the dark, dank crypt, descending deeper and deeper into the gloom.

It took us all of half a minute to realize this wasn't a potato bunker or a bomb shelter. In the dim light, the complex was enormous and went on for possibly hundreds of yards in all directions, with rooms large and small, a maze of corridors, and strange contraptions left to rot in the dark. Wow! Lacking flashlights, we all agreed to return the next day with candles, but listen up, crew: no one was to tell the grownups! And return we did, with candles held high. We never came to the end of the complex. No sooner did one of us believe we'd come to a cul-de-sac, then suddenly a small door would open up to another corridor, which in turn led to another set of rooms and yet further corridors. Thinking about this design years later, I realized the military logic of building not a single cul-de-sac. Were the Germans to get this far, there was no trapped dead end, just another door to pass through and fight on. I don't believe Eisenhower ever used this bunker, but we later ascertained that it had been built during the Battle of Britain when the likelihood of a German invasion remained high.

By the time Eisenhower took command of the Allied forces, there was little fear remaining of Luftwaffe strafing, and still less of a German invasion. The man-made caverns we explored obviously had fallen quickly into disuse, and were given over to bats and rats by the war's end, soon to be forgotten in final abandonment. We may have been the first explorers there since the war's end, which made it all the more exciting.

British boarding schools, alas, weren't half as much fun. Indeed, they were Dickensian in the manner of Oliver Twist, where young boys apparently are tossed about like inconsequential dust motes to fend for themselves. I was seven when my ordeal began in 1959. Prior to boarding, my brother and I briefly had gone to a day school named "Mrs. and Miss Fish's School for Boys." The dowdy headmistresses were sisters, you see. Quite how these two Fishes came to be a Mrs. and a Miss we were not made privy to. I don't recall much about this school except for gazing out the window at a magnificent weeping willow most days, its crown adorned with jackdaws. But one day when my brother and I came home with ballet shoes from the Mrs./Miss Fishes, jazzed about dance lesson where we had practiced our croisé in a pas de deux, with other boys no less, my father, who in so many ways was a typical square of the Great Generation, wasn't having any of it. Ballet? Obviously, this was a pirouette too far. Forthwith we were enrolled, as all English boys of means were supposed to be, in a proper British boarding school. We went to Papplewick in Ascot, where the imperious headmaster was the right honorable Peter Merrick Knatchbull-Hugessen. Going away to school means finding a new compass as we lose our former world. All compasses at Papplewick pointed straight to draconian strictures and properly washed ears. These were pulled like stretched socks to peer inside for dreaded signs of wax flakes, then scrubbed again should such offending detritus be found.

As the middle child in the family, as is often the case with that familial role, I became the rebel at an early age, the quintessential "overlooked middle child"—not with a chip on my shoulder exactly, but certainly with a bravura in my beanpole bearing. As such, I rather enjoyed Papplewick in a perverse sort of way, even its more draconian parts, Dickens' Oliver be damned. Throughout my time there, I took British prep school as a sort of challenge to outwit, in puerile fashion, seeing in it the British Empire in microcosm. Such schools have boarding children who are barely six years of age, if you can imagine, ranging all the way up to thirteen. One hapless little tot named Witheridge only seemed able to say, when asked pretty much anything: "How now brown cow." Today, this is a sign of autism, but it was the occasion of mocking camaraderie from us. Schools such as Papplewick prepare the upper crust for the ridiculously named "Public Schools" of England, be that Eton College, Harrow, or Winchester, where the average working sods of the true public schools, cockney accents and all, are certainly not welcome, at least they weren't in the late 1950s. Of scholarships for the toiling classes, there weren't any. Who could afford the tails and white-tie dress expected to be worn for High Tea anyway?

English boarding school life in the post-war years had some of the character and high dudgeon of Harry Potter's school Hogwarts, but with absolutely none of the charm nor any zip of the magic. It was largely a rote sort of quasi-military academy minus the saluting. Teachers were called "Master" or "Sir" and all wore tweed coats with school ties over which were draped black damask gowns, open in the front with roomy sleeves, flowing magisterially behind them as they strode past. Even at six you started on beginner's Latin: amo, amas, amat, absent the love of course. Then there were classical Greek myths, and Roman and English history. The latter, surely, was the only history that mattered, with a focus on glorious battles which, with the advent of Alfred the Great in the 8th century, the Brits always seemed to win—never mind the routes at Castlebar in 1798 and Gallipoli in 1915. My favorite subject was geography, which was mostly a grand lesson in empire, but I traveled the globe as a child upon a magic carpet of maps to the far-off Mughal water gardens of India, to Aboriginal Australia, to the wild Canadian frontier with its mounted police. All the world beckoned. All in all, it was, by any standard, a rigorous classical education.

Two masters stood out to me, Mr. Kidson and Mr. Penny. Both of them seemed so dashing and debonair and handsome, so witty and fun in the classroom, ever erudite, ever serving as role models. Mr. Kidson, the older of the two, was forever flirting with the school nurses, which my callowness thought very rakish and daring of him. Miss Beckwith, the younger nurse, had a particularly hour-glass waist and fine bosom. It was the first inkling for me as a lad that this sort of daring-do with the ladies not only had, as they say, panache, but that it seemed to work a spell on the ladies too. Miss Beckenwith would pretend to blush and tease back in return. The smiles between the two spoke volumes. Obviously, nurse Beckwith welcomed Mr. Kidson's attention. In any event, a sort of secret door to sexuality opened in my young mind as I watched Mr. Kidson work the gracious art.

Mr. Penny was entirely of a different fiber, even if cut from the same pattern. He was smiling, kind, engaged, good-humored, perhaps all of twenty-something—so perhaps he could see in us grubby little toffs something of himself just a few years prior. He was the magician who, almost single-handedly, helped me realize that within the thin pages of books, you could actually hop upon the magic ride of your own imagination and thereby travel to distant and exotic continents merely by the simple act of embarking twixt the covers of that humble artifact of paper, boards, and typeface. One term, I recall that Mr. Penny read aloud to us T.H. White's remarkable *The Sword in the Stone* (Putnam's, 1939), about young Prince Arthur,[1] lord of his Knights of the Round

---

1. My grandfather, a scholar of old texts of literature such as Mallory's, told me that the story of Arthur's mercurial ability to pull the sword Excalibur from the stone was actually a hidden allegory about a young prince bringing metallurgy (and thus advanced weaponry) to the British Isles. Whoever

Table, and his fair maidens, wherein whole enchanted realms of gallantry and mystery sprang to life. And then there was magical, irascible Merlin the Wizard. My gratitude is fathomless for this gift of enchantment that Mr. Penny bestowed upon my illiterate self at age seven. I have been a bibliophile ever since.

Pretty much from the start of boarding school, my brother and I were teased as "Yanks" with our peculiar Portuguese-inflected American accent; worse still was the way we held our forks (pointing up, rather than down as in England) and all the other quirky, unfathomable habits we'd gleaned from the tropics. But as a kid, one adapts quickly: by the age of eight, I was all but a proper British chappie, my accent transformed to proper upper-class English diction. But otherwise, I never fit in. I was forever being dragged by the ear to the headmaster's study for a tongue lashing and, later, the cane. Whether it was for pillow fighting after lights out or insolence in the classroom, the cane became my not-so-irregular corporal punishment.

This form of cruel and unusual reprimand came in four levels of severity, all visited on your tender bum by a switch. "Three of the best pants up," then "Three pants down (bare bum)," on to "Six of the best pants up"—well, you get the picture. The master who administered the cane at Papplewick was not our Headmaster, Mr. Knatchbull-Hugessen, but rather Mr. Roddy, a rail thin crow of a man with a shock of hair rising round a bald top. The "boss" in the cartoon strip Dilbert is perhaps a chubbier approximation. He had suffered polio as a child, a consequence of which was that his right foot was encased in a black boot with a three-inch sole and heel, giving the withered appendage the appearance of a black peg with an anvil on the end. Mr. Roddy thus clumped through life with a visage I never once saw smile. Mr. Roddy! Lordy, what

---

Arthur may have been, his ability to elevate the peoples of Briton into the Age of Iron is part of the delight in this ancient tale.

irony, that this sadist administered the rod. And the rod? Rather a long thin switch of pliable bamboo.

I was lucky, I suppose, that the worst I ever got, albeit on several occasions, was "three of the best pants up." The fabric of my trousers spared my bare bum, though ripping a distending flatus in Mr. Roddy's direction, while it might have been fun in imagination, was not advised in practice. I wisely kept my flatulence to myself. And there you'd be in the headmaster's oaken study, with his shiny cricket trophies on the mantle, bent over double holding your ankles, looking at Mr. Roddy upside-down through your knobby knees as he began his clumping trajectory toward you, cane held high, taking aim. Yes, imagine it, as his massive black Polio boot goes clomp! clomp! clomp! across the floor, then with the grimmest of visages—THWACK! Owwwww-wch! Oh god, two more! And then you had to thank the bleeding blighter when it was over, shake his clammy hand as if you were now best of pals, supposedly with the shame of your infraction thereby removed from your soul, and with head slung low, you walked the long interminable hallway out through the headmaster's quarters to the dining hall, thence to your mates who were pruriently awaiting your verdict of the beating. By the third beating, I had learned to put at least three or four sheets of blotting paper inside my underwear. Ha! So there, piss off you beastly old pervert! My bum certainly much appreciated this accommodation. But, by the second of my pained retreats from a caning down the lugubrious corridor of the headmaster's offices, my youth's heart had filled with disquiet and loneliness, and something inside me knew I was no longer a child.

The food at Papplewick was equally atrocious: greasy slop, vegetables boiled to mush, unidentifiable meat chunks that had come the long way round from market, cabbage pie, and, more often than you'd care to remember, maggots. Yes, maggots. British boarding schools like Papplewick had six forms, roughly matching grades two through eight in American elementary schools.

Each form ate separately at long scrubbed wooden tables with benches to sit on, with perhaps ten boys to a side. A master sat at one end and served up the day's gruel. At least Oliver Twist had wanted more of his chewy oats, which is more than I could say for myself on most days. But back to the maggots, biological name Musca domestica, the indomitable larvae of the annoying common housefly: harmless little blighters. Let us say a master happened to be absent from a meal and a sixth former was called upon to sit in his place, serving up the slop. Maggots seemed particularly fond of the thirty-and-one ways the cooks served up cabbage: chopped, diced, stringy, boiled, baked in pies, filler, fodder, and so on. And once upon a meal a lively little wiggler, who had survived the over-cooking, would be found by an enterprising lad on one side of the table. Then if another, praise be, were discovered on the other side of the table—O callooh-callay, how we chortled in our joy. Two maggots, what largesse! We were snotty seven- and eight-year-olds recall, so of course we loved our maggots. The master's daily duty was to have one side of the table clean up the dishes. Groaning, the chosen side would have to take the greasy plates and spoons to the washer's grimy window with surly sighs of forbearance. So, a lively little wiggly maggot in its prime was a welcome sight indeed, and be still O my heart, a miracle to have two! Its very own twin on the same day, in the same cabbage—surely this was cause for celebration, as it provided us precocious lads with a splendid way to sort this chore of the greasy plates out for ourselves.

Each side would size up the health and vigor of their particular racing maggot, then unscrew the salt shaker and pour the contents over their contestant in equal little conical mounds, and whichever maggot wiggled fully free of the dry brine first, won. The other side was forced by custom to concede and volunteer to clean the table. Oh, to be seven again! The real trick, of course, was keeping the inherent rowdiness of such a magnificent insectoid Olympiad to a minimum, in order not to alert the haughty sixth former at table's end to what beastly business the under-formers were up to at the other. Such were the fun repasts to be had at Papplewick.

Was there homosexuality at the school?[2] Of course, some of it endearingly non-sexual. The dorms were nothing but large, long attic chambers with gabled ceilings and ancient toss-off army cots for beds filled with young boys. Each of us also got one chair beside our beds, upon which we had to neatly fold our clothes at bedtime each night. Inspections were the norm. At lights out, a master would usually lead us in some sort of bedtime prayers. You know: "Bless us tonight, Jesus, give us a good night's sleep" etc., which of course became "Undress us Jesus, give us some good white sheep to bed..." and so on. How anyone remained the least bit religious after the withering scorn with which we young lads heaped upon the head of poor Jesus is a miracle unto itself. This enjoyable mockery certainly made me a budding atheist, and a nonbeliever to this day. Though in truth, I'm probably nothing more than an apatheist, someone who just doesn't care a fig if god exists or doesn't. In any event, each morning your bed had to be made with military precision in all its ten exacting steps. Drilled into me to this day is a neurotic obsession with tidiness.

But with lights out, some of the youngest of the boys, all of six years old and terribly lonely, would crawl out of bed and go to sleep with another boy of six for nothing more, I suppose, than the embrace of honest human warmth. I don't recall being particularly surprised, still less offended, by this. To about age six, my brother and I had often shared the same bed. Though I never felt the urge to do this myself, I can vividly recall that in that attic darkness during my first years at Papplewick, many a night I cried

---

2. This author's pronouns: He, Him, His, hetero, given at the request of LGBTQ activists I admire. And to paraphrase an author I love, Paul Kingsnorth: I am 75% English, 25% German/French, 100% European. and 0% Corporate Apologist. I share 96% of my genetic material with chimpanzees and 60% with bananas. And, of course, my oldest ancestors came from equatorial Africa and were, by all accounts, rather hairy and big browed. That should cover it.

myself to sleep for loneliness. It felt to my dark, unformed soul as if no one in the whole world loved me. It's hard to imagine that this isn't the experience of the majority of young boys dragged to boarding schools at such a tender age.

The first dorm I lived in was in the main schoolhouse adjoined to another at a dogleg. They were all, apparently, renamed after British WWII bombers, such as (Vickers) Wellington and (Avro) Lancaster. At least that's what we interpreted the names to mean. In each dorm-house complex, a master had his own rooms in order to keep an eye on his flock. And yes, once in a rare moon some older boy crept into these rooms after dark. We were all too young to really understand what was going on, but that it was somehow naughty and not proper was the general consensus. None of us, of course, had a clue as to the word pedophilia or that such reprehensible behavior occasionally occurred. But being callow, we never breathed a word of it to either Mr. Roddy or Mr. Knatchbull-Hugessen, that I recall. When I rose to being a fourth former (third from the top), my dormitory was in the Cottage, a semi-attached building whose four rooms surrounded a central stairway and bathrooms. These rooms held only four to eight boys apiece, unlike the long attics full of twenty or twenty-six boys. My escapades were decidedly more daring by this time. I was forever climbing out the dorm window up onto the roof at night to gaze at the moon or spot those first human satellites. Tiptoeing outside hither and yon after lights, out and about like a cat burglar with a few close mates, became a regular peregrination. And so, inevitably, I was caught and again dragged back to the headmaster's study for three more of the best. This further cemented my burgeoning antiestablishment mistrust of authority.

I do recall one master being caught flagrantly *indelicato*, though I'm sure it was more common than just this incident. He was booted out. Today, of course, it would be more than just getting the boot: it would be arrest, trial, and imprisonment for sex with a minor. Yet there he stood upon dismissal in the long fading light of a late spring evening, battered suitcase in hand, awaiting some sort of ride into his new life elsewhere, shamed and stigmatized. And there all the lads in my Cottage dorm room were, crowding the window to watch him go. At last, a small black sedan arrived in the wan light and swallowed him up. I can still recall the keen sense of empathy I felt for the chap, as he stood alone in the last light of day. I had no particular judgment toward homosexuality at that age, still less since. Truth be told, I actually didn't really know what this "homosexuality" was, though it was obviously frowned upon by the masters in oblique terms, as they pretended to huff and cough into their hands.

This strange prejudice toward homosexuality (again pedophilia was unknown to us, so the excoriated act back then was indeed homosexuality), this censorious view of homosexuality may have actually formed in me, as early as this, a keen sense of identification toward groups of the oppressed, as I, too, felt oppressed by the system. It's not comparable, of course: my childish chafing versus the master's disgrace, but a young boy's emotional intelligence at age eleven in 1963 was hardly dignified by critical thinking. Putting aside my cluelessness of the criminality of sex with a minor, that evening, the poignant sight of an expelled master, forlorn and fallen from his pedestal, body slouched alone in the school yard, was a scene bathed with such pathos that I truly felt for the man. In my chest empathy just welled up unbidden, and in wordless acceptance I forgave whatever his sins may have been. What did I know? I honestly didn't know what the details were, just that the whole sordid denial exhibited by the school's grownups seemed part and parcel the bane of polite society evasions and a hypocritical dodge. Recall that this was Britain in 1963, with the faux innocence of "Love Love Me Do" and "Please Please Me" filling the airwaves and the girls still in bobby socks. After the taillights of his ride vanished into the gloaming, each of my roommates crawled silently back into his bed, each with his brooding thoughts, mine being one of honest compassion for the man and his mysterious transgressions.

Speaking of the Beatles, England in 1958 to 1965 was a magical place, or so it seemed to me growing up there at that time. The zeitgeist of the Sixties was soon in full swing, with winkle-picker shoes and skinny ties. There were castles and Gothic crypts everywhere for a young boy to explore, and great palaces like Blenheim and Hampton Court to be baffled by: why did one family need so many ridiculously ornate but sparsely furnished rooms? There were grand privet hedge mazes to get lost in, too. By 1963, the Beatles and the Mersey Beat were all the rage. I particularly liked the Dave Clark Five, Peter & Gordon, and Herman's Hermits. The first inklings of the anti-war movements pushing against the conformity of the 1950s were also popping up like a sore. Suddenly in trendy London there were lovely "tarts" wearing mini-skirts and smart young chaps with long hair dashing merrily about in Aston Martins. Lovely Catherine Gale was Mrs. Peel on *The Avengers* back then, then heaven itself opened and it was the divine Diana Riggs doing the karate, which was twice as better. Roger Moore had barely bought a razor as *The Saint*, a weekly spy thriller, as he raced across the telly saving the world. And of course, dashing Sean Connery was having his martinis shaken not stirred.

Every summer during the time I was ages eight to thirteen, my mother would take my brother and me on summer holiday car tours about the isles in her drab, pale green Ford Anglia. Up through the Lake District to Scotland we went, where a lost lamb I once picked up had the temerity, for my good deed of saving him (from what I didn't know), to shit all over me. Then the next summer it was to Cornwall and the magic of Tintagel. Castles, ruined abbeys, stone circles, weird gothic manors that appeared haunted, Hadrian's Wall, and Stonehenge in the evening rain: these brooding places of wild mystery set my young mind afire. But if I am ever asked to enter another bloody medieval grand cathedral, no matter how touted it is in the guidebooks, please shoot me. Those dreary monuments to interminable wounded statues of Jesus hanging on his eternal cross, as bland plaster saints by the baker's dozen look down from every cornice with perpetual approbation! And the wretched mortuaries of interred long-dead nobility, their hands invariably clasped in prayer over marbled chests, and the grand men always in suits of chiseled stone armor above funereal casket clutching unsheathed swords. Ugh. The cloying stricture in these hallowed halls of horror that misbehavior was *strictly forbidden* simply infuriated me. I felt like howling out loud. I did, however, quite like some of the magnificent stained glasswork, in York Minster in particular, especially if a sudden sun-bolt shot through the glass and you could skip over the colors reflected on the holy flagstones underfoot.

But to dash madly about the wind-torn barren bluffs of Tintagel in Cornwall like one of King Arthur's wayward knights, with the sea wind whipping the waves below and gannets soaring above, was to be in heaven. To chase the wild ponies on bleak Dartmoor, oh, what glorious fun! Or Glen Coe, where the dastardly Clan of febrile Campbells slaughtered Clan McDonald on a winter's morn in 1692—to see those high moors under threat of thunderclouds, that was to be alive in the world. These adventures our dear mother took us on were decades before tourists came to Merry Olde England by the busload. We drove the lonely narrow roads of wild Northumbria out of sight of village or lorry, singing silly songs and passing no other vehicle for hours it seemed. I felt as free as a bird, exhilarated, as if I was suddenly a dashing explorer of the unknown. The wild moors of the northlands filled me with a sense of hushed awe. Every night we found a bed and breakfast somewhere, almost always by happenstance, usually a lonely farmstead, and found a humble berth for the night. Crowing roosters would awaken us at dawn. Indeed, the evening we visited Stonehenge in a fine slanting rain, we had the entire haunting place to ourselves. The stones sang as the drops beat down and I just knew the magic of Merlin was still alive in the world.

On one adventure of note, I met Peter O'Toole in London at the ripe age of eleven. This was on a trip led by the aunt of Papplewick's Headmaster Mr. Knatchbull-Hugessen, the dowdy Mrs. Gordon, a stout and imperious matron of a certain age (think Maggie Smith in Downton Abbey). Her position at Papplewick was to teach us delinquents good manners and the superiority of Anglo-Saxon European culture. On occasion she would take a select group of boys to some cultural affair or famous site and, in her nose-lifted manner, regale us as to why whatever we had been dragged to see was of the utmost cultural importance to our proper education. Why I ever got to go on any of these outings, as I was more miscreant than obedient schoolboy, I never understood. But chosen I was, as a gaggle of boys were one day bused from Ascot to see Peter O'Toole star as Hamlet at the Old Vic theatre in London. Doubtless this was to provide us privileged, if callow, chappies with a taste of the real Shakespeare in the peerless personage of an actor that Mrs. Gordon had probably rather taken a fancy to, given that all the ladies at the time seemed to swoon over the blue-eyed movie star.

I don't recall anything of the bus ride or much of the play, sadly. But at intermission between the third and fourth acts of the great tragi-melodrama, I was doodling around the front of the stage when I caught an enormous splinter of wood as I ran my hand along the stage front. It was an ugly wedge jagging out like a sword from the webbing between thumb and forefinger on my right hand. And there I was, a wounded lad. Bleeding profusely, I made it out to the lobby to find someone, anyone, who could extract the wooden dagger from my hand (to this day, I still sport a noticeable scar). An aged if kindly theatre employee took pity upon me and spiritedly announced that the "stage nurse" would soon patch me up handsomely.

So clutching my wounded right hand at the wrist, dagger protruding, I followed the kind docent into the bowels of the storied old theatre. We came at last to a vast area of thespian gloom, with a thousand ropes rising like serpents into the dark empyrean of the backstage, a cathedral it seemed to me, where all the magic of set changes obviously occurred. I was dazzled.

As my eyes grew accustomed to the shadows, whom should I see there, in an open space, but the great Master O'Toole himself, practicing his upcoming swordplay with whomever was playing Laertes. Swish, swish went their rapiers until O'Toole suddenly saw a real wounded hero, rivers of blood running down an upheld arm, a wee lad pale as the ghost of Banquo.

"Good grief lad!" he exclaimed, calling off the practice suddenly. "Whatever have you done to yourself?"

Sheepishly I said, "Um, I believe I caught a splinter, sir" and waved the offending three-inch dagger. Close up to the thespians, I was surprised at how much make-up these remarkable actors had lathered on their faces.

"I see," said O'Toole putting down his rapier. But makeup or no, his piercing blue eyes were electric; no wonder the ladies swooned. They bore right into me as he put a kind hand on my shoulder in a fatherly fashion, saying "I'm sure they can patch you up young man! Be brave!" He winked in assurance.

"Thank you, sir," sez I, altogether dazzled by the solicitude. At which point a foursquare battleaxe of a matron arrived from her cup o' tea, thoroughly displeased by my carelessness since her cuppa would now grow cold. Once in the tiny broom closet of an infirmary, she roundly scolded me for being such a careless twit, yada-yada. Without so much as a "this may hurt," she yanked the offending dagger from my hand with not an ounce of concern for my yelps of pain. Such a failure of her Hippocratic oath, it seemed to me. Iodine, bandage, and she soon sent me packing "out the back way if you please, fshaw!"

Suddenly I found myself in a back alley with instructions from the Valkyrie to re-enter the theatre again from the front as the fourth act was soon to start. Anxiously I made my way along the alley that opened out on the corner of The Cut and Waterloo Road. But no sooner had I turned the corner to re-enter the theatre when I was confronted by, of all things, a double-decker bus that had somehow hopped the curb and gone crashing into the Victorian era glass and iron awning at the front entrance of the old theatre. What a kerfuffle. Oh, but I loved it! This was all becoming such a wonderful adventure indeed.

Being an enterprising lad, I stepped lively over the tangled shards, around bystanders and bobbies, all the while looking for the kind gentleman who had led me backstage in the first place a half hour earlier. Luckily my savior was at the door to keep the gawking riff-raff out. Recognizing me with a beamish smile, he welcomed me back into the lobby of the Old Vic like some long-lost hero. "All patched up then, are ye? Good lad. Come along." Whereupon the kindly man snuck me into the back of the mezzanine in time to see the swordplay and, I was snobby enough to sniff, the fake blood.

It was in England, though, where I doubtless came by what the Reverend King called "the content of [my] character." In my case, such character as I had was doubtless an odd mixture of insouciance, empathy, burning curiosity, childish daring-do, and a lifelong suspicion and eventual outright mistrust of pretty much all authority. I realized soon enough that I could use my wits to maneuver through the grown-up world rather cleverly, and found, moreover, that truthfulness was best adhered to rather loosely, especially if one had landed into hot water. Hot water was a common state of affairs for this miscreant, pretty much all of my life. I could feign being the proper little chappie when a show of innocence was needed, while at the same time I used my beanpole height with an air of insouciance to impersonate a more mature lad whenever exigencies warranted such a turn. The insouciance, of course, was all show. Inside I was often a very lonely child, although I adored and looked up to my older brother through my formative years, and had a lively and engaging sister. In the literal homelessness of British boarding school, my loneliness, such as it was, grew out of forever feeling the misfit, always the outsider, the indifferent observer even as I was sometimes willing to risk all by doing very foolish things. This brashness stemmed more from a desire to bust out of my self-imposed isolation, thereby gaining the applause of my mates, rather than from some inherent fearlessness. Bravado, in short, masked my insecurities. I felt abandoned, I suppose, bereft of any physical contact one might remotely call parental love. So I built about myself a wall of protective attitudes to insulate my sometimes-desperate feelings of aloneness, so that a cocky veneer, it seemed to my callow self, would mask the inner wounds of that sense of being forsaken. Where did this odd contortion of character traits come from? This is hardly the place for the therapist's couch, but certainly part of it was my parents, part of it the stark lack of human affection at Papplewick. Mom and Dad were never emotionally demonstrative, still less physically affectionate, and the act of packing us off to boarding school at such a tender age seemed singularly unkind. It was always, "Now remember Pete, we love you..."—it was all matter-of-fact, never the first-person singular "I love you" and absolutely never a genuine loving hug as they packed us off, yet again, to the gloom of boarding school.

But it was a fair bargain, all things considered, because at the same time Mom and Dad were wonderfully funny, literate, ever-curious parents whom all our childhood friends, and even later our grownup friends, saw as "amazing," "so fun," and "totally cool"—to the point they often seemed more loved and admired by these pals than by us kids for whom they were just the quirky parental units. Yet in retrospect, I can certainly see how they would appear this way to others. They were always willing to engage in conversations of any stripe, invariably engaged with solicitous questions, and were true regalers of tales given the fabulously idiosyncratic lives they had led. They were also kind and generous to a fault, my father being particularly generous of spirit though not, sadly, of his emotions, except perhaps to exhibit a persistent, lifelong, grinding anger at the unethical meanness in the world. We grew accustomed to the fact that Dad would go to inordinate lengths to lend a helping hand to virtual strangers.

Nor can I forget how we children were exposed to political and cultural discussions at the dinner table at a very early age, given their solidly liberal leanings and wide reading. Furthermore, in all matters related to child-rearing, they were lenient to a fault, a blessing which a kid of seven might easily overlook as heaven sent. If there was a golden age in my childhood, our sojourn in the British Isles was it. During our holidays we largely had the run of the environs and were indulged in our escapades without challenge. Other than a sort of pervasive, if unspoken, worrying about our general wellbeing, my parents had not a clue about how to actually parent. Perhaps in their wide reading they had picked up the tidbits we experienced, but that was about it, until we all finally left home for good and were out in the roiling world on our own. My father, throughout my twenties and thirties, would needle me on occasion about my undisciplined "vicissitudes," which he'd intone with exasperated mockery. Yet he rarely said "no" to my misadventures ahead of time—a martinet, he wasn't. I think what he saw as my aimlessness struck him as somehow hedonistic, at a time when the world so needed smart young men like myself to buckle down and set it aright. He believed in the noble crusade against the iniquities of the world and his children should care, too. Yet to their dying days, when I came home to my parents from my worldly peregrinations, the homecomings were almost always wonderful returns to bonhomie and intellectual nurture. Arguments between us were rare, with fewer knockdown doozies than the fingers on my left hand,

Born in the tropics I may have been, but something in the barren moors and fens of the British Isles, its magical stone circles and mysterious tombs, feretories, burial mounds, undercrofts, and barrows of primeval allure, its perpetually winding roads through bucolic country both beautiful and ancient with flocks of sheep seemingly grazing upon every green hillside, this panoply filled me with a love for the odd beauty of ancient farmlands that stays with me to this day. And the fact that this great landscape was essentially sub-arctic with Scotland protruding, like a crown, into the polar seas, as far north as southern Greenland, all the while still bathed by the tropical waters of the Gulf Stream, just seemed so magical—with palm trees at Lands' End in the west and cold unforgiving fens in the eastern shires of Northumberland. Southern Greenland you ask? Look on any map, the Hebrides, certainly. I consider Scotland, to this day, the most hauntingly beautiful country in the world. So I am eternally grateful to have become a "little man" in England, where my callow being was filled with perpetual astonishment. The capacity for wonder became my joy, especially toward nature and the ancient stone ruins of early peoples; this was a gift beyond measure. Whatever trauma boarding school had inflicted seemed hardly worth the bother of elevating it to the status of neurosis. Anyway, to this day, the word Druid conjures realms of megalithic mystery. The tropics of Venezuela and Brazil no doubt made fallow my spirit for this sowing, but something in my highland heritage has always been drawn to barren landscapes and desolate wilderness, where what might pass as my soul sowed small shoots of wonder in the kingdom of British kings and queens. The happiest days of my life that I can conjure were of my childhood in England. I hold now, as then, to the Bard's own words: "Against the envy of less happier lands, this blessed plot, this earth, this realm, this England!"[3]

---

3. *Richard II*, Act II, Scene I (Spoken by John of Gaunt).

Back to the Tropics and the Feathered Serpent

We left British Isles in the summer of '64 when my father was reposted back to Venezuela as a top executive in Shell's agricultural division, managing distribution of soil amendments and pesticides for crops such as sugar cane, bananas, papaya, and pineapple. Doubtless, too, he had a hand in Shell's growing influence in Venezuela's burgeoning oil industry. I was still too young, all of twelve to thirteen, to really take an interest in my father's work affairs, but even as early as 1965, I sensed my father's growing discontent with the corporate pressures of endless work and conformity expected at the British office, whereas in the tropics things were looser for him; you could let your belt out a notch or two, allow your personality to find expression, move at a slower pace in the languid siesta time of equatorial latitudes. Mañana was an actual business ethos in the tropical heat of midday, that even the most laid-back hippie might appreciate.

We left England as we had arrived: by steamship. Except this voyage was across the equator, through the Caribbean islands, to our port of call at the Terminal de Pasajeros del Puerto de La Guaira on Venezuela's northern "gold coast." After six plus years in England, this first reawakening to the tropics rushed back through my sense of smell as I stepped down the gangplank to the tropical soil of my birth. There is no other olfactory experience like it. It is, at first whiff, almost overpowering as it bursts upon the memory centers of the brain. It's a hot, rich vegetative scent that's spicy, sweaty, and sweet at the same time, and hangs heavily in the equatorial air like an incense. It envelopes you with a sort of unidentifiable lassitude, as the haphazard if benevolent anarchy of how humans go about their business between the horse latitudes drags you back into a world of *que sera sera* with its enticement of poolside deck chairs in the land of Nod. And through it all, here blow the trade winds of the Caribbean with names like bayamo, suestado, and alisio that grow stronger the nearer one approaches the equator that bisects Venezuela right down the middle. Yes, I had come home.

Years later, when I was Dean of Library Services at Fresno State, I often took my wonderful dog Otter, a part-Labrador, part-border-collie, and part something else mix, out to a county park in the Central Valley of California. On my first visit, with Otter happily off leash, I saw across a wide lawn a small grove of royal palms (*Roystonea oleracea*) whose fronds rose up high on their stalks, swaying in the morning breeze. I was suddenly and viscerally transported back to Venezuela. The sight of those slender palms bending to the wind, their green flags volleying in the March wind, truly took my breath away. I was transported, palpably, back to being thirteen again on the bright sandy beaches of Macuto. That was where our family went on holidays to get away from the grinding horn-honking intensity of Caracas. For ten years I walked Otter there at that humble park, and the wonder of those slender palms never diminished despite a thousand dawn trips to watch them.

Upon arrival in Venezuela, I was soon enrolled in the British School of Caracas, nestled in the privileged section of town called Altamira, an expat neighborhood under the high imposing massif of Mount Avilla which forms a bulwark between the Venezuelan capital and the coast. Our "fifties modern" house was within walking distance of the school, located in the streets above; with my satchel, I'd climb the steep Avenida 12 where we lived to the school each morning. My sister was a fellow student; my brother was two forms ahead and had been shipped off to boarding school in Connecticut. In some respects, the year I went to school there was a sort of lost year. I don't have too many memories of living in Caracas as a precocious teen, although a few stand out. One was at age thirteen, when my dad turned me on to Ian Fleming and the James Bond series. My father had actually met Fleming twice, once in Jamaica sometime in the 1950s and then again at some swank soiree in London in the early Sixties. Mom told me that she recalled Fleming had been three sheets to the wind at the London shindig, an inebriation driven home a few years later by his death caused, as the papers reported, by a deadly cocktail of heavy drinking, chain-smoking, and a congenitally weak heart. And yes, for me Sean Connery is forever 007, the true Bond, whom I idolized throughout my teens.

Six years at a British boarding school for boys can make of any lad's character a mud wallow. Lucky for me, I was promptly spared this porcine fate for there I sat, as if upon some boyish half shell, in a tropical classroom with *girls*. Yes, *girls* for crying out loud. Jeepers, the fairer sex. Imagine that. You never so much as saw a girl in British boarding school. They were infinitely alluring, yet as untouchable as porcelain urns in a museum showcase. My first attempt at a novia, or girlfriend, was a black-haired Iberian named Consuela, the daughter of an attaché at the Spanish Embassy. Despite my being appointed Head Boy, a sort of topnotch hall prefect, by the headmistress at the British School after my first term, with a little pin to match, and despite being tall for my age and, I thought, rather debonair and amusingly rambunctious, all efforts to woo Consuela failed miserably This was a traumatic conundrum, perhaps reinforcing an uncertainty around women that's dogged my life. So you counterweight the conundrum, as men are wont to do, with a false exterior of bravura, assuming at a stroke all the usual ridiculous prerogatives males simply assume they are entitled to. If you have an ounce of sense going forward, of course, you spend a lifetime thereafter shedding these dead skins of assumed superiority like a self-whelmed male python who has swallowed a horse.

There's another small matter I should mention here, for what happened one school day in Venezuela was to have an enormous impact on my life over the years. In itself it was perhaps no big deal, but it opened in me a doorway into what one might call, as shorthand, the mystical realms, though I don't care for the word "mystical" much. My sister and I went to see the somewhat sappy movie, *Mary Poppins*, just out from the States at the time, with Julie Andrews striding along with her enchanting umbrella. Anyway, as for the mystical realms, the big joke going around school that year was a parody of the film's famous song: "A Super Callused Fragile Mystic Hexed by Halitosis." The sentiment resonated. The mystical, in any case, seems by deduction to connote there isn't a perfectly sensible and biological, possibly quantum anomalous, reason that weird things happen, be they precognition, lucid dreaming, or astral projection. The cognizati, those so-called initiates of these things in their colorful robes and smoky sweat lodges, love to gussy up psychic phenomena in all sorts of magical mumbo-jumbo, which only they, through some deep spiritual guidance, arcane knowledge, and hefty fee paid up front, can help you to attain to an understanding they alone are the gatekeepers of. I don't need a tinfoil hat to doubt such folderol. Notably, in telling the stories I share here, I shall touch on the works of scientist and cetologist Lyall Watson throughout, in particular, those fascinating and empirically grounded books on these topics that in my reasoned opinion are just a marvel to read.[4] I cannot think of any other author, alive or dead, who has influenced my thinking as much as Watson, nor who has helped me better understand what happened to me that day in the classroom of the British School.

So here it is: upon arriving at the British School one balmy day, our class of maybe twenty-two students was told that since it was Guy Fawkes Day (he of the Gunpowder Plot), there would be drawings for prizes, boys one prize, girls another. No sooner did I hear this announcement than I became certain beyond shadow of doubt that I would win the random drawing. There was no wishing or hoping. No invocation to imaginary gods somewhere

---

[4]. My favorite quote of Watson's comes from the book *Lifetide: A Biology of the Unconscious* (Simon & Schuster, 1979): "I make no apology for a fascination with the soft edge of science. It is here, it seems, that we get fleeting glimpses of strange shadows just beneath the surface of current understanding." He introduced me to a passionate belief in the miraculous based on analytical skepticism. He is an amazing mytho-scientific raconteur of which more anon.

in the aethyr above, O me me me, please me! Nothing like that. The certainty just popped up like a memory, like it had already happened sometime in the recent past. All I needed to do was scoop up my prize that was preordained and sit back down. All of our names had been written on little chits of paper and placed in plastic pails, boys in one and girls in another, to be drawn randomly by someone in the class. A student in the front row, a shy boy with a stutter if I recall, was asked to draw out a name from the boy's pail. He rummaged around, pulled out a chit, and haltingly read off the winner. Yes, of course, it was my name. I felt no giddiness, no real surprise; it just did happen as I knew that it would. Indeed, I felt no surprise whatsoever, which is odd for a thirteen-year-old winning a prize. Everyone turned and clapped, though I could tell all the other boys were disappointed they had not been chosen.

And so, with a calm and sure demeanor, I walked up to the front of the class to get my trophy, a new red cricket ball. The winning of this prize did not give me any particular sense of joy nor relief that I'd been so lucky, still less of any accomplishment on my part. Instead, what bothered me over the next few days, and does so to this day but for different reasons, was that I wanted an answer to the question: how had I known with such calm assurance that I'd win the prize even before my name was drawn out of the bucket? I vaguely knew about precognition. So, I immediately read up more on the subject in the school's battered *Britannica*, but only found stories on Delphi and Cassandra. This was not much help, but it was a start on a lifelong quest. For me, though, the certainty had been implacable, a foreknowledge known well ahead of the drawing. There were no "ifs"—I was the winner, just like that. It was that foreknowledge which rankled: how had I known? From that day forth, I became convinced that there must be some sort of underlying and invisible weave beneath the outer trappings of everyday reality to which only the few were invited in to feel the sacred fabric directly. But what was that weave? Where did this magic fabric reside, in what hidden dimension? How could such a strange thing actually happen? Who was the weaver? And why me?

Throughout my life answers to these conundrums have come to me in insightful tidbits, and with each answer more questions pop up like a hydra. It has not been for lack of seeking. I have lived with Thelemic magicians steeped in Aleister Crowley. Studied under Native American shamans. Gone on guided psychedelic journeys in far mountains, flying high on ayahuasca. Meditated at Zen temples. And lived the life of a hermit for months on end. So I have had my spirit quests. Perhaps these all boil down to nothing more than a searching for an understanding that, though our human mind-consciousness may be limited, it is still capable of great spiritual freedom to explore the far realms if we so chose it. I'll delve into all this further on.

At this time in my life, I was also slowly becoming politically aware of the larger forces of history and social upheaval unfolding beyond the blinkers of my youthful myopia. These were the riotous 1960s after all. My father mentioned something about an "International Day of Protest" against some sort of conflict being waged by US forces in an Asian country named Vietnam. There should be no war anywhere, he railed, unless Congress declared it. I then heard about the struggles in Palestine, as Israel and Jordan battled for the Hebron heights and its environs. My great uncle Grover, my grandfather's older brother, had been Israel's first American ambassador, so my parents took a keen interest in the Middle East. The American spacecraft, *Surveyor*, landed on the moon about then and I recall my father showing me pictures of the lunar landscape in a glossy spread in *Life* magazine. I recall being disappointed at how barren and dull it looked. How could the moon shine so brightly like a white doubloon in the night sky, and yet be so dusty and gray up close? And in 1965, and more so again in 1966, most of Latin and South America tumbled into social and revolutionary turmoil to roil the world.

The Cuban Revolution of 1959, for one, had doubtless galvanized other disaffected leftists, put-upon workers, and beaten-down farm peasants, in countries as diverse as Mexico to the north and Argentina in the south, to seek redress for their grievances. In Venezuela, the most passionate partisans of revolutionary struggle were the "notorious" Las Fuerzas Armadas de Liberación Nacional (FALN), arguably the best organized and most successful guerrilla group in Latin America in the early Sixties, post Cuba, at least for a brief flare. In response to their growing political clout in the countryside, the rightist government of Venezuela called for martial law in many outlying states where the newly formed guerillas of FALN were active.[5] Yet all efforts by FALN to influence the 1963 general elections proved futile. Their increasingly violent conflicts were doubtless a turn-off to the generally pacifist rural poor who might otherwise have supported their aims. For American families such as ours living in Venezuela, and even more so for the corporate interests doing business there, the bombings, kidnappings, armed attacks, and even executions associated with FALN were an obvious and present threat.

Several episodes of revolutionary fervor, which I witnessed first-hand, may explain some of my growing curiosity pertaining to leftist causes across the globe. I've been an ardent lefty since. Though I am interested today in most all insurgent struggles, I can say all the same that I eschew all calls to violence and have done so since my twenties. The fantasy of taking up a machine gun and mowing down the crypto-fascists of racism and petty hatreds is best left to Hollywood directors. On one occasion, though, during a

---

5. The real fear, of course, was that rural peasant-guerrilla conflicts would join hands with student-led urban uprisings, and squeeze out the grifter class of exploiters who were enriching the powerful oligarchs. A refurbished Monroe Doctrine (Kissinger. McNamara, Dean Rusk) was patched together, to institute reigns of terror intended to silence, and in some cases, assassinate those who dared to question the cozy and exploitive cronyism so rampant in Latin America at the time.

Boy Scout camping trip to the Parque Nacional Guatopo southeast of the capital, I heard a firefight in the mountains, which the well-armed government militia claimed was with rebels associated with Ernesto "Che" Guevara, who was giving tactical aid to the FALN. I had not a clue at the time who this revolutionary miscreant Che Guevara was, of course. It's highly unlikely that the claim that Che was fighting in Venezuela is remotely factual, but for a thirteen-year-old, it was an enthralling experience nonetheless.

A truck had dropped our scout troop at a small rainforest waterfall near a turn-around at road's end. From there, we headed up into a wall of tropical vegetation. Suddenly, we were enveloped in a strange otherworldly stillness, encircled by the rainforest's velvet glove. We saw ferns as tall as floor lamps, emerald cups of pitcher plants, soft mosses everywhere steaming with humidity, and vast banyans towering into the cathedral gloom above. Soon enough a ruckus in the canopy started up as red howler monkeys bellowed their annoyance at our intrusion.

A monastery, long abandoned to malaria and the monkeys, had collapsed in ruin at trail's end; this was our final destination the next day. For the first night, we pitched our camp on a gravel bar by a soft stream tumbling through verdant castles of ferns and vines. The troop had barely finished its meager dinner, when suddenly—my god! We were not alone. In a thrice, we were surrounded on the burning ground by armed gunmen who appeared out of nowhere. I counted fifteen in all, dressed in fatigues, their shoulders laden with guns. Wary and war-weary, they seemed care-worn from conflicts I could only imagine, with great straps of bullets slung over their shoulders. The gunmen, for their part, had at first thought that we innocent campers were the gang of ruthless rebels they were looking for, seen by woodcutters the week before. They all burst out in hollow laughter.

"Hijole! Rico gringos! Pfft. Meros niños pequeño." They spat the words out derisively, seeing nothing but piss horn gringos. "Bah! soló niños!"

The alarmed scoutmasters leapt up gallantly, quick to confer with the taciturn leader, a hawk-nosed capitán in camouflage pants and grimy t-shirt. He lugged some sort of oily machine gun over his collarbone like a toddler's toy. He nodded a sullen welcome. The heated conversation was quick and to the point. The words heard in the brief exchange were clear of ambiguity, bell-clear and sinister.

"Si, si. Ernesto Guevara. La guerrilla Che. Pendejo! Cabrón!" like a bullwhip. At this the hardened leader spat into the dirt, then clamped the stubbed cigar back between brown teeth. With a nod to his lounging men, they all lumbered on up the mountain into the gloom. The alarmed scoutmasters were left to wonder, what to do? As if in answer, a new sound pattered through the jungle, the coming splotch splotch splotch of evening rain, and listen, distant thunder.

To us boys, Ernesto Guevara meant nothing. Who was this man whom the soldiers seemed so keen to kill? We didn't have much time to ponder, because the jungle canopy above us began to dance; it was both life-giving and macabre, under the baton of the coming storm. It was suddenly a full-on tropical downpour. Well, duh, it was rainy season, what were the scoutmasters thinking? A moment later, the heavens opened up in earnest, hissing and pelting, shower squalls soon lashing the wind-tossed trees with the storm front. The once gentle stream soon became a torrent seething so rapidly with white teeth that it swept away our flimsy campsite from the gravel bar with a broom of raging water. Much of our gear was suddenly gone.

Huddled under the ineffective umbrella of a banyan, our troop counted off, screaming our names above the roar. Hours seemed to pass. Finally the last showers dwindled to pitter-patter, as a strange black peal of receding thunder echoed into the far valley. But was it thunder? Listen. No, not thunder... "Good grief! Gunshots...!" muttered the scoutmasters. Explosions! Unmistakable rata-tat-tat of gunfire echoing down the vast rain-drenched valley of the broken mountain. What should we do? Then, just as suddenly, the gods took back their fire bolts and the drenched jungle sighed with sudden relief. There was silence despite the rush of the subsiding torrent in the creek bed. Ghostly wraiths of morning mist drifted in like shadows. Somewhere a scarlet macaw squawked a morning tantrum. Still no one moved for a good long while. The scoured sandbar, we saw, was swept clean. And we sad-sack scouts were sodden through. Not a word was spoken, and in dead silence our troop broke what was left of our camp, collecting up ruined gear where we could find it. How tedious it was fetching blankets, kettles, tent poles, food tins, and an endless jumble of bric-a-brac lodged from amid the tree stumps.

At mid-morning on the long muddy climb down, the scoutmasters having advised retreat, we suddenly heard voices again. Now they were coming from above—booming voices again ordering everyone to step aside. "Oye muchachos! ¡Basta!"

The band of weary soldiers abruptly reappeared, like gaunt jackdaws. We stepped aside as they slumped down the slippery trail in a grim patrol. They stank of sweat and gunpowder. Three apparently were wounded. One moaned upon a makeshift stretcher made of a wet blanket tied to a cut pole, his leg mangled. Another tended a head wound as he stumbled pitifully down on a comrade's shoulder. In the rear, barely older than us scouts, a disoriented lad held a bandaged hand at the wrist with a grimace. His pistol holster yawned empty; he had also lost a shoe. None acknowledged us in their grim descent. No other words passed between the soldiers and our silent troop. I felt a mixture of astonishment and quiet dread. Suddenly the phony gunfights on TV series like *Gunsmoke* and *Bonanza* were made vividly real and horrifying. In my memory, it was a dreadful passing, without acknowledgement from any of the actors in this Dantean drama. We wretched scouts just stared dumbly: here marched our first processional of death.

Childhood

The second encounter I had with the FALN was in downtown Caracas itself. A German-owned art gallery in the center of town had an annual "Children's Show" of paintings and sculptures curated for "European-descent" children under fifteen years of age, like myself. This was not a juried exhibit by a long shot, but rather a means for A-B-C-G (American-British-Canadian-German) expats to celebrate their little Sally's and Johanne's artwork as a grand social event on the annual calendar of non-Latino celebrations.

There was an extensive German immigrant population in Venezuela at the time, mostly of Jewish intelligentsia who had fled the brutal grip of National Socialism in the 1930s. I recall one such household, where my mother and I saw an enormous print of Johannes Brahms playing the piano while smoking a cigar. In the famous print,[6] the smoke from the stogy sends a curl of smoke wafting above the composer's bushy head. My mother proudly exclaimed to our hostess that we, too, had that same print, hanging in our living room. "Oh, no, no!" exclaimed our hostess somewhat dismissively. "This is the true original! See it is Willy von Beckerath's first handprint, hand-tinted, signed here in his own hand with dedication to our family, lower right corner, dated 1904. A personal gift from Willy, himself, to my grandfather, of course." She waved at the portrait imperiously with a proud smile.

A budding artist I was not. Even so, I was encouraged to submit to the Children's Exhibition my own painting of a yellow flowering Guayacan tree (*Tabebuia chrysantha*) silhouetted against a pale blue sky. I still have the damn thing. On the day of the opening, my mother was driving me downtown to the gallery, me chafing in an outgrown school jacket and necktie, hair spiffed up, when suddenly, as we approached the gallery itself, we saw a scene of chaos, with people everywhere dashing madly about,

---

6. Ergo the cover of this very book, and its title, with no little irony, and in true revolutionary homage, to Thelonius Monk's sublime LP and cover—*Underground*—photo-shopped onto Johannes B.

some bleeding from head wounds. Not ten minutes before, FALN revolutionaries (so the Venezuelan government said later) had apparently sprayed the gallery with gunfire. Several people were wounded, none too seriously, though the gallery with its precocious artwork was essentially wrecked. Hearing the sirens of approaching police and ambulances, my mother promptly did a U-turn without stopping to investigate further and dashed me home. I was deeply disappointed when my painting was returned to me a month later without a single bullet hole. Harrumph. Can't they even shoot straight?

But no matter how much my mother or my father tried to gloss over what had happened, my curiosity as to the "why" only grew in proportion. Certainly when talking about it to me, my parents' approbation towards the "rebels" ("terrorists" as yet was not an epithet in current vogue) was more for the mindless damage to property, and the danger to children's lives (none of whom were seriously hurt in either the gallery shootout or the Scouts' outing) than a fundamental political disgust at the Leftists' aims. In any case, my own take-away was somewhat different. Tinged as these affairs were with a sort of wild-west adventure to them, a la OK Corral, which to a thirteen-year-old is a *big*-potatoes allure, this asymmetry between Leftist aims and bourgeois response caused me to become oddly attuned to the latter's ineffective censorship on the topic. I knew vaguely that there must be some sort of deeper grievance than just wanton destruction; somewhere there had to be underlying iniquities as yet unspecified. I was beginning to surmise, perhaps because pervasive social inequalities so evidently existed, that these in turn had brought on the rebels' violent reactions. I was thirteen and my thinking on such matters was callow and clumsy, but nevertheless sincere. As anyone who has travelled in Latin America well knows, slums are everywhere: these grim rubbish-strewn shanties are impossible to miss. I recall once as a teen in Mexico when my mother felt obliged to drive me to one of our maid's homes "in the barrio" to honor their daughter's quinceañera—the coming out at age fifteen. I was stunned at the maid's shack, its beaten dirt floor, their abject poverty. I was maybe sixteen and blithely ignorant about such hardscrabble living. But the "what" of the matter with regards to FALN escaped me despite my nascent curiosity.

Other than a momentary boost in my street cred among fellow students for having seen the gallery wreckage first-hand (some of my classmates had had artwork in the same show), our British School was singularly hush-hush about the insurrection, extinguishing any exploration of the topic. My mother simply didn't engage my enquiries after a bit, perhaps to insulate me from her own fears. More to the point, ensconced as I was in the lap of white ex-pat privilege in Caracas, with a lovely home, a Venezuelan maid who came and went, the might of American imperialism at our collective back, and so on, nowhere in my life was there anywhere to triangulate an insight into why the rebels were fighting as they did, still less a heuristic inkling of why I was so privileged and the rebels so angry. The weekly land grabs that the FALN decried, the mistreatment of peasants, the disenfranchisement at the ballot box, the arbitrary searches and seizures, the rounding up of student Leftists who were then tortured, these were unknowns to me at that time, though I patched bits together over time.

All in all, perhaps it was a blessing in disguise that I was left naïve and ignorant. However, these explosive events, experienced so early in my life, prepared me in ways I could not fathom at the time for far greater acts of political violence I was to experience first-hand in the years ahead.

Chapter 2
Like Life Without Parole

Boarding Schools in the States

The difference between boarding schools in the US and those in the UK were remarkable to the degree which they seemed to mirror the trajectories each country took to put the war years behind them. America boomed and England struggled; it's as simple as that. Where maggot races out of cabbage heaps at Papplewick proved the norm in England, we had more of everything, and even ice cream, in America. Where dorms in the UK were filled with dreary rows of creaky, lumpy, toss-off army cots in rows of twenty, boarding schools in America offered sensible bunk beds or real twin beds for upper formers with only one roommate, and after your second year, rooms of your choosing. You might not end up liking your first roommate, true, but at least there was only one of the offenders, not twenty whining brats, you among them. Luckily, I rather liked most of my roommates.

Doubtless because of their fears of the revolutionary fervor spreading across my birthland, by the fall of 1965 my parents had sent me packing to a boarding school outside of Hanover, New Hampshire (home to Dartmouth College—not yet a university at that time). My great uncle Lee, whom my father loved as a man of kind dignity and deep probity, lived in Hanover at the time. He was the retired Dean of the College (1952-1959), and was then kicking about in retirement for things to do when I came north.

He had recommended Cardigan Mountain School, which took in boys in grades four through nine. It was situated on beautiful Canaan Street Lake, east of Dartmouth by fifteen miles, with the eponymous mountain and surrounding state forest beautifully etched as a green-carpeted peak in the distance. Both I and my brother, two years ahead of me and at another boarding school in Kent, Connecticut, were spending our teenage years studying abroad from where our parents lived. My younger sister was the only sibling left at home through the rest of the 1960s.

Cardigan Mountain School was perhaps not seminal in my maturation to a boisterously political adult, but it did afford me my first glimpse into life in America, even if cosseted in a New Hampshire boys' school. As a middle school for boys, Cardigan was considered one of the best, I suppose. In some ways I barely remember my two years there, though a few highlights stand out. For one, in my second year at Cardigan, the school chaplain sexually assaulted me. It never came to much, since I was both bigger and stronger than him, so I was able to rebuff his ardent, if inept, advances by the simple expedient of pushing him aside and dashing away. But I did become aware, first-hand, that my own behaviors in response to the molestation followed the observed clinical pattern of not telling anyone anywhere of the attack. Being bigger than my abuser even at thirteen, I was able to withdraw from the abuse through self-protective measures, in short shoving the man off me and avoiding him on campus. I can hardly imagine what sort of hell other less fortunate kids suffered as they navigated their own dark paths of self-loathing and fear. Around the chaplain I quickly put on an air of haughty defiance such that the bungling man eventually kept his distance. Yet a young boy can never really wash off the dark taint of such an experience. One comes away feeling like a sinner covered in ashes that no cleansing can rub off. Ever after there is this chasm that cannot bear one's soul as weight.

What a sad story of human failing and deceit. In truth, it is here in writing about it that for the first time I make this public. I'm guessing the chaplain is well into his nineties now or dead. I mourn that his subsequent abuses may have been traumatic for other boys, but I never thought to report him. I was convinced it would have gained me nothing, while at the same time might have caused me to be ostracized as a "queer" myself. Besides, in a he said/she said world, how do you prove it? Retaliation from the accused, especially with him in a position of power as chaplain, might well have been ruthless. So, you remain stoically silent and carry on, even as some inner lightness is extinguished forever.

At the same time, I became aware of a strange sense of pervading pity for the poor chaplain. It informed my growing emotional intelligence, I guess, prompting nascent critical thinking skills to dwell on my feelings beyond just revulsion. His whole predatory fumble seemed so inordinately pathetic that I just couldn't quite bring myself to hate the man. He had a young wife and a new baby after all. He seemed so abjectly lonely in his fake life that his tortured sexual identity seemed like a malignant manifestation of a larger sickness of societal prejudice and hypocrisy in the world. Had he been allowed a same-sex partner at that time, none of his predations would likely have happened. Such crucibles of experience can instill in a young heart, as it did in mine, some notion of empathy. Whatever this odd empathy may have been, though, it did not extend to my bitter feelings toward religion and the church as symbols of this repugnant hypocrisy. The perversion had occurred in a church school, after all, by no other personage than the chaplain himself. Where was God while this assault unfolded? I saw this as the rankest sort of swindle of convoluted logic—where the evasion of "God is but testing you, my child" seemed so utterly pathetic and dishonest. I could see right through these sorts of sanctimonious pieties and pretenses masking this heinous behavior, made worse in a purported place of worship and sanctity. My lifelong antipathy to all religions, to churches of every stripe, to gods for whom there is no evidence, was sealed for life at Cardigan. I realize in myself today a tendency toward withering mockery of "gods" of any sort. Obviously, the ecumenical god of Cardigan was singularly absent and indifferent to this child's plight. The convoluted logic that molestation was somehow "God's Will" seemed utterly ridiculous. I deduce with philosopher Bertrand Russell, a mirroring quip that there's absolutely "insufficient evidence" that any divinity is ever likely to turn up to change my mind on this point. As First Secretary of the Communist Party, Nikita Sergeyevich Khrushchev said when visiting the UN in 1959: "Sputnik go up. No heaven!"

I may as well come clean on my "beliefs" here as anywhere in this narrative. This is not to say that I don't see that all sorts of gods live on, figuratively lodged between people's ears as belief systems. By this criterion there is evidence that gods certainly do exist for many people, probably billions of them. Doubtless, too, there has to be something in how the human mind evolved, in tandem with our early hominin emotional states of fear and awe, that made our species prone to believe in magical beings, if only to answer the existential "whys" of life. The need for such beliefs is almost universal. So I accept that religious faith is inarguably real; perhaps long ago it was even an important evolutionary meme for early hominins to thrive. A survival strategy, if you will, that cohered tribal bands together under a banner of common beliefs and ritual. Truth be told, even as early as Cardigan, I actually had a permeating curiosity about most all religions, especially their earliest forms in paganism and shamanism. I kept jabbing at these mysteries like a tongue probing a cracked tooth. My sojourn at Cardigan Mountain School made me a nascent, if curious, doubter, and thence into the budding humanist and disbeliever I am today. Actually, I prefer the word "apatheist"—I just don't give a fig leaf if God exists or not.

On the upside, Cardigan stands out for another reason, which would play an outsized role in my formative twenties and thirties. I came to rock'n'roll brother, amen. Suddenly all the boys had LPs of the Monkees, the Beatles, the Beach Boys, the Troggs, the Mamas and the Papas, the Rolling Stones, and all the Merseybeat 45s you could want to spin on cheap turntables like the ubiquitous and handy Dansette portable. The glorious sounds of nascent rebellion blared out of every dorm room. I owned no records of my own at the time, and was envious, though when I finally bought the Monkees' eponymous first album in a Times Square subway station record shop in 1966. Confirmed atheist I may have been, but as I walked back into the city's sunlight, heaven opened up for me.

Back in Venezuela, my father had a faux veneer 1950s record console with built-in speakers. Lift up the top, plop down your record, place the needle, and music filled the living room. We had an odd assortment of LPs: Herb Alpert and the Tijuana Bras (*The Lonely Bull*), Trini Lopez (*La Bamba*), Sergio Mendez and the Brazil 66 (*Mais Que Nada*), Etta James (*Fool That I Am*), Petula Clark (*Downtown*), the Ramsey Lewis Trio (*The In Crowd*), Getz/Gilberto (*Corcovada*), and many amazing samba vinyl records, one-offs pressed in Brazil from the 1950s (artifacts which would inspire Paul Simon twenty years on, of which more later). Also, there was the inimitable Tom Lehrer, whom my dad adored, cheek by jowl with Allan Sherman LPs. My mother most definitely was partial to classical music. This is why she had bought the Brahms print from a stall seller along the Seine and had it framed. Cheek to cheek with the lounge music of my father's were stacks of Ludwig Van and Pyotr Ilyich with all the usual big wigs of nineteenth-century romantic movements piled in stacks with Bach cantatas.

But then along came the Lovin' Spoonful on their late 1966 tour. Sure, I liked other bands better, the Stones for one, and had my first wholly-owned Monkees LP in my covetous hands. I had heard a few Spoonful songs on the radio, "Do You Believe in Magic" foremost among them. In September of that year, we boys seized the opportunity to go by bus to Hanover and see the band play live in concert, I was just giddy with excitement. Who among us doesn't remember their first rock concert? The crowd, the crush, the loud music, the blazing lights, the trying, and usually failing, to look cool. In my case, I busted my concert virginity on a band that even my mom thought wholesome and cute. Dartmouth College was all boys back then, and Cardigan was all boys, too. But heaven-sent, there was amid the crowd this miraculous smattering of cute girls in short skirts huddled together like flocks of wondrous birdlife. Oh my.

But even as that night in the Dartmouth gym imprinted an experience of pure delight on my dazzled mind, it also etched in me a nascent recognition that the reckless power inherent in rock'n'roll would blaze a path for my 1960s generation. I may not have known it would set me on a career path as a punk rock promoter from the late 1970s on, but one must start every journey somewhere. The Lovin' Spoonful revved up mine. The hypnotic power of the crowd was not lost on me in my first encounter with the counterculture. I didn't know it then, but the inherent power of "we got the numbers" as Jim Morrison would wail on the Door's "Five to One," was a powerful precursor that would influence the anti-war marches of my generation. Rock'n'roll dragged that transformative decade forward to Nixon, to the Tet Offensive, and on to Altamont. In fact, ever since, rock and rebellion have been inextricably linked, from "Chimes of Freedom" to Farm Aid to the riotous "Full Disclosure" of the Fugazis.

The night of the concert, it wasn't John Sebastian who drew my gaze the most, as it happened, but rather the drummer, Joe Butler. Up on his podium with the cymbals and tom-toms surrounding him, I just couldn't take my eyes off the way he pounded those skins, the flurry of his drumsticks. He had this habit of swinging his head back and forth to the beat such that the marvel of his long quasi-pageboy haircut flew wildly from side to side in a tail-feather span. I thought that the whole gestalt of his "look" was the coolest thing I'd ever seen.

By the time I graduated from Cardigan in the spring of 1967, not only had the world of Vietnam-era America changed forever, making mockery of my sort of cloistered boarding-school innocence, all shattered as it would soon be, but my father had been re-posted from Venezuela to Mexico, as the head of Shell's office of petro-chemicals for Latin America. *México aquí venimos!* Returning from Cardigan in the late spring of 1967, now to Mexico where my parents had moved again, was the turning point in my becoming a full-blown, if puerile, anti-war activist. Back in the cosseted world of Cardigan, news reports about American "incursions" into Vietnam were spotty. Most of the time it was just whispered rumors. But by 1967, with me being a less-than-worldly if ardent fifteen-year-old, the palpable ferment that simmered beneath the coming summer caused my inherent antiestablishment predilections to fill me right up with a thirst for more. Newspapers blared grim headlines. Casualty numbers filled the airwaves. Flag-draped coffins on the tarmac seemed to be an iconic if forbidding backdrop to life. CBS News anchor Walter Cronkite became the nation's avuncular oracle of the debacle. Dove-footed peace signs became ubiquitous. The first stories of "hippie communes" appeared, and of course the Age of Aquarius and Haight-Ashbury filled me with curiosity. Our whole family even went to visit that shaggy mile of hippiedom in the summer of 1967, where Jefferson Airplane sat on the stoop smoking their joints of weed in that Peace & Love neighborhood of San Francisco. How I longed to be just like them.

Before our family's trip out West during that summer holiday, I remember spending a day in New York City that spring on my way home from Cardigan. I arrived in Port Authority by bus from Hanover, on my way to catch a flight out of La Guardia home to who knew what in Mexico City. There I suddenly was, on the big bad streets of Gotham brimming with vibrant, cool, loud, laughing, face-painted burgeoning non-conformity everywhere, which mesmerized me to my loafer soles. The songs of Simon and Garfunkel "Live from NYC" blared from car radios. Hippies with goatees smiled back at me, granny-glasses perched on their noses. Flower-power rockers and long-haired girls in flowing dresses seemed everywhere, these visions of norm-busting-defiance striding up and down the avenues like walking billboards to freedom. The palpable battle lines between staid fifties culture and sixties explosive counterculture were electrically evident everywhere, not just in Greenwich Village. And so, I caught my plane to my new "home," arriving in Mexico City on the cusp of arguably the most blazingly brutal and bloody of all counter-culture revolutions and clashes of the 1960s, culminating in the horrific Tlatelolco Massacre of October 2, 1968.

The City of Tenochtitlan

What to say about Mexico City in 1967, and its 1968 Olympiad, on through to 1971 when Familia McDonald left the tropics for good? Caterwauling world it may have been, but it began in fine fashion for me with one long litany of firsts. In the wider world, you had black athletes Tommie Smith and John Carlos at the Olympic Stadium raising their fists in defiance on the medal podium, while stoner me was purchasing quarts of liquid peyote in washed out bottles at the massive downtown Mercado Central—all for less than ten pesos a bottle (about seventy-five cents). Mexico introduced me to sexual seduction and drugs. It made me a connoisseur of rock'n'roll as never before, since as a gringo it was easy to purchase cool *álbumes de "rock" música* in New York City, thence return from the land free of the brave and impress all the local girls with rock's latest hip LPs. *Las canciones mas nuevas de Los Beh-at-les! y Los R-r-r-oling Stone-es!* as the Mexican DJs pronounced the British wave on blaring radios coming out of every cantina and bodega. Mexico also opened me to a sort of mysticism of the *Indios*, to those pagan spirits as I saw invoked by arid-land farmers when they tossed out the local priests as ineffectual louts, turning instead to ancient folk gods to bring them rain. I had become a habitué of a sort of expat teenage hedonism, but I became existentially aware of my dismay at seeing peasant squalor and poverty on rides to and from the airport. The shantytowns stretched for miles.

When I turned sixteen, I was of an age and certainly of a privileged enough group to be considered fully an adult in that vast metropolis. Everywhere we went in Mexico City, we were able to walk into any bar and buy a drink without a blink, as long as we gringos had the money. We could drive the great glittering avenidas of the city, essentially without thought of having a driver's license, and pay off a cop if he stopped you—twenty pesos were more than enough. I remember treating two scruffy beggar boys to a meal at the finest sidewalk café in Mexico in the famous Zona Rosa, with two hippie girlfriends of mine from school. The waiter was mortified. When we waltzed out, we climbed the massive Ángel de la Independencia monument at the central traffic circle in the city, smoked some pot and danced amid the bronze mermaid statues fifteen feet up. Traffic stopped to ogle. But down we leapt like monkeys when half a dozen police cars came blaring, and we vanished into back alleys howling. The beggar boys had a blast.

My parents, in any case, were just beginning to make new friends among the ex-pat business class in the city. My brother, sister, and I were reaching out more tentatively, but soon enough we had our own gang of troublemakers to make do with anywhere in the city we wanted to go. Our first house in the old district of San Angel was built precariously above a dirty *barranca*, or dry gully heaped with tossed bric-a-brac, tires, and busted toasters, and was forever patrolled by mangy dogs who roamed for scraps. Yet the house was nice enough.

The neighborhood we lived in was filled with many eighteenth-century haciendas with great oaken gates sandwiched in between more modern urban homes. All of the houses were built behind high walls topped with glass shards or barbed wire. There was a Trumpian mentality that the *peons* would storm our bedrooms absent these deterrents. Up and down the cobbled streets, bicycle vendors selling every imaginable ware called out to the servants in the big houses to come and sample their merchandise or their services. Fruit vendors, knife grinders, odd-job mechanics, cook pot sellers, cobblers, *"Tortillas! Tortillas frescas ya calientes! Tortillas vienen a buscalas!"* on and on. Each peddler-vendor, I came to realize, had a different, product-specific sales call, be it a different bell, horn, whistle, or song. It was a remarkable cacophony, as the daily cicadas took up their rasping choirs in the high trees. Maids often huddled in the stout doorways chatting shyly with their novios, or boyfriends, taking their two-hour lunch break. The jokes about siestas were entirely true. Lunch everywhere in the city began at 1pm and went to about 2:30pm. Sated workers would then sack out and nap under any shady tree they could find. There you would see them, straw hats over their heads, lazing for an hour. Then by some silent spell, up they'd all get and go back to work till six. After that the great city seemed to sigh for a spell only to come together for supper at about 8pm, a festive repast that usually went straight through to midnight in gay camaraderie on patios and out of doors. Rich and poor alike ate late under the strung lights. Few went to work before nine the next morning.

    I didn't realize it at the time, but the teeming Distrito Federale (or city proper) was slowly being given a colorful if paper-thin facelift for the XIX Olympiad to be held all over the metropolis the following summer (1968). The miles of shanty towns out by the airport all the way in to downtown got a veneer of bright stripes of paint, the whole Avenida Gonzalez long. This façade provided gringo tourists with some eye candy to cover over the slums as they were whisked without discomfiture to the tony Zona Rosa, where all the posh hotels and shops were. Even in the 1960s, Mexico City was one of the largest burgeoning metropolises in the world. On weekends, to get away, my father took us exploring by car on back roads where we'd get thoroughly lost. Half of the dirt roads we rumbled over weren't even on a map. How I loved these excursions into the unknown, where we'd been told *banditos* would rob gringos without a thought.

One thing I have always loved about England, once one fled the dreadful roil of London, is that the residents of her countryside dales revered the tranquility of their ancient routines tied to the rhythms of their upland farms. Three-hundred-year-old houses stood fast in the hallowed ground against suburban encroachments. The old ways were fiercely guarded for their inherent humanity against the soulless shopping plazas and townhouses of New Urban Planning that were popping up everywhere. At least that was true in the UK during the 1960s. In Mexico, it was truer still. Anywhere outside the larger cities, the rural communities in the dry, sun-burnt countryside seemed not to have changed a jot since Emiliano Zapata's time. Quaint villages abounded around every turn, where fields of tended agave grew in blue-green rows to the foothills. From the squeezed pulp of these sharp succulents the locals made their pulque, mescal, and pretty darn good local tequila, too. The totality of the whole seemed to thrive quietly with sleepy contentment, at least it seemed so to privileged outsiders like us.

Doubtless the lives of the peasants were difficult enough, dry and hardscrabble as the stands of maize in the fields, but they always seemed so ready to smile in their shy fashion. The small towns were invariably built round a formal square or zocalo, where some eighteenth-century church would throw open its oaken doors to call the faithful to prayer. There was a timelessness about these earthen townships, which scarcely counted the years as generations came and went, barefoot and insular into the new day of the waning twentieth century. The men wore traditional sombreros and ponchos, leading laden burros down crooked streets; the women wore colorful skirts, their jet-black hair in ponytails down embroidered blouses of washed white. Bathed in silver sub-tropical sunshine, these hamlets seemed always caught in an eternal and ethereal glow as you stepped out of some dark bodega onto the wooden porch facing the square. There you could behold the village anew, like an explorer coming out of the gloom of a Mayan temple into the sun. In some villages, a fountain drew youngsters to sit by the coolth of its rim. Pigeons cooed. Throughout it all, the tranquil beauty of the plastered walls, the dark tiled porches, and the church bell tower seemed by some strange magic to keep all intrusions by progress at bay, thwarting the vile commercialism of the burgeoning century from further rude intrusion. In tranquil habitats such as this, Mexico lived out the hardscrabble life of its peasantry, unchanged and seemingly unchangeable, enchanted even, to bless her requited concord through the centuries with a steadfast adherence to the rhythms of an unchanging life. This quietude, this time of forgotten human-scale history, forever instilled in me a countervailing horror at the endless geography of nowhere that is America, the billboard horrors of commercialized strip malls blighting every town off an American interstate, from Maine to Malibu. The outback villages of Mexico, as indeed in the staid British countryside of my childhood, gave strength to these stolid folks, blessedly emboldened to spurn the hijinks of progress with its empty promise of bigger, better, newer, and the pabulum of dubious commercial benefits that progress supposedly would bring—a Jiffy Lube!

I recall vividly one trip we took to Volcán de Parícutin, a geologically anomalous cinder cone volcano in the far state of Michoacán. What made Parícutin peculiarly odd was that in 1943 it suddenly started bubbling up molten lava into a farmer's cornfield—just like that. No one had seen anything like it. The poor farmer doubtless thought it would eventually subside, but month after month, then year after year, then into decades, the lava monster grew, eventually engulfing the nearby village and beyond. The church tower to this day forlornly sticks up out of a dusty lava field. Eventually the central lava flow formed a massive cone, which today stands seven hundred feet high. And for several hundred square miles, a drifting blanket of pumice ash lays thick upon the land. We rented horses to go into the lava fields since all roads had gotten swallowed up by the drifting grit of the effluvium. The horses were a moth-eaten lot: forlorn, skinny, hang-dog, swatting flies lazily with their tails. One was barely able to take my father, who at 6'5" and some 230 pounds, seemed ready to crack its swayed back. But swing up we all did into the ornate vacquero saddles, and off we plodded into the hellish landscape that late afternoon. I didn't find the ruined and gutted village particularly interesting, and was disappointed that they wouldn't take us, or at least their horses, up to the unstable rim of the far-off cone, smoldering with dark foreboding. It seemed the true embodiment of Mount Doom from *Lord of the Rings*. But on the way back, the horses in single file plodded up a steep bluff to have a last view of the volcanic valley. I'll never forget what I saw below.

An evening breeze had come up when we stopped in a small copse of dry pines at the rim and dismounted. Suddenly out of nowhere wheeled an enormous flock of green monk parakeets (*Myiopsitta monachus*), circling out of the evening sky to alight in a whoosh in the pines overhead, all the while carrying on like a schoolyard of screaming kids. It was miraculous and very noisy. It put me in mind of the parrots in Rio. But when I turned back to look down over the gray valley in the last long golden light of sundown, I saw two riders crossing the vast ashen plain below. They cast enormously long shadows over the drifts as they trotted gingerly along. And the wind, as if in concert, whipped up low clouds of pumice ash that funneled off the horses' hooves in the direction of those shadows, making them seem to emerge as if out of a whirlwind. The two men each wore colorful ponchos and wide-brim straw hats. The plain was Ozymandian—boundless and bare, the lone and level sands stretching far away—a poem I knew by heart. With the screeching parrots above, and the chilly wind blowing as if summoned by Merlin himself, into my ears howled Jim Hendrix's anthemic version of Dylan's "All Along the Watchtower." I was thunderstruck.

A Preppy and a Miscreant Perp

I entered my new boarding school in Connecticut that fall (1967), ill prepared as a sophomore for upper-level studies. My brother was already a senior by this time. Kent School, perched dramatically on the banks above the Housatonic River, and surrounded by the verdure of the Berkshire Mountains, was to prove forever seminal in how I became an out-and-out rebel for the rest of my life. I devoured Camus and Herman Hesse. Tackled Sartre. Stumbled upon Henry Miller via the *Colossus of Maroussi*, arguably his finest and most lyric book—I still have a signed first edition in immaculate condition. It was at this time that I came to read J.R.R. Tolkien's grand trilogy, and the contemporaneous yet even more amazing, darkly gripping if marvelously macabre, massive *Gormenghast Trilogy* by Mervyn Peake, first published in 1950. As Anthony Burgess says of this little-known opus: "There is really no close relative to it in all our prose literature." I have been a fan of fantasy and the other-world dystopian genre ever since. By mid-term of my first semester, I had cottoned on to the Beats, Alan Ginsberg, Jack Kerouac, Kenneth Patchen; devoured *Catcher in the Rye*; tripped out on Genet; dug into dystopia with Orwell and Huxley; and blew my mind with *The Teachings of Don Juan*. My tastes in music became more psychedelic and eclectic, leaning toward Hendrix, Jefferson Airplane, Pink Floyd, the Zombies, Iron Butterfly, Beau Brummels, and the Dead, as well as the hard edges of The Doors. I took my first toke of pot up in the wooded hillsides of nearby Algo Mountain and had little pot-induced journeys into the odd worlds of floating woodland fish and talking rabbits. I became curious about LSD and read about the antics of Timothy Leary. In short, it was late 1967.

I rather fancied myself, in the manner of a starved garret poet, a bit of a tortured soul through much of my teens, with the flotsam of Rumi, Leary, Janice Joplin, Vietnam, pirate radio, lunar orbiters, and so on all stuck together in a pastiche of my budding found-art personality. Kent, surprisingly, did have a girls' school five miles up Skiff Mountain to the north. Smaller than the boys' school in the valley, it nevertheless began to provide regular contact with the opposite sex. This was certainly something new and intriguing. By age fifteen or sixteen, most guys in regular American high schools would have been around girls for a good nine-plus years. Other than tussling with my sister, girls were largely terra incognita. To my surprise, though, I found they rather liked my smart-aleck, devil-may-care antics. I was never into sports, despised the jock crowd, postured a lounging disdain toward all authority, and was a middling academic at best. I took up guitar that fall and by the mid-Seventies considered myself rather good in the folk-blues genre; I played around, had coffee house gigs, and tried to impress girls. I also took up writing poetry and even won a poetry prize, the Alice B. Nutter Prize, for best poem. Over the next few semesters, I became an on again/off again junior editor of the school newsletter and joined the photography club. I tried out for a few school plays and got parts, including in *Under Milkwood*.

The long and the short of it is that most every teenager in the Sixties was up to his or her own shenanigans of crazy. Yes, I became a pothead and took LSD on many occasions, once wearing out the vinyl on *Abbey Road* during an eight-hour cosmonaut excursion through inner space guided by John, Paul, George, and Ringo. Uncounted were the number of times I walked the five miles in the dark up to the girls' school at night to smoke pot with a gaggle of fine lasses in the woods. I snuck out of school one weekend and hitchhiked to Cambridge, MA, where my brother was a freshman at Harvard, and saw the Stones, with B.B. King opening, at Boston Gardens. Another time, with a school chum, we commandeered the math teacher's car one night and drove over the state line into New York to visit some girls we knew at the women's college at Millbrook, where Timothy Leary had his estate. The math teacher had foolishly left his keys in his Dodge Dart. Hours later, when my friend and I emerged like sated satyrs from our respective paramours' dorm rooms, to our astonishment, it was snowing up a storm. How we made it back to the school through that blizzard escapes me, stoned out of our minds as we were. The next morning at Assembly, the Headmaster thundered that he knew someone had taken Mr. [let's say Doodlehead's] car because telltale tire tracks were imprinted in the snow, dammit. "Will the miscreants please confess?" he demanded. Confess? Seriously? No, we didn't confess—both my friend and I singularly lacked the necessary moral fiber to cop to such a crime. And so it went for three rebellious years.

Looking back, I can only think that this sort of behavior was rather feckless, selfish, recklessly anti-authoritarian, and, well, stupid—but then that's the nature of hindsight. What if we'd run the math teacher's car into a snowy ditch? We never gave that a thought. But being stupid, like pliant bones, allows most teenagers to muddle through their various tumbles without too many lost appendages, all with a modicum of growing maturity fermenting our heedless souls.

I mentioned Timothy Leary and his estate a moment ago. By the late Sixties everyone had heard of Leary, of course, especially those inclined to drugs and modes of anti-establishment posing. Leary's sayings, themselves too often childishly inane in hindsight, nevertheless resonated with a spoiled, disaffected, world-weary cadre of youth defiantly unwilling to go fight old men's wars. Peace, love, and all that. I read Leary's pronouncements myself and must confess they resonated for me with their aphoristic catch-phrase rebelliousness. Leary's estate was not far from the house my parents had bought in Salisbury, CT, not far from Kent. One school vacation in the spring, I even snuck into his Millbrook compound, known as the Hitchcock Estates, with a friend and wandered about. I'm not sure what we expected to find, maybe a meal ticket to the tuned-in guru's road show. One of Leary's female acolytes called the place "a cross between a country club, a madhouse, a research institute, a monastery, and a Fellini movie set."[7] Spot on if you ask me. The manicured lawns led to a big house, a sort of pastiche French chateau with murals of Hindu gods emblazoned on the exterior walls. A porch ran round the entire front of the house, where more than a dozen zonked-out young folk lounged about laughing with aimless bonhomie. Which is to say, they seemed not to care one bit who we were, nor why we were there, but welcomed us to "Spaceship Leary" with well-rolled joints and goofy banter. Maybe they, too, had hopped the fence and found themselves in this fool's paradise at Leary's expense. The great man, as it happened, was away. So after sharing a few joints, my friend and I drifted away, dropped out as they say, then wandered through the grounds, out the elaborate wrought-iron gates, and thence back to our car on the side of the road. It wasn't these forays while at Kent that particularly set me apart from my school chums, but rather that every vacation while at boarding school, I would leave the hardwood valleys of Connecticut and catch a plane out of New York City to the roiling tropical effervescence of Mexico. I felt that my life had the quality of a yo-yo to it.

The summer of 1968 in Mexico City was a turning point in my life, as far as drugs were concerned. I fancied myself a full-on radical by this time, open to any and all drugs and experimental forays, a wildly flailing lost soul, in truth, as if in all my worldly two dimensions of experience I was now some tortured soul torn like a page from a Gogol novel. Make that Kafka. Being "conflicted" on just about everything seemed all the rage, so I was conflicted. I recall a lovely British girl who drove me down to the Mercado

---

7. Nina Graboi in her autobiography, *One Foot in the Future: A Woman's Spiritual Journey.* (Aeiral Press, 1991)

Central one time, where for a few pesos you could purchase a washed-out bottle of squeezed peyote buds. It was the vilest stuff imaginable, tasting a bit like drinking used engine oil laden with chalk powder. But the mezcaleros at the market topped off the quaff with a layer of thick coconut oil to coat your throat and stomach on the way down. My chaperone and I drove out of town to the ruins of an eighteenth-century monastery in the foothills west of the city at Rocas Xinter National Park. Here I took two or three enormous gulps of the vile stuff, doing everything I could not to gag the concoction back up. There I sat under an enormous Montezuma pine (*Pinus montezumae*) to await enlightenment. But vomit I did, as is customary even on guided peyote trips. You retch out the pulp, wipe your face, then lean back and gaze like Gulliver into the color show of a transformed world. With these cactus bud compounds now coursing through your blood, the hope is always that you might actually meet the god *Peyōtl* (meaning "the glistening one") and be given entrance into the realm of the Nahuatl gods. I was so blessed and was sure that, in the guise of a startled rabbit I came upon, it was *Peyōtl, for sure,* clothed in earthly fur. But alas, unlike Alice, there was no hole to the underworld.

Mescaline is an inducer of a bright, brilliant kaleidoscope of colors heightening an awareness of all things visual to an acute pitch of experience. The jitteriness associated with most synthetic LSD compounds is absent. The high, such as it is, has the quality of the beatific to it, pillowed as you soon become in exotic states of wonder. "It was without question," wrote Aldous Huxley to his editor in describing his first mescaline trip in Mexico, "the most extraordinary and significant experience this side of the Beatific Vision." Huxley is correct, the mundane is opalescent with inner light. Trees come alive. As it had been for Huxley, my hallucinogenic experience amid the ruins that day gave me access to realms of existence that were extraordinarily vivid, curative, and strangely invigorating. I must have wandered the ruined abbey for hours, entranced by every leaf and root. As evening came on,

I recall looking heavenward, seeing the first stars of the constellation Cassiopeia shining like a necklace of opalescent pearls in the evening sky, and was transported as if to heaven itself. I have absolutely no idea how the day ended from there but here I am to tell it, so I must eventually have come back to reality.

Since that day, I have taken most hallucinogenic drugs known to western pharmacology and the DEA,[8] but rarely, if ever, as a recreational drug. There have been one or two exceptions, like a night with Eric Clapton, which I'll touch on later. By contrast, I have taken hallucinogens like psilocybin, mescaline, LSD, DMT, opium, and ayahuasca scores of times with a deep sense of reverence, invariably out in nature or alone in some quiet space. From the age of twenty on, I never "popped pills" in order to dash out into the public arena to dance the night away and behave like an idiot. Nor have I been the least bit interested in party drugs like cocaine, speed, or heroin, which seem so inexorably to lead to abject addiction. By contrast, all the recent studies on hallucinogens, as Michael Pollen elucidates in his fine book on the subject, *How to Change Your Mind* (Penguin Press, 2018), show a path forward for them to be used as curative medicines for most all types of spiritual and psychological malaise, such as PTSD or death vigils in hospice care. The expert collection of essays on the topic edited by J.P. Harpignies, *Visionary Plant Consciousness: The Shamanic Teachings of the Plant World* (Inner Traditions Bear and Company, 2007) is a great primer. From the forward: "[All] indigenous people claim nature speaks to humans through these plants; and entertaining such a dialogue...helps keep our human

---

8. There are now dozens of authoritative books on psychadelia. But to really grasp the gestalt, there's no better place to start than Hunter S. Thompson's madcap dive into the gonzo realm, *Fear and Loathing in Las Vegas: A Savage Journey to the Heart of the American Dream* (Random House, 1972). The first sentence of the book begins, "We were somewhere around Barstow on the edge of the desert when the drugs began to take hold..." and it's bats out of hell from there in a red convertible all the hundred miles to Vegas to attend a Drug Enforcement Agency convention while high on mescaline.

community healthy." Many hallucinogens, in any case, show great promise in allowing depressed sufferers to cope with their trauma in a safe holistic environment under professional guides.

The summer of 1968 in Mexico City was a watershed for me in other ways, as the great lumbering city tried, as I've mentioned, to give itself a facelift as national host of the '68 Olympics. My father and I even went to an exhibition soccer game between Brazil and Mexico (yes, I know my own prohibition on mentioning sports) and saw the magnificent Brazilian soccer star Pele score three goals to beat the home team head on. I recall wild nights of parties with my friends in magnificent houses in the hills. I remember hanging out with radicalized university students at hip clubs and cafes. The worldwide student revolt against authority and militarism, indeed a violent antipathy to the whole rampant edifice of capitalist cronyism so endemic in Latin America, drove one of the largest student protests in the world to surge forth throughout Mexico at the time. And because the revolt was so overwhelming and widespread, the grievances so palpable, the government's response grew more draconian in proportion. It rose to a crescendo as the Olympiad approached, with the fear that visiting suburban sports enthusiasts in the tens of thousands would shun the games, alarmed at the uprising. The city was an odd choice for an Olympics, in fact. Mexico City sits in a valley a mile and a half high in the tropical air at an altitude of 7800 feet. No wonder that in that thin atmosphere, the furthest long jump ever recorded, at 27 feet, 4 inches, was posted that fall and has stood since.

Throughout that summer, students in Mexico marched, boycotted, and demanded that the government sit down and answer their many grievances. The core demand, in all cases, was a fierce call for a reduction in statewide authoritarianism, and a fairer shake for poor students to afford college. Communist factions vied for attention. While the students were the most vocal, many middle-class professionals joined the movement as well, notable among them medical staff, doctors, some lawyers, and the building trades. Huge crowds took to the streets regularly, I among them.

On the beautiful sunny day of July 26, 1968, I took the daughter of a Canadian embassy attaché, a pale redhead also of sixteen, to the town of Puebla situated to the east of Mexico City, on the far side of the massive volcanoes of Iztaccihuatl and Popocatepetl—a two-hour bus ride away. This was to be my first outing as a "proper young man of means," approved by both sets of parents. In short, I was apparently now mature enough at sixteen and sufficiently alert to the task of squiring a date to a far-off town. A summoned cab drove us past the city center to the bus terminal to buy roundtrip tickets to Puebla. Our bus left at 9am, and after a day in Puebla we were to re-board the 4pm return bus, where we'd pick up another cab and return the Canadian attaché's daughter into safekeeping.

It was a glorious day, and I was feeling every inch the mature young gentleman. We arrived in Puebla and had a wonderful time walking through the colonial downtown with its stucco cathedral and quaint stucco-covered sidewalks under tiled roofs. How soon 4pm came—but there we were, back at the bus station, she with some knick-knacks bought at the Mercado. Back off to the sprawling city we went, only to arrive to a city aflame and in utter chaos. It was one of the summer's bloodiest student-government protests, and became known as "The Youth March for July 26." It had been organized by a Communist youth organization, Estudiantes Democráticos, and was a massive mobilization to commemorate the 15th anniversary of the 1952 assault on the Moncada barracks by Fidel Castro during the Cuban Revolution. How were we cosseted gringos to know?

Even on the outskirts of the great city, my date and I knew things were not aright in the great metropolis of Xochimilco and Tenochtitlan. Whole sections of the immense city seemed to stand in flames as the bus passed smoldering barricades; we saw students everywhere, eye slits white with terror over masking kerchiefs, running like a battered rabble in the rubbled streets. Already older women were weeping for the wounded. Within minutes the bus was commandeered and the bus driver thrown out with the rest. We suddenly found ourselves on the street in a world of chaotic mayhem, with masked muchachos yelling for bloody insurrection. Unsure what to do, I clasped my date's hand firmly, and we set out to look for a cab through streets of chaos and fierce struggle. Bullhorns bellowed: *Viva la revoluçión, compadres!* We came at last to the zócalo at city center where a bankroll of grimy pesos in my pocket managed to commandeer a taxi at precisely the moment it pulled out of the back gates of El Presidente's palace, past the terrified guards. In we piled, terrified ourselves, exhaling relief in the back seat, ensconced and presumed safe by the stout cab doors which we promptly locked. I cried: *Oye Viejo! Ándale, andale por favor!* And yet hardly a block later, in the cobbled streets, through curtains of acrid smoke, so laden did the taxi become with other people fleeing the conflagration that the muffler of the old jalopy scraped against the strewn pavement as it labored on under the weight of hangers-on as desperate as us to get the hell out. *Fuera! Fuera! Soldados! Soldados!*

And so the improbable coché lurched out of the fire zone on flattening tires. Several peasant women with bundles pleaded to be let in and we obliged. Then students began to pile on, front, back, and roof. Finally, the world returned to some semblance of normalcy as we left the city center down emptying streets with not a soul out walking. Our stout motherly riders in the cab said they had witnessed a few young men they assumed had been beaten to death. We soon sat in stony silence. And slowly, very slowly, the avenidas became becalmed. The normal sounds of city life at night returned the further we got from the conflagration: laughter in a cantina here, lovers in the shadows there, and thus through slow miles the smoke cleared. We'd made it out. The once distraught students on hood and boot disappeared; the roof clingers slipped away under a veil of silence, till at last those who had found a seat inside the cab beside us, they too bid us "buenos noches" and vanished into the darkening streets. We wished them luck. Suddenly, my gal and I sat alone, dumbfounded, in the back seat of the taxi with no one save the driver as companion, intoning a peon prayer. We thanked our lucky stars.

When at last we arrived at the iron gate of the attaché's hilltop residence, servants had been posted at the door. A hue and cry went up when we arrived. My date's mother, in her housecoat, came down the sweeping steps and wept outright as she greeted the prodigals with great gulping gasps of hyperbole. Far below in the autumn night, fires still smoldered in the vast city and gunshots rose like exclamations in the distance against a canticle sung by a million cicadas in the garden trees above. Within the hour, my anxious father picked me up. We drove home in a sort of strained silence. I'm not sure Dad knew what to make of it all. We could see that, down in the inner city, fires were blazing everywhere like some macabre Bosch painting. "Wow..." was all he managed to say. Ambulances flew by and traffic was backed up on the Periferico, the city's ringing freeway, as many were fleeing the mayhem. We never learned how many students were killed or wounded that night.

In mid-September, reluctantly, I returned to boarding school in America. Two and a half weeks later the Tlatelalco massacre occurred in a park near city center named La Plaza de los Tres Culturas. This small memorial oasis to the country's history celebrated Mexico's three great cultures, the Indians past and present, the Conquistadors and their Spanish colonial rule, and the mixed-race independent Mexico of modern times. Tlatelalco was the Aztec name for the park. It was the early evening of October 2, 1968, when the military opened fire on roughly 10,000 student demonstrators who had gathered in the plaza downtown. Hundreds were massacred in cold blood when they became trapped in the square and government soldiers opened fire with machine guns stationed atop nearby buildings. The student movement "was nothing more than a disgusting ring of infiltrated pro-communist conspirators," according to then-President Gustavo Diaz Ordaz. Many hundreds were slaughtered, although no one knows the exact numbers of the dead. At least 2,000 youngsters were also stripped naked and beaten in military prisons that night. From the last gunshot on, there was an ironclad cover-up, and the shattered corpses of the poor bullet-ridden students were buried secretly in mass graves the next day. It would take more than four decades before the Mexican government even admitted that the massacre had happened, though rumors and eyewitness reports were widespread. How prescient the words of Mexican poet and writer Octavio Paz echo still: "Cold rapid hands draw back one by one the bandages of the dark/ I open my eyes, I am living at the center of a wound still fresh."[9]

Back and forth I went to and from boarding school, a resigned if rebellious preppy. My junior year at Kent, and then my senior, followed a familiar pattern. I was in and out of trouble. I was excoriated by some teachers as a bad seed, but loved by others as creative and engaged. I did drugs. I got caught drinking. Academically at odds, I was mostly a middling student. I found too many of my teachers dull ventriloquists parroting lessons they knew by rote, year after year after year. There were, of course, some wonderful teachers: in English, music, and oddly, biology. In these I came alive and got A+'s. I made lifelong friends amongst my schoolmates, too, with whom I still gather every few years to reminisce. We were childish rebels back then and still are, I suppose, as we continue to champion every revolutionary cause under the sun. Something in the crucible of the Sixties created a spiritual bond between us that has lasted fifty years and counting.

Back in Mexico again, my parents had moved from the barranca house to an eighteenth-century hacienda in San Angel with great oaken doors everywhere and a carriage house. Except

---

9. From the poem "Dawn" in *Selected Poems* (New Directions, 1984).

for the bedrooms, huge shutters alone served as windowpanes throughout the house, where redolent and rosy bougainvillea vines covered the archways. We certainly lived the privileged life of expat Anglos, insulated from the wild anti-war riots north across the border and the burgeoning counter-culture in general. The riots in Mexico were enough of a distraction. North in the US, the battles for black civil rights hardly made the news in Mexico as the Olympiad approached. On vacations from school through those hectic years, my brother and I would return from boarding school with all the latest cool albums, brimming with the patois and chit-chat of radical hippiedom, introducing our parents to the lingo of far-out, groovy, bogart, dope, weed, truckin', mellow, drag, fuzz, freak out, and whatever else has been lost to my hazy memory.

I have noted that my parents were staunch liberals. They were also avid readers. Our house was always filled with books, with many hand-me-downs from my grandfather's large library of scholarly tomes. I, too, became an avid reader, and remain so to this day, an unapologetic print-in-hand snob. I have mentioned my grandfather the English scholar. Several times on my journeys to and from Mexico City, I would stay at my grandparents' house in Lansdowne, PA, for a day or two. Grandpa's collection of books, which I often perused, was amazing. Browsing through it, I felt like the Benedictine novice and tale narrator in Umberto Eco's cracking good novel, *The Name of the Rose*, a lad by the name Adso of Melk, who follows the impious detective William of Baskerville to the heart of a scriptorium's mysteries. While hardly as extensive as the library at the heart of Eco's tale, my grandfather's bookshelves also held hundreds of holograph letters from great writers hither and yon, such as Dos Pasos, Norman Douglas, Santayana, Huxley father and son, and Homer Pound, Ezra's father. I loved the letters from Homer Pound especially. I have had a lifelong love of Pound's *Cantos* and all that he did in championing avant garde English letters in the early twentieth century. But his father

Homer, a Master of the Mint at the federal repository in Philadelphia, was forever decrying to my grandfather that his son's antics through the First World War, as the prodigal provocateur, made him despair from exasperation. In these letters, pa Pound made clear that he was particularly incensed that his son had taken to wearing an earring, "of all things!" and was a showoff who now seemed bent on parading around London, along with the earring and a silver-knobbed cane, draped in a black cape. This wasn't the hip Sixties but rather the staid Edwardian 1916, when the shadow of Victoria still loomed over a Europe at war as her progeny duked it out from gilded palaces. In any case, a corresponding aspersion was echoed by none other than D.H. Lawrence in one of his letters to my grandfather. The collier's son considered Ezra a "detestable young man," decrying as had Homer the affectation of an emerald earring, floppy French chapeaus, and black cape. Pound, by contrast, acknowledged Lawrence's genius from the start of their acquaintanceship. I'll give him that.

In any case, my grandfather's crown jewel came from his decades-long correspondence with D.H. Lawrence. As far back as the early days of the First World War, long before America entered the fray, my grandfather reached out to Lawrence and became a champion of his work in America. Grandfather had a dear friend in Harold Mason, proprietor of the Centaur Bookshop and Press in Philadelphia, whom he persuaded to become Lawrence's American publisher, at least for the non-fiction works. The first of several books by and about Lawrence to be published by the Centaur Press was Lawrence's delightful book of essays, *Reflections on the Death of a Porcupine and Other Essays* (1925). It's a truly lovely limited edition with marbled boards. I have a copy I inherited, inscribed by Lawrence to my grandfather. From the 1920s on, my grandfather was to write the first literary compilations of Lawrence's work, *A Bibliography of the Writings of D.H. Lawrence* (1925), with a follow-up in 1931, *The Writings of D.H. Lawrence 1925-1930*, both put out by the Centaur Press as well. Lawrence himself wrote the introduction for the first book and my grandfather, of course, had the great author's holograph manuscript of that introductory essay amongst his many papers. Biographers have written that Lawrence was careless about his manuscripts. Once his books saw print, Lawrence rarely bothered to haul the manuscripts around. Indeed, in the introduction to my grandfather's bibliography, Lawrence roundly pooh-poohs the whole fetish of manuscripts and first editions. Nevertheless, out of gratitude to grandpa for the 1925 bibliography, Lawrence mailed from the UK (where he was recuperating from a near fatal attack of malaria and tuberculosis caught while on his third visit to Mexico), the hand-written manuscript of *Women in Love*, which David Herbert L. had turned up in a closet while visiting his sister in Nottinghamshire. I recall with what reverence I held that very manuscript as a teenager. The great novel was penned in a tidy stack of three-dozen ruled, blue British schoolboy essay books. That was the first book by Lawrence I read, in the author's own minute and precise penmanship. Later, my grandfather gifted me a few paperback copies of the author's work, *Twilight in Italy* (1916) in particular, as far back as my freshman year in boarding school. Those luminous works gave me insight not only into Lawrence's genius, but also how writing could exude such beauty and majesty to transport any reader to Sicilian sunsets as if in a dream. *Twilight* is arguably the most jaw-droppingly gorgeous book of prose I have ever read. Indeed, there's nothing like it in all of English literature for sheer power of lyric prose.

The *Women in Love* manuscript resides now at the Ransom Center at the University of Texas, Austin, and is in critically frail shape. Lawrence tended to write all his books in these crappy-paper, cheap, ruled, stapled, blue cover, schoolboy essay books. The paper was never intended to last beyond the essay exam. His penmanship was extraordinary, though: a tiny cursive hand, both compact and assertive. I was taken aback by the manuscript itself because Lawrence never went back to edit a word here or a phrase there as I have in writing this memoir. He never finagled a sentence by rewriting it in the hopes of making it more eloquent, never fussed with an erasure here, or a sentence further on with arrows and insert carets. None of that. It's almost as if they were typed in perfect cursive.

I have seen other holograph manuscripts, for example those of Charles Dickens, when I worked at the New York Public Library. Dickens' manuscripts by contrast are just inky blotches of spider crawls, page after blotchy page. Pity the poor editor and typesetter! Not Lawrence. The only rewriting he ever did was to pencil out the occasional paragraphs here and there in its entirety, and in even tinier script, write in a new paragraph above the cross out. I suppose part of Lawrence's genius, and perhaps why his loquacity sometimes grates, is to be found in the manuscripts themselves. The verbiage, the elegiac prose, the sheer poetry of his language, seems to flow like a torrent as if directly out of his creative mind, to pen in hand, to ink on paper, to completion as a holistic and wholly contained artifact, marbled and polished like statuary by the sheer force of his genius. His books seem willed into wholeness with hardly a correction anywhere. Pretty amazing as I sit here struggling to pen this memoir. But there is consequently a lot of repetitive turns in Lawrence's work, looped phrasing that gets wearisome at times. In any case, say what you will about the great novels, Lawrence's travel books have no peer anywhere, in any language, in any era. Yet poor Lawrence himself, consumptive, frail, ever withering to nothing inside a rebellious body—how he suffered! He was like some sort of lost wanderer about the globe, seeking some spark of the Original Fire in the soul of humankind, stopping on each visited continent like the stations of the cross, to die of tuberculosis in Vence, France, precisely a thousand years after Christ, who was himself tacked to his cross at about the same age as Lawrence. On more occasions than I can count, turning to Lawrence's writings and poems has proved a soul-restoring consolation in my life.

Kent School, where I boarded 1967-1970, obviously had its share of "sons and daughters of famous people." Hell, Henry Kissinger, the execrable world meddler, has retired to bucolic Kent after his decades of slaughter across the globe. In fact, in the surrounding townships and countryside live a veritable who's who of A-list society pagers, including the conservative William F. Buckley clan. The most notorious clan to have members become classmates of mine at Kent was the Somoza family. Forgotten now, no doubt, but in their day the brutal son and nephew of the dictator Anastasio Somoza Debayle, of Nicaragua c1967-1972, were notorious and arrogant classmates to match the totalitarian rule of their homeland. Papa was later assassinated in Paraguay in 1980. The reign of Somoza terror through those years was one of the most brutal, egregious, and heartless in all the centuries of such depravity in Latin America. And for several years in the late 1960s, these hoodlums were my erstwhile school chums.

Any reader can delve into the horrendous history of the Somoza rule of Nicaragua, and understand why their overthrow under the Sandinistas was such a victory for social justice. I'll only add that while the given name of dictator Sr.'s son, Anastasio Jr., was foreshortened familially to Tacho, everyone in the radical crowd I hung out with at Kent called this smarmy future torturer "Taco" to his face, much to his seething annoyance. The entire Somoza family was despotic, cruel, and kleptomaniacal, ruling Nicaragua for a generation with an iron fist. I am glad to say that the repulsive tub that was Taco was soon run out of the country following his father's assassination. The Sandinistas even managed to confiscate some of his billions of ill-gotten gains, which they distributed back to the workers. Sadly, Taco remains alive and well in Miami as of 2020, rotund as an oak cask and just as bloated with booze, says the *Miami Herald*.

I recall, in my final semester before graduation, planning all sorts of ridiculous midnight sorties to the far corners of the campus to inflict, a la the Weathermen, fire and brimstone on hockey sheds and the cow barn. It all came to nothing in the end, of course. But in early May 1970, came the news that four students at Kent State had been shot in cold blood during an antiwar protest. My classmates and I were stunned. I immediately organized a vigil to be held in the graveyard of the school chapel. About a hundred students showed up. I recall strapping on my guitar and leading the crowd in "Where Have All the Flowers Gone," but having partaken of the devil weed I got the verses all mucked up. It took someone with aplomb to have the wherewithal to get a hook and haul me off stage lest I repeat the whole silly song again. Then a month later, on the day of graduation itself, with happy moms and dads front to back cooing over their little wonderfuls, the radical wing of our class handed out a mimeographed broadside excoriating the school administration for every imaginable sin that angry, if puerile, eighteen-year-olds might dream up. Life's history books, alas, have not yet recorded this brazen, mutinous, and utterly superfluous deed, so it is inscribed here for posterity.

Chapter 3
Adulthood

Yes, My Vicissitudes Were No Solicitude

My father had a favorite expression which he used to describe my wayward life to about the age of forty. As often as he could find an audience, and feigning an English accent, out would drawl: "Those were the years of Pete's vih-sis-ih-twooodes!" An interesting word, "vicissitudes," meaning, of course: "a change of circumstances or fortune, typically one that is unwelcome or unpleasant." Hard as it is to admit it, Dad and his favorite descriptor weren't far from the mark. But I have no regrets for wandering so far afield through my twenties and early thirties, as if finding my footing meant striding with alacrity any which way, as long as it was in the opposite direction from that pestiferous conformity called "a career." It was a good run of anarchic exploration, I'll say that for myself, and whatever merits this book may have, they are largely due to those vicissitudes.

Unfortunately for your narrator, the path forward through these odd life choices with their wayward travels to the far corners was not always easy, growing crooked more often than not by following the bohemian paths of least resistance, absent the traction to succeed on the straight and narrow. By the summer of 1970, my father had had enough of Shell, and Shell apparently had had enough of him. There was movement in his life to find some other career path for himself. He'd had a good run with Shell, he'd say, but it was time to move on. While I am largely a fierce critic of capitalism in all its forms, my father's working abroad for a world-spanning company like Shell in the 1960s meant the company helped subsidize his children's schooling, offset costs of rather posh housing, provided a company car, paid for servants as needed, and so on. This sort of corporate largesse didn't last much beyond the Sixties. By 1970, with Shell's headquarters' move from London to boomtown Houston, emergent business culture in America became ever more ruthlessly profit-motivated, emphasizing cost-cutting, work quotas, exacting bottom lines, and in short, adopting a callous winner-take-all ethic. All of this was to my father's dismay, a sea change that has today ramped up to the obscene inequalities we see in all neoliberal nations. Earnings reports demand that executives meet exacting profit margins. Cut costs. Bust unions. Hit profit benchmarks. Fire people at will. My dad just balked, and Shell noticed. The year I graduated from high school was his last year with the oil conglomerate.

That year, too, I had been smitten romantically by a British exchange student at Kent. We had met at the school dance. Her name was Linda and, as teenagers will, we started a tortured groping not uncommon to clueless eighteen-year-olds everywhere. While the flames of first love lasted barely a calendar year, they did form the impetus for me to assert a sort of probing independence as a young adult. Lucky for me, despite what my father thought of my failings, Linda and I did manage to remain lifelong friends until her untimely death from lung cancer three decades later.

So it came to pass that with high school graduation behind us, British exchange student Linda was called back to merry olde England by filial duties and anxious parents, and I was meanwhile set adrift. Having eschewed heading immediately off to college, I was suddenly left utterly bereft by her absence. Young love is headstrong and foolish in that way. I was also not keen to get a job at the proverbial car wash. So in the time-honored tradition of many freshly-minted high school graduates, I implored my parents to let me have a summer in Europe at their expense, a gift for my having weathered three dreary boarding schools in a row. I promised that, upon my return, I'd figure out the college thing. They bought this ridiculous ruse. I had absolutely no intention of going to college, at least not then. Be that as it may, I was well aware that the Vietnam War draft was in full swing, that I was now eighteen and eligible, and that college might confer a deferment. My number in the draft lottery was ninety-six, borderline for induction. As luck would have it, though, my draft notice came via the US embassy in Mexico. They forwarded it to our Mexico City address. Handing it to me, my dad made me swear I'd fill it out and send it back to the embassy as required. Plumb my memory as I might, I have absolutely no idea what came of this request, but I'm guessing that with my burgeoning revolutionary fervor against the war, I simply tossed the form in the trash after long procrastination. From that day forward, I was, by my own account and by US law, officially a draft dodger. I was blessed with no local Selective Service Office to track down this act of defiance, and the disorganized embassy certainly did not seem to care. It's amazing how ineffective the young mind is in critical thinking skills, for I had an almost laughable fear that some sort of fedora-wearing gumshoe might at any moment pop out of the woodwork, hot on my tail, and off I'd be dragged to boot camp. This scenario played like a film noir in my mind. I also came to the conclusion that the better part of valor would be to slip across the border to live in Canada as a war resister at some point. As it turned out, in this hair-brained idea I was quite clairvoyant.

But I was too naïve about such matters that first summer of freedom as a diploma-wielding eighteen-year-old to care much about the Selective Service. As to my future, my modus operandi was clearly to make it all up as I went along. I held to Rimbaud's pithy saying, "Everything we are taught is false." This gave me justification to say aloud that I was the captain of my own soul even if I should plummet from grace and, by turns, hence land on my face. My parents, bless them, rescued my soul by their willingness to pay for my airfare to the UK with a wad of cash thrown in for good measure. Sometime that July, I boarded a BOAC flight and landed triumphantly at Gatwick, a very natty and ever-curious chap ready to reacquaint himself with the British Isles of his childhood. My father had arranged ahead of time for me to stay with Linda's parents in the town of Guildford for a week or so, and then I was to do what American kids were doing all over England at the time: blow the soot out of my pipes, have a merry olde time, quaff a few pints, then return, fulfilled, to settle down to college, hence a good job, a wife, two kids, and a car in the garage. Or so it seemed to me. None of this appealed to me in the slightest.

I must say, though, that with proper British aplomb, Linda's parents feigned mock delight at my arrival and put me up in a room "in the back of the house," doubtless to be neither seen nor heard. It was a fine room to me after twelve years in boarding school. As often as we could get away, Linda and I would sneak down into the bracken fields and, as they say, fiddle about. I rather enjoyed fiddling about as it happened. But when my stay stretched to three weeks, then four, and looked to be going on to five, me being in the lap of luxury with no inner decency to move on, Linda's father called my father to say "enough." The phone call came just as Mom and Dad were beginning the arduous planning involved in leaving Mexico to go back to their final home in Salisbury, CT. Linda's aggrieved papa made it clear that I'd overstayed my welcome. Besides, his daughter needed to prepare for teacher's college, so he intended to put me on the road to London that very day and good luck to your son. Dad apologetically mumbled agreement, doubtless shaking his head that once again my intransigence equaled my self-manifesting, repeating misfortunes.

So, that morning, I was unceremoniously summoned by Linda's father the banker, and informed in clarion terms that I was to be deposited on the great Guilford Road to London that very day, where I could either catch a bus or hitchhike into my future life. "Good riddance to you, you layabout Yank" was the message.

I was a bit put aback and suddenly much bluster went out of my young life. I was rather enjoying these cushy days, living in Linda's Guildford home with mama and papa. In any event, I pulled my meager effects together and stuffed them in haste into my rucksack. The good banker shuffled me to his waiting car, but not before I tried frantically to say a fitting farewell to Linda, assuring her in no uncertain terms that I'd be back in touch as soon as I could find a shilling for the phone box. And this is how I met Eric Clapton for the first time.

Linda's father drove me, rucksack slung over shoulder, out to the Guilford Road. I'd already decided to save my dwindling money and hitchhike back to London. He said a polite if firm "goodbye and good luck," and there I was, suddenly alone like a beaten dog by the side of the busy road, not exactly destitute but certainly disoriented. My starting point by thumb into my new life, as it happened, was at a traffic circle with the quickest route to London being the second turn. I had a schoolmate, a Kent friend in London at the time, by the name of Penrose. Somehow, I had managed to reach him (there were only landlines back then) and he had given me an address. He said it wasn't much, but I could sack out on the couch and we'd go from there. So I stuck out my thumb and started hitchhiking. The first vehicle to pick me up was a van with a plastic Mickey Mouse as a sort of weathervane attached to the roof. The side door flew open and a cloud of hashish smoke wafted out, choking me with its familiar beckoning, a sweet pungent aroma indeed. Well, this looked very promising, I must say, so in I piled with my kit and thereby met the furry freak brothers, one of whom has remained a friend for life.

Inside the bare van were five lads and a lass, rather pretty in her short skirt, go-go boots, and Twiggy bob. Two mates were sitting up front: the driver Terry and his gap-toothed chum Devin riding shotgun. Eric, my friend still, was the voluble one in the back. They were all totally stoned; they promptly handed me the most gargantuan spliff I'd ever seen and off we went, I knew not where. I have never smoked cigarettes and find tobacco smoke somewhat nauseating, so have never been a big fan of the British spliff, a honking big joint of loose tobacco leaf into which one crumbles giant gobs of hash. But I was hardly about to quibble about a bit of tobacco smoke in the back of a very fine freak van that day. One must keep up the American standards of excess, after all. I inhaled with gusto and passed the drooping doobie on. We had hardly gone through introductions, when a minute later we screech to a halt at a bus stop to ask two fetching nurses waiting patiently for their bus, little white caps perched on their hairdos, if they might fancy a lift "down the road a piece." They were young and adventurous, so shrugged a "why not" and piled in, although they declined the burning spliff. Barely a minute after that, we came upon a wedding unfolding at a church up on a little hill. So the furry brothers did a little U-turn, zoomed up the church driveway, and Terry rolled down his driver's side window and shouted: "Don't marry that worthless bloke, my darling! Marry me, I've got the Mickey Mouse van!" The assembled guests, bride and groom included, stood wide-eyed on the church steps and seemed utterly perplexed by this unwarranted utterance. And with that, howling giggles coming from all of us in the back, Terry jammed the van into gear again and back we zoomed to the main thoroughfare and continued on our way. Even the stunned nurses had a giggle.

Somewhere our angels of mercy got off, relieved, I am sure, to be of a piece, but thanking us all the same profusely. They'd had "a bit of a lark," they assured us. So on we went. Eventually, as if it were an afterthought, one of the blokes in the back asked where the hell I was going and would I like to tag along on their adventure. I said, "Hey, no problem, London can wait. Grand!" To which Eric said, "We're going to a party at Eric Clapton's house down somewhere in Surrey." "Yeah, cool stuff, mate!" they all concurred. Stoned as I was, this seemed so outrageously unlikely that I held little store that their wild assertion had the slightest shred of veracity. But, having nothing better to do, I said, "Sure, why not?" The rest of the ride was a jumble of laughing fools with tall tales, peppering me with questions about the latest cool bands in the US. Had I ever been to a Dead concert or seen Janis Joplin? Alas, at that time, no, though I rattled off some of the bands I had seen: Hendrix, Vanilla Fudge, Paul Butterfield, Muddy Waters, Stones, Spoonful, and others. So chatting happily as we trundled on, bouncing, bouncing, and bum sore in the back, we at last arrived in a quiet corner of the British countryside at an imposing gate on a dark, narrow lane.

Turns out the party wasn't actually at Clapton's heap (Hurtwood Edge) or whomever's Italianate mansion it was, but rather at the gatehouse belonging to a groundskeeper named Colin. He was a jolly soul if ever there was one. As I recall, he had the appearance of a demented and rather toothless Walt Whitman, and drank tankards of ale like a Viking. But his impish smile could melt the heart of even the dourest of matrons. I took to him immediately. He had a thick accent, which I surmised much later was a northern sort of "Geordie," he being from Newcastle—such as "Howay man! You gan doon the road to the canny dodge, mate! Areet! Foon neet we'll haff. Lots o' nice hinnies! She's geet lush that one, eh? You lads knackered? Clammin a banger?" I'll spare my readers a rough translation. Ah, Colin, how he loved to talk.

The party at the gatehouse wasn't that big, maybe twenty people in all, but what we lacked in numbers we gladly doubled in quaffs of ale, hard cider, skank whiskey, and spliff. The fun really took off when one of the lads pulled out a packet of LSD hits in tiny cut blotter squares and placed the purple microdots onto our lolling tongues as if it was the Eucharist.

"Giz a deek at that, will ya! Bonny nappa, lads!" chortled Colin, wolfing down his hit with ale. (Translation: "Will ya look at that! Feed your heads, lads!"). We each took our hit, then carried on. Someone brought out a battered guitar and we began to sing Dylan songs. Laughter, more grog, fetching lasses dancing. About an hour later (it now being past sundown and getting dark outside), with all of us acting out the usual LSD satyricon, Colin had the brilliant idea that we should sneak up to the swimming pool below the big house, get naked, and have ourselves a grand old time by way of cooling off in Eric's pool. The refreshing oasis toward which we stumbled in the pitch darkness was where George Harrison had, in fact, written "Here Comes the Sun" not long before, himself on drugs. He had sought a blessed breather there from noisy London and the interminable legal wranglings with Apple, Inc. solicitors, which he just loathed. Good old George.

So off we went, fumbling through canyons of black swirling hallucinations, hushing each other not to make a racket lest Clapton (& The Dominos, as it turned out) should hear us, oops a bush! Hoh, a tree! Smash, stumbling on a root. Ha, quiet? Finally, we came upon the pool, with all the stars of heaven above making diamond twinkles in the sky. A goodly number of us stripped in the gloaming and splashed into the glorious water of the pool like a bunch of monkeys relishing the water, all silky sheen, the sheer joy of life high as a kite, water—O how glorious. Like river otters we were, slithering about nekkid and all. Tumbling in glad heaps, too. Eventually howling. We must have made a hell of a racket, I am sure.

From our watery vantage, we could see the big house up the grand lawn through the trees and certainly could hear musicians practicing. What we didn't notice, because we had turned into a fiendishly happy troop of monkeys, or was it otters, was that at some point the rock'n'roll practice came to a sudden stop. And lo! Quick as a blink, a new set of people were circling round the pool and gawking amusedly at we the naked ones cavorting in the water. It was Eric the guitar god, of course, and his musicians, wondering what the hell-in-blazes was going on. They didn't seem too upset, as they could hear Colin's gleeful exclamations from the verandah after all.

And there they were: Clapton, Bonnie Bramlett, Jim Gordon, Bobby Whitlock, even Duane Allman, and many lithe and lovely hangers-on. The furry lads said later they were sure Greg Allman was there, too, but I have no recollection of him. Duane Allman stood out in silhouette with his leather brim hat. Colin finally realized we'd been busted and hailed Clapton, jumping out of the pool like a beached walrus on hind flippers, and went off stark naked to have a confab with his boss. From our vantage in the pool, trying not to giggle, it seemed a serious conversation indeed. But the silhouette that really stood out as it came down the lawn was a 300-lb outline with a four-foot Afro. It was no less than drummer Buddy Miles.

Apparently, and lucky for us, yanks Duane and Bonnie were of the opinion that sweaty as they were from practicing for hours, who cares, Eric, let's join the damn revelers for a cool-down. And so they did. What harm, eh? And quick as a wink, off went their clothes and in they dove. We all had a grand old time splashing about into the wee morn under the sparkling stars. I don't really recall talking to Clapton that night, nor Miles, nor Jim Gordon, none of the latter at least had jumped in. But Whitlock, Allman, and the Bramletts were game, and smoking their own spliffs by this time, seemed to be having a grand old time with us. It was a pool party to die for. That's what comes back to me whenever I have a lysergic flashback listening to Derek and the Dominos, with "Layla" blaring from a stereo (it's a sad fact that Duane was dead within a year, the man whose electric guitar and slide on "Layla" is just 24-caret gold). Grand old time, did I say? Not so much at actual daybreak, awakening on Colin's stone-hard floor with a ten-hammer hangover and shivering for the cold.

Through much of the rest of the summer of 1970, I lived with the furry freak brothers in their squat in Guilford, southeast of London, county Surrey, which was handy. Linda wasn't but a quick bus ride away until her college started. The lads had a marquee tent business, providing everything from cover for dog shows to the food tents for the musicians at the second Isle of Wight Festival later that summer. Tents large or small, that was their business. For two months I travelled England with them, from Hammersmith to Hull, putting up enormous, near circus-sized tents as a "canvas lad" and they even paid me a fair wage. Best of all, I got in free to the Isle of Wight Festival, backstage tag and all.

    I eventually did hitchhike from Guilford to London to visit my friend Penrose whom I had intended to visit before the furry freak brothers whisked me off into guitar-god-heaven. The first thing Penrose did when I arrived was take me round to meet his good mate, Prince Gypsy Lee, a grizzled old fart with a beard to his belt. Yes, he was a veritable gypsy, a prince in fact of the Romani tribe in the UK. Penrose had been a year ahead of me at Kent but we'd always gotten along, bad peas in a crooked pod, I suppose. That year he had been the Yank exchange student at the posh British boarding school of Eton, which, upon arrival, he had promptly dropped out of to become a layabout bohemian. This seemed rather rakish to my young mind. In fact, being a layabout, chatting up girls, smoking spliffs, seemed a jolly good lifestyle to me. My friend seemed to know his way about London like a local and knew every trick to get a free shower, cop a free meal, nick a cup of tea, or find a bed for the night with a lass and a spliff of drugs. Lots of drugs. That pretty much covered the basics. Life was simple but ample back then.

    Penrose's tawdry room was in a cold-water squat not far from Euston Station, and was full of long-haired layabouts like himself and not a few heroin addicts—a drug which neither he nor I had ever taken a fancy to. On the afternoon Penrose first took me round to see Gypsy, picture London in 1970 at the height of bellbottom hippiedom. The powdered Georgian wigs of 1750s London paled in comparison to the hairstyles of the burgeoning young in London at the time. Beards and beads were all the vogue. Gypsy, in fact, lived just off Carnaby Street, arguably the most wacked-out half mile of pavement that London has ever seen. He had a motor caravan for sleeping in, which he parked in back alleys where there was a garden faucet to do his dishes and wash up, wherever the neighbors didn't drive him off. They still did this with sad regularity, intolerance of "thieving" gypsies being the norm even in 1970. His other caravan, his "office" as he called it, was a more traditional hand-carved, horse-drawn carriage on Carnaby itself, where he'd haul in the gullible, do a palm reading, pull out the Tarot cards, or peer like Merlin into a scrying stone with great deliberation—all to predict your future, as long as you crossed his palm with a pound note. This carriage seemed to have a permanent spot in the middle of the Carnaby thoroughfare, and was always busy. Everybody loved Gypsy. He was over seventy at the time, I am guessing, smoked a curved Sherlock Holmes pipe, wore a colorful silk bandana that flowed down his back with his very long gray hair, and always wore a leather vest over which was laid one of the finest bushy beards you could ever imagine. He was every inch the Gypsy Prince.

I spent several weeks there in London with Penrose and Gypsy, going back periodically to Guilford to share surreptitious meetings with Linda. One day a letter came from Manchester addressed to Gypsy, who had a letterbox at the nearby post office. It stated that the city wanted to highlight his hand-carved, eighteenth-century Romani caravan which was in storage in a warehouse there. Might Gypsy allow it to go on public display for a while? Apparently, there was going to be some sort of Renaissance festival and it would make a great addition. Might he come north and deliver it to them? Gypsy loved this sort of attention, so of course he said yes. He said that on grand Romani festival days, when the clans met in Manchester or York, they would all bring their horse-drawn carriages and parade them around, and he was always there. These events often coincided with horse shows and auctions.

Gypsy asked that Penrose and I stay in his live-in caravan while he would be away, and feed and walk his two dogs. He said that he'd be back in three days, with swan eggs. Apparently, Romani gypsies could take a certain number of swan eggs from the banks of the Mersey each year and Gypsy promised us the "omelet of our lives" when he got back.

It didn't take long for Penrose and I to ascertain why our absent host needed someone to watch his caravan, besides the two flea-ridden grouchy dogs. Every, and I mean every, nook and cranny had a fat roll of pound notes in all denominations hidden there—under his socks in a drawer, under the mattress, behind the frying pans, in tins in the little built-in ceiling cupboards, on and on, all because Gypsy had no use for, nor trust in, banks. We estimated there must have been at least ten thousand quid stuffed in sock drawers and whatnot all over the bleedin' caravan, and this in 1970! Gypsy had been very specific that he wanted us there in the caravan upon his return by train, so we could have his heavenly swan egg omelet. We promised, and to our credit we never nicked a single quid from Gypsy's piles. We feared his evil eye, and with good reason it turned out.

Penrose was nineteen and I was a year younger—what the hell did we know about time and responsibility? The afternoon Gypsy was to return, we had been invited to a wild party with Procol Harem as the draw, promptly took too many drugs, including my one lifetime hit of heroin with a needle (not bad as it happen, but not enough to lure me again), drank way too much, and didn't get back to the caravan till well after midnight, zonked. A scowling Gypsy greeted us, the dogs growled, and a pan with a cold swan-egg omelet screamed "guilty." Oh dear, shit, the fucking swan eggs. Not surprisingly, Gypsy turned into a snarly old grump and promptly booted us out.

At 1am we stumbled back out into the cold night and somehow made it to Paddington Station, where Penrose knew you could catch a wink on the great railway station benches on the upper level without the coppers bothering you. A teashop was open 24/7, so in we went to get warm. We sat there gloomily tendering our tea and bemoaning out loud about our stupidity with

Gypsy, when a well-dressed middle-aged gentleman came up to us with an inquiry. He was a Yank like us, it turned out, in a posh suit and coifed hair.

"Couldn't help overhearing," he said, "but are you referring to Prince Gypsy Lee, by any chance, the fortune-teller?" We rocked back stunned, though in truth Gypsy was always a self-promoter and widely known by many folks. He'd even had his own BBC2 television show for a while. We said yes. The gent then took a seat with us at the long communal table. He told us his name, which I've forgotten. We shook hands and he asked why two American boys were stuck in Paddington past midnight talking about Gypsy. We told him our tale of the swan eggs, and then asked him what his connection was to Gypsy. Here's the American businessman's rather amazing story, the tale of "Gypsy and the Yank Soldier." A spun tale perhaps it was, but a damn good yarn in any case.

It was 1944, and our Yank was a drafted soldier in the US Army. On the day in question, his company had been given one last day pass, so live it up, boys. Back by o-six hundred crack of dawn, sharp. And no hangovers. Right. He had hitched a ride to London to be with a British lass he fancied. At the time, being about our age and inept in love, he was foolish enough to claim that he was absolutely sure he wanted to marry the girl. Might they do that before he was shipped to France, he implored? She demurred, of course, being smart enough to know that years of fighting and much killing lay ahead for nice lads like him. She'd survived the Blitz and knew all about death and destruction. A dead husband would do her no good whatsoever. In any event, our Yank had just attained his sergeant stripes that week and felt brash and invulnerable. Rumor had it that his company would soon be shipped away for the long-awaited invasion of Belgium, perhaps even Holland—none of the foot soldiers actually guessed, still less had been told, that it would be Normandy. It was nevertheless a giddy if terrifying prospect. His sweetie worked in some government office and for her part was distraught at the thought that her Yank would soon be ducking German mortar fire. So on this the last day of his freedom, she asked if he'd be willing to visit a gypsy chap she knew who lived in a horse-drawn caravan behind her council flat. He told fortunes, she said. Not knowing what to say to this, our Yank put on a brave face: "Uh, sure, honey cakes."

It was a spry Gypsy Lee back then, of course. The lass, who had dabbled in séances with her girlfriends and religiously read the horoscopes in the magazines every week, sincerely liked Gypsy. It never bothered her that a Romani had taken up residence in the alley. She had moreover beseeched him to read her sweetheart's fortune, her handsome Yank soon to be off fighting in France or wherever it was they were going. At first Gypsy was very reluctant, but he finally relented, in part because she was the one who had convinced the neighbors to let him stay in the alley, as long as he scooped up the horse poop every morning and hauled it away. As a rule, Gypsy did not read soldiers' fortunes, no matter the pleading. Calamity was too close at hand. But on this reading, at her insistence, he used the Tarot. The Yank told us he was utterly baffled, if a bit enchanted, by the longhaired Merlin look-alike, dashing in his way. But in truth he was also horrified as a good Presbyterian that he was partaking of something that was possibly black magic, quasi-satanic, and certainly mumbo-jumbo. What would his devout mother say? Oh, he suddenly rather rued the pickle his girlfriend and Gypsy had landed him in.

The prince read the cards, but halfway through he simply packed them up with a look of true alarm ("a big scowl" said our story-teller) on his face. He said "The cards are playing tricks" and that he just couldn't read them then. The reading was at an end, free of course, and he shooed them out the door. The unhappy couple stumbled out into the alley assuming the worst. As he was the one soon going off to war, surely the Yank would be in harm's way and should expect the worst. The undercurrent of their last night together was troubled. Before dawn the next morning, the lass clung to her Yank soldier all the way to his transport back to barracks on the coast. The Yank himself shared that he'd been truly discomfited by the reading for all sorts of reasons, not least that it possibly suggested he'd get a "Kraut bullet" in the stomach. Less worrisome, but nagging all the same, he feared that by partaking in this devilish nonsense he'd somehow brought God's wrath upon him. And finally, maybe a lass who believed in such claptrap wasn't the gal for him after all. Sadly, he and his girl had argued that last night.

The next day, off he went to a new bivouac with his battalion. He did indeed land on the beaches at Normandy (on Omaha, he said, the worst of it) and was wounded by a graze on his thigh, but otherwise survived to fight on. He fought at the Bulge (as did my father, but in a different location) and joined in the victory battles on up to Berlin. In January of 1946 our soldier returned to London, deeply concerned because letters from his lass had suddenly ceased, and he had not even received a "Dear John" letter. His own letters had been returned to sender. On his second day back in the UK he learned from his lass's younger sister that his sweetheart had died not long after he'd deployed, blown to bits from a direct hit by a V2 rocket. There was no postal address left, ergo the returns. He was stunned.

All those years later, in the train station that night with us, he still looked disconsolate. He added, gravely, that he had seen so much death by that time, he confessed his mental state was more numbed resignation than any hollow feeling of loss. All the same, something gnawed at him to find Gypsy, to ask the man what the hell the cards had said. He'd spent months brooding about it when a quiet hour between bivouacs came. It took him almost a month to track the Romani prince down, as Gypsy was never in one place long. It had always been thus for the Romani in England, and for those lucky few who survived the holocaust everywhere else. When our soldier finally reconnected, he said that Gypsy apparently wasn't in the least surprised to see him.

"Well, if it isn't our Yankee, eh!" or some such in his thick Midlands accent. "I thought I'd be seeing you again, lad! You look of a piece."

"Yes, I survived." the man said grimly. "So, you thought you'd see me again?" He was flummoxed. How could that be?

"Yes, of course, mate. No question of that. What of your sweetheart, pretty lass if I recall? She let me stay by her flat."

"She died. V2."

Gypsy was pensive a moment. "Yes, well, I was afraid that would be the case. I had to dodge a few V2 meself." He then said. "You know lad, the cards foretold her death, not yours. I said nothing because I wanted a brave young Yankee lad such as yourself to have a damn good reason to go fight like a bleedin' lion, to live on and give those fascist bastards a swift fookin' kick in the arse... and come back to your intended as a war hero!" Gypsy despised fascists, Hitler, Mussolini, Franco—they had all persecuted gypsies through the 1930s and 40s. The Yank and Gypsy spoke for nigh on an hour.

By the time the Yank had finished this tale at Paddington, almost two hours had passed in the blink of an eye. By tale's end, the first dawn commuters were showing up to catch their trains, filling the platforms where engines steamed. The man also shared rather sheepishly that Penrose and I were the first people in twenty-three years that he'd talked to about it, well, since telling his brother back in 1947. His brother thought it was all nuts, cavorting with gypsies was talk with the devil. So our Yank from Nebraska just buried the tale all these years. He thanked us and said that it felt great to finally tell someone. Amazing, he said, that he should connect with two American hippies talking Prince Gypsy Lee in Paddington Station. What a coincidence, we all agreed with nervous laughter. The man gulped down the last of his umpteenth cup o' tea and shook our hands. "Must catch my train to Manchester," he said. Surprised, we told him to go to the fair and see Gypsy's old wooden caravan; maybe Gypsy would be there. "Hey, thanks for the tip." He waved and walked away.

Penrose and I just looked at each other incredulously. A few days later we made up with Gypsy by offering him a huge bribe of hash as our penance. He harrumphed but took us in for tea. When we asked him about the tale we'd heard from the man at the station, he just frowned.

"No real memory of it, sorry," he intoned, as it was going on twenty-six years. "Listen lads. I talk to twenty fookin' people a day about their miserable fookin' lives and loves, read their palms, listen to all their weepy shyte. Bleedin' goin' on forty years now. Gets a bit tiresome it does, know wot I mean, though it's always fun to chat up the pretty birds in their mini-skirts. Loose lot them." And he left that hot potato at that. "See I forget most of the twaddle I hear by teatime. Unless there's a connection, I just tell them any old shyte that I can read from lookin' at 'em and take me quid and top of the day to ye. But sometimes the cards come alive. I can it feel here..." he tapped his chest, "...that I'm on to something and the bloke or bird is on my wavelength. The spirits can speak to you, see. It's fun when that happens, like it means something. But listen lads, I had what? Maybe three hundred soldiers come to see me during the fookin' war asking if they'd come back alive. All weepy like, hated it. Mostly said no!" He was pensive for a moment. "Was he a nice chap, this Yank? I vaguely recall his bird back during the war. Nice lass. She let me stay a few months behind her flat if I recall."

"Yeah, that's the guy. Totally sincere," we said in unison. "He asked us to say 'Hi.'" I always wished that either Penrose or I had been able to remember the man's name, but we couldn't. We were coming down from a drug high as we listened to our Yank, and I always felt there was something terribly surreal about the whole encounter, a nagging that some sort of opportunity had been missed. I very much doubt that Gypsy is still alive today, as he was over seventy in 1970. Fare thee well, old Draba Ataman,[10] into the mysteries. There's a photo of him on Carnaby Street in the ornate doorway of his caravan: longhaired, bearded, wool-vested. Google his full name "Prince Gypsy Lee" and it should come up.

That same summer, in July, Linda and I went to a concert in Hyde Park featuring Canned Heat, Pink Floyd, Eric Burdon and War, and my first rocker, John Sebastian. There must have been several hundred thousand people there, a mass of flower power and hash smoke. We had also attended the Bath Festival in June with a dynamic lineup of Led Zeppelin, Johnny Winter, Frank Zappa + the Mothers of Invention, the Byrds, Country Joe, and John Mayall with guitarist Peter Green, co-founder of Fleetwood Mac, as backup. My most memorable of all concerts that summer, though, was the Isle of Wight festival at the end of August, 1970. My mates with the marquee tent business had scored the gig to put up several tents for the attending musicians. Our lorry packed to bursting, with several lads, Eric, Colin the groundskeeper (who'd gotten us the gig through his boss), and myself on top, and the Mickey Mouse van loaded with our own kit and gear in the lead, off we went to Southampton to catch the ferry to the island, a good week before the concert was to begin. Already hundreds of foot-loose hippies and bell-bottomed mods were lounging about the docks when we arrived at the ferry terminal, a scruffy lot trying to cadge a ride or panhandling for a fare. We bought round-trip tickets and drove the van and lorry aboard the ferry, arriving on the isle at the little port of Cowes, then driving to Afton Down where the stage and much of the backstage were already starting to take shape. We were ushered in and lumbered down the grassy incline to the staging area.

The *Guinness Book of Records* calls it the largest rock festival in history, with some estimates of the crowd topping 700,000. It was certainly ridiculously huge. While the site for the festival was

---

10. A "spell-casting chieftan" in Romani.

dramatic, the hillside slope was at such an angle to the prevailing winds from the sea that those zephyrs cut across the stage at a relentless clip. Indeed, putting up our damn food tents, with pegs and guy wires, was hellish. About thirty roadies from various bands had to pitch in to raise the center poles. Heck, even Marty Balin of Jefferson Airplane, Joe Cocker, and Bob Dylan at one point deigned to lend a hand. Nice blokes. With the back of the lorry now cleared, we put a canvas awning above the flatbed and turned it into our private caravan pop-up, parked at the back of the bus lot behind the stage. During sound checks, it was clear that the concert stacks, large as they were, just couldn't project sufficiently, with complaints from the soundboard a hundred yards up the slope that the crosswind just stole the sound away. The Who came to the rescue. Their vast army of roadies, plus us canvas lads, plus Keith Moon and John Entwistle (drunk on their arses), were roped into turning their massive kit stack of full-on speakers into a second tower of sound. I remember that Pete Townsend, two sheets to the wind himself apparently, became our erstwhile concert-stack director, laughing uproariously when one stack toppled over in the wind before we could latch it down. Perhaps it reminded him of smashing one of his guitars to smithereens. Luckily no one was hurt. While it never rained, the incessant wind made for a very chilly festival.

My personal highlight came when meeting the politically radical, innovative Brazilian maestros Gilberto Gil and Caetano Veloso, who were slated to play their fusion Latin jazz. The two men were long associated with the Tropicalia Music Movement, which was formed by a variety of young and rebellious artists as a direct response to the Brazilian dictatorship of the 1960s. Wikipedia says of the movement that it was "fiercely anarchistic and anti-authoritarian" and that members of the movement had a "passionate interest in the New Wave of American and British psychedelic music of the period." The 1968 album Tropicália: ou Panis et Circencis is a classic and well worth a listen, and iTunes has a wonderful documentary featuring Gil and Veloso by cinematographer Marcelo Machado. Because of their fearless defiance against the dictatorship and its censorship of decadent pop music, Gil and Veloso were imprisoned for three months in 1969. The condition of their release was exile, so they emigrated to London. Veloso was to say later that London at that time "was a cold dark period in my life." Both he and Gil felt at sea, having braved the same Rio to London shock that I had experienced eleven years before, exiles with no vibrant community to join or become a part of, palm trees and sandy beaches suddenly a receding memory. In addition, in hipster acid-rock London there was no real following for their unique music. To the festival's credit, they were invited to perform at Wight.

They, and their conga and flute musicians, didn't have much equipment, and certainly not the mountains of Marshall amps that most big-name bands had, but I and my mates nevertheless saw them struggling with their kit and lent a hand. Their set was Thursday. I came to meet the two great virtuosos, and some of their band members, after I had made the acquaintance of their road manager. I was introduced to Gil and Veloso and some of the others, who seemed set apart from the throng of bell-bottomed riotous rock stars. Some of the Tropicalia musicians only had rudimentary English; the roadie in any case introduced me after I shared that I'd lived in Brazil in the 1950s. I spent a wonderful evening before the festival start chatting with these two lively, politically-savvy maestros. To this day, they remain true progressive luminaries, as with the rest of their jolly band of outlaw compatriots at the festival. The highlight came when they invited me to join them as they went to find a quiet corner (ha!) in the tour bus parking area. Sitting on upturned buckets behind rows of buses, I listened to the ensemble do an impromptu set of Brazilian classics on their beautiful nylon-string guitars, with panpipes and congas flailing. Sadly, I don't know how or why (probably because I was tearing around being a stoned fool), I entirely missed their stage set. A crappy video of it is available on YouTube for those who may have an interest.

Though at the time it chafed me terribly, I had to leave the festival early. I had an interview with the college admissions team at Wroxton College in Oxfordshire, where I had promised my dad I'd enroll to get credentialed with my A and O levels, essentially the more rigorous SATs of British university prep. I was then to apply for entry to Oxford. I had heard about Wroxton from a variety of Kent School sources, as it was then a struggling effort to provide a study abroad experience for students and allied affiliates of Farleigh Dickinson University (FDU) in New Jersey. The son of its founder, Farleigh Dickinson, Jr., had been at Kent in my first year and had graduated with my brother in 1968. Farleigh was a delightfully fey and devil-may-care boy who, sadly, was the first student from Kent to make a splash by dying of an "acute morphine overdose" at Columbia University (later to be my alma mater) in March of 1969. It made the headlines. As it turned out, though, leaving the Isle of Wight festival a day or two early was propitious for me. When I hitched a ride to the ferry at Cowes, there were only about a hundred passengers waiting to get on, plus the usual line of cars and lorries. By the day after the festival, all 700,000 attendees, even the big-name rock stars, were left trying to get off the island for forever. For some it took a month or more.

Wroxton and Monty Python at the Oxford Assizes

How exactly I wrangled my way into Wroxton I do not know any more; it is lost to old age and memory loss. But I do recall the college itself. The entire student body couldn't have been more than thirty or forty students in 1970. The manor where the college was housed was a seventeenth-century red brick heap with great lawns and enormous beech trees as a backdrop. Rumor had it that one grand room embossed with leather wallpaper came from tanned horsehides, flayed by some Russian prince. The dorm that I stayed in was above the converted carriage house next to the manor. My classmates were an odd assortment; many were from FDU itself, looking for a chance to study in the UK not far from Oxford University. But there were also a number of sad sacks such as myself, for example fourth or fifth sons of peerage etc., who were admitted in the hope that these layabouts might eventually pass their A and O levels and go on to university and thus make something of themselves. Well, not so much was my experience. We all seemed to remain devout bohemians and contentedly so.

One friend I made at Wroxton was Francis Ormsby-Gore, the sixth Baron Harlech, yes, very toff. But he was a bright and anarchic soul, striding around like a Welsh laird in his thick woolen sweaters and Wellingtons. He also had ready access to awesome drugs. But what got us together was that his sister, Alice Ormsby-Gore, was at that time Eric Clapton's girlfriend. When I shared with Francis my story of Colin and the pool, he was absolutely delighted. He knew Colin well and had on several occasions visited Hurtwood Edge House to tromp around with the groundskeeper to get tips on how one wrangled the upkeep of a grand house. He would himself eventually become the Lord Harlech upon his father's demise and inherit not only Harlech Castle in Wales, but several other heaps besides. I thoroughly liked Francis, mostly because he was absolutely without affect, never took his title and peerage seriously, and was only interested in being a gentleman farmer when all was said and done. I met Clapton again as Francis' guest at a nice pub outside Oxford, where Francis went to spend some time with his sister, who was clinging with sweet adoration on Eric's arm. Eric vaguely remembered me from the night in his pool. We quaffed a beer or two and that was about it. In any event, conversations with Francis, invariably enveloped in clouds of hash, would suddenly turn to sheep rearing and fen pasturage. Years later, when he was a peer in the House of Lords, the poor embattled man gave a rambling speech of some notoriety that began: "Medicine, my Lords, can come from both music and dance just as surely as from a bottle!" I believe it went downhill from there, though I think as a premise his assessment sounded about right.

I cannot remember attending a single class at Wroxton. Not one, though doubtless I warmed a chair. I do, however, remember several fun LSD trips in which Francis, some girls, and I hiked all around the countryside and went skinny-dipping in the nearby Fish Pond. Emersion in psychedelics, unfortunately, did not have sufficient magical or prophylactic properties to ward off the subsequent vampiric visit to Wroxton by a certain Officer Tucker of the Oxford Constabulary. He was summoned by the headmaster to root out the rumored drug-crazed goings-on at the college. Ah, Officer Tucker—stomping around in his trench coat, a bit like Peter Falk's Columbo. But instead of Falk's clever LA patois, Tucker expostulated with the inebriation of his loquacious verbosity in the thickest of cockney accents. Besides, Falk as Columbo was at least self-effacingly brilliant. Officer Tucker, by contrast, was a dimwit, with handcuffs dangling absent-mindedly out of his coat pocket and licking his pencil as he jotted notes. Even my dad, in the weeks ahead, thought him a buffoon.

My dearest pal from Kent, Joris (pronounced "your-iss"), a Dutch lad by birth and to this day still my best friend, came to visit me at Wroxton. Francis, Joris, and I, along with the rest of the gang, smoked up a storm of hash and had a grand old time. Unfortunately, the college headmaster at the same time had got wind that a certain unsavory set at Wroxton was carrying on, sleeping around, and doing drugs, of all things. Sorry business. Mustn't blight the name of newly-minted Wroxton College and all that. So, he called in the Oxford constabulary to investigate, ergo Officer Tucker. The morning before Officer Tucker arrived for his drug bust, Joris had with warm goodbyes set off on his way back to London, by hitchhiking and train-hopping. Unfortunately, stoned fool he that he was, Joris had left his passport behind in my dorm room.

The gods, such as they are, briefly smiled on me because, while I may have been one of the worst offenders, when Officer Tucker did his sweep that day I was blessedly without a crumb of actual hash or other drugs. All I had was "paraphernalia"—several long Moroccan pipes I'd picked up on Carnaby Street while visiting Gypsy. Through their long stem the harsh hash smoke passed up the pipes and was cooled to a fine temperature. Never one to give up a chance for theatrics, upon spying these malevolent objects Officer Tucker put his hands behind his back in affectation of Sherlock Holmes, leaned over with a sniff of the air, all the while peering at the pipes on my bedside table and said (again in the thickest of cockney accents): "Wewl, wewl, wewl, wot do we have here, den?" His voice rose with each word to the query mark.

"Pipes," I said. "Wewl, I can see vat! But wot ky-and of pipes might dey be, eh?" And with a flourish he lifted one up and sniffed the bowl. He immediately made a grimacing face as if the residue of hash was too much for the poor sod's offended nostrils. He was obviously delighted to have found a smoking gun. "Ah ha! Wewl, den. Smells like hasheeesh to me, does it not! I shall be taking dese, if you don't mind!" And so it went. I think poor Francis was caught with a gram of hash or something later that week and was expelled, if memory serves. But I was summarily cuffed and hauled down to Tucker's waiting police car with a great flourishing ceremony of police work. It was as if he'd found the hideout of the dastardly thieves of the Great Train Robbery itself, not some layabout with a tube-pipe from Morocco. Ugh. In his search of my room, Officer Tucker tossed my possessions about, lifted up the mattress, and did a theatrical sweep, just like on the telly! Finally, the great detective landed on, ta-da, Joris's passport on my desk chair. Good work, copper. "Eww, wot's dis, den? J-OR-is STY-K!"

It was early evening by this time, and I recall sitting cuffed in the back seat of the police car as Officer Tucker drove me to the police station to book me for drug paraphernalia. The whole interminable way there the bastard never shut the fuck up, smoking fag after fag out the window: "Wewl den. Wont ta know wot I fink?" "No actually I don't," sez I to meself, "give a shit 'wot you fink.'" "Wewl, wot I fink itz da red Chinees doin' it, dat's who. Yes, da red Chinees is da ones sendin' over dese bleedin' drugs to hook our good lads on dat demon 'eroin! Nasty business, dat. Red Chinees, mark my word. Bleedin' blight, it is. And you lot, oi, carryin' on and lookin' like 'ippie tramps. Bleedin' disgustin' it is. And you! You a guest in our country! Wot da bleedin' 'ell you finkin' ov? Should be ashamed ov you'sewf! Bleedin' red Chinees, mark my words!" Yadda, yadda, on and on. As for myself, I knew precisely "Wot da bleedin' 'ell I wuz tinkin ov." I was tinkin', "Piss Off You Bleedin' Imbecile!" I was hauled down to the cop shop and booked.

Unfortunately, the good sergeant had taken with him my mate Joris' passport. When Joris realized halfway back to London that he'd left his passport at Wroxton, 'round he turned, hitchhiking all the way back to the college, looking for me. After being booked, I was sent back to the college by cab around midnight. Joris was there awaiting my return. Taken aback, he had heard from other students of the grand bust. We were certainly glad to see each other. I told him of my travails, but shared that his passport, alas, was in the grimy mitts of a certain Detective Sergeant Tucker of the Criminal Investigation Department, Drugs Division in Oxford. He'd have to go to the police station and retrieve it. Joris, poor lad, looked crestfallen.

"Wewl" Tucker was certainly very glad to see my mate J-OR-is the next day after the latter had said his fare-thee-well to me. Joris now received Officer Tucker's sermon on the Red Chinese. Ah, to have another unwitting ear to regale! Even priests of the windbag variety usually wrap up their tedious homilies in under an hour.

Joris was not so lucky. He had to sit through an interminable harangue that ticked off the minutes past the hour. He was let off with a stern lecture to stay away from drugs, criminal reprobates such as myself, and for emphasis, "dem red Chinees." Sensibly, Joris fled to Paris the next day by train, only to get busted for drugs there, more the fool he, and spend several months in a miserable Bastille-like jail cell. The crapper there was nothing more than a little concrete ditch running through each cell in one long trough, tilted at an incline, where a never-ending freshet of sewer water wafted the poops at the high end of the cell block down to make the acquaintance of the cellmates at the lower end, thence out a hole to the famous underground sewers of Gay Paree. Yuck.

By contrast, my brief time in the cell at the constabulary establishment in Oxford had been rather nice and clean actually, even had me a spot of tea, thank you very much. If I were to spell out my relief, and were I the least bit religious, praise the lord might have passed my lips. But it didn't. Besides, I didn't much care about being caught with paraphernalia. I knew enough from my marquee tent mates, themselves always one step ahead of the drug "copsicles," as they called coppers on bikes, that paraphernalia was never more than a stern warning and a finger wagging. What worried me the most was that my father at that very moment was traveling from Mexico City to London to be feted by the nabobs at Shell for his twenty years of service, just one more cog in their global ambitions of market share. Shell would trot him out as a loyal servant of capital, give him the short end of a golden parachute, a cheap watch, perchance, and see the back of him.

When Mom and Dad arrived back in England, after many years away, they traveled to an old family friend's house down in county Kent to stay for the visit. Alas, the night before they arrived, the headmaster at Wroxton had called my father's friend, as he was listed as my legal UK "guardian." The headmaster gave Dad's friend the sordid details of my ignominious arrest. Welcome to your retirement party, Dad. I was mortified for my poor father.

Rightfully he was furious, less about my ridiculous hash pipes than that he feared word of my transgressions might somehow percolate up to the big wigs at Shell and in some fashion compromise the negotiations of his retirement. And to have dragged his own old friend through it—really, Peter. He picked me up at Paddington Station with barely a word of reproach (though in truth simmering in annoyance) and drove me down to Kent where I met the old family friends and my more sympathetic, if equally aggrieved, mother.

The upshot of my transgression was that I had a summons to appear at the Oxford assizes (court) to face charges of "possession of paraphernalia with intent to use illegal drugs." My father and I met my court-appointed solicitor in his chambers and I was relieved to hear from him that indeed I was very likely to get off with no more than a stern warning from the presiding judges. So into the grand courtroom we trooped. Holy moley. It was absolutely straight out of *Rumpole of the Bailey*. I nodded to Sergeant Tucker, who was reading the horse race stats in his folded newspaper, ticking off his bets with a pencil stub. He nodded curtly to my father as if to say, "Glad you've got dis miscreant on your short leash, sir!" Back to the stats with his licked pencil went this detective.

The interminable trial began. Upon the high dais, three imperious and elderly judges, all bewigged in ridiculous white flowing hairpieces, all with spectacles on their long noses, all twits or so it seemed to my rapscallion's mind, intoning with long upper crust "ahs," and "ohs," and "ews" a singularly clueless legalese about pretty much everything going on in their own court—this is what greeted poor Dad and me. My solicitor at least had a sense of humor and kept reassuring my father, "Won't be long now. Won't be long." But long as a furlong it was anyway. Case in point: the court brief before mine had to do with a rambunctious fox beagle that had somehow gotten loose and made its canine way, as dogs will, into a neighbor's sheep pen and thereby giving the aggrieved woolly heads a run for their money. All six of them. Very upsetting. Even gave one of the domestic herd a good chomp on the leg. Bad dog. The facts were clear though. One dog, six sheep, all survived, the suffered wound all patched up. The issue was that it had happened before, and could the dog somehow be constrained? But the central judge, bewigged and benighted, spectacles perched upon nose, couldn't quite seem to grasp the complexities of this canine-ovine donnybrook. Fit to be POTUS by Trumpian standards.

"I sehy. So, I em confuuused, sir. Wahs it one dog and six sheep or one sheep and six dogs? Might you clarify, please sir!" The peanut gallery tittered with quiet mockery. Even Sergeant Tucker looked up from his racing pages to smile with wan forbearance. The poor dog owner's solicitor, hand to the collar of his black gown, his own diminutive white wig no match for the nabobs on the dais, started the whole bleedin' litany all over again. At last, the dog owner was let off with a finger wagging, and the shepherd of the six sheep departed with a loud "Harrumph!" My bewigged solicitor immediately stood up and motioned me into the docket, nodding to Sergeant Tucker to bear witness to my manifest depravities. Tucker folded up his paper, stuck it in his trench coat pocket where I was sure the handcuffs still dangled, pencil in pocket, and made his way forward to testify. My case number and crime were read off, and the center judge asked if Detective Sergeant Tucker might care to amplify.

"Wewl, yes, yu'onor. I'm 'appy to oblige. On de day ov my visit, Mr. McDonald was app-re'ended in 'is dormitory room at W-oxton College outside Oxford. Let me add W-oxton is a school for chappies like 'im who 'aven't yet found der way in life, you'onor. Bit of a party school if you ax me. I appree'ended de suspect wiv possession of drug parapha'nalia. To my mind, it's da red Chinees to blame yu-onor, but I'll keep dat to meself..." Thank heaven. "I will say doh, de suspect came quietly, sir, and eye'm not aware he 'as misbehaved since dat time. 'Opefully he is ready to repent. Ere wid 'is favver I believe.' He turned to me with a ridiculously counterfeit smile and waved toward poor Dad, who was sitting glumly in the cheap seats. My court-appointed solicitor then rose, thanked Sergeant Tucker for his diligence, and launched into a rehearsed speech that he obviously eulogized on behalf of all the miscreant clients who shuffled his way: I was but a misguided youth, that youth do make silly mistakes now and again, but inevitably these mistakes lead the penitent to be a far more worthy adult do they not, that paraphernalia, surely, was not a crime but a minor misdemeanor, and so forth and so on, *et cetera ad nauseam et factum est in vobis*. Not Shakespeare, but sufficient. He sat down. I stood stone-faced in the dock facing the bewigged old coots up at the dais who peered at me as if I were some odiferous rat, held by tail, to be thrown out with the day's rubbish. The central ogre took a deep breath as if he were already tired of dealing with, yet again, another miscreant such as myself who felt drugs were the new dram of whiskey and we could do as we damned well pleased. Well, not in his assizes. In the thickest of posh Oxford don accents, he became suddenly eloquent again.

"Young man!" he began, clearing his throat. My mind drifted. By this time in the UK, let it be said, Monty Python's Flying Circus was on the telly for the first time, and all the stoners were watching it, myself included, howling with laughter. Just then I could not get the grinning mug of John Cleese's pinched face to come unmasked from the legate's imperious mug. "Mr. McDonald, is it? Well, young man I must seh-y that I ehm very disappointed to hear Sergeant Tucker's report of your wanton ways. Yeuw dew know that drugs are illegal in Brit-ohn, is that correct, young man? Know yeuw this?" I nodded and muttered "Yes." "I see. So why is it then that yeew stand before us accused of partaking in such drugs if yeew knew they were illegal in the first place, hmmm? Ahehnd may I add, yeuw an American, a veritable guest to her royal majesty's fair shores, yes?" To which the other two judges nodded their gruff assent, both of whom I was surprised had actually managed to stay awake through all the many dogs and sheep.

"Yehhs, young man. Moe-st disappointing. What yeuw exhibit, young man, is obviously Low Moral Fibah!" The last word "fiber" clipped for emphasis. Then very slowly for emphasis. "L-o-w M-o-r-a-l Fibah young man, do you hear me?" I nodded vigorously. That would be me, low moral fiber. Sure thing. The judge looked around expansively to the largely empty courtroom as if he were old King Lear upon the moor, soliloquizing at the Globe. "Yes, oh yes! Once again, we see visited upon us a case of LMF! Dew I make myself clear young man?! Low Moral Fibah!" Again, I nodded vigorously, all the while thinking, enough with the fucking LMF, already! Enter John Cleese and a giant Terry Gilliam cartoon boot, ker-splat! Squished wigs. Now for something completely different.

After a brief conferral with his fellow wigs on the dais, the sentence was then passed. He would be lenient as this was my first offense, but I was to absolutely and emphatically stay away from drugs, did I hear? Yessir. I could remain in England through the remainder of my visa, but must register with the police wherever I went if I was staying in any one place for more than two days. Understood? The police! Yessir. And he threatened me with fire and brimstone should I be seen again in the docket of his court. Yessir, and there I stood, duly chastened, thinking all the while, "Jesus H. Christ will the pubs still be open after this geezer waffles on to his bitter end?" And so I was set free. Officer Tucker came over all friendly-like to shake my hand, glad that I was now properly admonished, yes, put to the straight and narrow, and giving my father a congenial nod, tapping his law-enforcing forehead with his racing paper as if in salute, he left the courtroom.

Out in the lobby, Dad looked at me sternly. But then he smiled. "Well...glad I don't have to buy you a damn cake and saw!" He then added exhaustedly, "Wow, what a pompous ass!"—meaning the judge. "Alright, let's go see your mother, she'll be worried." And out we went, yours truly now marked like Cain as a penitent criminal. I had a fierce thirst for a pint about then, but thought better of asking my father if we could just pop 'round for a quick one at my favorite university pub. Maybe Francis Ormsby-Gore and Eric might be there for a farewell toast.

I never did register with the police. I rang Linda that night and gave her the news; we had a giggle. Nor did I return to Wroxton as an enrolled student again except to pick up my effects. From Wroxton, rucksack in tow, Dad took me to a London hotel that night where he and Mom were staying near Shell's HQ and his farewell party. They had to order a cot for me, shunted off by the window in their swank hotel room. The familial energy between my parents and me, for a while, was strained, but only for a few days. My father was taciturn, my mother tiptoeing around my father's disappointment. Mom tried to muster sympathy for her wayward son. Had I not been hauled in front of a judge for drugs the very week of Dad's retirement party, I'm guessing both he and she would have let my "low moral fiber" slide with a listless two-minute lecture. At the retirement party, which I didn't attend, I don't think my dad got so much as a pen or even a Lucite brick in thanks from Shell. No odds, Dad was ready to cut all ties with the big oil giant and find something new to do in his life. He chose a lump sum rather than an annual retirement annuity and that was that. From that time onward my father became a passionate advocate for all things environmental. I guess he had had enough of poisoning the planet for profit.

I do have one sweet memory of being with Dad at that time, before he left the UK for home in Mexico. He agreed I could stay on till Christmas when my six-month visa would expire. I had another Kent friend there, a British exchange student John H., and we'd been best of pals for quite a while. John's father was a don at one of the colleges at Cambridge University—the college, in fact, which holds the secret to where the head of Oliver Cromwell is buried. Each Don in turn tells the newly elected one, and the secret has been kept for centuries. I had asked John if I might stay with him and his family while I sorted out my plans, no need to tell me where the Roundhead's head was. The don readily assented to

John's pleading, and agreed to a mid-December turnout when I best find other lodging or return home to my parents. Dad drove us to Cambridge to drop me off. The don invited us to spend the night and my father, now essentially retired, called my mother who was fine if we stayed.

Several weeks had now elapsed since my ignoble appearance at the Oxford assizes, so Dad's smoldering ire had largely dissipated. In any case, though we'd previously lived in England for many years, he had never gotten to hear the King's College Choir at Cambridge, arguably the finest all-male choir in the world. So that afternoon we went to the university and parked by King's College; we were early, so found a quiet bench beside a lovely willow on the River Cam, from which the university itself derives its name. The King's College Chapel, which we could see across a great lawn, is considered one of the acoustic wonders of the world. By American standards it could almost be called a cathedral. But something in its sixteenth-century high-vaulted ceiling lifts the choir's voices into the empyrean to bring their evensong down to earth, as if from heaven itself. There is something truly mesmerizing about the angelic sound of that boys' choir, all a cappella.

It was a lovely late fall day, with the river murmuring behind us, and a soft breeze in the willows. Birds were singing. Dad and I were engrossed in our own thoughts. Suddenly a figure appeared out of one of the far cloistered buildings, a tall thin man whom we could see was studiously reading from a sheaf of paper as he strode our way toward the river. On and on he came, this imposing figure never once looking up from his papers. When he was about twenty-five paces away, Dad said suddenly: "I'll be damned... that's John Kenneth Galbraith!"

For his part, Galbraith, a world-famous economist at that time, still hadn't looked up as he strode along, all the while muttering to himself as he clutched his sheaf with rapt attention. When he was barely ten feet from our bench, he suddenly realized he was on collision course with us on the obdurate obstacle of the bench. My father stood up with alacrity and put out his hand. Galbraith, in truth, seemed a little taken aback. He was a very tall man, as tall as my father, but leaner and more chiseled. At first, he seemed confused as to how we had so suddenly appeared, as if out of thin air.

"Mr. Galbraith," said Dad, stepping forward. "What an honor! You are the last person I expected to see at Cambridge."

Galbraith took Dad's hand. They exchanged pleasantries. "And this is my son, Peter." I shook the great man's hand.

"So, what brings you two to Cambridge?" Galbraith asked congenially, unsure I think if he was supposed to know who Dad was or not.

Dad looked at me. He fibbed. "Well, my son Peter wants to go to college here in England. We've seen Oxford." Only I heard the barb in that.

"Both damn good schools," Galbraith said turning to me, "but I'd say Cambridge is a tad less stuffy. But you can't go wrong either way." I actually knew who Galbraith was. My father had several of his books in his library, and had mentioned Galbraith here and there at the dinner table. As with most of my dad's books, I had browsed *The Affluent Society* (1958), arguably the economist's most influential tome. I think "dry" best describes it.

"So, what brings you here?" asked my father in turn. Galbraith smiled wryly.

"William F. Buckley!" he replied with a droll harrumph. "We are here to debate tonight. I'm reviewing my notes!" He waved the sheaf. It was, I later learned, the first of several annual debates between the old rivals: Buckley, the archconservative, and Galbraith, the Kennedy-era liberal. One of the debates is available via YouTube. Buckley went for the jugular and had a wickedly quick wit. Galbraith was always the forbearing gentleman, but hardly less nimble. It was pretty clear who "won," even if the students' hearts were for the liberal underdog.

"I'll be damned," my father exclaimed. "You know, Buckley lives just a few miles down the road from a house we have in Salisbury, Connecticut. Everyone says he's a son of a bitch!" The two men chuckled. Prescient, as it happens, because my father and William F. went head-to-head in the years ahead, and my mother with Buckley's snarky wife, Pricilla. I like to think that in those skirmishes both gave as good as they got.

"Well, you might be right there," said Galbraith, not quibbling. "The man's a real bastard on the debating stage, though. But if you don't mind, I won't mention a fellow American called him a son of a bitch by the river Cam." They laughed. With parting pleasantries, Galbraith wandered off muttering again, his lank frame stooped over his papers.[11]

We went to find seats in the chapel. It was cool and gloomy inside. Everything was candlelit and the long light through the fabulous stained-glass windows gave the church a warm glow. The smell of incense was thick in the air. Eventually the choir, in pious gowns of red and white, entered the great chapel, filing two abreast behind the choirmaster as they sang a Deus a cappella. Up the center aisles went the processional until at last the choir took to their ornate seats in the nave by the alter. My last memory of the service was Dad leaning back with his eyes closed as the choir sang with such exquisite beauty, a beatific smile on his face. I closed my eyes, too.

I stayed on in England for another month or so, on the lam mostly, sometimes at a cottage up on the East Anglia coast, other times with John in Cambridge, sometimes back in Guildford, once down to see Linda at her college, and one day with Penrose again, when he and I got caught up in another anti-war march in London.

---

11. I have found mention, and even YouTube footage, of the famous Galbraith-Buckley debates for several years around this time, but not for 1970 itself. Perhaps Buckley failed to make it, or withdrew for health reasons that year, or maybe it was less remarkable than the others, and hasn't endured on grainy footage.

It was a small crowd of maybe ten thousand. I wasn't near the front, but somehow my particular group of American youth marchers was siphoned away by some sort of fracas ahead, ending up in a cul-de-sac off Marylebone Road, near Regent's Park. The coppers had planned this very thing. We were surrounded, and asked for identification papers. Clearly many of the marchers were Yank troublemakers. Presenting my passport, I was asked to step aside, and shortly after was hauled in a paddy wagon to a city magistrate, a white-collar bureaucrat as it happens. No white wigs this time, but rather all business, with the man behind the desk suggesting, all things considered, that it was probably best if I just up and left the United Kingdom post haste, how about within three days or else? The "or else" was that if they caught me again, they'd just chuck me on the cheapest night flight to Kennedy with a mark on my passport that would signify to immigration officials in America—troublemaker or draft resister? And laissez-faire draft resister that I was, I had not an iota of proof that I'd ever registered, and I certainly didn't have a draft card. My number 96 was nail biter—leaning toward crew cuts, this way soldier. My parents had returned to Mexico by this time, my father tying up loose ends at the Mexican office before packing up for the States. Once I was let go from the magistrate office, I called home asking if they'd wire me airfare to Mexico City. At least in Mexico no one would care whether I was a draft dodger or not. I didn't mention my second haul before the magistrate whose office I'd just left. I was still on the straight and narrow after all and simply said I was ready to come home. They were relieved.

    I never had the chance to return to Guildford to say goodbye to my canvas tent mates, though I kept in touch with Eric, the liveliest of the bunch, by letter for many years. I took the train to Cambridge to gather all of my things, thanked the don and his son for their hospitality, good luck with Cromwell's head, and returned by train to say goodbye to Linda at her women's college in South London. For her part, I think she was rather tiring of me. Understandable, as her father's surmise was that I was a draft-dodging, college-shirking, hash-smoking, Marxist-spouting layabout with low moral fiber and dim prospects for amounting to much of anything. Her college, in any case, did allow boys to visit the dorms during the day, but at the witching hour, all the XY chromosomes were to leave the girls to their dorms and hightail home. I never paid the least attention to this dorm rule.

On my last night in England, airfare to Mexico City in hand, I had a hankering to have one last amorous night with Linda, but what I envisioned as a dance of dalliance instead turned into a harrowing marathon of distress. It was raining when I arrived early that evening, a good hour I'm guessing before the curfew. Shaking off my umbrella, I strode up the stairs two at a time to the second floor where Linda's room was, limber in my youth despite the heavy rucksack. But rather than finding an expectant and ardent girlfriend, what I saw as I turned from the corridor into her room was a panicky huddle of college girls gathered around one seriously distraught schoolmate with mascara streaming down her face and carrying on as if she were having a seizure. Turned out she was literally freaking out from a bum LSD trip she'd foolishly embarked on. The poor woman was bawling in distress, as the circle of friends and dormmates crushed in from all sides, doubtless trying to be helpful. But this jabbering cohort was clearly just making things worse. Linda leapt up, suddenly glad to see me, and asked if I had any idea how to calm down the poor distressed lass. Was there some magic antidote to a bum trip? Alas no, the only antidote to a bum trip, I knew, was a good trip and that the poor lass wasn't having.

Approaching seventy years of age as I am now, I have taken uncounted numbers of hallucinogenic trips through the years, but Linda knew I was a pretty fearless frequent flyer even at eighteen. I have also never had a "bad trip" in my life, so other people's terrors are known to me only as a spectator. I have certainly taken heroic doses and lost touch with reality, but that's rather the point, isn't it? I've never freaked out just because the psycho-dwarves were carting me off into the underworld. Once on Belladonna (*datura*), I am told I sat in a closet at a friend's house talking to a very wise gorilla about the mysteries of the universe for nigh on two days and two nights, pretty much straight through. No amount of coaxing would get me to leave my comfy closet. Instead, it was they who had to bring me sips of water so as to wet my whistle through my edifying conversation with the ape. Consider the Navajo, the Havasupai, the Paiutes, and even the ancient Aztecs: they all speak highly of *datura*, and I'm with them, though it can be psycho-tropically dangerous in overdose. Anyway, here I am today, happily typing away these tales of excess, no worse for the wear and tear. I became very fond of my companion the gorilla. As an aside, perhaps this is why I've always loved Daniel Quinn's marvelous novel *Ishmael* (Bantam, 1992), about one of the world's great teachers, a black mountain gorilla named Ishmael, who speaks with a wisdom as old as the hills. Quinn does a remarkable job of making it believable that the ape speaks like a prophet. Read it if you haven't; it's a remarkable and enlightening voyage of sheer joyful imagination.

But where, pray tell, was my big hairy ape when I needed him now, eh, Fay Ray? Most of the girls seemed relieved that I had arrived, as doubtless Linda had gossiped that I was a worldly psychonaut who had never seen a hallucinogen I didn't want to ingest pretty much immediately, anywhere, anytime. Calumny, I say. I much prefer to be in the woods, thank you very much, and had learned some prudence in my eighteen years, to moderate my dosage. Well, at least some of the time. Gathering my wits, I took off my rucksack crammed as it was with all my worldly goods, put down my wet brolly, and then promptly asked everyone but Linda to leave the room. I quietly closed the door behind the departing gaggle. Before me I recognized the poor distraught girl from prior visits, as she, in a crumpled heap on the floor, looked up at me with dark-streaked, pleading eyes. She was certainly in a bad state.

"Make it go away!" she said, over and over. She was pulling at her hands frantically as if to remove imaginary gloves. Her face was a mess. With Linda gently holding her shoulder, I came to sit next to her on the floor. I realized intuitively that the circle of freaked-out girls I'd seen upon my arrival, well-meaning as they may have been, were suffocating rather than soothing the lass. Their gasps and wide-eyed anxiety were probably partly to blame for the intensification of their school chum's bad voyage to a sky devoid of all diamonds. What this poor girl really needed, naturally, was some Kenny G. on the stereo and a bunny-rabbit to hold. Alas, I had neither to hand. So I asked her to take five big deep breaths. Just breathe. Yes, in and out, that's right, there you go, breathe. The broken record of "Make it go away!" dissipated, as I anticipated. I made it clear that she was safe and was still the beautiful wholesome girl she had been before the trip had suddenly ripped her from mundane reality. With a nod to Linda, I began to sing the nursery rhyme, "Row row row your boat, gently down the stream..." Over and over, merrily and quietly and soothingly. Merrily Linda followed suit. Eventually her friend took up the song, if haltingly, as if it were the last lost end of a lifeline on the storm-tossed gale of her mind. The three of us just sat there, for a good ten minutes, singing the soothing rhyme. I even began gently to chuckle like a child with a bobble-head, as did Linda, until the clouds parted a bit in our ward's mind. In slow stages, our charge managed a wan smile, looking at her two friendly nurses sheepishly. She took a huge breath as if a thundercloud had indeed passed. Her bunched shoulders sagged; her hands fell to her lap.

"I have been silly, haven't I?" she said at last, which was a very good sign indeed since it meant some modicum of her normal self had taken back control of her fraying neurons. She kept breathing deeply. Over the next half hour, we talked the poor girl down to where she was able to walk to her room. With Linda on one elbow, me on the other, we got her to lie down on her own bed, shoes off, pillow fluffed, mind calmed. Another girl came to sit by her at this time, and the drama in the dorm quieted down. As for me, it was a mixed blessing, for if I hadn't been the hero that last evening, I am quite certain Linda would have asserted her growing independence, and with tear in her eye and kiss to my cheek, have asked me to leave. She needed space. But suddenly I was the day's fine hero. LSD trips aren't exactly like lamp switches; they don't just turn off with a flick when you might want them to end. Indeed, you might calm down but still be tripping for hours. The entire dorm of girls pleaded for me to stay, just in case. I agreed. Be this as it may, Linda still requested that I sleep on the floor and fetched some blankets.

My flight from Heathrow left midday, as I recall, but Linda wanted me gone before 7am when the morning bell went off. Daylight it would be by then, so I could hardly just waltz out the front door the way I had come in, so it was down the trusty drainpipe. This would be my second go at this handy contraption of an exit. I had climbed down once before when Linda first arrived there for college a few months before. There was a window at the end of a little cul-de-sac corridor where the girls' lavatory and shower rooms were. Slide up the window and you could look down upon a foot-wide ledge, which led to a large, well-attached iron drainpipe coming down from the roof. To each side of the drainpipe, all the way down, there were architectural flourishes of alternating and protruding stone blocks that could easily give your feet a purchase as long as you rappelled down holding the drainpipe with both hands. The last I saw of Linda (until a decade later) was her giving me a sad sweet wave goodbye as I clambered down. I waved a kiss.

This time, unfortunately, I had the heavy rucksack on, so getting the balance and weight right was the devil. The umbrella I had stuffed haphazardly into the rucksack suddenly popped out, clattering down to the sidewalk. It emphasized that there was always a danger of falling. I didn't notice that by this time Linda had been joined by other girls, all of them gaily watching another paramour daredevil descend the handy drainpipe. The crowd in the window suddenly took up giggling, but I was too focused on my clumsy descent to really notice. Granted it was only the second floor, but still it wasn't that easy. At last I landed on terra firma and turned to pick up my brolly, but who should be standing there but two fine British bobbies in their blue-black bobby helmets emblazoned with their constabulary badges, all their fine buttons polished, and their handy bobby whistles dangling. My very own Tweedledee and this must be Tweedledum. Hmmm. Damn.

"Mornin' squire!" said one of the jovial duo. "I do believe you dropped your brolly." The sight of these two roly-poly Bobbies with my umbrella was so ridiculous I suddenly burst into a ridiculous grin. I reached out to take back my brolly but the copper said, "Uh uh uh. Now squire it's a good fing indeed, sir, dat your para-moooor, who I may assume is she in de window up der," indicating with the brolly. "Yes, a good fing indeed, as I say, she be smilin' down upon us like an angel of mercy givin' us a little wave. Mornin' luv!" he called up, at which point I too looked up and of course, there was Linda and two of her beaming dorm chums giving little ta-ta waves and giggling uproariously.

"Wewl, wewl," the copper mused, returning to the matter at hand. "Lucky fo' you, as I say. Good fing dey're wavin', cuz me fellow constable here and me might uvverwise fink you was up to some mischief. Know wot I mean? But obviously a fine chap such as you'self is just gettin on wiv his day, isn't that right, young squire? Getting on wiv your day?" At which point he handed me my brolly with a stern "don't do it again!" look. "Go on den! Blow your lass a kissy goodbye! Atta boy. Off wid you den!"

And so off I went, waving at Linda and her pals silhouetted in the receding window. What a wonderful send off from the British Isles. A young squire, imagine that! As I learned in subsequent letters from Linda, this pair was often at the bottom of the drainpipe at dawn to welcome back to terra firma other amorous frequent flyers. I was hardly the first in their rogue's gallery who had scampered out at dawn, down the infamous drainpipe. "Mornin' squire!" Busted.

Chapter 4

Mixcoatl—The Cloud Serpent Is Angry

Under the Knife

I returned to Mexico in December of 1970. The spring before, my parents had moved yet again, from the unwieldy if quaint 18th-century hacienda to a beautiful Parra house literally across the street. Manuel Parra was one of the most influential 20th-century Mexican architects, his focus being residential homes built so that natural light filled shared spaces, with spiral staircases to upper floors. Living rooms flowed organically into gardens, and he used many materials from colonial haciendas mixed with modernist motifs. The room I shared with my brother was on the topmost floor of the house, that itself had a bold stairway leading to the roof where our cook kept potted herbs, pepper plants, and the like. I even found a pot plant growing there once, score one for the cook.

    What was perhaps most remarkable about this extraordinary house, though, was that from the upper verandahs and the roof you could look over toward Calle Diego Rivera and see into that famous artist's home. The rear of Rivera's studio and house faced our lush garden, where it abutted ours at a right angle; all of its surfaces were painted an electric blue, with splashes of other colors in peacock splays. By the late Sixties, the house had been turned into a small museum. To this day, Calero Street remains cobbled, the stones having been laid down some two centuries before. The old hacienda we had lived in is gone now, but the neighborhood retains much of its old charm.

Sometime around the New Year, my brother and I decided to climb Mount Toluca (Nevado de Toluca in Spanish), a ragged volcano whose elevation rises to about 15,350 feet, a good 3,000 feet higher than Mount Fuji. In winter, the summit peaks around the caldera are often draped in snow. Guidebooks say it is the fourth-highest peak in Mexico. To the indigenous Indians it was known in Nuahtl by the name of Xinantecatl, the Naked Lord. Its ashen slopes are pretty much denuded of trees which may explain the name. In 1970, a narrow and sometimes precarious dirt switchback road could get you by jeep within several thousand feet of a gap in the caldera, though the worn-out track may well have gone into the cone at one time. What makes this dormant volcano famous is that within the caldera there are two lakes: Lago del Sol, the larger, and Lago de la Luna, nestled like a mirror near its twin. The waters of these lakes are gin clear, famous for how they shimmer with all the streaked colors of the caldera's steep inner rim, rising several thousand feet above the ancient floor of the volcano. These slopes have all the sulfur, copper, and cobalt colors of volcanic chemicals in them. Here, in the deep gloom, a unique species of transparent, blind fish has been found, about four inches long at maturity. They have vestigial eyes and are found nowhere else in Mexico. When the Spaniards finally took control of the Toluca valley in the sixteenth century, early explorers who arrived with a fabled priest from Córdoba climbed the peak, and with stone they found strewn in abundance, built a small chapel over the site of the indigenous shrines. The ruins of this little chapel were evident when my brother and I came to this haunting place that chilly winter day. What happened next was to shadow my life to this day. Near the peak, my left lung collapsed. Here is how it happened.

After coming down from a perch just below the inside of the crater peak, I stood deep in that fire cauldron, high on a rise between two mountain lakes where nothing save sagebrush and cactus grew and a few low, thorny weeds in a chilly wind. To the west lay Largo del Sol, whose depth plunged down to abyssal darkness. And to the east, the smaller liquid oval the local Indians, so I've been told, called The Lake of the Coyote Moon, Lago de la Luna Coyote. I was a stranger in that thin air, as the whole vast cone of the mountain about me flared like an Aztec sacrifice in reddish hues on the sheer caldera walls that rose straight up twenty-five hundred feet. The palette was bilious with sulfur bands, green streaks like tarnished copper, rust red blotches, and everywhere huge boulders colored almost cobalt, lava dark, coughed up in some prehistoric explosion. The crater rim as I recall was aflame with the red tongues of the slanting sun, all reflected as in two mirrors in those mountain tarns below. In most winters the volcano lay deep in snows, a vast white volcanic thumb rising from the plain. This winter it was cold, but with only rains; even at this height, the snows had not yet come.

We had left literally a half hour before sundown and by the time we were on the north slope down, night stars circled Polaris, and a cold wind suddenly came up. We found shelter in a herder's hut with his bell-clanking goats. All night the wind beat the hut's tin roof with an angry fist. The clinking goats were restless. Then in the howling hour I awoke bolt upright with a searing pain that suddenly seemed to rend my gaping heart in two. With no warning, I felt like a man drowning for air in his sleep, gulping for the life in me at thirteen thousand feet. My brother awoke, and with concern held my head against his chest, for we both thought, not being wise in the ways of medicine, that on this night atop the world, I for one was a goner. What a bitter night of terror listening to the Olmec winds outside howl about the weeping mountain. I could barely breathe a gulp of the thin air, and there was an arctic chill in every bone. We made no coffee, but chose instead to descend the mountain as fast as we could, given my grave condition. We bid the goat boy adiós, and my brother, bless him, lugged both of our gear-packs, for even the weight of my own coat caused agony in my left shoulder and chest. A mile above the tree line, the great volcano was an endless undulation of alpine meadows with stunted shrubs and swoops of scolding crows.

The long climb down was excruciating. It was at least six miles to the nearest hamlet. We found refuge at last in a doleful *taberna*, or cheap beer joint, in a little village that had a single bus stop where we could catch the autobús to Toluca. We waited in a little brightly-lit bar, which turned out to be the finest stinking piss hole of a rundown cantina I have ever stepped foot in. Folk music blared out of tinny speaker. But the cantina design was sheer genius. The bar at which we took our seats was also a tiled urinal with tinkling water running down the front, so from your stool you could pee and gulp your icy beer at the same time, with a drain hole at the far end taking the pee-water out to the rutted street. Never in all my life has a cerveza tasted so good, and there I sat, numb from shooting pain, while on the blind pig radio a mariachi band sang, "Feliz año nuevo!"—that long-ago Yule spent weary, beaten but intoxicated on sweet old pungent planet earth with a grand urinal gurgling.

The trip from this marvelous cantina to Mexico City was sheer agony. It took many interminable hours to arrive back home, where I literally collapsed on the doorstep. I was promptly driven to the ABC (American British Canadian) Hospital across town. After ruling out pleurisy or a heart attack, and with most of the gringo doctors away for the holidays, a very kind intern, who seemed barely older than me, struck upon a collapsed lung, as it is called. A quick X-ray confirmed the diagnosis of a "spontaneous pneumothorax." I was immediately wheeled into surgery and, without general anesthesia, they cut me open in several places and inserted rubber tubes to inflate my sagging lung. It was horrible. By mid-January, it was agreed that my mother and I would go by bus to Dallas to get an authoritative diagnosis; there was a thoracic surgeon there who had been recommended. I couldn't fly since I was inordinately sensitive to pressure differentials. No one at the Laredo border-crossing so much as asked for my draft card since I was not only "with my mom," but she made a big show that I was a wounded bird on my way to a doctor's appointment in Dallas. The butchered surgery done by this witless Texas "cuttin' doctah," as he called himself, actually attached my lung onto the upper pleura (lining) of my lung cavity. I have a huge scar under my left breast to show for it. A few years later, the right lung collapsed while I was hiking in Big Sur. I had the same operation again. To this day, while I can now fly, I cannot take a backpack of more than a few pounds over either shoulder.

Post-operation, I took a train from Dallas to Philadelphia and spent several months recuperating at my grandparents' home in Lansdowne. It was certainly an interesting transition. I often took the commuter train into the city to visit Kent friends who were at Penn. We palled around, smoked weed, and went to some shows, including my first Grateful Dead concert. I also went to lots of movies, alone with my popcorn. My stay with my grandparents was blessedly uneventful, even fun in a weird way. I came to know both of these engaging, well-educated, and literate elderly grandparents as fully embodied human beings. Unfortunately, modern life in the West today boxes generational experience into Thanksgiving meals and not much else.

When my parents in Mexico were finally packed up to move to the States, I bid my grandparents goodbye and headed up to Connecticut to the house that had been purchased five years before. Semis were on the way with all of their effects. They were coming by car, stopping to visit cousins of my father in Ohio, and would arrive later.

Gittin' Me Edercated

That fall I entered the University of Connecticut, Torrington, hardly more than a postage-stamp-sized community college in 1971.

But it was a start, and served mostly to get my dad off my back. I rented some digs in the bucolic village of Norfolk, ten miles north of the campus. My first roommate was a Vietnam veteran, the first of many vets I was to meet over the years who helped me to understand what, back then, was still going on overseas. His name was Tod. I am sure Tod suffered from PTSD because if you drove much over fifty mph, he'd clutch the armrest, the tendons in his neck taught as bowstrings. And with any loud bang, like dropping a book, he'd flinch visibly, go stiff as a board, and whip around. Helicopters drove him bonkers. Before getting to know Tod, the war had always been an evil abstraction for me—a quagmire of American imperialism. In the words of Kurt Vonnegut, "Vietnam was a country where America was trying to make people stop being communists by dropping things on them from airplanes."[12] All of these descriptions were ripped from headlines, while the actual grit and grimness of jungle fighting and of acts of grim survival, I knew virtually nothing about.

Tod didn't dwell too deeply on what he'd seen. He'd get hauntingly quiet, with a sort of caged anxiety when he spoke about it. The man described sweeps his platoon had done through jungle villages, shooting those who fled, rounding up the rest who cowered. Burning the huts was a common enough occurrence upon orders from superiors. Afterwards, they'd march the hobbled old men, women, and terrified children to staging areas, many miles away. Stanley Kubrick's dark film *Full Metal Jacket* gets to the heart of it. I sat listening transfixed to these grim stories, with a sort of "Mr. Kurtz, he dead" horror. On the upside, Tod and I managed to plan several protest marches. One began at the college and wended its way into the town of Torrington, CT. Maybe thirty-five people showed up, but six were 'Nam vets so that felt good. It was a disappointing turnout, but this was the northwestern boonies of CT, so we consoled ourselves that we

---

12. *Breakfast of Champions* (Delacorte Press, 1973).

were giving people a voice. Down with American imperialism! At our next "action" in nearby Winsted, CT, the following week—hey, we had over a hundred! Yet even in rural "polite" Connecticut, the hostility to peacenik activities such as ours was palpable as farm-hats shouted obscenities as they drove by in their pickups, middle fingers punctuating their sneers.

Oddly enough, I was a straight-A student at the branch college in Torrington. One PoliSci professor sat me down to have some heart-to-heart conversations about my future. She felt hopelessly stuck in a backwater like Torrington herself, but she needed any teaching job she could get. She had been broke at the time, with student loans to pay off, and even with a new PhD diploma was not a ready hire. Her hope was to maybe move to the main campus at Storrs at some point, get tenure, and move up. So she just could not fathom why a smart young man like me was piddling about in nowheresville where she herself felt so trapped, rather than attending Stanford, Penn, or the University of Virginia—heck, even a good four-year college like Wesleyan or Dartmouth. Wasn't my brother at Harvard, for crying out loud?

I could have probably gotten a scholarship to all of them, and actually did get one to the "hippie" Reed College out in Portland, but never attended. Naturally I had no ready answer to these earnest exhortations, certainly none that satisfied my professor's exasperation, except to say UConn@Torrington was an easy holding paddock for my restless soul. I'd sort out what I really wanted to do in time. Clearly, the cost and hassle of entering a real four-year "kawledg," as Ezra Pound was wont to call them, seemed daunting and totally constricting. I had had twelve years of being a caged inmate at boarding schools behind me; university and its cookie-cutter freshman dorms just seemed like a hellish extension. Maybe I'd go on, maybe not. But I did understand that being in college was a 1-S student deferment for the draft. Were I to be picked up by a draft board somewhere other than the US embassy in Mexico, a decision on whether to send me to 'Nam could have gone either way. I'd certainly be punished for failing to register, a criminal offense in itself that might well have tipped the balance for a one-way ticket to eight weeks of basic training, then a troop carrier to Saigon.

Sometime during my sojourn at Torrington, a group of radical friends of mine at Yale were forming the Attica Brigade, which would be a "let's trash Wall Street and get arrested" cadre within a much larger anti-war march planned for NYC in April of 1972, partly organized by John Lennon and Yoko Ono. I decided it would be fun to attend. So during spring break, I hitchhiked from my apartment in Norfolk down to New Haven to meet up with these good-humored, irreverent radicals. The march in the big city was fun if cold and blustery, though our self-proclaimed Attica Brigade, with trashcan shields and face bandanas, was summarily relegated to the rear of the tens of thousands of marchers. This is a PEACE march, we were told. Fair enough. I don't recall if this was my first big march or not in the US, but it was certainly one of the most memorable to an impressionable twenty-year-old, not least to see John and Yoko doing their sing-alongs in Bryant Park. The huge procession of fifty-to-sixty-thousand marchers began up by Columbus Circle, wended down Broadway, and ended up in Bryant Park on 42nd and Sixth Avenue, where the ex-Beatle and his bride led everyone in chanting "Give Peace a Chance" with fiery speeches. No one in the Attica Brigade was arrested, luckily, though we did manage to spray-paint "REVOLUTION" in big red letters on a Bank of America window. We also told at least six USPS letterboxes what's what with red paint: "The People's Revolution!" Pretty silly stuff, really. There were a few scattered arrests that I managed to avoid that day, even though it's a badge of honor for me that I've been arrested for political actions at least six times in my life. Once was in NYC, where the thousands of arrestees were carted off in buses to a holding pen in either Shea or Yankee stadium. I forget which, not being the least interested in baseball. But not that day. Back in Norfolk, I tried hard to finish out the school year in good standing. All the same, I remained my angst-filled self, at a crossroads with no real plan for "my future" whatsoever. I just knew I was tired of being stuck in northwestern Connecticut. Give me the revolution! Give me urban guerrilla movements! Give me a crowd of agitators! And, not least, where were the girls?

It was my brother, bless him, who managed to quash these vacillations that seemed to have me by the scruff end. In the spring of '72, soon after my brother graduated from Harvard, he took off for Alaska, the last Thoreauvian frontier left in America—where we were both convinced that the Walden Pond life still beckoned. He wrote that he'd found a wonderful cabin on a bluff above Cook Inlet, with three volcanoes in the distance across the wide and surging waters. Life was grand and peaceful. I had no idea what heaven looked like, honest sinner that I was, but a wilderness cabin on a bluff above the ocean in far-off Alaska seemed pretty near to God's green pastures to me. My brother then wrote me asking if I'd fly to Seattle that June, pick up a camper truck he'd bought, drive it up the Alaskan Highway, then head to the fishing hamlet of Seldovia (Seldovoi in Russian means "herring") and deliver the truck into his keeping. He'd met a girl whose father had built the camper shell, and sold him the truck. She and bro wanted to leave Seldovia and explore the rest of Alaska before heading down to the lower forty-eight to visit various family units and attend to other sundry responsibilities. I could then stay on at the cabin and get a job at the crab cannery. Let's see, sez I, of course, of course.

Into the Last Lost Frontier

So I flew to Seattle and picked up the truck. I didn't know it then, but a decade later, Seattle would play a pivotal role in my life. Turned out, the father of the gal my brother was dating, the same gent who had built the camper shell above the Ford truck flatbed, was a genial if gruff old coot. He showed me around his home neighborhood of Ballard, where the salmon fishing fleets were moored. Today the dwindling fleet is but a sad whisper of its former glory, as the salmon runs have pretty much collapsed everywhere below the Alaskan panhandle. My brother had sent me a check to pay for gas as well as camping provender. Finally geared up, I headed out of Seattle one early summer morn, first to Vancouver, BC, thence to frontier cities like Prince George in British Columbia, and eventually up Route 97 to Fort Nelson and the true wilderness beyond. The whole trip was a revelation.

Outside of Vancouver, I picked up a hitchhiker named Gary. He must have been more than fifty at the time, had long hair in a braid, a hermit's beard, a big peace sign patch on his backpack, and a Japanese bamboo shakuhachi flute in a leather case slung over his shoulder. Gary was the first among many teachers in my life to introduce me to Zen Buddhism, which I have practiced like a truant ever since. I hold Gary in my heart, for in so many ways he blew open my mind to the spiritual beauty of Asian cultures, their art, poetry, and music, and to the quietude of Zen. He carried a small cache of books by Ryokan Daigu, Muso Soseki, and Dogen. Gary was fastidious, knowledgeable, aloof, pretentious, and generally a great companion on that 1700-mile slog through what is, outside of Siberia, the wildest and least-populated highway in the world. We rarely spoke on most of the long journey up, but were instead enraptured as the great summer light of the northland heralded a change in the inner lives of both of us. I had never seen such beauty, nor such sweeping vistas to far-off peaks. For most of its length back then, the Alaskan Highway was unpaved and rugged, though today the endless dirt washboards are paved end-to-end. The Army Corps of Engineers built the original two-lane gravel road in 1942 to connect the lower forty-eight with Alaska, so that all types of war equipment and personnel could be shunted through the Yukon to thwart any possible invasion by the Japanese in what back then was still the Alaskan Territory. The curves in the road, such as they were, were well banked so that trucks and jeeps could cover the distance at full throttle. The occasional semis we saw did the gravel road at a good sixty-mph clip, kicking up showers of pebbles that could crack your windshield and pop out your headlights in seconds. To avoid this, I had purchased special clear plastic covers for both.

With the camper canopy on the flatbed as our erstwhile hotel room on wheels, we never had any reason to spend time in the frontier towns we drove through in the wild west provinces of northern Canada. Each successively got smaller and smaller until, fifty miles from the gas station at Fort John, the truck stops were nothing but a few weather-beaten buildings huddled together against last winter's wind and a single gas pump for weary travelers like us in our dusty vehicles. Every evening, and evening is relative as you approach the Arctic Circle, since the sun barely sets, Gary would sit on his little mat and meditate while I cooked up rice and beans or other simple fare. Then he'd play his beautiful flute, also a sort of meditation. Finally, he'd rise like a penitent monk and join me for our meager, if nutritious, meal. The deal was that he got a free ride, meals included, as long as he paid for every second gas fill-up. The further north into wilderness we went, I began to have intimations of a return to some primal sense of myself, as if as each mile passed behind us, a corresponding chip from my weighty ego fell off to reveal a quiet abiding innocence beneath.

If you have never driven the Alaska Highway (sometimes known as the Alcan Highway), I can only say: saddle up your camper and go. To spend days on end, miles from anywhere, on a lone highway that stretches half a continent into more of nothing but wilderness, the whole experience is akin to a revelation. Magnificent scenery greets you at every turn. Dirt tracks off the main highway wind into wild hills and beckon as remote campsites. Vast glacier-studded peaks seem to rise up every hundred miles like cragged scrags of rock and ice, then vanish into your rearview mirror. But bring the mosquito repellent, as they are fierce. Lake Kluane, for example, is arguably the most beautiful spot I have ever seen on this battered earth. To the west lie the Mount St. Elias Mountains towering to 19,000 feet like jagged sawtooths. The icy turquoise blue of the lake mirrors the perfectly clear sky, all cradled in the lap of the verdant undulating mountains to the east. The land is shorn of all the detritus of human interference. Here the "peace of wild things" as Wendell Berry called it, lets one "feel above [you] the day-blind stars waiting for their light. And for a time rest in the grace of the world, and [be] free." Finally, after the slings and arrows of human civilization were left far behind us, my long-forgotten soul brimmed at last in sheer primeval being. I was transfixed and intoxicated. Would that I were an alpine god, I said to myself, to gulp all this splendor down like a vast tankard of honey mead.

    The sheer amplitude, the vastness of true wilderness, was driven home one afternoon when Gary and I took a side trip off the highway down some lost track into who knew where. Five miles down the rutted road we came to the willow-and-alder-lined banks of the White River in flood. Here there was a small campsite with old firestones growing moss. The White flows out of the Yukon highlands carrying 19 million tons of glacier sediment to the sea each year. Its color in June flood is a dirty egg white. A raging river it was, too, a good two hundred yards wide, but rushing so forcefully through spruce-forest tundra and ripped bluffs that it filled me with a sort of unbridled terror at the force and majesty of nature unleashed. As we stood upon a small bluff looking down at the sheer riverine power of it, a far-off skiff suddenly appeared to our left. A single oar flailed about in an oarlock. By the look of it, the boat was empty. Skimming by at a good twenty miles an hour mid-river, flying over huge waves, twirling like a bobbing top, it shot past us like an apparition and was gone. Had its rower collapsed into the hold? Fallen overboard? That bizarre vision remains with me to this day like some strange Man Ray film clip. It was one of the most hauntingly surreal things I have ever seen. That roaring place of ungodly power was suddenly enveloped in a menacing pall. I had an instantaneous realization that in wilderness nothing is forgiven, no small mistake absolved, indeed the human ego, our innate sense of specialness, all mean absolutely nothing to an indifferent rough-hewn country a hundred miles from civilization. One misstep and you, too, are tossed onto the white seethe never to be seen again. Sean Penn's film *Into the Wild* (2007) gives a taste of how one mishap (such as forgetting the nature of spring floods) will kill you as it did Christopher McCandless, the unprepared protagonist. Nature is implacably indifferent to all human aspiration or sense of self-importance and true wilderness will quash a human life as fast as an avalanche can bury it. It was a lesson I have learned to my core. The White River in full flood drove that home for the first time in my life. We hurried back to our truck and rejoined the lone route north to Alaska.

    I did have some anxiety about crossing the border from Canada into the US since I was still without a draft card, though I had my driver's license and passport with me. Alaska, in any case, was the jumping-off point for most all soldiers heading to Vietnam in the bowels of those enormous Ghostrider troop planes. If you look at a globe of the Earth, and not a map, you'll see that the arc from California's Fort Ord to Anchorage, hence to Saigon is one logical grand arc and essentially the shortest route to Asia with one stop for the huge troop carriers. Gary had asked about my status, fastidious as he was. I shrugged his concern off. But as we approached the border station, suddenly on a paved road again (ah, the quiet—no more washboard), I felt a pang of anxiety. But my momentary trepidation came to naught. At the kiosk, we both said we had jobs lined up at a cannery in Seldovia, and with that twaddle were summarily waved back into the US of A by an indifferent border guard reading a paperback.

    Anchorage was a miserable bust, with more seedy bars per capita than any other city in North America at that time. Until then, I had had virtually no contact with Native Americans, but up and down all the tacky prefab avenues, one after another, under harsh street lights and on the grimy curbs, the local tribal Indians lay littered like tossed bottles of hooch. I learned later they were mostly Athabascans of various tribes. I was just stunned. So much for the Noble Savage of my high school American history lessons. The burly white lumberjacks and offshore deck hands from the salmon trawlers weren't one wit better. Everywhere, drunken men in uniform mocked the supine Indians. Gary had said his goodbye back at Tok Junction, taking the Richardson Highway north to Fairbanks where a cousin had a cabin outside of town. Back in tawdry civilization again was a shock that battered my fledgling soul-sense of the wilderness. After wandering aimlessly around the burg of Anchorage for a few hours and buying a few needed items, I got back in the truck and headed south through the Kenai Peninsula to the little fishing hamlet of Homer, famous for its long spit poking out into Kachemak Bay like a pencil with an eraser on the end. The eraser was the ferry dock and fishing harbor.

My destination was Seldovia, a picturesque fishing village with an eighteenth-century Russian church above it, on a hill far across the bay. There are still no roads connecting Seldovia to the mainland highway system; it is reachable only by ferry, boat, or small plane. I remember my excitement as I stood against the ferry gunwale, brisk sea breeze in my face, gulls crying, crossing the choppy waters of Kachemak Bay. My final destination would be, as it turned out, my home for the next year and a half. My brother Dave met me at the ferry dock, took command of the driving, and wheeled us out to what was then called the Outside Beach, past the gravel air strip, the two canneries, along fresh water lagoons to a little turn-off several miles out of town on the Jakolof Bay Road that wound out to a small logging mill. All the roads at that time were nothing more than puddled tracks of dirt. Every car and truck we passed was caked in mud. From the turnout, it was several hundred yards by foot along a wooded trail to the cabin on the bluff.

Honestly, I've never seen a more spectacular site for a home anywhere, not in all my travels. The cabin itself, made of stripped spruce logs, was large at two stories even by Alaska standards, with a big wing given over to a workshop-cum-skiff house-cum-wood shed. But the 270° view from what is now called Seldovia Point—the panorama was simply breathtaking. The bluff here faced northwest out over Kachemak Bay to the larger body of water known as Cook Inlet, named after the eighteenth-century British explorer who sailed along these far coasts on his many voyages.

Straight across the gleaming waters, Mount Augustine poked up, a perfectly conical island volcano smoldering at 4,000 feet from sea level with a lariat of ash and steam smudging the sky. Beyond, as far as the eye could see, were the Chigmit Mountains of the Lake Clark National Park region, crowned by two more massive volcanoes towering to 10,000 feet. The closer of the two was Iliamna with several peaks, the further one named Redoubt was more cone-shaped, think Fuji. They both gleamed in the far haze. Bald eagles (*Haliaeetus leucocephalus*) were soaring about the point, where below on the rocks horned puffins (*Fratercula corniculata*) squabbled with their familiar guttural squawk. It was as breathtaking as it was glorious. The cabin had glass windows on the lower level, clear tarp plastic on the second. Blustery day that it was, smoke curled up from the chimney and we went inside. The cabin had a fifty-gallon barrel stove but only an odd assortment of furnishings, a rudimentary kitchen, and three bedrooms (one small one downstairs, two upstairs). Lacking real beds, grimy mattresses lay on the floor and a reading chair downstairs was releasing its stuffing. The toilet was an outhouse out back. Lighting was provided by oil lamp or candle. Water was hauled in by two five-gallon cans that were left by the side of the road at the turnoff whenever empty. A kindly nearby neighbor with a flatbed Ford would pick them up, fill them at the cannery spigot, and then drop them off on her way back to her house later in the day.

I liked my brother's new girlfriend Moira, a handsome, strong limbed, auburn-haired young woman with beautiful eyes. My stay with them was hardly more than a day; the cabin living room in fact already held much of their effects packed. They were off to what was then known as Mount McKinley (after the president, today called Denali), then they'd head down the Alcan Highway to points south. Dave was unsure of a return date to Seldovia but wanted to explore a sixteen-acre parcel he'd heard was for sale on the Kenai Peninsula. Moira was more emphatic, saying she would come back before summer's end to return to work at the cannery. Cannery pay by lower 48 standards was great, five times the usual rate. Upon their departure, I would inherit the cabin. Moira asked that I "keep it for her" until her return, though I was never quite sure what that meant exactly. You might ask who owned this slice of paradise. Apparently, no one either my brother or I could ever discover. Over the years it had become a first-come, first-served squat. Granted, the cabin had fallen on hard times through neglect, but the basic structure, large as it was, was sound.

And so, as if by some strange magic, I had the whole glorious place to myself within thirty-six hours. I was also nearly broke, and now without a car. Luckily there was a path off the bluff point where the cabin was situated, which wended down to the long curve of the Outside Beach. The far end of the gravelly beach came to another promontory, where the northern outskirts of the village started. Go down a quick path through the woods and you would soon pick up the main road into town.

I got a job at the cannery the very next day. I had a ponytail at the time and had certainly inhaled by this point, looking for all the world like a hippie. My brother warned me that Sal, the Filipino cannery manager, was an ex-Marine drill sergeant who for reasons unknown hated hippies. My brother said that it was best to appear as straight as possible, so I took the hint to shape up for my "job interview" for cannery work—about the lowest bar for employment south of North Pole. If you can stand on your feet ten hours a day and move your arms, you're hired. It's a stereotype, but Sal's demeanor had all the psychological markers of a classic Napoleon complex. He stood barely five-two, was almost as wide at the shoulders, with hulking sinews and sculpted muscles busting out of his T-shirt. I had no doubt that he was a fierce pugilist. So, I always went to work with my hair tied up under a wool cap, and tried to avoid the loud-mouthed git as much as possible.

I was put on the crab processing line, running sliced Dungeness crab halves over a whirling brush to scrape off all the gills and guts. What remained of the edible carcass, encased in exoskeleton, you'd dump onto a conveyor for inspection, hence a last spray wash with salt water, then into big waxed boxes for weighing and flash freezing. All workers wore enormous waterproof pants with suspenders, big rubber gloves, and boat-sized rubber boots. It was miserable work even at five times the minimum wage, and the hours were long. I don't know why Sal and I didn't like each other, maybe my long hair, maybe I was too aloof, too tall, too everything Sal wasn't, who knows, but from the start we just bristled around each other. "You! Put up hair in girlie cap! Put up hair!" he'd yell at any guy with hair past his collar. He was brusque, barked orders, seemed eternally pissed off at the world, and treated all his workers like we were Marine recruits. I balked. Besides, standing ankle deep in crab guts all day, it all too soon wore thin. I think I lasted all of a month. I had heard that one of the two local bars in the village, the Night Spot, needed a roustabout who would do everything from cleaning the stinking dive every morning, to hauling out the night's garbage, to hauling in stacked beer and restocking. After one of Sal's umpteenth episodes being a tedious martinet about something any normal supervisor would have just shrugged off, I told the nasty little shit to fuck off, and quit on the spot. I thought he would clock me on the chin, red-faced as he shook with rage and clenched his fists.

"You deadbeat! You deadbeat!" he yelled. "No good! You hippie deadbeat!" And there, at last, was the dreaded epithet. Me, a deadbeat. Of course, I couldn't have cared less what this idiot thought of me.

He then spat at my boots, and sent me packing. Little did he realize that, behind his back, half of the crew was giving me their thumbs up. Doffing my grimy gear, I picked up my "pay-owed" in cash on the spot and never went back. So, there you have it, I was officially now a deadbeat. Being called this epithet by an asshole with anger management problems didn't bother me much; I'd been called worse. Besides, if being a deadbeat for not wanting to slaughter crabs all day for an Asian conglomerate, under the hawk-eye of an ex-Marine martinet from hell—deadbeat I would be then. I walked down to the Night Spot, and got the job that same day. Swabbing out that piss-hole at 9am every morning was vile, but I had the place to myself and could play the best country music there was on the jukebox while I swabbed. For all intents and purposes, I was now my own boss once I learned the ropes. The urinals admittedly were a challenge as they doubled as ashtrays and contained mystery gunk.

The bars in Alaska all seemed to have jukeboxes spinning 45s. During my Alaska sojourn, I came to love many country artists who until that time I had never heard before. These included Patsy Cline, Hank Williams, Tex Ritter, Loretta Lynn, and the young Johnny Cash, Buck Owens, Roger Miller, Merle Haggard, Tammy Wynette, Porter Wagner, and a new star on the rise back then, Glen Campbell. Heck, I even enjoyed that old drunk womanizer, George Jones—what a silken voice the man had! As I Waltzed Across Texas, I could have sung "Okie from Muskogee" backwards I heard it so many times. I've had a soft spot for what I'll call *real* country music ever since, electrified acoustic if you will, where catchy melody, clever lyrics, and simple orchestration drive the down-home songwriting. Watch Ken Burns' six-part documentary on PBS, *Country Music*, for the back-story.

I did meet a few lads in Seldovia, at the cannery, the Night Spot, and the fishing crews, who became chums. One in particular was

Patrick, a strapping lad about my age, whom I came to admire. He drove a black 1941 Ford Super Deluxe with white rim tires and how we teased him for fussing about the mud splatter. Lost cause, Patrick. He also had a great bounding mutt named Adam, some sort of Rottweiler-Black Lab-something mix. The two of them, dog and man, had been sleeping in Patrick's car to save money so I invited him to join me at the cabin. He and Sal for some reason got along, at least longer than Sal and this deadbeat did. Patrick was thrilled by the offer. In return I got a roommate and a sometime ride—Super Deluxe and all. I picked up a stray dog myself, Nanook, a Norwegian elkhound who just wandered into my life and decided to stay. I fed him on scraps and whatever game we could hunt. He mostly came and went as he pleased, obviously cadging scraps from all the neighboring cabins on his rounds as well. He was a sweet dog, but mostly feral. Patrick and I set about fixing the cabin up. We made several four-poster beds out of found driftwood to get the mattresses off the floors. We hammered together a dining room table. We cleaned up the workroom, and built a greenhouse out of bent alder poles and tossed plastic tarps from the cannery. The summer days were so long that sun didn't set until 11pm, and it rose again around 4am. We managed to grow some squash and potatoes, and one sad cabbage, while most other seedlings made a gallant show of dying slowly.

Out of a total population of 350 in Seldovia at that time, there were maybe all of ten or fifteen people who had the spirit and the look of hippies about them, myself included. Sure, many of the cannery workers were college kids working their summer get-rich-quick job, but they mostly stayed to themselves in the cannery bunkhouse, trying to save every last dime for the fall semester. The rest of the Seldovians were mostly a bunch of ham-fisted uneducated rednecks, as best as I could figure. They seemed to have only two personality switches. One was getting piss drunk back and forth between the town's two bars every night until they were thrown to the curb, and the other was working themselves to the bone at unforgiving jobs: a skipper here, deckhands there, or loggers up at 5am chain-sawing out at Tutka Bay. What wives there were worked at the cannery office or the logging company, others at the town hall or the store. Men outnumbered women three or possibly four to one, and I met nary a single woman outside of the college kids. There seemed to be no other sort of life. The notion that you might actually sit quietly by the fire of an evening in your bucolic log cabin and actually read a book, or play an instrument for your loved ones, or even sit outside to listen for great grey owls (*Strix nebulosa*) hooting through the forests, anything but drinking, seemed never to cross their minds.

Knuckleheads they may have been, but I admired the fact that they all seemed to know how to fix every manner of thing. They could crawl into a boat hold and fix an inboard trawler diesel in an hour, frame/plumb/string electricity through a house or cabin in a day, run machinery of any type, rebuild their truck engine, hunt their dinner, and skin a moose with deft knife cuts and haul it all home over broad shoulders. Seldovia was 100% DIY for it had no plumbers, carpenters, car mechanics, or butchers to hire. You did it yourself or your busted-down vehicle soon sprouted fireweed out of the tattered seats.

A couple of stories will reveal the odd schizophrenia of the place. Alaska was hardscrabble, illiterate, dotted with loud living humanity, and out in the woods, the vast wild lands outside of the towns, were cut like sharp glass into dark fjords and icy crags ringed in snow. Patrick finally quit his cannery job and got better work as a crew lead with the Forest Service running flag lines through the forests where next year's logging roads would be cut. A barebones crummy (passenger work van) picked him up out on the road promptly at 5:30am every morning, took him out the logging road and beyond. He sometimes worked ten-hour days as long as the light held. My own work at the Night Spot was usually done by noon. I'd cop a free meal and beer then head back to the cabin. Adam the dog was kept on a long chain while we were away. Oh, how he'd jump with excitement when I came home, as dogs will. Since Patrick didn't get back till real late, it was often just me and the dogs. Man, I loved Adam: such a wonderful canid. But one day around Halloween, I came home to find he had wiggled out of his collar and bolted free, probably with Nanook. There lay the collar on its chain in the grass, minus a dog. I wasn't too worried. If he was with Nanook, they'd circle back by sundown for a handout.

Nanook was never chained up; I considered him a wild dog mostly (which was silly in retrospect). He'd just shown up one day, a stray, coming by several times a week thereafter for scraps and bones, sometimes enjoying the comfort of my bed at night. After several months, he'd swing by every day, and if we ran into each other in town after my shift, we'd walk home together. Adam and Nanook were pals so it made sense they'd probably gone off together. But Nanook came back home that day, alone, seemingly agitated. That was weird. Where was brother Adam? Nanook, in any case, had an annoying habit of chasing down porcupines. He'd then slink back yelping, his snout full of quills. What a painful ordeal, as we wrapped him up like a burrito in a blanket. He'd squirm and yelp all the more, as we pushed the worst of the damn quills through his skin and out his gums. They're barbed so you can't just yank 'em out, unless they're literally hanging by a tender hook. A deeply lodged quill will rip a hole in any animal if you yank it loose. The whole operation could take an entire evening, as the poor boy whimpered helplessly. When the last quill was worked out, Nanook would be so cross with us for this torture, he'd bolt out into the night and we wouldn't see him for several days.[13] Then two weeks later another snout of quills, sigh. Anyway, the afternoon Adam got loose I had a bad premonition. Nanook

---

13. As I mentioned many pages before, D.H. Lawrence's first book ever published in America was his wonderful collection of essays called *Reflections on the Death of a Porcupine* (Centuar Press, 1925). It was my grandfather who negotiated the book deal. In the porcupine essay, Lawrence painfully describes an evening in Taos, New Mexico, spent pulling out porcupine quills from Mabel Dodge's poor hound. If you're a dog lover, it's a tough read.

was whining incessantly, sniffing the empty collar, as if to tell me something. But what? It wasn't like he was Lassie who had the wherewithal to tug me by the pant cuff and lead me to the scene of some crime. Then our friendly neighbor came bounding down the path, she who so thoughtfully picked up and filled our empty water canisters. Custom had it in Alaska, that you always shouted out a loud "Hello!" from thirty yards out—you didn't want some mad-hat cracker shootin' your head off for an unannounced fright. I knew immediately something was wrong; the poor woman was wound tight. Here, in a poem I wrote at the time, is what happened. It was Patrick though, as Adam's dad, who got the gun. Please forgive the poetic license. By the time the neighbor came over it had begun to rain. It was a grim night to remember.

Samhain Eve
for Patrick

As I was walking home along the evening ridge
down logging roads to the bay, out where the abandoned
tanners' camp once stood, a neighbor came running,
saying you better hurry, your dog's been shot
by a logger in a pickup whom no one to this day will name.

Adam? Jesus! I suppose I set out running, growling
to the rundown country store, how I feared I'd be too late,
where someone had laid him to rest on the tailgate
of a flatbed Ford, in the rain, the life in him limping
out through a bubbling wound in his big black snout.
I guess the bastard meant to shoot him and leave old Adam dead,
instead a small red hole, made by a .22 through the nose,
tongue and gurgling throat, and a firearm burn between
big brown eyes, and a look of incomprehension
between pained brows. All the same, old Adam managed
to thump his tail when I arrived, and lift a wet and bloody head.

Truly what a terrible night and stormy from the north
by the time I hauled him home, a black fist of rage
wringing blood from my dead heart as the wound bled
him out. With pick and shovel and a propane lantern

> I climbed the rim of the wild crags in the gloom to dig
> a gaping hole, shirtless to the waist, cursing God
> and all His worthless creation to explain the awful grave.
> Yet the old boy deserved no less, I'd have dug to China
> to lay old Adam to rest in his burial hole above the bay.
> And still the rains came down against the angry surf out
> in the tormented brine that lashed the black night.
>
> Somehow he was still alive when we laid him matted
> in the mud under the swaying lantern. Ignoble end
> to the noblest of friends. And blind from crying,
> we fetched the hunting rifle, and cradled his head
> in a soaking lap one last time. You know the rest.
> Down in the town, the loggers keep saying it ain't
> nobody's fault at all that he was shot. Dogs off their tether
> don't deserve a second thought. But you know,
> it's funny, I don't reckon it that way. And here I stand
> on a vacant shore, caught between spit in their face,
> and the rain's redemption on this bleak all hallowed eve.

What a grim night to remember!

The sad fact is, Nanook, too, was shot less than a month later for grabbing some drying salmon strips from a native Athabascan's smoke rack. I never saw his carcass, only heard one night at the bar that he'd been shot dead and tossed into the ocean. Poor boy, I could only pray he'd had a good free life. I tried not to blame myself for his death since my efforts at adoption had been half-hearted. Mary Oliver wrote in a prose poem about these canine friends, in her wonderful book, *Dog Songs* (Penguin Press, 2013): "Dogs die so soon. I have my stories of that grief, no doubt many of you do also... We would do anything to keep them with us, and to keep them young. The one gift we cannot give."

These twin tragedies were the harder truth of knucklehead Alaska, then as now. It's why, in the end, I never chose to live in the northland for good, much as I loved the wilderness and its pristine solitude. When intractable American individualism bleeds into the hardscrabble realities of living in rural Alaska, all sense of community, of solidarity of purpose, of humanity in concert with egalitarian communion and acts of kindness, the whole lot just bleeds out into a hard-fisted insular individuality. People seem to grow hard as the winter freeze. All that remains is a sort of bitter isolation so rife among the rednecks, where drink and alienation go hand in hand.

My other strong memory of Seldovia is less doleful, but no less poignant. As winter came on toward the middle of November, I was heading into town one morning when I saw a lone Canada goose (*Branta Canadensis*) in a tidal pool out along the Outside Beach. When I approached, I then saw another goose, dead in the barnacled pool. The standing goose, other than giving this muttering series of squawks, didn't budge. If I approached, he'd just dosey-doe round the tidal pool's parameter always equidistant from where I stood. But if disturbed, he'd stir up a ruckus. But his webbed feet never left the ground. The goose was there when I returned later that day, forlorn and alone right by his dead mate. Five days on and pining, he was still there. I say "he" though in truth, Canada geese are monomorphic, impossible to tell them apart. Most geese mate for life in any case. As Thanksgiving approached, I finally had a heart-to-heart with the wasting goose, who should have long since headed south in migration. "Go home!" I said. But again the next day, the goose was there mourning for its decomposing mate. I finally told the goose if he/she was still there the next day, I was going to shoot it before it starved to death. The goose heard not a word of my threat, just kept on keeping on with its vigil, now going on three weeks. So I fetched the rifle that Patrick had shot Adam with, and saying a farewell, I shot the forlorn beast clean. It seems cruel, I know, but it was now twenty-one days into its vigil.

Patrick and I had been invited for Thanksgiving dinner to our kind neighbor's home up on the hill opposite us on the road. I told them proudly I'd bring a goose for roasting! But when I plucked the poor beast, never have I seen such a scrawny thing. It had already wasted away. I brought it to our Thanksgiving repast early and we cooked it. But in the end it was just shoe leather inedible. Poor goose. At dinner I heard that there was an aging sourdough who lived alone in a remote cabin at the head of Seldovia Inlet. He'd been ill and was looking for someone to bring him supplies. The very next morning, my day off at the Night Spot, I gathered the needed supplies on the list given to me by my neighbor and hiked the four miles (two as crow flies) of shoreline up the inlet to his cabin, dragging a lumbering backpack of goodies. It had snowed. The way up at low tide was icy and hazardous, the stranded kelp slick as can be. It seemed to take me hours over the slippery boulders. Finally, I arrived. As was customary, I called out my presence at thirty paces. Out of the cabin came a diminutive old man, shaggy haired under a tatty wool cap, unkempt, with a sheepskin vest and wellies, but smiling like a happy elf all the same. He waved me in. And so I met, and then spent that winter with, Tony Martin.

Tony was eighty-one when I met him that day. My cabin back west of town may have been more dramatic on its towering bluff, but Tony's small one-room cabin on the shore of the bay was the most heartwarming home I've ever spent time in—it was picture-perfect beautiful. In time it became my borrowed paradise beneath brittle winter stars, the grand wheel of the sky an axle of circling waterfowl during the day. He had built the low-slung cabin in the 1950s, so by the time I came by he had been living alone there for more than twenty years. He was essentially self-sufficient in his enforced solitude. He did have a rowboat and once a month would row up the inlet at ebb tide the two miles into town. He'd buy a few sundries, cartridge shells for his rifles, lamp fuel, and batteries for his shortwave radio, and cash his Social Security check. He'd pick up some onions, some cans of diced tomatoes, and then row back on the flood. I gave him the bottles of pills for his heart that I'd picked up at the tiny post office in town that doubled as a sort of 24/7 drop-off in its cramped foyer.

That first day of my arrival, as if I were a strange lanky gift from the surrounding forest, he cooked up a delicious hare stew with the carrots, potatoes, and a tin of diced tomatoes I'd brought. We chatted for hours, though he was not by nature talkative. Tony had fled the Armenian genocide perpetrated on his people by the Turks during the First World War. From Palestine he traveled to Lisbon, and worked as a stevedore until he could afford a steamer to New York. At Ellis Island, he had stated his name to the unctuous official: "I am Tevan Mooranian." His entry papers stamped him as Tony Martin, now his legal name. In the 1920s, he worked for Rockefeller's Standard Oil, digging pipelines in Pennsylvania for the new-fangled oil wells. But when the Depression struck, he hitchhiked to San Francisco. The vicious pogroms he'd witnessed as a teen in his homeland, and the brutal indifference of the oilrig bosses, had mostly soured Tony on humanity. He was a hermit at heart. He eventually caught a steamer to Cordova. Ever since, he had lived in Alaska doing odd jobs until he landed in Seldovia and built his cabin with his meager earnings.

I stayed with Tony on and off through that entire winter into the spring. Our big cabin out on the bluff was impossible to heat as winter came on, with the inefficient woodstove it had. The log walls leaked the bitter sea wind like a sieve, gales seemed to howl through every crack. Besides, with neither Adam nor Nanook to keep us warm, both Patrick and I started looking for winter digs elsewhere. My brother's girlfriend Moira had returned in early November and seemed put out that Patrick was staying there, too. But the umbrage didn't last, luckily; Patrick was such a nice guy it was impossible to hold a grudge. Anyway, I got an attic room in a little house in town, from a summer-salmon/winter-crabbing skipper I'd befriended. It was just a gabled little room with one window, bed and chair. But with the heat wafting up from below it was always toasty. My rent was simply an exchange for being the caretaker while the skipper went out into the inlet crabbing for Dungeness (*Metacarcinus magister*) for weeks through the winter. It was a dangerous and messy business, I knew, since once or twice a crewmember of his fell ill. My landlord would ask if I'd go out as a substitute, which I did. The pay was great. Honestly, it's not a life for the faint-hearted, out in those freezing seas, ducking 250-pound crab pots as they swing up onto the deck, dripping water and seething with crabs in a five-foot swell. Just crazy dangerous. Be that as it may, through January, February, March, and April, I spent at least five or six days a week at Tony's anyway, bushwhacking through the forest to get there on snowshoes, or if it was low tide, stumbling over the slippery rocks. It was a hell of a slog either way.

It was Tony who taught me "right mind" when it came to solitude and living right. Mindless chatter was frowned upon. Sitting quietly in contemplation was encouraged, be it for hours on end. Fussiness and antsy behavior were wasted energy and he'd frown. He taught me how to cut wood (mostly red alder [*Alnus rubra*] and some Alaska willow [*Salix alaxensis*]) along the Seldovia River that formed the long inlet where he lived. He taught me how to keep the water hole in the frozen river clear of ice. In all things, he taught by example, by doing the chore deliberately. You were to watch and learn. With the alder cutting, always thin the copse, never clear-cut it. Keep the cut wood poles at least nine feet long. Strip the branches in situ by the river. Drag two thin trunks at a time the 200 yards back to the cabin. At the cabin he had four large piles of wood leaning on a bar between two large Sitka spruce (*Picea sitchensis*—the most common tree throughout the region). The piles were laid out in order of their drying times. That way, you always had stacks ready for the fire and, as you replenished the piles every day, the stock never diminished. The new green poles started at the left and were re-stacked in stages to the right as they dried, in a sort of musical staves over many months. He also taught me how to snare rabbits—we caught at least two a week, sometimes more. As early spring came on, and the first chum salmon (*Oncorhynchus keta*) appeared, he showed me how he worked his shoreline gill net at the mouth of the Seldovia River, which had a small run of leaping fish until summer, maybe 5,000–10,000 fish a season. The word "chum" is derived from the Chinook Indian word *tzum*, meaning "spotted." They aren't the best eating by sockeye comparisons, but the river was full of them and you could brine barrel a winter load in under a week. Once picked from the net, Tony taught me how to clean them for the brine barrels. Others he smoked on alder wood racks the way the Athabascans did. Finally, he taught me how to shoot a rifle and never waste ammo.

Once every ten days or so, we'd bag a willow ptarmigan (*Lagopus lagopus*), a type of grouse, when we went out hunting. At eighty-one, Tony was still a crack shot. I commented the first time he shot one of these birds—Bang! Right through the head!—that they seemed dumb as dirt. When flushed they just flew up into the nearest tree and peered stupidly down, which of course made them an easy target. Tony grunted. Their evolutionary predators, he scolded me, are the fox, weasel, and wolverine. Heading to the nearest tree is precisely the correct strategy from which vantage the bird can immediately see what the hungry predator is up to. Weasels and wolverines could climb, but once the bird was in a tree, any hope of stealth was lost. All three predators would give up. Besides, in winter when food was scarce, why expend energy flying two hundred yards when that might not be necessary. The "stupid" willow ptarmigan went up three notches in my estimation. In his quiet way of being, Tony taught me the art of keen observation, how just seeing the way nature unfolds in the moment is the key to living alone in harmony with wilderness. Not least of this was how to stay safe from heedless calamity. Implied without a word in all this was his tacit preference to give all civilized opinions a rest. Yes, you, he'd indicate, your opinions, let them go, they are not worth a pile of bear shit out here, my friend. He'd wink, but he meant it.

Despite his age, and slowing reflexes, Tony was nevertheless hardy. True, he did tire on hikes that went much beyond a couple of miles. He was getting old, had a bad heart, and he knew it was perhaps months, not years, before he'd have to relinquish living in his cabin and move on to some sort of old folks' home for withered sourdoughs. As a precautionary measure, he was also always deliberate, intentional, slow moving and observant by nature when he was out of sight of the cottage. When we went out together on whatever woodland errand was called for in the wilderness, he never explained things, he simply taught by slow and meticulous example, using motion to express himself. A word here or there, and you had to just pay attention and learn. Words for any hermit are largely wasted breath. His deliberation in all things was necessary because if he slipped and broke a leg out in the wilds he'd die for the cold if he were unable to find shelter by nightfall. For emphasis he ran his finger over his throat. Everything was therefore choreographed for maximal, intentional safety and economy.

There was something majestic to living in wilderness, to feel nature in the raw, to see how the whole earth-centered ecosystem fits together in harmony. But there was also a cold-eyed unsentimentality about it, too. My run in with a wolverine perhaps best describes that dichotomy. One of these solitary predators, arguably the fiercest in Alaska, had come down out of the mountains that winter and was picking off the snared rabbits on Tony's trap line. The traps were just loops of wire on the little highways the bunnies cut to hop along through the snow. The hares would catch their necks at night in the loops, and still be there alive at dawn. You dispatched them by a swift torque to their neck. That wolverine had Tony mighty peeved. We saw it several times from a hundred yards out, scuttling like a dark bushy broom as it bolted over the snow. It seemed far larger than I had imagined, even at a distance. If threatened, they will go on the attack against a nosy brown bear or even a whole wolf pack without a thought. Fearless and vicious, they never seem to get the wrong end of these encounters. Backing down seems contrary to their nature. They are also lightning fast, the largest member of the weasel family, with sharp three-inch claws. Later that winter, another sourdough, a man who lived two miles up the shore on the far side of the inlet, snared the poor critter in a brutal bear trap. The wolverine chewed off its own paw, but soon bled to death several hundred yards further on. I saw the carcass. This is quintessential wilderness living in Alaska. You can't be squeamish, sentimental, or compassionate, even less so toward animals stealing your dinner. You track them down and kill them, as I was to do later with a pesky black bear.

I mentioned that Tony had wanted batteries for his radio. It was an ancient Korean War-era vintage short wave. With its tall antennae rigged by wire to his metal stovepipe above the roof, he was able to pick up each evening at 6 o'clock sharp Radio Moscow, which was the Russian counterpoint to Voice of America. It was broadcast from a remote naval listening post on the Russian Lavrentiya Peninsula, barely forty miles from coastal Alaska. The news was delivered in good, but accented, English, the announcer always making it sound like, "Guhd Evenink free world. Thees is Rrray-dio Moss-cow. Now de Noose!" But what was reported was invariably soberly given with probing analysis. The erudite announcer was never chatty, and never delved into gossipy things. It was squarely about politics, world events, Kremlin news, and American capitalism, with an emphasis on the imperial boondoggle and quagmire of Vietnam. Tony would sit at his little table with its oilcloth cover, lamplight flickering, and lean his head against a hand and listen intently every night. When the broadcast was over, and some sort of music or cultural program was to follow, he'd turn off the radio to save his batteries and deliver a brief insightful commentary on what he'd heard. He was fiercely socialist and pro-union, an ardent anti-capitalist, hard-earned in disgust with the oligarchy of the Rockefeller sort. He prided himself in being a "man of the people," though as a gentle misanthrope he nevertheless mostly shunned those people as a hermit. Clearly, he sympathized with the struggles of the communist bloc, though he didn't like Stalin for some offense the dictator had committed. I gathered it had to do with Stalin collaborating with the despised Turks on some oil pipeline through the Caucasus. He also talked about having once gone to a rally, Chicago he thought, back in the 1920s to listen to Emma Goldman, as a stellar line-up of anarchists and communists regaled a crowd of thousands. If I had an opinion, he'd listen politely, but never got into debates. He had no interest whatsoever in winning an argument, scoring a point, or even making me see his point of view, still less in wanting to appear more clever than anyone else. He stated his own point of view and had done with it; that sufficed. We'd soon fall back into silence until bedtime unless I prompted him with questions rather than comments.

I came to greatly admire this taciturn hermit, with his deep earth-wisdom, his revolutionary politics, and his quiet dignity. I breathed them in. I came also to appreciate the acuity of his silences, how he approached everything with foresight and acumen, his deliberate intention. He lived to be still and be. To observe nature fully without judgment or thinking. To be self-contained in spirit and being. But by the spring, I was basically broke, antsy to migrate on in my young life, and felt that poor Tony was paying me in food as an indigent, not the other way around. Through the Second World War, he had worked for the U.S. Forest Services in the Tulkeetna region along the Sustina River. He now received a small pension every month, his sole income. I'd pick up his checks at the post office in town, then cash them at the Night Spot with a forged signature (which was sort of the black-market local bank with loose rules anyway). Cash in hand, I'd hike back up to his cabin with a new bundle of goods. But more and more, other than being helpful about the cabin, I was contributing less and less. I hung around the docks a while but no one was in need of a deck hand, so with my last pennies, I caught the ferry to Kodiak to work in the canneries there. I never saw Tony again after our last farewell. He cooked a stew that night and we listened to Radio Moscow and then, as always, we went to bed. At daybreak I was gone.

I arrived on the island of Kodiak with the flu and spent six days in a leaky shack with nothing but a blanket, virtually penniless, shivering for the blustery cold, wet drizzle racing through broken windows, thinking I was set to die. A hippie dude I'd met on the ferry had gotten a canary job and brought me scraps of food. He brought several spent cans of Coke, which he filled with water. I was so grateful. Somehow, I got back on my feet, joining him a week later in processing halibut at the canary. I was still feverish, but just had to get out of the drafty shack and into cannery digs. Halibut processing was my meal ticket. After working non-stop for six weeks in Kodiak, I caught the ferry back to Homer, and hitchhiked up to Anchorage. From the outskirts, I caught rides all the way back down the Alcan and across Canada on Hwy 1, landing scruffy and smelly two and a half weeks later in Montreal. Hitchhiking down the Alcan proved easy, as I caught a single ride all the way from Tok Junction to Calgary with three young mountaineers fresh off an ascent to the peak of Denali. They were the nicest guys. But once on Canada's Hwy 1, the country's only east-west highway, two lanes wide and endless as it was, that portion by turns became a sort of hell. You could spend two whole days under a single telephone pole with thumb out, dawn to dusk, with nary a nibble or brake light. One time a semi pulled over. I'd never climbed inside one. I was happily surprised to see they had a bed behind the seats. The driver was from Regina, Saskatchewan and we weren't a mile down the road when he pulls out a big ol' jug of fizzy gin and takes a swig, handing it off to me as if there was no tomorrow. Not wishing to offend I too took a small sip. Yuk. Gabbing away, the driver took another gulp and handed it back. I faked a second swig. Eventually as he jabbered, he forgot about me as a drinking buddy, and just started taking one swig after another. Soon he was soused, the upshot being that he missed a curve twenty miles down the road, crashing the whole rig through a barbed wire fence and careening into a wheat field for about fifty yards. The whole rig lurched to a shrieking stop. All he managed to say as we sank to a stop in the mud was: "Gosh darn it! Now why I done that?" And he took another swig. I hopped out, thanked him, and went back out to the road and continued hitchhiking. Maybe the damn truck's still axle deep in that field to this day.

Somewhere outside of Moose Jaw, after another fruitless day of hitchhiking with at least four other guys at each succeeding pole, I decided to hang it up. I jumped a barbed wire fence into a cow field and threw out my sleeping bag to crash. I'd start early the next day, I thought. I awoke to find eight enormous milk cows around me in a circle, their wet nostrils inches from my face, breathing like humidifiers. It was surreal and, for a second of disorientation, terrifying. Yikes! I leapt to my feet and they scattered. Just then I saw a small wiry guy about twenty yards away also getting up from his bedroll. He waved at me. As if synchronized, each of us rolled up his bedroll. At that precise moment, we heard a train whistle and the clanging lurch of freight cars. Looking across the field, we realized we'd both bedded down next to a big freight yard. The kid said loudly, "Alright! It's heading east! Let's catch it!" And by gum we did.

The two of us rode that freight train all the way to Thunder Bay, Ontario nigh on a thousand miles down the tracks. Every evening it would stop somewhere to fuel up for a couple of hours. We tossed a coin, and one or the other of us would dash off to reconnoiter some food and sodas. Our sleeping quarters were two seven-foot end-car cubbyholes to each side at the hitch of some sort of fuel or closed grain car. Except for the endless screeching of the metal wheels, and the thundering clack of the steel rails, it was rather comfortable. Out on the plains we'd climb up the little ladder and sit atop the car and watch the world go by as the shooting stars in the heavens above raced across the prairie night. The ancient brakeman, his hand bones glinting with coal dust and oil, took us all the way to Thunder Bay, the terminus of the journey. It was an hour before daybreak, and we'd been riding the rails for three days straight. From there they'd ship the cargo east through the Great Lakes, and out the St. Lawrence by tanker. My companion told me he was an AWOL Canadian sailor. Weary of military discipline, he'd up and left his station in Victoria, unwilling as he was to go with his supply ship to southeast Asia in some sort of capacity to help with the conflict overseas. He was heading home to Newfoundland. We snuck out of the rail yard together back out to Hwy 1, where I wished him good luck and we parted ways.

The chronology of passing years for the next few sections will deviate somewhat, since my various stays in Alaska are of a piece and so they logically seem to belong together. They form the bedrock of my spiritual practice, and were in aggregate formative to how I experience the world ever since. I did make it to Montreal that first return from Alaska. I had heard from a hitchhiker I'd met that McGill University had a great summer hostel with dirt-cheap rooms. Furthermore, from Montreal down through Burlington, Vermont onto Rt 7 south was the most direct route to my parents' home in Salisbury, CT. It seemed like it would be an easy hitchhike, and if I got stuck somewhere along the pike, perhaps my parents would even come and pick up their prodigal. I will pick up Montreal and my attending McGill University in the fall of 1973 later in my story. For now, let's U-turn back to Alaska and finish up with a story of how I came to meet a fifteen-thousand-year-old ancestor by a glacial lake.

The Zen of Home Alone in Wilderness

It is now the Yuletide of 1976 in this narrative, with my graduation from McGill University behind me, of which I'll say more in a bit. Once again, like Balaam's ass, I am undecided between this and maybe that. My brother David had returned to Alaska himself during my sojourn at McGill, and had indeed bought sixteen acres of land from someone breaking up their much larger homestead holding, erecting a lovely one-room log cabin several miles out in the middle of nowhere in the village of Kasilof on the Kenai Peninsula. It was made from spruce trees felled on the property. My brother also found the time to enter graduate school at the University of Alaska, Fairbanks with an emphasis on biology. To support his budding graduate student elder son, my father gave Dave the family VW bus, a well-loved vehicle we'd all taken to over the years. When I returned home from my peregrinations in Virginia (of which more later) after graduating from McGill, my brother asked if I'd like to return to Alaska. As a newly minted college graduate myself, I was kicking aimlessly about wondering what to do with my life next. Might I want to head up the Alcan Highway again to Alaska over the Christmas break? It would be cold, he said, but with the two of us sharing the driving it seemed doable. Besides, I could spend the winter in his cabin, fix it up and make it homey, while he went back to school in Fairbanks. I wasn't entirely sold on the idea, especially a winter trip, but after some thought, I said yes. One particular impetus was that I wanted to try my hand at writing a novel, as I had several ideas rattling around. A winter alone in a cabin with my trusty Olympia portable sounded like a capital way to get those ideas on paper. Indeed, half of my luggage seemed to consist of boxes of typing paper, ink ribbons, the typewriter, plus books—lots of them. Besides, at that time I had no intention of going to graduate school. What would I study? My life hung on that question mark.

So sometime before Christmas, with our VW bus filled with gear, bro Dave and I headed west to Seattle, and then up the Alaskan Highway to Kasilof. I don't recall much of the trip across the US, on the northern route through Chicago, Minnesota, then buffeted by icy and blustery North Dakota, Montana, and on to Seattle. We may have arrived in Seattle on Christmas day, for all I can remember. We stayed with friends of Dave's, bought supplies for the long haul north, and got geared up. A Volkswagen bus may be a sturdy vehicle and fun to drive, essentially one of the earliest versions of a small vanigan suitable for camping, but as with all VWs in those days, the engine was in the back. We'd taken the back seats out, building in their stead a sort of platform which served as our makeshift sleeping cot. We knew it would be cold once we turned from the coastal region of the Pacific inland into the hinter world of the Yukon. So with some sort of insulating tape, we wrapped the heat ducts that ran from the engine in the rear to the vents in the front, along the chassis pathways beneath the van. We also bought an electric oil pan heater to plug in if we stopped the engine for more than an hour in the sub-zero weather. I think we also had tire chains, one per wheel, clanking rhythmically every one of those 1800 miles. We may even have bought warmer clothes in preparation for the bitter temperatures ahead. Then out we ventured to northern British Columbia and the far underbelly of the Arctic Circle.

The temperatures until around Fort St. John, BC were tolerable, getting down into the twenties at night. In alternating shifts, we pushed our driving time to upwards of ten to twelve hours a day. At night, most hotels and lodges had electric plugs along the frontage for guests to plug in their oil heaters. But from St. John north things got increasingly dodgy, as the temperatures in Fahrenheit never rose much above the twenties during the day itself and down to zero and below at night. Later on, temperatures dropped further into the single digits during the very brief sub-arctic days, then well below zero as the arctic stars came out. Some nights we drove into the magnificent veils of the northern lights, shimmering over the pole. It was often hard to keep your eyes alert on the endless white highway in the cold cone of the headlights. I have absolutely no memory of ever passing any sort of vehicle going our way after dark. During daylight, coming at us on any given leg of the journey, maybe a few semis rumbled by or the odd car of hoarfrost crazies like us.

Our little chugging VW heating system was no match for the cold, of course. I think in the end we cut the foot ends of our sleeping bags open and sewed the bags into body tubes, which we'd then pull up to our armpits, down jackets over, wool caps pulled low, leaving our feet free to work the three peddles of the stick shift. Once we reached the southern border of the Yukon around Watson Lake, the inside of our van never got much above twenty degrees tops, even at noon, with the sky blindingly bright on the endless fields of snow. After sundown it was just brutal. Our foam sleeping mats in the back, for one, got so brittle in the bitter cold they simply shattered into packing-sized peanuts. To say we were miserable would put a good face on it. Luckily, we were never swallowed up by a blinding blizzard. Massive snowplows and diesel trucks with spiked packing rollers kept the rock-hard surface free of slippery ice. We sometimes drove for three hours straight without seeing another vehicle through an endless winter wonderland stretching to the horizon on both sides of the barren highway. All of the stunted spruce were cowled in snow blankets, and the lakes were frozen solid. Outside Whitehorse, I got sleepy while driving and failed in my vigilance, prompting our little van to careen off the highway into a deep snow bank at the side of the road. Lucky for us it was daytime. Within the hour some sort of big truck came down the highway offering assistance. We could have frozen to death. The three of us, with chains on the rear axle, managed to haul the tottering bus back onto the hard-pack. On we went, arriving in Anchorage around 8pm on New Year's Eve. We were so utterly knackered we simply crawled into our motel beds and slept till noon, New Year's Day, 1977.

Winter in my brother's cabin that year, and the following summer on Kalgin Island, were perhaps the happiest times of my life, certainly the most carefree. To live absolutely unencumbered by the constraints imposed by industrial civilization, the tedium of a work-a-day job, and all the media distractions of modern life: halleluiah! I had absolutely none of that over the next eight months. I could just live my life with the rhythms of the day and of the night, the surrounding wilderness free of all constraints. All of those compromises which living in civilization demanded were gone. Living in wilderness is an act of apprenticing yourself to yourself. You yourself become your own experiment in living fully, never driven by some external push manufactured by society. For food, I had big tubs of raw rice, beans, other dried foodstuff, racks of canned diced tomato, etc. For heat there was a fifty-gallon stove. Wood came from the surrounding spruce forest. Water at first came from pans of melted snow, then boiled spring water. Because of the cold, the outhouse seat was kept by the inside door. You'd bundle it under your jacket, head for the little wooden crapper where, ta-da, your bum got ensconced on something rather toasty, as otherwise you shivered to point of constriction. Life, in short, was brilliant and bum warm.

It was here, that first winter back in Alaska, that I spent sixty-one days and nights without seeing a single other person. I've only met three other people, Tony among them, who can say the same. Alaskan poet John Haines is another. For most city dwellers, driving to a mountain getaway with our significant other is the most alone we've ever been. Maybe for a day here or there, hiking the Pacific Crest we don't meet other hikers—that sort of "being alone." But being truly alone for an extended period of time, living intentionally for weeks on end, miles from anyone or anything, is not for most modern western humans. The cabin was out on Crooked Creek Road, five miles off the Sterling Highway. At the end of the Crooked Creek turnoff, you took a forest service fire cut into the woods about a half-mile. Our cabin stood on a little rise, a hundred-yard hike off the cut. It was the only cabin within a mile radius in any direction; back then it was sparsely populated into the surrounding boreal woodlands, draped in icy cowls over ghostly trees. Today, of course, it's all built up and unrecognizable on Google Maps (I think the rough forest cut of 1976 is now a graded gravel road called Sunset Drive, but who knows.)

So what does one do through those long winter nights, living in a cabin in the middle of nowhere? Well for one I came to study the stars, to observe night after night how the wheel of heaven moved in relation to the moon and the planets. I had a wonderful little rotating star chart (still have it) called a Star Explorer, created by the Junior Astronomy Club of America. With the cardinal points on a fixed square, inside the star chart there was an oval window and a spinning replica of the night sky. The constellations were all laid out, with names of the most prominent stars. You could then find at least one constellation you knew, Orion say, and line it up in the chart window with the wheel of stars, get your compass bearing in line with the four-cornered compass, and suddenly there was your perfect chart of the heavens. In time, all the scattered stars coalesced into meaningful groups, Cygnus (my favorite), Leo (my second), Scorpio (third), Cassiopeia, Orion, and Boötes, on and on into the mysteries of Messiers and rearing nebulae. Wandering across the Milky Way, the magisterial planets traversed the diamond-studded sky where, night after night, I watched transfixed under the dome of heaven. I had a favorite clearing in the forest where I lay down in the snow to watch the show, a flashlight lighting up my little chart.

Easiest of all the celestial mechanics to comprehend are the phases of the moon. Then the visible planets, and why they go retrograde in relation to earth and sun. I studied how some moved more stately across the sky, while others were more fleet until there was a passing conjunction The great orrery of our solar system somehow all fell into place from nothing more than dazzled observation. Into my vocabulary came such wonderful words as syzygy, an unusual alignment of plants, or celestial coordinates, whose declination and right ascension are the celestial equivalents of latitude and longitude. The great Andromeda galaxy was perfectly visible, and faintly the Magellanic Clouds. A few of the great nebulae shone reddish in the velvet darkness. Many nights, too, the northern lights, the Aurora Borealis, swept the northern skies with colorful curtains of light dancing in hues of electromagnetic blues and pale greens. In short, through many nights of visual study, and hours at a time at that, I came to understand how the sun, the planets, and the earth triangulated, how the heavens wheeled, and how the phases of the moon happened. I fell into my lifelong habit at this time of calling the moon in all her phases, Selene, the Titan goddess of the moon in Greek mythology, sister to Helios the sun, to whom I always gave (and still give) obeisance in her cyclical journey round the earth. Odd as it may sound, I have never seen the moon since in all my years without saying aloud, "Selene, beautiful you, three bows!"—a habit burnished in wilderness.

D.H. Lawrence in his book of poems *Pansies* has a poem called "Lonely, Lonesome, Lonely – O!" in which he decries how so many people he meets feel "lonesome." The poem ends thus, reflecting exactly my own sense of precious solitude:

> But what is lovelier than to be alone?
> Escaping the petrol fumes of human conversation,
> and the exhaust smell of people
> and to be alone!
> Be alone and feel the trees silently growing.
> Be alone, and see the moonlight outside,
> white and busy and silent.
> Be quite alone, and feel the living cosmos softly rocking
> soothing and restoring and healing.

With me always on my sojourns in Alaska was a tattered Penguin Editions paperback copy of D.H. Lawrence's *Collected Poems* now held together with tape and a prayer. Other nights, I wrote into the wee hours, frantically clacking away on my portable, the words, phrases, sentences, paragraphs all in the service of what

I could only hope would become the next great American novel. I imagined cute nerdy girls throwing themselves at me at book signings. As the sheets piled up, the ribbon rolls running dry of ink, sweat and toil rose in stacks on the floor telling a sprawling Tolkien-esque tale of magic and daring-do set in Viking Norway circa 800 AD. The protagonist was Elgar the Woodcarver, and I typed a good two hundred and fifty pages of his adventures, the last hundred, alas, without the letter "E" as the key end had snapped off at the head one night and my portable typewriter suddenly had a gap tooth. So much for the great American novel. It puts me in mind of French author George Perec's infamous novel *A Void* (*La Disparition*, 1969) written entirely without the letter E as the protagonists go looking for Monsiur Vowl. With my own gap-toothed prose, I am sure experimental novelists like Perec might well have approved. I still have the manuscript in a shoebox somewhere. In any case, I grudgingly conceded that the Pulitzer wasn't in the offing, despite my gallant efforts at mead-filled flagons of imagination. Effort ceased entirely when my brother came south to visit, read an early draft, only to howl in derisive delight at the phrase "scurrying dwarv s" (sic) after which my typing sort of "p t r d" out.

But one does read voraciously in wilderness if one's inclined, as what else is there to do? Thus we may well turn to Shakespeare's Polonius, who asked of Hamlet (Act 2, Scene 2): "What do you read, my lord?" to which the Danish prince replies with a weary riposte: "Words words words!" When Polonius further inquires as to the subject of the words, Hamlet brushes his question aside with, "Oh just lies!" There's a certain truth in this, for all writing is a fable of sorts, an invention, even as some may claim a moral plot. I have never felt inclined to Hamlet's self-pity. Reading, in any case, returned me from my hermitage back into the world of humankind, if only in imagination. "Conduct and character are largely determined by the nature of words," wrote Aldous

Huxley, "[those] we currently use to discuss ourselves and the world around us define who we are."[14] Ergo if you listen to fake news, you become a fake. Turn to the classics, and therein one might find insight into the human condition. By listening to Nature, you become a naturalist and so on. As companions, I had a stack of Steinbeck, several books each by Henry Miller, Loren Eiseley, Joseph Conrad, and Faulkner, *I Claudius* by Robert Graves, *The Cloud Forest* by Peter Matthiessen, and mid-century works by the likes of Norman Mailer and other titles forgotten. Letters home pleaded for more books and a month later a cardboard box of them would arrive at the Kasilof post office. Bundle under arm, I'd hitch back to the cabin feverish with expectation. I wish here to make a plug for one particular classic, indeed one of the finest books ever published, yes, the singular one-volume, *The Columbia Encyclopedia* (3rd edition preferred, published by the university, c1963). Running to 2,388 pages on rice paper sheets, it is miles better than Google in a box, and far more authoritative and concise. Not "three million hits in 0.0003 seconds" (whatever the hell that even means) when searching on Henry VIII or what an "isotope" is, but rather a single pithy, dependable, trustworthy, scholarly. and accurate entry: voila! Granted you need good eyesight. Anyway, it's a marvelous tome that needs no improving, never crashes, has no click bait, no false leads, no colored whirligigs endlessly spinning, eschews fake news and dubious leads, there are no Comcast, AT&T, or electric bills to pay, and not one crap advert. Instead, there are just the vetted facts in brief eloquent entries available 24/7, rain or shine, no Wi-Fi or cell service required, power outage preferred as it doesn't ever need electricity. What's not to adore? In short, I never slept alone a single night of those sixty-one days without contact to the history of our civilization at my fingertips.

---

14. Aldous Huxley, *Words and Their Meaning* (Ward Richie Press, 1940).

A smaller tome, but no less authoritative, was my father's 1952 gifted copy of *The Concise Oxford English Dictionary of Current English*, edited by F.G. Fowler. I remember reading it from front to back, and then from the front again. Now as it happens, I have often been accused over the years of using way too many "ten-dollar words," and not a few worth a whole twenty bucks and change (oh, commination!) to wit—"mnemonic," "sequacious," "natatorial," "perstalith," "strabotomy" (after Buñuel's Andalusian Dali-dogs, of course), or easier ones—"lugubrious," "avuncular," "uxorious," "unctuous," and so on, ad infinitum. I do indeed have a hefty vocabulary. My problem is, in truth, that the words were all learnt from reading that dictionary like a novel, page after page, even in the outhouse. As a consequence, to this day, I generally don't have the slightest clue about how most of these fancy words are pronounced. Sad it is, but here I have been sounding stuffy, as they say—verbalizing my loquacity with highbrow verbosity, yet inevitably with lowbrow delivery. Not a few far better scholars than myself, sententiously seated in their ivory towers, have over the years listened to me expound eloquently about this or that, only to raise an eyebrow and furrow a frown at my awful pronunciation of these wonderful, if challenging, twenty-dollar words. Even as an exalted library dean, I was once politely scolded by my provost, a rhetoric scholar of whom I was fond, that "behemoth" wasn't pronounced "beh-hee-moth" for heaven's sake, it was pronounced "beh-heh-moth," the aspirant middle "heh" pronounced with apposite alacrity. Ah, the incomprehensible world and fathomless absurdity of the English language. To those learning English for the first time, sepulture I say.

I remember one howling blizzard night at the cabin, long after I'd gone to sleep, stove crackling low with the night's firewood, when I was rent from slumber by a cabin-rattling clatter. I sat bolt upright in the dark, fearing a tree had fallen on the roof, or the tin chimney had blown off (which it had, as it happened, for I found it the next morning twenty yards away in a snow bank). Shaken, I bundled up, grabbed my handy flashlight and peered outside into the storm. Good grief. Of all things, I was dumbfounded to see an enormous bull moose (*Alces alces*) standing on the porch, doubtless trying to get out of the howling gale. We sized each other up. Even a 1200-pound brown bear (*Ursus arctos*) won't take on an 1800-pound male moose. Size aside, moose always seem so long-faced and forlorn, do they not? The mournful eyes of this enormous ungulate were rimmed with ice, its fur caked in snowy clots. Well, hello there, big fella! He seemed equally astonished by my sudden apparition; I think he was more startled by the light beam than by some little sleepy-eyed human. He promptly loped off into the howling gale and was gone.

Black bears, coyotes, weasels, martens, and occasional wolves were everywhere but usually only seen at dusk or daybreak, unless they happened to be regular denizens of my immediate diurnal habitat. The naturalist Loren Eiseley put it thus in his book *Firmament of Time* (1959): "If we are to penetrate nature's secrets, we have to come to an animal with a knowledge of his various habitats. We have to know something of the place in which he lives. Then, and only then, we may, if we are lucky, be able to glimpse in slow and scarcely perceptible motion how the living form flows and transforms itself through time." To live alone in wilderness for any length of time as a castaway from careworn civilization, is to "penetrate nature's secrets," there to glimpse in scarcely perceptible motion how an ecosystem flows all together in the dancing reel of wild life: to read the clouds for a weather report, to know which snowfalls will soon rage into blizzard, to sense which bogs will carry your weight on a hunt and which will plunge you to your armpits in peaty water. There is no one there to come and rescue you if you are foolish or take a bad fall. Around you always is the great unfolding of nature in its perfect, heartless harmony. Jack London's story "To Build a Fire" should be the cautionary Bible of all who trek alone in unforgiving wild lands beyond even the vapor trails of airplanes.

One day, out of some crevice in the cabin, a little ermine weasel (*Mustela erminea*) arrived unannounced. He was fearless, inquisitive, snakelike in how his long silky body curved effortlessly around corners, and I at first welcomed his company. It was winter and he was now all white except for the telltale black tip to his tail. He soon became a regular, and because I didn't chase him away at first, seeing in his cute little inquisitive self a sort of odd and comforting companion during those long winter nights, this fierce little hunter soon became fearless around me. There must have been a chink in the base logs of the cabin somewhere, just the size of his skull, through which his shoulders and hips could collapse like a sock pulled by sharp claws through the hole. It is possible that in the sidereal realms of nature, such clever mammals as weasels are in fact life forms as intelligent as us, since this particular little chap had mastered our shared habitat with synchronous harmony. He'd gnawed into the beans, tasted each onion, knocked everything over, and been a general pest when I was trying with little success to sleep at night for his racket. This mischievous blighter finally crossed a line of intrusion to beset my peace of mind.

I killed the annoying, if "tame" ermine with a swift fierce smack to the head using the flat side of a heavy cleaver. How strangely beautiful he was draped over my hands in death. As it was winter and the earth was frozen, I couldn't bury him. So I skinned him, and made little booties out of the white winter fur for the baby of my nearest neighbors. Killing the handsome guy may seem cruel, but in wilderness neither sentimentality nor squeamishness are your friend. Another time, the unwelcome intruder was a black bear boar who broke into the cabin through the window—just bashed it in like a tinfoil sheet—and proceeded to wreak absolute havoc inside the cabin, tearing open big cans of diced tomatoes like paper cups. My neighbor shot the son of a bitch, and there was stew meat all round.

In all, though, my time spent in wilderness was generally an abiding contentment, far from the madding crowd and the grating chainsaw of human commerce. I saw in nature, in the words of Loren Eiseley, an "elusive and indefinable divinity," an open-ended labyrinth to my true self. I was never bored, never got cabin fever, didn't think to miss companionship, and was absolutely never lonely. I dreamed of women here and there but didn't much mind my aloneness. The downside was that I did get in the habit of talking to myself out loud, as if for some innate psychic need to hear human speech. So I filled my "lonely" ears with a sort of running commentary. To this day my bemused wife will call out from the next room, "Whom are you talking to, dear?"

The most miraculous day of my life came that spring when I came face to face with the ghosts of Pleistocene explorers, somehow stepping through a door of Deep Time into an intangible realm of astonishment. I had gone to the Fish and Game office in Seldovia at winter breakup, having heard they were hiring for the summer. I immediately got a job as a salmon weir operator on Kalgin Island in Cook Inlet, with a start date in two weeks. On the evening before heading out to the island for the summer, I decided to leave the cabin at dawn and bushwhack east through the bog lands, around thin stands of boreal spruce up to Tustumena Lake. The lake was about four trackless miles away, with the morning sun as my compass. Tustumena itself is about fifteen miles long and five miles wide, fed by a number of glacial rivers that wend their way out of the Garfield Ice field of the Kenai Fjords National Park. This pristine body of water is a magnificent expanse, colored a robin's egg blue by the bluestone granite crushed to silt beneath the ice field under the weight of those distant glaciers. Miniscule particles of the blue-tinged bedrock float suspended in the lake, giving its distinctive color. At the western end toward where my cabin was, the Kasilof River comes to sudden life as the lake's single rushing egress to the sea, a swift river wending but a short run through rocky banks to Cook Inlet some seven miles away.

In case I encountered bears, I set out with my ten-gauge shot gun loaded with massive slugs. I had a bundle of good nosh in a satchel, a water bottle, and my feet were shod with rubber boots for the patches of melting slush and thawing bogs. The day was glorious, a balmy forty-five degrees maybe, veritably hot for Kasilof in early May. After about an hour, I came upon two black bears eating the carcass of an ungulate, probably a deer, possibly a woodland caribou. Someone may have shot it, a poor wounded beast struggling on to that spot to collapse where the bears likely found it dead or dying. Grizzlies can run fast enough to take down a galloping elk with a single swipe to its back legs. But I somehow doubted these yearling black bears had it in them to take down a deer. They were two young males, likely brothers by the look of them, not yet off on their separate solitary journeys into adulthood. I felt safe enough because a ten-gauge slug can blow a hole through a bear wide enough to see through, though the math of my armaments wasn't lost on me. I could only fell one if they charged. I'd be left to swing the butt end on the second, precipitating a less encouraging outcome. They both raised their grizzled snouts, looked over at me sniffing the air, grunted as if to say "this rotting carcass is ours," then simply turned back to ripping the flesh off the poor dead animal. I guess for them it was a veritable feast, fresh out of hibernation as they were. I walked on.

Within the hour I came into a beautiful grove of paper birch trees of enormous girth, white whorls almost two feet wide at the base. I felt I had stepped all of a sudden into a Maxfield Parrish painting, and would scarcely have blinked had a unicorn stepped out of the copse into the sunlight. I sat beneath the leafy branches of one of these lords of the realm and had a snack. Immediately I felt something was watching me. It was an uncanny sensation, but looking round I could see nothing but some gray jays (*Perisoreus canadensis*) who'd been following me. Gray jays are very inquisitive, the tamest of North American jays, or as the Cornell Laboratory of Ornithology is wont to put it, they are "deceptively cute." As a survival strategy in the cold north, they have retained adaptive behaviors learnt from eons of foraging for food near the camp middens of Native tribes; the latter obviously tolerated these "deceptively cute" camp robbers. I had four regular jays at the cabin all winter myself: Geek, Beak, Zeek, and Freak. Damn birds, sometimes even before sunup, they'd tap at the front door (tap-tap-tap-tap-tap-tap-tap!) until I hauled my groggy ass out of bed, grabbed a few bits of bread, dopily tossed the provender onto the porch to shut them up and went back to bed. By this act of charity, of course, I simply encouraged more of the annoying behaviors for which they are famous. Why in the name of Dickens do scientists ponder if birds have birdbrains or are manipulative, smart, and cunning? One time I left the cabin door open to let the smoke out as I'd burnt something, probably a baking loaf of sourdough, when in came two of these bossy pests to see if the burnt repast might be salvaged to their advantage. Out! They would happily alight on my wool cap while I was outdoors, often perched upon my head in mimicry of a hipster top-knot, from which soapbox they scolded the surrounding forest with jay chatter. Feeding them by hand was a daily chore; I had all four on me hopping about regularly. Yet how wonderfully did they provided me with companionship that long winter, each of the four having distinctive avian traits of behavior to easily tell them apart. You have no idea what joy they brought me even as they trained me to keep them plump and fed. A fair question to ask: who was domesticating whom?

In any case, on my amble to the lake that long-ago day, I was sitting beneath the birch trees admiring the jays and listening to a flock of boreal chickadees (Poecile hudsonicus) flitting about in the budding branches overhead. There was nothing untoward besides. And yet...yes, what was this eerie sense I had of being watched? Then I looked up. There, from out of a huge circle of sticks thirty feet up and directly overhead, were three peering great grey owl chicks (Strix nebulosa). They were looking down at me out of their nest with eyes of affronted surprise, as if I were the oddest thing they'd ever seen in their short lives. Soon momma arrived, soundlessly out of the forest, with a meadow vole or other small rodent in her beak. Although momma glowered at me with her own enormous yellow eyes accentuated by feathered rings, the chicks were too hungry by then to care anymore about the weird hominin below.

When I got to the southwestern edge of the lakeshore about a quarter of a mile from where it flows out to the sea via the Kasilof River, high up I saw three Vs of snow geese (*Chen caerulescens*) winging north to their barren arctic breeding grounds. I gave thanks that from where I stood winter was, at last, in full retreat. Though a perfectly clear day, a fierce "sun wind," as they're called in Alaska, had come up so I found shelter beneath the curve of a low-bluffed cove by the lake. I could see the glaciers and peaks of the ice field clearly in the east. The lake was choppy with waves. Then the strangest thing occurred. I can honestly say it changed my life forever. Once hunkered down out of the wind, I was eating my lunch, when this shiny object about twelve feet out in the lake seemed to bob in and out of the choppy blue waters. I looked through my binoculars and studied it. It was shiny, streaked reddish black, and looked for all the world like a largish oval, sticking out of the lake like some preterhuman version of Arthur Rex's sword Excalibur. Was it the sharp tip of a branch of a submerged log? That didn't register as likely. I got up, rolled up my pant legs and started to wade out into the freezing water to have a look-see, but soon found the water too deep. To reach the object I'd obviously be in well over my knees in no time, and I had eight feet to go. So I clambered back to shore, took off my trousers and underpants, and waded out again, buck-naked.

The lake water was frigid; it couldn't have been more than thirty-six degrees, just a tad above freezing. My ice-cold feet meanwhile sank into the blue-gray clayey silt. It got as deep as my thighs. Freezing though it was, I tiptoed on into the lake. It seemed surreal, but with a start, I suddenly realized I was now making an ascent up a little silty bank, with the lake water coming first only to my knees, then my ankles, then barely an inch deep. And there, as if by some ethereal magic, clasped in the blue silt like a gem, was my quarry. I reached down and picked up a magnificent large Stone Age spearpoint gleaming wet in the sunlight, about seven inches by three. To say that I was astonished beyond words doesn't describe my mind—it was on fire. I just couldn't get my head around how the damn thing a) had gotten there; b) was sticking point up in a lake bed of muddy clay; and c) why hadn't it long ago toppled over into the fathomless mire hence to be lost forever to the world of prying eyes in a fathomless lake. Yet here it was, glistening like a hidden treasure in my freezing hands.

By this time I was shivering for the cold, so I hightailed back to shore, got dressed and huddled in the lee of the little bluff to admire, wide-eyed and wondering, the magical object now in my possession. I could answer none of the nagging uncertainties that filled my mind, even though I can now say that it was for me the most perfect day in the world, safely retained in memory from all encroachment. Sitting on the little stony beach miles from anyone, I was simply overwhelmed by my find. My restless mind sought some way to answer the questions that would explain it—an answer in any case that could satisfy any skeptic who might question the veracity of what happened. Not one thing of it makes rational sense. To this day I cannot excise the certainty that the stone floated upon the milky blue waves like a message from beyond, a gift from some Stone Age ancestor. Direct me to a single verifiable report of a floating stone anywhere, unless it be porous pumice, and I will file my stone point under "scientific fact." It wasn't until sixteen years later, when I read the absolutely wonderful book by Lyall Watson, called *The Nature of Things: The Secret Life of Inanimate Objects*, that I came to understand how such "inanimate objects" actually do have secret lives, and more often than we might care to admit. My own experience that day could have been torn from the pages of that book.[15]

I no longer ask the "why" of that day's miraculous find, there by the glacier-fed lake in the lee of the wind when I was all of twenty-five. I came to see from reading Watson's book that these sorts of implausible happenstance actually happen all the time in the lives of normal people. We just file them away as some quirky and momentary synchronicities soon forgotten to memory. Yet there are tales of rings that get lost overboard on a boat outing, then return to the owner in the gullet of a hooked fish years later. That day was marked nevertheless by several sensible observations. For one, I was in a state of wide-awake and joyous consciousness; it was springtime after a long winter of darkness, with the sun shining and migrant waterfowl returning. Second, I also felt a keen sense of participatory day-born wonder in all that unfolded in the forestlands about me. I was wading through the morning like a swimmer through bracing currents. Is it thus impossible to imagine that in this state of grace, on a glacial moraine long ago, I had come upon evidence of an ice-age wanderer passing this way fifteen-thousand years ago? That it floated like Excalibur above the lake water somehow makes perfect if indelible sense, which in the end perhaps needs no explanation. That day I was in a state of "no thought" as Zen practitioners call it. I was alive in my being without a deliberation in the world. Peerless English author Tony Parson perhaps sums it up best in his book, *As It Is: The Open Secret to Living an Awakened Life* (Inner Directions

---

15. Watson, as perhaps I've mentioned, is the most influential author that I've ever read in my variegated life of reading, a life moreover chock full of read tomes of all shapes, sizes, and genres. He's a magnificent writer: engaging, curious, eloquent in every one of his dozen or more books, including his authoritative *Guide to Cetaceans*. Do check him out. His book *Heaven's Breath: The Natural History of the Wind* has just been reissued by The New York Review of Books (2019). It's another classic. Or even better, the shamanic chronicles in *The Gift of Unknown Things: The True Story of Nature, Healing and Initiation from Indonesia's Dancing Island* (Destiny Books, 1992). Wow.

Publishing, 1995): "Home is simply oneness, my original nature. It is right here, simply in 'what is.' There is nowhere else I have to go, and nothing else I have to become." Perception that this home is already and forever our existing nature allows the miraculous things in life to self-express. No striving marred that long-ago day, no longing for some achieved result, still less any doing, froing, invoking, measuring, praying, hoping, wanting, worrying. Just an enveloping Beingness. If only the Danish prince had left it at this: To Be, with no questions to follow—he and Ophelia might have married happily ever after, and had a brace of kids. That was the essence of that far off day. In the raiment of a curious teleology, the spearpoint then appeared, as if handed down by some forbearer through trackless ages into my keeping. A Gift so to speak. "The harvest of symbols in our minds," John Steinbeck once wrote in his marvelous travel book, *The Log from the Sea of Cortes* (Viking, 1951), "seems to have been planted in the soft rich soil of our pre-humanity."

I gave the spearpoint to my brother at some point, to have it analyzed at the University of Alaska in Fairbanks. Not sure much came of that. When I finally ended up at library school at the University of Washington a decade later, I had a geo-anthropologist there study the knapped point. It was made from a glossy red-black shard of jasper, he was sure, itself an odd if symbolic choice from which to knap a spearpoint. It is a handsome, semiprecious stone in any case. The professor was very dubious about my description of how I had come by it. He dismissed the woo-wooness of it with a wave of the hand. Raised brows, oh, come on? He was surprised, nonetheless, after more research to realize this type of jasper is only found in quantity within any remote striking distance of Alaska in Japan and the Korean Peninsula, where it is mined to this day for ornamental carvings. There are mineral pockets further north around Kamchatka and the remote Lavrentiya region of Russia. But odd pockets might be anywhere, he felt obliged to add. If truly it was of Old-World origin, then whoever made the point had carried it all the way across the Bering land bridge (Beringia) during glacial maximum, c15,000-20,000, a lowland that connected Siberia and Alaska where trumpeting mammoths doubtless still roamed the tundra in shaggy herds. All those thousands of years ago, an unknown hunter had somehow let it fall from his grasp, perhaps on a coastal ice-sheet of the New World, where over the aeons, the odd object melted down through the miles of ice, thence into the clay of Tustumena Lake, veritably an heirloom past down into my hands. Good enough an explanation for me. The professor looked at me. Might I donate the artifact to the Anthropology Department, he asked? Uh, no, I said emphatically, grateful though I was for his analysis. To his credit, he understood that it was the find of a lifetime. Perhaps I'll bequeath it upon my sad demise, I said in parting, though half in jest. Too late for that now, as we shall see.

My route back to the cabin that day took me to the banks of the Kasilof River, where I saw a playful group of river otters (*Lontra canadensis*) belly flopping down a mud chute into the roiling flow. The river was in flood with break-up and milky with silt, carrying mysteries of the cold glaciers to the springtime sea. Over and over, the playful otters would pop up out of the water, clamber ashore, and scamper up the bank to wait their turn like children to slide back down the chute again. It was sheer delight. How I envied the exuberant hearts that beat in their riverine breasts, born free as brothers and sisters in a playful band of camaraderie: curious, communicative, and content in the quick of life. Wilderness for me that day was an intoxication, as if I had been graced by *Anima Mundi*, the soul of the Earth, enveloped as it were in a field of pure wondering consciousness. Thoreau wrote that "in wilderness is the preservation of the world" adding "to apprehend it, we cannot be naked enough." It was that psychic ability "to be naked enough" before the whole cosmos which was so exhilarating for me that day. To be alive and alone in a grown-up state of innocence, to be unguarded, open to whatever the great web of life might deliver into the moment, to experience the whole cosmos floating homeward into me as the cold day awoke from winter sleep. While I did not miss human commerce, I confess I often dreamed of how wonderful it would be to share this wilderness with a hardy girlfriend who would be the guardian of my solitude just as I would be of hers. But Alaska in the 1970s was a "man's world."

Wilderness, in any case, surely preserves the soul of our planet, as Thoreau intuited, weaving Earth systems into a harmonious whole. It certainly gave substance to my soul in my formative years. As James Lovelock sought to probe in his Gaia hypothesis, [16] all parts of the Earth's multifold systems regulate a Gaian equilibrium for all other living things, each doing their part for the sum of the whole. For some it's the survival of the fittest, for others it's a mutual symbiosis, but it is in the totality of an intact ecosystem across the globe where Gaia finds her pathways to endless flux, fecundity, and change. I am eternally grateful that I was given the chance to witness firsthand that intact wilderness ecosystem of the northlands, to live there as just one inhabitant amid the myriad. How sad that in 2020, Gaia in her luxuriant offerings helps ravenous humans in their inhumanity to thrive every day of the week, while we return the favor by ravaging Gaia's every limb in return. Yet each day, without a grudge, she continues to give and give again. Plumb that. Had you asked me that spring day back in 1977, along a lost wind-blown shore of a glacial lake, yes had you insisted to inquire if I knew about the climate chaos to come, in truth I would have thought you were mad. I wouldn't have known what you were talking about. Nature seemed so vast, so alive, so intact, and so full of wonder back then.

Yet in full disclosure, by the time I left the northlands for good the following year, the Alaska pipeline was tearing up 800 miles of tundra, as stubborn men in hard white hats built massive oil

---

16. James Lovelock. *Gaia: The Practical Science of Planetary Medicine.* Gaia Books, 1991.

rigs out in the arctic thaw of Prudhoe Bay. Even as I walked back to my cabin that day, surveyors were at that very moment measuring this once pristine wilderness to bring it under the rule of plumb bobs and vast diagrams of conquest. Well, enough. More on my years in the environmental movement will come later in this story. Over the next year, I moved around Alaska quite a bit. That summer I lived alone on Kalgin Island counting red salmon. In the fall, I took a fishing boat down to Sitka on the eastern shore of Baranof Island in southeastern Alaska, where I spent the next year and winter. Then I fished up and down the coast, for salmon and halibut mostly. I made good money and pissed it away, my life a cycle of boom and bust.

In the late summer of 1978, I flew home to visit my parents, and then spent three months living in New York City. This sojourn in Gotham essentially launched my career into the music business the following summer of 1979 in Seattle. But in order to keep my time in Alaska as a single narrative, I have skipped the period in my life in which I got my "real" college education, from 1973 to 1976 at McGill University in Canada. The next chapter returns to pick up that thread from my first stay in Montreal in 1973, after returning from my first sojourn in Alaska, through to my leaving for Seattle in 1979.

Chapter 5
Dudley Do-Right to the Rescue

Montreal, McGill University, and the Summer Olympics of 1976

Before I dive into the various sagas of my punk "daze," I obviously need to get myself "ederkated at a kawledg" (as Ezra Pound put it in the *Cantos*), else how did I ever become a library dean? So the progression of my chronology does, at this point, do a u-turn to fill in an oxbow of backwater tales and peregrinations covering the years from roughly 1973 to 1976. Remember the AWOL sailor with whom I hoboed across Canada? Soon after I said goodbye to him, I made it on to Montreal by thumb. After my long travails of hitchhiking across the continent, those first two days at the McGill University hostelry were surprisingly delightful. The accommodations at the university were, by my recent standards of sleeping at roadside for several weeks, truly splendiferous. They even fed you a simple breakfast. And the city was utterly charming.

The solution to my growing sense of being at a thorny crossroads in my life, both as a draft evader and without a college education or prospects, came together at my stay in the McGill hostel as I explored the city. Draft dodger that I was, maybe going to school at McGill in friendly Canada would be a sound and viable option, the veritable two birds of education + draft evasion being solved with one proverbial stone. I'm rotten at math, but this simple equation seemed to add up. I found the admissions office while I was there and got all the appropriate applications for admittance. I was assured they still accepted Yanks, although the following year they put the kibosh on that, what with all the thousands of American draft dodgers in Canada looking for their social services to support them as a pastime. Once I got to my parent's home in Connecticut, I filled out the forms, sent in my transcript from U-Conn, and awaited a reply notice which came a month later. Reprobate and deadbeat I may have been, but I got accepted for the fall class, 1973.

I think I entered McGill University as a sophomore that year (all dates through the Seventies are a bit sketchy). McGill was a brilliant choice though, as I had intuited on my first visit as a hobo. It's Canada's sole "Ivy" after all, arguably with the University of Toronto, the premiere school in Canada—at least back then it certainly was. The focus was entirely on academics and, other than a few desultory intramural sports for the sound building of body, mind, and character, McGill had no varsity sports. It was here that I was finally challenged academically for the first time in a setting that matched my inherent thirst for learning, for explorations into arcane knowledge, and, who knew, perchance even a dollop of wisdom might fall my way.

Excellent professors walked me through the Spanish Civil War and the depravities of Leopold II of Belgium's genocide of Africans in the "Belgium Congo" circa 1890. I took evolutionary biology and learned about Alfred Russell Wallace, who devised his own thesis of natural selection probably before Darwin himself. My major was English so we delved into Thomas Pynchon's *Gravity's Rainbow* and Ezra Pound's *Cantos*. I learned Pound's poem "Hugh Selwyn Moberly" by heart. I got stoned often enough, following Pynchon's protagonist Slothrop down a figurative toilet to find the infamous flushed harmonica through the surrealist lavatories of that grand tome. I studied art history and came to admire Pollack, Robert Motherwell, de Kooning, Braque, Kandinsky, Frida Kahlo, Judy Chicago, and Helen Frankenthaler. My minor was in film, so I watched Godard, Fellini, Louis Malle, and even more far-out experimental filmmakers such as Stan Brackage, Andy Warhol, and Kenneth Anger. I went to lectures by Howard Zinn and Michael Harrington. They were heady times.

I never lived in a dorm. My apartments, living sometimes alone, sometimes shared, were always in quirky parts of town. In all my life I have never experienced such ethnic diversity as I did in Montreal. There was a restive, passionate Quebecoise French population for one, and a thousand disparate immigrants from Portugal, Spain, Germany, Greece, the Balkans, and beyond. Boulevard St. Laurent, just two blocks from one apartment of ours on Rue de Bullion, seemed to have a thousand delis from half a hundred ethnicities. There were cheese joints from Portugal, sausage shops run by German émigrés, and brimming markets run by Turks or Czechs with rabbits hanging by their rear paws next to braces of full-fledged pheasant, tubs of pickles in wood barrels, wheels of local cheese as big around as your arms, olives ripening on propped metal mats, spices, exotic fruits, tins of dates and fig jams, baklava and revani, Italian salamis, ripe tomatoes, bizarre vegetables in heaps amid braids of garlic, and everywhere there was blaring music from Morocco or India. Everyone coexisted side by side without any apparent ethnic abrasion whatsoever. What a relief to be so far away from the dreary political and social angst wracking America, with its Vietnam war chaos and Watergate shenanigans rumbling interminably south of the border.

Here's a fact: I stopped by my favorite local coffee shop on Rue Saint-Dominique one evening on my way home from classes at McGill. The place was tiny and it was twilight. There was only one person in the cramped little coffee shop, Leonard Cohen (himself a Canadian) as it happened. He sat at a small round table with a chessboard on it. He was reading...of course, Camus. I bought my coffee and, thinking what the hell, asked offhandedly as I stepped to the door: "Wanna play a game?"—indicating the board.

With those deep beautiful feminine eyes, Cohen looked me up and down, saw I wasn't some crazy person, and somewhat listlessly said, "Sure." He smoked like a chimney throughout. I guess in his mind the board created both a barrier in space, as well as a purposeful lack of need for conversation between us, only concentration. He was fiercely intent on both counts. Puff, puff, puff. We barely said a word and he showed not the least interest in who sat across from him, I was just—The Opponent. I became a board game abstraction for him, who must be thwarted at all costs.

He was a deliberate player, and often rested his chin on his palm. We never said a word; his cigarette dangled, curls of smoke rising, blown clouds buffeting me as if I didn't exist. The outcome? He cleaned my clock. He was very sweet in saying goodbye as the victor, and asked about me finally, as if concerned that his fierce concentration might be misconstrued as sullen disdain. "Student," said I, "McGill." "Ah, I see, well then, do good things, Peter, is it?" I thanked him for the match and walked out into the night. Anyway, he wasn't that big of a hotshot back then, you could see him strap on a guitar often enough in small clubs here and there about town. One can see Cohen's interest in chess from his slightly odd but engrossing short film, "I Am a Hotel," a collage of his songs filmed in a single hotel room, produced by the Canadian Broadcasting Corporation. A chess set is front and center throughout.

My mother, bless her, ever trying to make me respectable, encouraged me to "be a gentleman" with an acquaintance of hers, a woman younger than Mom by twenty years, but certainly older than me, in her thirties. Sally was in the vanguard of the Olympic Committee that was preparing for the 1976 Olympiad in Montreal. I became Sally's "gentleman caller," if you will, squiring her to a fabulous jazz super club downtown where we saw B.B. King, Thelonious Monk, Horace Silver, Herbie Hancock, Keith Jarret, Howling Wolf (one year before he died), my fave bluesman Willie Dixon, Stan Getz, Art Blakey, and more. All the blues and jazz greats came through Montréal at that time. Sally, bless her, always paid for the tickets—as I was always broke. I even remember standing outside the club one night with her in a fine drizzle, waiting for the second show when Roland Kirk, the headliner, blowing two clarinets through his nose, came waltzing out a side door with his whole band, playing like gypsy minstrels, entertaining the crowd waiting in line, then reentered the club via the front door to finish up his set. Two clarinets through his nose: I didn't know such a thing was possible. I felt so suave paying the maitre d' a fiver for a better table up front. Today anything under fifty and you'd probably be shunted to the cheap seats. I am eternally grateful to Sally for introducing me to jazz, a genre I have loved and cherished ever since. I must have over 500 jazz CDs now. Through her met all the local jazz musicians in town.

Once again in my life, by sheer happenstance, I was living in a city hosting an Olympiad. The cosmopolitan city of Montreal was the host to the XXI Games. They say that protecting those 1976 games from potential terrorist attack became one of Canada's largest military operations in its history. The 1972 Munich games had been a disaster, with Palestinian Black September gunmen attacking the Israeli athletes. Germany had been humiliated, and Canada did not intend to have that happen. Naturally the city came alive, with tourists and troops patrolling the avenues. Several of us got jobs driving ABC courtesy cars, ferrying elite athletes and mucky-mucks hither and yon. After hours, we'd nick these same vehicles, ABC logos and all, and tear around town, once getting as far as Mont-Tremblant National Park up north with two British blokes keen to watch a three-tequila sunrise in the hinterland. Yet I made it back to the ABC lot by sun-up; I'm not quite sure anymore how we did that.

Here's an example of how tight military security was in the city that summer. Taylor, my old Kent School pal Joris who was now also at McGill, and I pooled our meager cash reserves to buy some hash to sell, with a stash set aside for ourselves. Joris said he had a friend with a load of hash down in New York City, an easy day's train ride south; he could make a big score and head back, toot suite. Our addled thinking decided that since Joris knew this dealer and also traveled under a British passport, it should naturally fall to him to cross the Canadian border with fewer questions and hassles. So off Joris went, promising to return with a major score. Back in our dive on de Bullion Street we soon forgot all about Joris.

    I loved that two-story apartment we lived in on de Boullion. Our aged landlord, who lived downstairs in the basement with his rolly babushka of a wife in colorful headscarves, still had a picture of Nicholas II Tsar of Russia on the wall. He had been a Cossack soldier, he proudly told us, back in the 1920s fighting on the side of the White Russians. Bad Bolsheviks, he'd say, Lenin no good! Trotsky terrible. Stalin worse. Given how awful Trotsky's pogroms of the Tsarists became, our landlord and his babushka somehow escaped to Canada. In any event, about seven of his burly male relatives from the motherland were allowed to come to Canada for the Olympics. The Soviet Union only allowed one member per family to visit Canada for the games, assuming correctly that none would defect, since that would cause vulnerable family back in the USSR to be hounded by the KGB. The bullnecked gents on furlough seemed all to be named Boris, Igor, or Ivan. They dragged enormous battered suitcases into their granduncle's basement when they arrived, each with one change of underpants but about thirty-five one-gallon bottles of vodka rattling inside. If my math is right, thirty-five times seven, that's about 250 bottles of hooch on the wall in all. To say they drank prodigiously is an inadequate understatement that may actually be taken as an insult to the Motherland. Despite the fact we were in Canada, to punch-happy Ivan, Igor, and Boris everyone was nevertheless our "Amerikinxs fren!"—including Taylor and myself.

    Foolishly we invited them up for a détente beer; instead, they each lugged up their own gallon jug of rotgut vodka and proceeded to drink them like soda pop, glug glug, forcing the backwash on us. Inevitably we all got smashed. I must say that I never saw evidence that Boris, Ivan, or Igor ever actually went to a single game in a single stadium to raise the hammer and sickle in solidarity with their "Amerikinxs frens!" They just kept raising their elbows to glug some more swill, it seemed to me, gills deep in their fish tanks of vodka. They were a friendly enough bunch, though none spoke a word of English except "Amerikinxs frens! Ypa! Ypa! Skol!"

About ten days after Joris' departure as our drug courier, Taylor and I finally surfaced from the floods of vodka to start worrying since we'd heard nary a peep from our southbound friend. Then it came to pass that one morning at crack of dawn, after a hellish night of quaffing the distilled Rooskie potato juice with our burly malchicovs, the old rotary phone clanged a hellish bell in the hall. There must have been at least ten lunks littered about, passed out in various poses and draped in assorted states of undress, when I finally got to the clanging wall phone, bleary-eyed. My hangover was no better than the rest. It was Joris and he was frantic. His rant went something like this, at a galloping clip of syllables, all in on one gulp of air, like a frantic five-year-old:

"Pete-it's-Joris-listen-I-got-thrown-off-the-train-wrong-papers-I'm-at-a-phone-box-down-the-road-from-the-border-station-only-one-quarter-left-listen-I-managed-to-hide-the-hash-in-a-toilet-vent-before-I-was-chucked-it's-in-lav-of-railcar-number [making this up] C847563819303891AO. Got-that? C847563819303891AO. Shit-last-quarter! Gonna-try-catch-bus-walk-border-maybe-blah-blah..." Click, wrnnnnk. The phone went suddenly dead as the last penny dropped.

Given the state I was in, I had absolutely no idea what he had just rattled off in my ear. I did vaguely understand that our precious cargo was now in limbo in some sort of lavatory vent on the morning train from Gotham. Beyond that, not so much. Anyway, when Taylor shuffled downstairs about then, I managed to convey the gist that our stash was in a moving loo twixt there and somewhere half way here; we both said: "Fucking Joris!" in unison, our erstwhile "pal" to a T. We managed finally to rouse the lumbering "arktiki" walruses clasping their throbbing heads, and chuck them out the front stairs to go bother their Tsarist great Uncle Vanya downstairs. Out went the lovely Polish tarts, too, and who knew who else. We lost count of the number of empty vodka bottles we threw in the trash, but nary a drop remained. Quelling our throbbing dis-ease in head and stomach ourselves, Taylor and I nevertheless strategized about what to do. We hit upon the brilliant idea to ring La Gare Centrale to find out when the Gotham train got in. That was Plan One of our hazy response. We'd scope it from there, and in the worst-case scenario, on to Plan Two—if we missed the incoming train, we'd head down to the freight yard several miles south along the Saint Lawrence River, where all passenger trains went to get cleaned. Here we'd sneak in unobserved, avoid the hundreds of coppers, the phalanx of machine-gun equipped army sods, give a wave to their canine unit of German Shepherds, dodge all the club-car cleaners, avoid the yardmen, pop open fifty lavatory vents unseen, and...well even we could see this was a witless scenario.

By the time we actually called the station, the train had arrived, so the two of us hopped on a single bike, with one gammy peddle and sketchier brakes, Taylor peddling with me on the bar. Down the busy streets we headed to our rendezvous with destiny on a one-peddle bike. On the Arrival/Departure board we saw which track the train was on, but also couldn't help but notice that armed soldiers patrolled the building from one corner to the exit. We felt we couldn't risk it. After all, we had wild hair, wrinkled clothes, and smelled of spliff. With both of us topping 6'4" with wild eyes and hangover wits, there was zero chance we'd somehow blend in with the upstanding middle-class hoi polloi piddling about in their nice Olympiad couture. Besides, we'd have to loiter onto the train unobserved, open umpteen lavatories, unscrew umpteen vents, and say to anyone who asked that we'd lost a camera, all without being seen or someone saying: "Your camera? In a lavatory vent?" Vodka had obviously dulled our wits, but that didn't mean we were utterly bog-rolled, gormless, or wanker-stupid. Dispirited, yes, I'll grant, but nevertheless determined to retrieve our one and only stash of hash. So, we decided to move on to Plan Two, which was to head down to the rail yard on our wobbly bike where the Amtrak train to New York would get its wash-up before returning to the station for the trip home. We already knew this was a fool's errand, but hope springs eternal. When we got down to the industrial district where the massive rail yard stretched to the river, our worst fears were confirmed. We saw soldiers and canine units patrolling everywhere. There was a high fence and every likelihood of being chased down at gunpoint. There was nothing for it we realized, but for one of us to buy a ticket to NYC for the return trip, and implement Plan Three! We'd jump aboard the Gotham Express at La Gare Centrale before it left southward, and scrounge through thirty fucking toilet vents on the off chance that bomb sniffers hadn't gotten to it first. Ah, dear readers, how is it only now in our dotage, that we can look back with such equanimity at the impossible dreams of our youthful inanity, and ponder from hindsight the utter ineptitude that youth is too often mired in?

The time for the New York-bound train to return finally rolled round later that afternoon. I was the logical one to go on this journey as I was the Yank. With a one-way ticket in hand, Taylor and I were now sitting on the waiting room bench, having spiffed up, with shoes and socks even, pretending to read a newspaper as we spied over the fold the uniformed fuzz. Our intention was to look completely inconspicuous, which of course to a trained eye would have leapt out as "PH-O-NY--BA-LO-NY!" Then who should waltz in all la-dee-da but Joris? We were not amused. He'd somehow finagled the border, gotten back into Canada, and caught a ride into town by thumb, coming straight to the station.

"What?!" he feigned with exaggerated affront, as if this was all part of some elaborate plan of his devising to keep us on our toes.

"Plenty of time! See, five minutes to boarding. Back off. What's the worry?" Yeah, right. Our confab made clear though that since Joris a) was the sorry wanker who had lost the hash, b) had memorized the complex railcar number, and c) was at fault, he could damn well go down and scrub the lavs for our lost loot. At last there was the boarding call for the Amtrak train to New York. So, ticket in hand, down Joris went to the tracks on the platform below. Agitated, disbelieving, rolling our eyes, Taylor and I felt like we waited forever, imagining Joris being hauled off in cuffs to some grim replica of an Orwellian paddy wagon. Then suddenly, lo! Thrice adream, he emerged from yon Stygian darkness, grinning, smarmy as ever with that "What, me worry?" look. Nevertheless, now our hero, good boy, he had the stash. We promptly forgot our umbrage, and all was forgiven. We cashed in our ticket for a refund and went careening back to de Bullion Street to partake of our stash. Oh, foolish youth! So happy were we at our sudden good fortune, we managed to smoke all our re-sale profits on the spot.

The Seed for Rock and Roll Is Planted

Some readers may recall that the mid-70s in Canada saw a fierce insurrection by the French-Canadian minority to secede from the commonwealth, with its rousing call to unite under the banners of the Parti Quebecois! They sought to make Quebec a separate nation, with a French-speaking national identity. The rebellion coursed through Montreal for months with fiery René Lévesque, the Parti Quebecois leader, orchestrating the charge. I went to several monster arena rallies to hear this passionate man preach secession from English-speaking Canada. The electric tingle of a second French Revolution was palpable in the air. Sadly, my French was never good enough to participate in these heady days of insurrection as more than a bystander. Anti-Anglo and anti-American sentiments ran high. I had a few flings with French-Canadian lasses through those many months, but they petered out for my crummy command of French, ardent separatists that these paramours (French word, that!) had become.

At about this time, my mate Taylor had started a little film company called Panic Productions. To anchor his effort in bricks and mortar, he rented a 19th-century furrier warehouse down in the old cobble-stone streets part of the city. Today it is called Vieux Montreal, arguably the most fashionable district north of the river. Back in Panic Production days, the vieux district seemed like a deserted backdrop to a noir murder scene, with whole buildings boarded up, the streets empty save for rising steam. Ever enterprising, and to capitalize on the influx of tourists for the Olympiad, Taylor turned the old fur factory into an illegal flash-mob speakeasy. The first night's gig, attended by about fifty people who were mostly friends of friends of the bands, was a raving disaster. Or, in Taylor's own words, "A fucking shambles." It was nevertheless a stab at the rising punk ethos in the air back then, the DIY approach, providing a glimpse into proper event management. It's hard to sculpt the essential shapelessness of a fuckup into any sort of learning experience, but a seed was planted all the same. I mean, come on, have a functioning lavatory, for crying out loud! How about some sort of liquid refreshment for thirsty revelers? And maybe a band that actually plays their instruments. In short, if we hoped to make any sort of money, doubtless a real bar was needed to turn a profit, selling cheap beer and booze at goodly markups. We'd need to have the wherewithal to create a checklist of sorts, writ up with some doable to-do's: Fix the loo, build a stage, set up a PA system, get some lights, maybe hire a soundman and a doorman, etc. In short, create some sort of risqué framework for thrill-seeking denizens to play out their fantasies. Gig two was a bigger success, as two hundred people showed up and the illicit gathering even got a sidebar write-up in the *Montreal Gazette*. Throughout the Olympiad, the place ebbed and flowed but it was always the place after hours if you had an ounce of hip.

Meanwhile, broke again, I went to work for six weeks in the arctic wastes of northern Canada, at an iron mine in northern Quebec called Shefferville. At the time it was the largest open pit iron mine in the world. You could only reach this wasteland of endless bottomless mine terrain by train or plane. The repugnant sores in the earth, a quarter-mile deep, and a mile wide at the lip, were like oozing cankers pocked for 1000 square miles in all directions and visible from space. My job, as a brakeman, was to ease a string of thirty empty rail cars, one car at a time, using only the wheel brake of a single car, to a crushed ore rock shoot opening beneath the transfer belt that came out like a devil's tongue from the crusher a hundred yards below. The first car filled up, then you gently released that one brake, eased the rail car string down one car, quickly turned the brake, and brought all to a stop so that another car could fill up. All I had for safety on this mad venture was a hard hat, a latch belt, and my wits. It was crazy dangerous work; one lad had gotten sliced in two that summer by a steel wheel. And I hated it.

I take this detour by way of setting the stage for how, by turns, I went from college life, to this iron mining gig, through various peregrinations back to the Alaskan outback, hence, who knows how, on to an alien world of the Sex Pistols, the Screamers, the Angry Samoans, the Social Distortion, and the Ruts, in short, the whole New York City late 1970s rock'n'rumble scene. This was the nascent impetus for my life in the music. It all began that summer in Montreal as the Olympics wound down. Panic Productions and the ongoing speakeasy scene continued well into 1977. I was drawn to it. It was anarchic, DIY, hip. Even after I had long since returned to Alaska in a frozen VW bus, something of the excitement of life in the speakeasy lingered. Before returning to Alaska with my brother, I did have an interesting six months living in the southeastern United States, starting on its borderline in the Shenandoah Mountains on the southwestern shore of the upper Potomac River.

This Ain't No K Street, No CBGBs, This Ain't No Foolin' Around

With the Olympics and Shefferville behind me as a newly-minted college grad, and before I headed to Alaska that coming winter, I wended south in an American Motors Rambler I'd bought used. I was rambling south to live for several months in Washington, DC. My school chum Joris, whose life and mine have been intertwined ever since Kent, happened to be looking for a roommate at the time. He'd moved to DC to join a theatrical group working out of the Church Street Playhouse, now known as the Keegan Theatre. Joris had an apartment in the Adams Morgan district, somewhere on Harvard Street and 15th, which in 1976 was definitely low rent and entirely African-American. In fact, when I moved into our large, airy, second-story apartment, Joris and I were the only white folk on the block. What I found was a vibrant, almost joyous street life up and down the block. Unlike whiter neighborhoods where people could afford air-conditioning in the swampy heat of the Potomac lowlands, on Harvard Street, absent indoor cooling, everybody just lived out on the stoop during the evening, with parties toppling to the sidewalk up and down the block. Kids played in the spray of opened fire hydrants and rivaling boomboxes blared from every stoop. On the corners, drug dealers huddled in suspicious knots, as big cars of every make tooled down the avenues, radios booming, parties on wheels. What a cacophony! It was a vibrant polis of fellow travelers in poverty, surrounded by crime, bad schools, potholed streets, and food deserts.

I realized the easy banter I shared with many of the black folk out on the hot summer streets had in its give and take a wary truce of reciprocal curiosity. Of me they must have asked: who is this white guy who keeps walking by? For me, by extension, it was more a failed attempt to somehow fit into that life, hanging out on the street that hot summer. I was woke enough to realize mine was a privilege that could sail through the 'hood, knowing that whenever I wanted, I could just pull up anchor and sail away to any white enclave in America of my choosing. The black folk on the stoop, they had no sailboats and still less the means to move. A different sort of leg irons firmly anchored these boisterous residents where racism planted their feet. I wasn't their "friend"—I was just some white guy everyone called Slim. Maybe a nice guy, but forever the interloper, just passing through.

The common refrain, in any case, was: "Say, Slim, spare a dollah? Join the party brotha," and so on, a sort of jest always with an asterisk. For a twenty-something white kid in 1976, it was like sitting atop a peak of national prejudice trying to describe the outline of the racist mountain that whiteys like myself were sitting on. It looked like a good view from where I was sitting, but not so much for my African-American neighbors. Today, of course, all of Adams Morgan is upscale restaurants and tony discos, with outrageous housing rents. Same as it ever was.

Man, oh man, was it hot in DC that summer, though! Lively as our street was, cops were always patrolling in their cruisers with hardly ten minutes between sirens tearing by in the distance. Often enough brothers from one stoop got into a fight with brothers from another stoop. I soon got a job making clay tennis courts out in the white 'burbs, one job in fact for depressive Senator Eagleton's gated estate, he who had been the disgraced VP running mate of George McGovern back in 1972. Those working days spent resurfacing the tennis courts of other ambassadorial heaps, and coming home to the 'hood by tube, sweaty and beat, was hardly the future I saw for myself. One night, as I came down our street from the subway a few blocks away, slouching toward our apartment, I saw a lone cop car outside our apartment building with flashers on. I asked the cop what the hell was going on. "You live here?" He was surprised when I said yes. "A man's been stabbed bad. Right in the foyer."

I was stunned, hoping that it wasn't Joris. As it turned out, the stabbed man was our delightfully gruff bear of a super, voice deep as a low note bassoon, from Alabama. He was a big man with a barrel chest, graying hair, and sharecropper hands. I'll give him this, no "trash street dealers" to that point had ever entered our apartment complex to deal or steal, at least that I ever saw. Our super just threw them out. Our building in fact had been built for an all-white clientele of federal employees back in the 1920s as the capital boomed after the First World War. Structurally, it was one of the better buildings on the block, nice enough to have marble floors in the foyer, a sweeping staircase on up, and large, reasonably well-kept apartments. All our building's black neighbors seemed to have day jobs. We all appreciated that our super kept the building clean, polishing that marble to a shine, sweeping the stoop every morning whether it needed it or not, and otherwise keeping to himself. He didn't allow the sort of all-hours revelry on our stoop that boomed forth up and down the block elsewhere. So there I was, this timid white kid, entering my apartment building with trepidation, cop car flashers streaking red and blue bolts of light against the foyer ceiling. The first thing I saw on the floor was a huge smeared pool of blood. The poor man had been stabbed by a drug dealer. All his fastidiousness had come to naught. The cop said our super was alive when the ambulance carted him away. I think that night I told Joris I was moving on. Within the week our super was dead.

Aliens There Be in Them Thar Hills, Sonny Boy

I then went south to live with friends in Virginia, first outside of Charlottesville, then on to Roanoke later that fall, finally returning home to my parents in November, and as described, up the Alcan Highway in winter with my brother in a VW bus over New Years. I had a college diploma in hand, though few prospects, and I still hadn't any real clue what to do with my life.

So when a friend invited me down to live on a "commune" farm outside of Charlottesville, VA, I jumped at the chance to leave the roiling heat of that city on the Potomac behind, with hopes of returning to a becalmed and cooler countryside of bucolic ease. Turns out the place was a farm house rental that came with two acres for the renters, while the surrounding 400 acres of the farm proper were part of a cattle ranch raising handsome white Charolais beef livestock. It was a herd of about forty steers, with one huge bull named Alfonse. He was a real pussy who loved nothing better than a snout scratch and a carrot, and the nicest bull you'll ever meet if you happen to be on the wrong side of the fence. Anyway, there were five of us in all living in that lovely turn-of-the-century farmhouse, me in a little room over the kitchen. Years later, I wrote a short piece of non-fiction about that time, and one day in particular that involved tripping in the mountains. I include a truncated version here because the inherent hubris of the United States to rule over the planet as its birth-written empire is so starkly etched in what I witnessed that day as to be worth repeating. It was a chasm between the natural world, if you will, and the madness of empire's dominion.

Conjure a sugar grove. What comes to mind? Perhaps a tropical hillside in Trinidad? Yes, imagine it, a summer evening with the cane fields waving their tassels to the far palms. Or maybe a biting day in March amid the White Mountains of Vermont with maple syrup taps flowing golden sugar into wooden buckets? Perhaps even the cheesy name of a retirement home near your local shopping mall; there's one in my hometown. Well, in this case, how about one of the National Security Agency's most secret surveillance posts in the world? The place is called Sugar Grove Station.

There is a vast area of the Shenandoah Mountains, a wilderness vastness in fact, where electromagnetic cell and broadcast pollution are forbidden, and most human development as well. Thirteen-thousand square miles in the northern sector of the Shenandoahs, close to where I lived outside Charlottesville, straddling the states of Virginia, West Virginia, and Maryland, the National Radio Quiet Zone (NRQZ) provides an eerie backdrop for two hi-tech listening posts, one belonging to the military, the other for astronomers. Most of the area is blessedly left to the wild creatures and old growth forests of Appalachia. By force of federal law as well as state regulations, all commercial radio and most cellular interference, even vehicular traffic in some cases, are prohibited within the enormous boundaries of this exclusionary zone. Yet how odd it is that the hills here are only a couple of hours drive from Washington, DC. In this largely pristine sanctuary, spared from almost all commercial development since 1960, the local fauna and flora thrive in odd proximity to the military's business and the frantic, if futile, ongoing search for extraterrestrial life in the cosmos.

One of the trippiest days I can remember was spent right there but a few miles from the NSA site at Sugar Grove. What a marvelous autumn weekend, camping alone on the banks of Sugar Run near the timbered borderline between Virginia and West Virginia. Having ingested an attitude-adjusting dose of *P. cubensis* (magic mushrooms), so happy was I that fine fall day sending fallen basswood leaves down the creek eddies and imagining them afloat on the cool waters like the Sunboats of Ra, that I, briefly wandering up a small ridge, stood absolutely stunned by what I saw through the shimmering trees. I have come ever since to call the vision Ominous Big Ears. Honestly, I did not believe my eyes at first. About a mile off there stood this monstrous circular thing gazing heavenward with steely implacability. Little did I know then, in my tripped-out state, that I was staring straight at the largest military radio telescope in the world. It was as if I had stepped suddenly through some sort of psychedelic portal into an alien world, one minute in the fall glades of the Shenandoah, the next confronting this ominous vision of a steel Cyclops looming out of the primeval forest like an alien dome. I immediately sensed there was something not only odd beyond reckoning about the vast space dish in the middle of a forest, but that it was also a place of forbidding malevolence. The sight of it was terrifying, I must say. Rather than feeling drawn to explore, I fled the ridge-top with a racing pulse, in a vain hope to return my seething mind to the quiet mystery of the familiar trees and falling leaves. The whole thing made me feel put out, nagged by a strange foreboding. On psychedelics it is sometimes quite hard after a scare to recalibrate your inner joy.

In those days, some forty-five plus years ago, there were no Google maps, no cheap video drones, and satellite capacity was still crude by today's standards. How was anyone to know? Indeed, when I had the chance a week later to investigate what I had seen in the forest, I thought the best place to start was in the map room of the library at the University of Virginia. A kind librarian pulled out the requisite topographic maps of the area where I had spent my day. I did not at that time know anything about the secret military surveillance post, who did? Honestly, I thought maybe the antennae belonged to some research station of the university, but I was assured UVa had no such post. On the 1960, and again on the 1970 United States Geologic Survey topographic maps of the region (scale 1:250,000), the NSA listening post is not even shown, its buildings and radio towers erased, nothing, not even the blacktop road from the naval base station along the south fork of the upper Potomac River on up to the NSA radio telescopes is marked. I was flummoxed; had I imagined the damn thing in my drugged state? I very much doubted that. Now, many years later, having investigated the site extensively, I realize the omission on the federal survey topos was clearly intentional to keep all reference to the place out of the Rooskies' grubby hands. But honestly, whom were they fooling? Well, me for one. My psilocybin-induced sunboats to Ra, I am sure, sailed down Sugar Run, past the radio dishes, all the way to the far swift currents of the upper Potomac, past the Washington Monument, thence to the distant sea, with no one in Congress still less the Jimmy Carter White House one wit wiser. To this day Sugar Grove remains very hush-hush.

But it is Nature herself in the NRQZ, as it happens, that has the upper hand today, just as it did in my wilderness sojourn that weekend in 1976. Absent cell phone towers and commercial radio signals, here where new construction has been strictly regulated since the 1960s, this vast region provides the needed space for the natural world in these eastern mountains to largely unfold unmolested. It is also one of the very few places in all of North America where people, and doubtless many creatures, sensitive to cell phone, TV, and radio-wave bombardment, can find relief from unceasing ubiquitous electromagnetic pollution. Except for the actual listening post in the heart of the Sugar Grove Station, jointly manned by the NSA and the U.S. Navy's Office of Naval Information Operations Command, and the Green Bank astronomical facility some miles south, this vast tract of wild land and small farmstead holdings has suffered little new human encroachment beyond the scattered homes that were grandfathered into the NRQZ in 1959. The largest of the antennae at the NSA facility is six-hundred-and-fifty feet across, arguably the biggest in the world in 1961, if you can believe it, hooked to NORAD-NSA-CIA centers across the globe. How we humans love our machines.

I have never been inside the Sugar Grove surveillance naval station itself, nor have I been allowed up to the inner circle, as it is called, where the radio dishes are arrayed, but I have since seen both from a nearby road and from the high hill of Bother Knob. But locally there are many reports of hikers in the surrounding national forest being followed by small military drones that can apparently make their way through the forest canopy with little hindrance, even at night. Indeed, if you follow Google's Street View (as of summer 2016) up the dirt rut of Reddish Knob Road that runs up to the back entrance of the surveillance dish array from the south, the Google car camera shows a wild dirt road and the eastern hardwood forests on either side stretching into wilderness. At about mile two, a government security vehicle comes into view ahead. You can see in the cam image that the vehicle passes the Google car on the left with the driver leaning out, saying something, and then suddenly the street view simply goes dead. No surprise, doubtless Google was ordered to cease immediately and turn round.

South on a beeline some twenty-five miles down the road from the NSA's Sugar Grove stands another listening post in this wilderness, this one given to science and the astronomers. This radio antennae array I have visited. It is located in the tiny hamlet of Green Bank, West Virginia, which gives its name to the largest rotating radio dish in the world, at the National Radio Astronomy Observatory (NRAO). This telescope has a long list of astronomical firsts to its credit. Perhaps its greatest coup, in its early days of operation, was the discovery of sugar molecules floating in the nebulae between the stars. Yes, sugar. Imagine that. And as astronomers considered this interesting if peculiar datum, the thinking grew that if complex carbohydrates were scattered through space, why not proteins, and if proteins, why not simple cosmic self-replicating life forms, ad infinitum? At any event, it was here in 1961 that a cabal of high-flying financiers and scientists gathered over whiskey and cigars and founded what they called the Order of the Dolphin. In these same stark mountains, they constructed the intellectual framework of what has now become the international astronomical search for extraterrestrial intelligence in the universe, today known as SETI.

The work of the Order of the Dolphin was the brainchild of Dr. Francis "Frank" Drake, who had penned a logarithmic equation on the back of an envelope to assess the odds of intelligent life in the universe. Drake presented his famous calculation, now known as Drake's Equation, to those assembled that night. As the lore goes, Drake's Equation "was developed to provide an estimate of the total number of detectable extraterrestrial civilizations in the Milky Way galaxy." The attendees at the Green Bank soiree that long-ago night were ten persons, including Drake, who was host and a professor of astronomy at Cornell. Also present were meeting organizer J. Peter Pearman, an officer on the Space Science Board of the National Academy of Sciences; Dr. Philip Morrison, ace builder of the atomic bomb, then communications technology specialist and President of Microwave Associates; radio expert Dana Atchley; neuroscientist John C. Lilly who studied dolphin communication, wrote the seminal book *The Mind of the Dolphin*, and, as Mr. Psychonaut, proselytized the beneficial use of LSD; UC Berkeley chemist Melvin Calvin; astronomer Su-Shu Huang, coiner of the exoplanet term "habitable zone;" astronomer Carl Sagan, also of Cornell; Barney Oliver, founder and director of Hewlett-Packard; and finally, Russian radio-astronomer Otto Struve, who believed avidly in extraterrestrial life, saying of it "we must take into account the action of intelligent beings, in addition to the classical laws of physics in understanding the universe." Quite the confab of luminaries, you will admit. These participants dubbed themselves "The Order of the Dolphin" on behalf of Lilly's work on dolphin communication.

I do have a real beef with Drake's famous if ridiculous equation. It fails spectacularly for the simple reason that it yokes the anthrocentric hubris that "intelligent life in the universe" will somehow long for this consumptive disease Drake calls "technologically advanced civilization." It posits the belief, a priori, that any life with a critically thinking brain in the galaxy not only would *want* to build what we call "civilization" but that any cosmic civilization would also clamor to invent *gizmo-technologies* capable of contacting other "pinnacles of creation" like *H. sapiens* across vast regions of interstellar space. Really? Consider physicist Enrico Fermi's famous paradox, which asks, in apposition to Drake's Equation, if there are uncounted billions of stars in the Milky Way, "Where is everybody?" Exactly. Here's my take. How odd is our fierce techno-fascination with alien beings in their spaceships, when you only have to look around wherever you might find yourself and be amazed at the largely unnoticed plethora of marvelously adapted alien species in all the phyla right here within arm's reach on planet Earth. Yet our vaunted civilization shows little interest in these living neighbors with whom we share the biosphere. Instead, the radio dishes like Big Ears look heavenward.

Let us posit a better question of inquiry: What sane life form, fish, fowl, or fellow mammal (or even freakish alien) would bother to get themselves civilized? Seriously. I mean planet Earth already has, give or take, roughly 8,700,000 and counting separate species identified (sadly alien to most people), all marvelously adapted to their myriads of environments, and not one besides "Man" has ever considered "technological civilization" an adaptive strategy for survival, still less a genetic benefit in procreation. This plethora strikes me as the true intelligence on planet Earth, whereas the thirst for power and national dominion over some vaunted first alien cosmic contact, this hubris of progress, strikes me as nothing more than a sort of rabidity approaching madness. Nary one creature amid the seas, mountains, deserts, or savannahs seeks to attain to "technological civilization," except us. Doesn't that tell us something? Instead, these fellow creatures live holistic lives in their own perfectly adapted ecological niches, watching in alarm as the vaunted *H. sapiens sapiens* makes a total hash of it. Successful evolutionary adaptation, as author Cristopher Ryan has stated,[17] doesn't presuppose that a species is getting better or more technological as it evolves, but rather that it is merely growing more suited to its natural environment. Technological civilization is in any case an unlikely, utterly misguided fluke, all things considered, ill-suited for adaptation, and hardly some obvious terminus of evolution. Besides, our industrial technologies inevitably destroy the natural environments they (and we) depend on. An evolutionary dead-end is more like it.

---

17. See his book, *Civilized to Death: The Price of Progress* (Avid Reader Press, 2019).

I got to know Carl Sagan, the astronomer and SETI booster, when I, too, worked at Cornell University in the 1990s. Several thorny environmental issues in our immediate neighborhood threw us together at various meetings. I shared that I was an amateur astronomer myself, and in his kind way, hearing I was to visit Virginia soon thereafter, suggested I take a side trip to the Green Bank NROA. He said he would be glad to set up a special tour for me. I took him up on his offer and went on that tour. I saw firsthand with what passion humans believe that SETI is vitally important to our survival as a species and that "advanced intelligent life" just has to be out there. And it is, it's just that the Carl Sagans of the world, bless them, always seem to look through the wrong end of the telescope to find it.

My purpose for this digression is to share, emphatically, how much I distrust technology and the nostrums of our false human definition of "intelligence" as if "human superiority" and "human progress," arm in arm with ever more clever technological wonders, march us forward to some singularly bright future. In his insightful book, *A Short History of Progress* (Canongate, 2004), Ronald Wright demolishes both beliefs as absurd, dismembering as misguided our human fascination with progress. He walks the reader through pre-history to the present ecological crises, giving examples of touted progress that invariably turn out to be "progress traps" insidiously destroying that which the progress sought to enhance in human lives in the first place.

So, there you have it. That was my Virginia sojourn, but it reveals in microcosm my burgeoning insight into the dissonances between the attainments of our grand civilization and its relentless destruction of the natural world, all predicated by the need for endless growth, consumerism, and progress boosterism. I thoroughly agree with evolutionary biologist Stephen Jay Gould who called "the very notion of progress a noxious culturally embedded, untestable, non-operational, intractable idea that must be replaced if we wish to understand the patterns of history."[18] Sounds about right. Anyway, from Virginia I soon went north as already written, in the middle of a bitter winter with my brother, up the icy Alaskan Highway in a VW bus, to return again to quietude and Nature that has long sustained my spirit. Here, as if by magic, I found the jasper talisman handed down to me through the ages by an unknown ancestral hunter. Here I came to understand the importance to the human psyche of solitude, and aloneness in Nature.

The Long and Winding Road: Alaska to New York to Seattle—A Punk Daze

After my sojourn in Alaska on various fishing boats during 1976-1978, I may well have been the richest Alaskan lumberjack in New York City upon my return to civilization. It was September 1978, and the fishing season out of Sitka, Alaska was drawing to a close. I had earned a princely sum fishing for halibut on longliners. Some of the halibut weighed in at 600 lbs. Today anything over 100 pounds is considered huge, but a hundred years ago halibut upwards of 1000 pounds were not uncommon. That's a big fish. I left Alaska with a conspicuous wad of $100 bills worth roughly $4000 bulging out of my trouser pockets, tied with a rubber band. I arrived in the big bad city of Gotham, banging headlong into a wall of glaring culture shock. I knew New York pretty well, of course, having stayed in the city dozens of times over the years. But to go from the pristine skies of Alaskan archipelagoes, watching the kittiwakes soar, to the grimy canyons of Gotham City, with sirens blaring and sidewalks teeming, was a shock indeed. Even though I hadn't seen a stoplight or a pedestrian crossing in many months, I popped out of my silver sky tube all the same like a man too long alone. New York is a long mile from paradise, but

---

18. Timothey Shanahan, "Evolutionary Progress?" in *BioScience*, v.50, 5, May 2000, p.451–459.

to gaze at the sinfully bright spires of Manhattan at sunset was a wonder in itself.

So into the roil I went. I caught a cab, looking for all the world like an unkempt sourdough in a plaid shirt, scuffed hiking boots, sailor's wool cap upon long greasy locks, and two weeks of scruff on itchy chin. I had no idea what to expect. I had been apprised that my friend Taylor and his British friend Arthur May had started a practice studio for bands on 29th Street (#43 to be exact, 2nd floor), between Avenue of the Americas (6th) and the Broadway Diner just up from the 4 & 6 subway station on 28th. The Broadway Diner and surrounding buildings are gone now, little more than a gaping hole today with massive cranes set to build another soulless glass and steel tower. For those who know the city, this neighborhood remains smack dab in the middle of what is known as the Flower District, just south of the Garment District. Back in 1978, hardly anyone lived there, at least not legally, as the zoning was commercial. There were flower and jewelry shops at street level, a few arty lofts, and many Korean fabric and clothing importers warehoused on upper floors. These 1920s pedestrian-looking row buildings often had high warehouse ceilings on upper floors, with grimy opaque windows that invited scant curiosity. Taylor's loft was on the north side of the street, with tall windows uniformly unwashed like the rest of the city.

He had somehow persuaded the landlord to rent them the entire second floor of this unremarkable six-story walk-up on that unremarkable street in an otherwise unremarkable part of town. For a while it had served as a photographer's studio, but her hopes at sustaining a business petered out. As a space, it was largely free of impeding wall structures, and was spacious by city standards. Rents were surprisingly cheap back then, maybe about $800. Taylor and Co. promptly turned the huge, open second floor of the warehouse, with its magnificent 14-inch wooden floorboards and 14-foot-high ceiling rafters, into a practice studio for rock bands, very similar to what he had done in the vieux quartier in Montreal. They had stripped all the remaining brick walls of plaster, built a wooden stage, hand-wired the electrical systems, put up the remains of the sound system, et voila.

The loft's house band was called Arthur's Dilemma, after the lead singer, songwriter, and loft mate Arthur May. We all knew Master May as Arfur. He was a talented songwriter and great front man who, with his wild female keyboard player, made a bit of a ripple about town for a few exciting months at the height of the NYC punk scene. Arfur and I hit it off immediately. He was funny, quick-witted, irreverent, creative, and fearless. First thing he did after I showed up from the airport with my mountain man scruff and long hair, was to sit me down under his scissors and give me a proper haircut. I was hoping to come out of this ordeal looking a bit like Rod Stewart; you know, teased hair fetching to the ladies and trey "mod." Ha. Instead, a glance into a mirror revealed a human toucan with newly-clipped tail feathers from an encounter with an electric socket. Arfur then dragged me down to some 8th Street leather and dog collar clothiers and had me buy a pair of tight black jeans and some hip shirts. And for heaven's sake, ditch the mountain man boots. Couldn't have a hairy lumberjack hanging about the practice studio scaring the wits out of his groupies. And just like that, I was transformed, into what exactly I was not sure, in a plaintive tale of Schadenfreude at my expense. True enough, I eventually did work with innumerable punk bands over succeeding years, but their anarchic culture never quite made any sense to me. It seemed nothing but a sort of donned costume all dressed up with absolutely nowhere to go.

Let's just say a counterweight to this vacuity came when a different sort of young lost soul, a teen named SAMO, came briefly into my life. When I first met SAMO that fall, it was in SoHo at about 10pm at night. Taylor and I were leaving the last dregs of some sort of gallery opening on Mercer Street, possibly of Donald Judd's work. In the brisk air we found ourselves kicking down the cobbles outside the old supermarket on Spring near Greene

Street. I spied this knotty-headed kid doing frantic chalk drawings on the sidewalk. We stopped and chatted. Taylor obviously knew the lad, having met him on several occasions via an actor/playwright friend by the name of Kate, whom I would date a decade later while getting an advanced MLS certificate at Columbia's library school. The lad, half-jokingly, asked if we'd like to have our portraits done in chalk on the sidewalk. We declined but as we were going into the Spring-mart to buy some beer we invited him back to the music loft on 29th. He was quick to agree and packed up his box of colored chalk. He said his name was SAMO when I introduced myself. I use caps because that was his tag signature.[19] Of course, SAMO was none other than Jean-Michel Basquiat, the famous painter-to-be. Prior to his rise to fame, his tag SAMO was how he signed his sketches, sidewalk street art, and scribbled notes.

I don't recall much of the rest of that particular night, but Jean-Michel as I soon came to call him, ended up living with us on and off in the loft from late August that year through to November, disappearing mysteriously for days on end, then popping round again for a place to crash. To be honest, I was so used to the silences of Alaska that I soon enough felt the pull of a much-needed respite from the clashing bands and reigning anarchy of the loft. Too many nights, after band practice, I tossed sleepless on a lumpen mat by the loft windows as sirens screamed down 6th Avenue and in the cubbyhole beneath the stairs some girl and Arfur were having a go of it. So, I wandered down to the Chelsea Hotel and rented my getaway.

What's to say about that storied establishment cum dive? When it first opened in 1885 on West 23rd Street, the Chelsea was a

---

19. Apparently, the name SAMO was actually that of a duo of graffiti artists, who tagged together, born from the stoned minds of Al Diaz and Jean-Michel Basquiat on a stoop in Minetta Lane. Little more than a goof on a street guy they knew whose response to "how ya doin?" was always, "same ol' same ol'. By some quirk in law, Mr. Diaz was to sell that tag name in later years for a bundle of cash.

beautiful boarding house of the gilded age, made of bright red brick in the Victorian Gothic style which was in vogue then, six stories high and getting on to half a block long. It was originally intended as a "home for artists," but this proved a bust, artists being what they are, and by 1905 it opened as a hotel proper. Many New York and world luminaries have lived there over the decades, including Mark Twain, Dylan Thomas, Arthur C. Clarke, Jack Kerouac, Allan Ginsberg, and Sid Vicious. By 1978, though, just about all of its former glamour had faded, along with the carpets and creaky beds. The ancient steam radiators clanged till dawn. A cabin in the wilderness may be a humble home by comparison, but the Chelsea when I arrived looked particularly threadbare. I'm not sure what I quite expected, though in truth its storied history had been a draw. Part of its charm for me was that, being on 14th Street, it was only a few blocks south of the loft. If we'd been out together somewhere, on more than one occasion I'd invite Basquiat up to my room. We'd sit at the little table by the window, drinking beer and talking art till the wee hours. I had no idea he was gay at the time, and our nights were chaste. Jean-Michel was rather shy, in fact, even an innocent in his charming way. He had an impish energy which was infectious. The cost for the room was something around $50 a night, at least for one of the "problem" rooms: small and unadorned, with a fire escape outside the large windows. The fire escape, as I soon found out, was where all the junkies hung out, thus the steep discount.

It seemed as if more nights than not, a tap-tap on the window would drag me out of my slumbers with a groan. Tap. Tap. Tap. Then the inevitable: "Hey man got a lighter to heat our spoon?" would waft through the window plaintively. Or they'd try to pry open the window and crawl in to rifle through my coat pockets, as one jonesing heroin enthusiast did my first night at the hotel. About the only time I've ever punched someone was at the Chelsea that first night there. Seriously. I had cracked the window open because of the stifling heat from the clanging radiator. Foolish me. Well past curfew, in crawls this pickpocket in the throes of withdrawal, looking for something to nick. Out of my half slumber I saw a dark silhouette through groggy eyes. I leapt to my feet when I heard him bang into a chair and clocked him one, and yes, my hand hurt for a week. Luckily it was just some tweaked-out junkie, for he flew back out the window to the metal landing, clattering down the iron stairs two at a time. I never opened a window there again, even though the permanently scalding radiator made the room stifling. But for that small inconvenience, you just stuffed moist toilet paper in your ears and made double sure the latch was tight. I learned to sleep like a baby. The junkies could take a leap.

Next to the many punk show posters hanging in the loft, SAMO covered the brick walls with jagged and frenetic drawings of his own. Most were in chalk, but some were taped sketches of loft mates in the scatter-shot style we've all seen. At the time, I must have had several dozen of his drawings, one or two with a "yo Peter—SAMO" sort of dedication, but who could have guessed? He seemed nothing more than some vibrant pimply-faced punk kid with haywire hair and a penchant for drawing on everything. Famous? It never entered my mind. My friend Taylor somehow managed to keep all of the Jean-Michel sketch books which the lad left behind, and a small trove of photos. Not in my wildest dreams would I have guessed that this weird prodigy would one day meet Andy Warhol and eventually paint paintings which now consistently sell upwards of $100M a piece at auction. He was just SAMO, the kid with crazy hair and disjointed speech, scribbling chalk in hand. I always thought of him as an orphan of the streets, not some upscale diplomat's son, which explained his mysterious disappearances.

In the years that followed, I misplaced all of Jean-Michel's drawings if I even actually kept any of them.[20] Anyway, I tossed SAMO's

---

20. I also lost some drawings by Andy Warhol before he was "Warhol!" They were sketches of Roman gladiator costumes he'd drawn when he was a costume designer assistant for an opera company. Andy's mom had given them

work aside thoughtlessly, through too many moves from flophouses to sublet apartments to shared squats, a crazy hopscotch of living arrangements over the years to save a dollar for beer and other essentials. Had I held on to the drawings, I'd be worth a pretty penny today, I am sure. Sometime around Thanksgiving, everyone in the loft had lost track of SAMO. Then years later, when I was a graduate student at Columbia in 1988, hearing of Basquiat's untimely death, I met Marvin Taylor, Head of Special Collections at NYU's Bobst Library. Marvin had begun a magnificent "Downtown Collection" on the whole punk/New Wave scene in New York circa 1976-1984, with the usual subject-headings of CBGB, Mud Club, Café Au Go Go, artists, songwriters, bands, photographers. I got him in touch with Taylor, who still had his collection of SAMO materials. I followed the correspondence for a while on what passed for crude email back then, but soon bowed out. I had no Basquiat archives to offer. Love ya, SAMO, you were a truly sweet man.

Not so much Sid Vicious and quite a few other punks of the era whom I variously met about town. While CBGB, the famous punk bar and music venue in the Bowery at Bleeker Street, today gets the press as *the* punk club, back then, anyone with an ounce of sense preferred a trip to a club that actually had a functioning urinal. There was no escaping the fact that CBGB was a dive. Often as not you had to climb over some whacked-out poseur sprawled on the floor just to find the nasty urinal inevitably so clogged with soggy cigarette scum that you were left to cringe at what pooled in the bowl below. The place stank of old beer stains and stale smoke. Instead, the cognizati went to Max's Kansas City, on Park Avenue South, which was far more hip, clean, and had cocktails for just $2—imagine that in New York today. In any case, Max's

---

to my mom, after his death, while cleaning out his room, go figure. They weren't signed, so were probably worthless. My mom would have been mortified in her world of polite society to have Andy's mom authenticate them, so she never asked.

served meals and those were actual cocktails shaken not stirred, thank you very much, rather than the thin plastic beer cups at CBGB. They no longer served bottled beer there, as too many musicians had been knocked-out cold by tossed bottles. Max's had none of that anarchy crap. There were posh booths, comfortable chairs, and a cute little stage. In the 1960s it had been a favorite hangout of artists from Rauschenberg to Brice Marsden. By 1968, the Velvet Underground had been considered the club band for many years. By 1975 it was the home of the city's burgeoning Glam Rock scene where Bowie, Iggy Pop, the New York Dolls, et al. hung out. And then from late 1977 on, under new management, it became the homeport of the early punk/New Wave scene. On any given night you could see the Patti Smith Group, Blondie, the Cramps, or Television. After the Sex Pistols broke up, it was here that bassist Sid Vicious played all his solo shows before he overdosed in 1979. And it was at Max's that I met him.

    He struck me as a lonely boy, trapped beneath several pounds of punk chains, a heavy leather jacket, and too-tight black pants. The snarl seemed a pose. His feet were always shod in enormous clunky motorcycle boots, also looped with chain. By contrast, although Taylor and I had these ridiculous hairdos, we chose instead to stand out from the pierced punk uniform of the day by wearing tweed sports jackets over tight jeans. After all, Malcolm McLaren, grandfather of punk fashion and manager of the Sex Pistols, often wore a tweed sports coat. But with Taylor and me both at 6'4", me with my rooster hair and Taylor with his shaved middle a la Bozo the Clown thing going on, all a shocking natural red, we were a sort of an inverse light-socket duo wherever we went. Vicious was inordinately shy with strangers. And sorry to say, but hardly a surprise, he never seemed to be the sharpest tool in the shed, often responding in monosyllables or just nodding off as you chatted. He was a full-on heroin junkie by this time, and Max's was his chosen hangout. Sometimes you'd see him there with his girlfriend, Nancy Spungen, a fraught teased-blonde addict-looking mess with round clown eyes and exaggerated lipstick. She drank like a fish, smoked like a chimney, and had a penchant to head-nod on the bar, whereas Sid was a tad more moderate with the booze, almost diffident in some gaunt way, and never acted out in my presence. As I was becoming a bit of a regular at Max's myself, Sid and I chatted on several occasion. I bought him a few beers, as I recall, as he certainly didn't offer to buy me one. Nancy just seemed zonked. The one time he did seem to perk up was when I told him that I, too, was a lodger at the Chelsea. I mentioned the junkies on the fire escape to pass the time. The only witticism I ever recall him saying was when I told him this, and he responded "Oh, sorry, mate; was that you?" with an ironic smirk and a wink. Was he joking?

That October, according to affidavits, the poor sod awoke in his suite at the Chelsea to find his poor dear Nancy sprawled on the floor, dead of a knife wound to the abdomen. He was arrested and charged with the sad waif's murder. A day later he tried to kill himself with a broken light bulb, only to be hauled to Bellevue Hospital for psychiatric observation and where, once again, he attempted suicide by trying to jump out of the window. These sorts of antics went on until Vicious was dragged to Riker's Island under court order for an enforced 55-day detox and 24/7 watch. Upon his release from prison on February 1, 1979, he killed himself with an overdose that same night. I don't believe "Sid Lives," alas. Perhaps it is my imagination, but I do believe staying at the Chelsea calmed way down post Sid and poor Nancy's departures. The losers on the fire escape, for one, seemed to fade away. In epitaph, I'll say sincerely, thanks for that tap! tap! tap! timeout Sid, and leave it at that.

My Alaska bankroll, such as it was, certainly helped to get the Dilemma's first 45' out, and covered other sundry expenses like loft rent. I was never good with money. It wasn't that I was a spendthrift on fancy kit, but that I was simply too trusting and generous. When I finally started using Facebook in 2008, all sorts of "old friends" from my promoter days popped up, thanking me for my generosity back in the day. To the last, their thanks for my various kindnesses during those reckless days of excess seemed utterly sincere and heartfelt, although I had entirely forgotten the nature of this repeated largesse. In any event, the NYC loft crew started to print peel-away, coaster-sized stickers that had just come on the market as the latest thing. In order to be *au currant*, we had 250 stickers printed up with the Dilemma logo and info on future gigs. You could peel off the back and slap them anywhere—and we did. It was not such a good of an idea at Club Hurrah, however.

Hurrah opened in 1976 as the largest dance club in the city, with pioneering light shows and nascent video technologies with monitors running throughout. Booming as a music dance hub months before Studio 54 even opened, and running band clips long before MTV on clunky wall monitors, Hurrah was *the* after-hours club for the late-night set until about 1980 when it closed. This quote from Wikipedia gives the flavor of its vibrant, if tumultuous, oeuvre: "The club became notorious for an incident in December 1978, where during a Skafish gig, Sid Vicious got into a fight with Todd Smith (brother of Patti Smith) ... David Bowie was filmed in the club for his music video for the song 'Fashion' in 1980." Well, you get the picture.

One night, Taylor and I got into the rave disco, as doubtless the bouncer had been told to let in gay guys who wouldn't hit on all the leggy models smoking their Silva Thins. It was a chaotic mix of disco strobes, video screens, and punk bands blaring, with a pre-Studio 54 Bianca in the corner with her coterie, and Liza Minnelli over there with maybe Truman Capote, and, "Oh, is that Cary Grant with Farrah Fawcett?!" Our brainstorm was to plaster this den of disco depravity with some good punk attitude and split. So, we stuck the damn stickers on the bar, in the men's room, you name it, then paid our tab and waltzed out into the night thinking what clever punks we were. Unfortunately, we hadn't read the criminals' handbook. Tip #1—don't leave the scene of the crime posting stickies with a contact number. Because the very next day, a very pissed-off manager of Hurrah, Jim Fourratt, called Max's Kansas City, which was listed on the stickies as where we'd be playing next. He asked Max's if they have a contact for Arthur's Dilemma, gets a number from some front-of-the-house Bruno, and next we know Taylor's loft phone is ringing. Whoever was on the line read the poor lad the riot act: "Come down and scrub every last fucking sticker off or I'll make sure the useless dumb Dilemma gets run out of town." That didn't sound good, as Brit Arfur was what we'd today call an illegal alien and Taylor was a past-your-sell-by-date Canuck also on dodgy grounds of over-staying his visa. So that afternoon, shoulders sagging, the two of us spent a good hour scraping off the damn stickers. Thank heaven Liza, Farrah, and Bianca weren't there to see our ignominious comeuppance. The stickers were nearly impossible to peel off, even with razor blades, brushes, and soapy water. What were we thinking?

Here's the thing about the whole punk ethos, if "ethos" isn't too highfalutin' a word. Maybe for Johnny Rotten and Sid back in working-class East London, growing up on the far side of the third track out, screaming invectives of "God save the Queen, the fascist regime, she ain't no human being" and so on made its statement of rebellion *real* (good song, don't get me wrong). But once the trendy shops started selling all those spiked leather jackets, dog collars, and blue hair dye crapola, it became little more than a pose. The fact that you snarled at the iniquities of the world, in the end, didn't add up to a hill of beans. At least hippies, a decade before, had dropped out to live on communes to grow their own food and raise cute kids. Peace, love, and all that. But among too many punks I knew, they seemed to spend their days doing scant more than sweet fuck all, hanging out in trendy shops oohing and aahing over the latest bit of spiky kit. It somehow smacked of vacuity with an ersatz attitude. To some of my old chums this is doubtless apostasy, but I'm OK with that. To be honest, nine out of ten punk bands couldn't even play their bleedin' instruments. Maybe that was the point, to create a loud messy muddy thrash a la Spinal Tap, with amp volumes set to eleven.

There were, of course, exceptions, my favorites being Black Flag, the Buzzcocks, Bad Religion, the Dead Kennedys, even the early Damned and the all-girl Flashbacks. I met Jello Biafra, lead singer of the Dead Kennedys, several times and always admired the fact that he ran for mayor of San Francisco in 1979 with a platform that stated that guys in suits, i.e., businessmen, had to ditch the suits and wear clown suits instead within city limits. Sounded reasonable to me. I think he garnered 15,000 votes. But contemporaneous with punk, suddenly along came the New Wave sound, in which melodies and musicianship mattered again. Thank heaven for Blondie, Talking Heads, the Clash, Psychedelic Furs, the Cure, Simple Minds, Gang of Four, the Stranglers, and Seattle's Blackouts. I worked many shows with these bands when I moved to Seattle the following year. They toned it down, wrote more thoughtful lyrics, and respected their musicianship, their guild craft. I was always an outsider to that 1977-1978 Sex Pistols thrash, into whose milieu I was dropped like a bumpkin, little more than a dazed and confused rube at that, who just happened to be solvent and drug free, in the right place at the right time to catch it all. Hell, by 1980, the department store Penny's was selling T-shirts emblazoned with "Juz lovin my Punk!" and some sort of lame graphic.

At the time, Taylor was dating a woman twenty-plus years his senior, Ruth Kligman, a doyen of the art scene, an abstract painter in her own right, and sadly most famous for having had a tumultuous love affair with Jackson Pollock in the 1950s. She was in the car when the inebriated Pollock, behind the wheel and "speeding wildly," crashed the car that he, Ms. Kligman, and her young friend Edith Metzger were riding in. Pollock and Metzger were killed at the scene of the accident. Kligman was thrown from the car and spent months in recovery with severe injuries. She was a handsome woman in her forties when I met her, with a wry turn to her full lips, frizzy hair, and unblinking eyes; she was also a heavy drinker. I remember seeing something so sadly haunting about those dark eyes, at once languid, then brooding, even jaded, as if she was set to peer right through you to gauge how dark your own shadows were. She'd sit on what was obviously her favorite armchair, bare feet tucked under her Capri pants, a sleeveless white blouse open to her bosom, and a glass of white wine always nearby.

At Max's Kansas City one night during a Dilemma gig, after having had one too many, she took to the tabletops to dance. Luckily Taylor was there to catch her as she careened toward the floor. He was twenty-four at the time he dated Ruth, she a spry forty-seven. When I reached out to Taylor for this memoir, he directed me to consider his affair with Ruth through the lens of Stephen Vizinczey's 1965 bildungsroman, *In Praise of Older Women: The Amorous Recollections of András Vajda* (Penguin Modern Classic, 2010) which approaches the Hungarian protagonist's love of older women with sympathy, tact, and delight. From what I've read since about Ruth, she had always been more famous as the muse for artists like Pollock, Mapplethorpe, and Willem de Kooning, than in her own right for the striking canvas work she'd produced. Taylor's story of the affair culminated in a huge row at de Kooning's studio on Long Island. Ever the hard drinker and yes, a former lover of de Kooning's, Ruth got in a row with the old man's new missus who had come back into de Kooning's life to care for him, what with his advancing dementia and all. Ah, the world.

The loft closed sometime at the end of 1978, after failing to scrounge the next month's rent. While my involvement was certainly peripheral, not one of us was much of a businessman and that lacunae does create an accumulation of too many loose threads by day's end. Things fray; people grow tired of scrounging. Friends avoid you in the street lest you hit them up for a fiver. While I did cover the rent while my money lasted, Taylor had a great flair for self-promotion, entrepreneurship, and, what's the hackneyed phrase today, the Art of the Deal? His Type A personality fit his abilities well, even if he was a bullshitter like the rest of us, making most of it up as he went along. Absent the dreary anchor of "sound fiscal management," the whole enterprise just blew to bits under the riotous and creative insurrections of trying to hold together a music loft for aspiring punk artists like musical prodigy and generally brilliant pain in the ass, Arthur May and his Dilemma. Money was always a hundred dollars short, and a rent check late. At least I got Arthur's free haircut.

Chapter 6

You Call This a Career?

Onward to Seattle: Punk Daze and Poseur Ways

Sometime around Christmas 1978, post-NYC-loft, I ran out of money. This was a recurring theme in my life. How were you supposed to hold onto it? The bulging wads were gone, and I was left again to ask my parents for a loan to tide me over. I will say that they never gave me a loan I didn't eventually pay off. My cheesy digs at the Chelsea were well behind me, my future uncertain. So, after a quiet Christmas at home and then living off my parent's largesse for several months, when early spring returned, I cadged the money to fly back to Seattle and do the only thing I knew how to do to make good money: commercial fishing. This would be my third trip back to Alaska, and a brief trip at that. But it was seminal all the same in how it played out. I went down to the Ballard docks in Seattle one day to see if anyone needed a deckhand. No one would hire me. All I could find was a ride on a large 48-foot ferro-cement fishing vessel heading for Cordova. The skipper said he was in a hurry to get north as herring season would be starting soon, so he was going to cut straight north around Vancouver Island, then cross the open seas of the Gulf of Alaska and make a dash for it. Only fools and desperate skippers brave the open seas of the Gulf in a ship much under two-hundred feet. Storms can come up suddenly with 95mph winds pushing forty-foot waves within a single weather cycle. Winds have been regularly clocked at 120mph. It's simple geophysics, really. Warmer winds coming from the west hammer the colder ocean currents heading east-north-east—it's a bad mix. Other than the anxious skipper, the only other people on board were an engine mechanic and a gruff deckhand. I made up the foursome. I did learn to play endless rounds of cribbage until the storm cut our playtime short.

Sure enough, somewhere out in the Gulf, a brutal howler came up. The skipper tried to persevere on north through the raging seas. A cement-hulled trawler of our dimensions might be able to do that in a lesser storm, but the gale-force winds of this mini-typhoon from the west caused such huge waves that we rocked sideways and back like a rolling pin. After a full day and night of this battery, with winds gusting to 90mph plus and sustained at 65, we turned east and high-tailed across the open gulf to the only port of safe harbor there is anywhere along the two hundred and fifty miles of the Mt. Saint Elias Mountains coast: Yakutat, AK. We made a harrowing maneuver somewhat in the manner of a surfboard turning to ride the huge waves down, breakers to stern. I've never been so terrified in my life. One massive wave, the skipper said it probably peaked at more than forty feet, punched out one of the windows of the wheelhouse as we turned to race eastward with the gale at our stern. With that intemperate wave, icy salt water burst into the wheelhouse like a raging fire hose. As the skipper held the rudder straight for dear life, the rest of us jury-rigged a piece of plywood we had ripped from the hold and somehow bolted it over the gaping hole where the wind, waves, and steely rain howled. My rubber boots brimmed with seawater by the time we were done, and I was absolutely soaked through. We then had to lash the side door of the wheelhouse open and try to push the sloshing seawater out onto the flying bridge. The skipper rightly feared that the water might somehow short a fuse, causing all the electrical systems to go dead. The boat would go down if that happened as we'd be at the full mercy of the gale, like a tossed cork. The only bailing tools at hand for this task were two wiry push brooms that served, with each starboard swell, to sweep the water back out. It seemed like it was "two buckets out, one back in" as we each took repeated runs at the flood.

Somehow, we picked up a buoy beacon. Limping by this time, after thirty-six hours with no sleep, we rounded Phipps Cape into the sheltered quays of Yakutat harbor. We had made it. I left the boat that day with a "thanks for the ride" and bought a seat on an Alaska Beaver prop plane to Anchorage leaving the next day. Yakutat back then was a fishing village of maybe 100 Anglos, and 200 Tlingit tribal members (about its size today, actually). By the next morning the skies had cleared as if the storm had swept the heavens clean. Glorious was the sight of that beautiful bay, the enormous sweep of the Malaspina Glacier rising up to the ragged sawtooth of the Saint Elias Mountains, with Mount Logan at 19,500 feet, the highest in Canada. This was arguably one of the most breathtaking sights I've ever seen. From the plane later that morning, I saw the trawler far below chugging north again, keeping sight of land to starboard as it plunged more sensibly north through becalmed arctic seas.

I was back at the cabin in Kasilof for barely a week when a neighbor told me he was heading down to Sitka, to work a purse seiner. He said I could call the skipper and find out if he needed another deckhand. It turned out that the man thought he just might, so I was soon back in the air, flying south to Sitka. I knew this fishing port well enough. I found digs down in the boat harbor on a leaky boat owned by an aging skipper I knew, who couldn't seem to part with his trusty old longliner but was now too old and arthritic to fish for anything "but my car keys out my pocket." It needed a good caulking but the skipper didn't have the money to haul it out to dry dock, still less to pay someone to hammer in the cotton caulk and tar it. My job, in return for free berth, was to keep the sump pumps running, or else that baby was going down to rest on the harbor's sandy bottom.

When I met the skipper who'd said on the phone that he might need another crew member, it turned out he didn't, as he'd already rehired an old deckhand. So I started to ask around if any other skippers needed a crewman. Within a week, I shipped aboard a salmon purse seiner as the low man on the pole. Turns out this was one of those decisions one makes that changes your life forever. Luckily, in this case, it was for the better. The fishing boat I shipped out on had a lapsed commercial fishing license. So despite a good two-to-three day catch of Kings and Silvers thick in the hold under shaved ice, no cannery would let us unload until the license was renewed. There we were, literally at sea with a hold full of fish that would soon rot to guts and mush. We were all flabbergasted by this downturn in our fortunes. I recall the skipper stomping up and down the deck, swearing bloody murder: "Suck Fuck Shit Piss Cunt Cock Crap!" Like a broken record. Priggish Comstockery wasn't a trait I experienced much around Alaskans of any stripe, though our good captain did omit asshole, dickhead, and butt-pirate. The long and the short of it was that since it would take upwards of a week to renew the license, the skipper decided we'd hightail down to Washington State and sell our load there. Apparently, they weren't as picky about fishing permits there. Point blank, the skipper asks: Who's game? That very day, we put that tubby little seiner into high gear and headed for Puget Sound after taking on a new load of shaved ice for the trip south.

We didn't stop until we got to Friday Harbor, the largest of the San Juan Islands dab in the middle of Puget Sound. But it turned out that our skipper got himself some bum intel. If you don't have a valid Alaska permit license you can't sell commercial to canneries in Washington, either. So again: "Suck Fuck Shit Piss Cunt Cock Crap!" But you could sell retail. So we chugged over to the mainland harbor at Bellingham, WA and started selling our fish right there on the dock, from the hold. Another deckhand and I went into town, found a print shop, and mocked up some handbills hawking our "fresh Alaska salmon." Then we wandered around downtown Bellingham handing them to anyone willing to take one. Meanwhile, back on the dock, the skipper was hawking whole salmon for half the price as the local fish market. All this was happening frantically, before the ice melted, or we'd have nothing but 1000 pounds of rotting fish to swab out. Word of mouth sold about 300 whole fish before the remainder got too rank to sell. We chugged out into the sound and dumped the rest, with clouds of seagulls following us out. It was a foul job, that, tossing the carcasses out of the hold up to the deck and over. It was a good day for the gulls, though.

I don't recall what my cash haul was but it was a bankroll somewhere in the vicinity of $500 or so, about a tenth of a regular salmon season payout depending on the boat you crewed. With the skipper apologizing again for the meager payout, I soon jumped ship. My brother David once again had come to my rescue. He'd entered a doctoral program in biology at the University of Washington, so I gave him a ring and headed south to stay with him. Thumb out, I stood on the ramp to US Hwy 5 south for Seattle, hoping for the best. And so, by a route circuitous in its many peregrinations, I began my erstwhile and largely checkered career as a rock and roll promoter.

In 1979, Seattle was hardly the hipster tech-world destination it is today. Nirvana and the whole NW grunge scene were a decade away. Microsoft and Amazon didn't exist. The city, though, was beautiful, a port metropolis with snow-capped mountains front to back (Olympics/Cascades), the expanse of Puget Sound on the waterfront, and a totally wonderful, funky, low-key, can-do vibe to it. And there was a vibrant local music scene still in its infancy to boot. With my $500 wad in pocket (in today's dollars worth about $2500), plus free rent at my brother's, I started to hang out at a club in Pioneer Square called the Bahamas as a vantage point to check out the music scene.

The Bahamas was lively enough, it had lots of cute girls in clusters up and down the bar, and the blaring music was tolerable, often with a sort of fake "south of the border" feel to it, sort of Jimmy Buffet stuff, ergo the name Bahamas. The proprietor of this establishment was a large, heavy ruffian by the name of Baptiste, with big rings on his fingers, shiny suits, disco-collar shirts, and burnished shoes. The thing that got this mugwump and me on the same wavelength was that he was a Quebecoise gangster from Montreal, my old hometown. Though I was wary of him, we hit it off. The short story is that he wanted to open a live venue in the basement, but what with running the Bahamas and three other cocktail bars about town, he needed someone he could trust to manage the room. He'd do the in-house business, stocking the bar and hiring the wait staff, but what he needed was someone to book bands, run the stage, and promote the gigs. Having cut my teeth in NYC, or so I pretended, I ran him a line of bullshit sufficient for him to give me a trial shot. Oh, lord, was that his mistake!

The first band I booked was the notorious punk riot combo Black Flag, with the infamous Henry Rollins as front man. They were a mix of hardcore punk, the Ramones, and a sort of atonal riff band with screaming lyrics. Rollins was a riveting front man. He was muscular, had great laryngeal pipes, and, on stage at least, was a whirlwind of banshee angst. He was also ardently political. His list of actions and arrests were, and remain, truly admirable in my humble opinion. Of course, I was a nervous wreck the night of that first show. I actually hadn't a clue how to do any of it, though I had spent at least half a dozen sleepless nights stapling posters for the inaugural show on every damn lamppost in Seattle. When this notorious Los Angeles punk band finally showed up on time for sound check, and some poseur opening band went through their dumb set without a hitch, I finally breathed a sigh of respite.

The show had soon sold out. Club venues in Seattle between the years 1979-1984 ran by either selling tickets at the venue ahead of time or people paying at the door. There were no online services back then, and Ticketmaster by phone barely covered more than its hometown in Arizona. The line to get in for my opening show went around the corner of the block. I was thrilled. The opening act (one of Baptiste's lame bar bands) did their big-hair spandex set to a packed house, with a few loud boos and tossed bottles of beer. I could handle that. Finally, on came Black Flag!

The Bahamas Basement, as it was called, was truly that: a basement. It was a great space, though: intimate, low-ceilinged, long bar up front, hot, sweaty, and smoky. How were we to know the open pipes running along the ceiling were to prove the end of it? Black Flag finally hopped on stage and started to thrash through its set of hits: "Depression," "Rise Above," and their demented trounce of "Louie Louie." The place was packed, the joint was a-hoppin', goin' 'round and around, reelin' and a rockin', what a crazy sound, when effing Henry Rollins decides to dive out into the mosh pit by swinging out into the crowd by grabbing onto one of the damn ceiling pipes. Yikes. Rollins certainly hit the mosh pit with a sploosh, but down came a water main with him and suddenly the Bahamas underground was soon under water. The screaming crowd fled for the exits in ankle-deep irrigation. What a freakin' mess.

Somehow the fire department managed to turn off the water main to the whole block. Sump pumps were hauled in. A grumpy plumber re-plumbed the busted pipe and Baptiste and I leaned against a paddy wagon trying to explain to the flatfooted cops how things had gotten so out of hand. Turns out that Baptiste hadn't actually gotten all the correct city permits for this side venture in the netherworld, beneath the tropical climes upstairs. I was mortified, sure beyond a shadow of doubt that my "one-night-old career" in the music business had been shot to hell. I saw it clearly: back to a stinky Alaskan fishing boat it would be; an atavistic outcome, to be sure. Well, it was certainly a real shitty night for Baptiste, who held the lease and was liable to the landlord for damages. He'd be hauled up, too, for lack of a permit, and whatever other officious bureaucratic crap he'd failed to file. But far from ruining my career in punk, suddenly I became a sort of streetwise hero. The two city papers, *The Seattle Times* and *Post-Intelligencer*, ran little sidebar spreads about the incident, with pictures of soaked concert-goers huddled on the sidewalk wrapped in police blankets. As good old Henry Ford is purported to have said about his Model T, "Don't give a damn if they like my cars or hate 'em, as long as they're god damn talkin' about 'em!" Rank capitalist Henry and I certainly came to an understanding on that overstatement in the weeks ahead. I suddenly had street cred in the burgeoning punk scene. Black Flag left town reveling in the notoriety. Doused concertgoers proclaimed it as a badge of honor, and within two weeks the crowd of maybe 200 had swelled to 2500 wannabes who swore they were there, too. Everybody who was anybody had been there, apparently. Baptiste was not amused, though to his credit he didn't blame me. We soldiered on, but the fire department closed down the basement that night and, to my knowledge, it never reopened.

Around the time of this fiasco, Baptiste had had his eye on another dive, one that he thought might make a good small club. The place was a sort of upscale Mexican-tequila-bar-cum-enchilada-restaurant named Pancho's (of all uncool things) literally across the street from the downtown department store district on Stewart and 3rd Avenue. Today it's some sort of hip dive called the Retro Lounge, yeah right. Baptiste took me round to see the owner. Sharp tejano that owner: his name was Emilio and he was jumpy as hell around this big shiny-suited Quebecoise heavy. The latter promised that he'll build a little stage, bring in bands, and quintuple the business most nights a week, and in return get 10% of the bar sales and 100% of the door. Also, Baptiste would pay the bands. Emilio just sat there, arms crossed, looking at the big guy with frowning skepticism. Back and forth they haggled, some of it in code language, which, at the time, I didn't rightly get the hang of. Silly me, I of all drug-prone people should have caught it. Finally, a tentative deal was struck and Baptiste handed off the details to me. It was all done on a handshake. But I watched every move of this cat and mouse with fierce vigilance, code aside, thinking: So that's how it's done, hmm, sez I to myself, that's easy. The upshot was that after I told the owner I had lived in Mexico City during the Olympics, this Emilio hombre cottoned to me, a "buen chico" as he put it, better than that "pendejo shit-for-brains matón" (i.e., a dickhead thug), that is, Baptiste. Sez Señor Emilio, why don't I just strike a new deal with him and tell Baptiste to piss off? The man offered me 7% of the bar, in return. I had to pay for "security" on show nights to prevent things from getting out of hand, a la the Bahamas underground. I'd book the bands and could keep 100% of the door take. We shook hands on the spot. Emilio called Baptiste and said he had second thoughts, so adios, amigo, no deal. I wish I had tapped that phone line. Word soon got out on the street that Pancho's owner was now working with me and Seattle had a new venue in town. Baptiste, again, was not amused.

I've shared that I'm no pugilist; I don't revel in street fights and I will usually turn the other cheek, generally being one who thinks with his legs when in peril. But pissing off Baptiste was something else entirely. On the upside, he seemed to be a loner in his sleaze-ball affairs; I never saw him with any sort of entourage. And while I was a good six inches taller than him, on the downside, he had 100 lbs. on me, with ham fists as big as pork loins. And those rings of his could doubtless take out your front teeth on the first pop. Our meeting of détente was straight out a noir movie. Baptiste had a loft office south of the Bahamas on First, that you reached by an ancient freight elevator to the third floor. Turns out that this was where he lived as well, on a cot, at least on nights when his clubs kept him at work past 2am downtown. We met on the sidewalk and up we rode in the open-grate, creaky freight elevator. We didn't speak the whole way up but, swear to god, I did notice the big pug had strapped on a little pistol, which he made no effort to conceal. Someone told me later it was probably a toy for intimidation, but it didn't seem like no toy to me that night. This wasn't good. However, it turned out that Baptiste himself wasn't in a fighting mood. We had a couple of drinks, he mentioned four or five other dives he would fight to keep, warned me off, and then magnanimously conceded Pancho's to me as if I needed his permission. He said I could have that "trou de merde Mexican shit-hole" and good luck to me. We parted on a handshake, and I went back to my true de merde shithole.

Pancho's was a bit of a shithole, but for six months it was the shithole about town. It wasn't large, with a fire marshal-approved capacity of 100 (but could be packed to 200), half-circle red Naugahyde booth seating, a too-small stage and a smaller dance floor, but had a great bar with a good view of the acts that played there. I had run into several band managers when I'd been little more than a barfly at the Bahamas, pre-Black Flag, so I called them up and started booking gigs. The first half dozen shows were basically a bust, with twenty to thirty paying customers and maybe a few Pancho's regulars. I started to book some of the hipper bands, the ones with actual followings and quirky song sets, who wrote their own and had some artistic credibility and good musicianship. Pretty soon I had door counts upwards of 100 regularly on weekends, with a more upscale well-heeled hipster clientele. Then suddenly, at about month two, big name stars on national tours started to show up, usually around midnight, as if Pancho's was suddenly the after-show dive in Seattle. These were monster acts by Pancho's standards, playing the biggest 15,000-seat venues all the way up to sports arenas.

The first of this ilk to show up was Pat Benatar and her band crew. I had no idea who she was in person until someone whispered her name in my ear. Cute, perky singer, maybe all of five feet tall, with a dark bob hairdo sweat-matted from her show, and skintight leather pants. But wait a sec, hold on! Whoa, whoa. What? You big-arena stars expect to get into Pancho's free, WTF? They of all people could afford the $5 cover (the 1979 price)! You're doing me some sort of favor by coming to my bar? But, why argue? So, in waltzes Pat & Co. Suddenly Pancho's was hopping, and it seemed like just the next night that it was Eddie Money showing up, and the following week guys from Def Leppard, then roadies from Motorhead, and then later Van Halen himself. What the hell? I didn't recognize most of these people, since they weren't the sort of bands I listened to much back then; nevertheless, the breathless groupies who followed these stars to Pancho's were quick to inform me just how cool the place suddenly was as the post-arena concert destination. "Like sooo totally way cool, like bitchin' yano?" Pat! Lemmy! Eddie! Whatever! So, the club had its run for the money for the duration of its allotted fifteen minutes. But I was soon to learn, like some befuddled dad last to find out his son is a coke head, or a naïve spouse that her husband is out shagging her best friend, that these honchos weren't coming to Pancho's because I was running this retro-cool club, no sir. Remember "the code" between Baptiste and Emelio? The code, such as it was, related to the fact, that unbeknownst to me, my bartender Tony was arguably the biggest coke dealer in town with the best blow money could buy. Y-e-a-h. His source was none other than Emilio himself, with his ties to south-of-the-border cartels. Bricks of coke were shipped into the city like wheels of French Brie. Ah-ha, duh, so this was the racket Baptiste was hoping to wheedle into. Crafty git. Clueless me. Yes, indeed, apparently every big-name road manager on the west coast now knew to send his acts to Pancho's after their Seattle shows for a score and a good ol' time quaffing Tequila Sunrises. Whoda thunk? Seriously, I was a cuckold. But, hey, by gum and by golly—Toto, I don't think we're in Kansas anymore. Ain't that how you learn the ropes?

Sadly, all good things come to an end, and someone, you can bet, soon takes their leave stage left. And so, true to form, Pancho's came to its untimely end. It was Tony, alas, who took the bitter end too much to heart, and made his abrupt leave first. My very astute great bartender got careless and took his iffy and illicit halftime job at Pancho's on home, dealing drugs out of his apartment or the trunk of his car, maybe even in some back alleys for all I knew. He got tailed by the fuzz and was summarily busted, which led like a fat cut line of cocaine straight back to who else but Señor Emilio. I think the latter skipped town, one step ahead of the law. Thus, my faithful readers, "si muy triste de hecho"—no more Pancho's. Pack up the sombreros. The last show before we closed was a raucous fare-thee-well party with local band favorites the Pudz. Neither Pat, Lemmy, nor Eddie bothered to show for the adios, sad to say. But hats off to Dave, Rob, and the Pudz; it was a great show.

It has been said that a wise man learns from his mistakes. Going through my own rolodex of my life's missteps it was clear to me that life in the fast lane of rock'n'roll provided insights into the facts that a) boys will be boys and b) don't trust anyone in the music business unless it's in writing, notarized, signed, sealed, and delivered. Anything much more complex would stump the best of us. It seemed like a simple list. Unfortunately, in the margins of the music business in which we all worked in Seattle at that time, none of this mattered for beans. I am no less a fool for recognizing how foolishly naïve I was. It was as clear as day, with every new show, that you had little choice but to make it all up as you went along. We were all the antic monkeys of our own one-man-show organ grinders. But through Pancho's, I did meet many of the streetwise music promoters about town, all scratching out a living as they, too, made it up as they went along. Some promoters, like the founders of Modern Productions with their fabulous venue the Showbox (on 1st Avenue and Pike Street), were better at making it all up than others. When I summon up recollections of that time, I am still struck by what a heady time it was. Music critics say the early 1980s was Seattle's heyday, with greater energy, more reckless creativity, and just plain old-fashioned chutzpah than the more famous era of Grunge that was to come a decade later with Nirvana, Soundgarden, Alice in Chains, and Pearl Jam. If these acts put Seattle on the map in 1990, we back in 1980 drew the map.

No better muse than Debbie Harry lays out the heady truth of the scrappy music biznez back then in her own memoir of those far-gone days, *Face It* (Harper Collins, 2019). Though she is writing of New York, the anthemic theme of DIY New Wave rings loud and universal: "We were struggling artists, scuttling around…just trying to get something going, walking home from work before dawn through the dark, dusty, sweet-dirt smell of the city. We felt like pioneers." I've seen her live, but I missed Blondie's Seattle show in 1977 when they opened (take a deep breath now), for Foghat and J. Giles. I was to manage or work at a dozen venues and clubs through to 1984. I even managed a few great working bands as well.

The catalog of great bands I met and got to work with is too long to list here. Certainly, working with the managers at the Showbox was perhaps the most fun, as the clubs I actually ran myself brought all the managerial headaches to the fore on a nightly basis. The Showbox, by contrast, was a great venue both for bands and audiences, an Art Deco palace with a 16-foot film screen in its heyday. It opened in 1917 as the premiere dance hall in the Northwest, but like many other joints selling liquor, it got shuttered as a dancehall during Prohibition. Post repeal, cum 21st Amendment, it reopened its doors to the swing set, bringing in many of the great wartime jazz artists and big bands, from Louis Armstrong and Duke Ellington to Gypsy Rose Lee. Over the years jazz seemed to peter out, and the Showbox fell on hard times; it reinvented itself, changed hands, and was even, briefly, a furniture store, then a bingo hall run by the Talmud Torah. In the late Sixties it became a pick-me-up venue for some big acts like Buffalo Springfield. But when Modern Productions took it over in September, 1979, with a show by the British post-punk band Magazine (a poster of the show still bills it as the Talmud Torah) with Seattle faves the Blackouts (whom I managed for several years) opening, a new era of great New Wave, British Wave, and artsy-post-punk shows made it Seattle's premiere destination. The bands simply trundled through, many just kids like us, including the Police, XTC, Psychedelic Furs, Gang of Four, Devo, Blondie, Iggy Pop, the Plasmatics, and even Willie Dixon and Muddy Waters. This is but a sampling. Daytimes at the Showbox, the space was rented out, as we had done in NYC, as a practice studio. The mega-band Heart was a regular.

We naturally make much of our own survival dramas, quick as I am to dismiss the fantasy that the lower echelons of the rock industry are somehow glamorous. It just ain't so. It all had a make-it-up-as-you-go-along chaos to it. The big promoters about town, the honchos producing arena-sized shows with Eric Clapton or The Who, or Pat Benatar and similar sorts of acts, had little interest in bringing in unknown (if electrifying) bands like The Police, who were tooling around in rented vans on their first US tours. Honestly, I don't think we sold more than 300 tickets for their first show, and I recall Sting in his trademark trench coat, standing in the back of the Showbox floor listening to the opening bands to a half empty house. He seemed like a nice enough bloke, and they ran through their sound check with expert professionalism. That's a big plus. Police drummer Stewart Copeland's brother, Ian, was in fact the grand impetus for all these great shows coming through the NW territories. Ian was a big New York music promoter booking all the New Wave and British Wave bands through US tours at that time.

But then bands like Devo would show up for a sound check in the mid-afternoon, wearing their ridiculous matching outfits and plastic orange cone hats. Eek. The usual street grunge crew setting up the show just laughed out loud, and off came the stupid hats. But a perfect example of the creative chaos which reigned at the Showbox was the November, 1979 show featuring a double header by James Brown. I was the front of the house manager that night, doing security (such as we had it), ticket sales, the door, and so on. There was an eight o'clock show and another at ten. It never occurred to any of us who'd been dealing with the sort of punk-dazed music we were putting on, that there was any need whatsoever for seats at a show, at least anywhere near the mosh pit at the front of the stage. For any punk show you might attend, stackable chairs would have been an unnecessary hazard, too easily weaponized and heaved onstage by the pit bulls if some opening band was too crappy. There was, as it happened, a raised section at the back of the Showbox with round tables and scattered mismatched chairs. It provided seating for maybe sixty or so people. In waltzed James Brown's mammoth entourage for the afternoon sound check: the members, horns and all, one humongous band, his hairstylist Harry Stall, his wardrobe coordinator Gertrude Sanders, his hefty handlers and body guards, the works. Hey, it was James Brown.

From that moment on, though, things went downhill. We Showbox managers were all in our mid-to-late twenties and our stage crews, light guys, soundboard manager, and so on were all either younger or a day older. Many were full-regalia punks with chartreuse Mohawks and nose bones. The Brown entourage didn't have any idea how to interact with these weird kids, nor in truth did we know how to interact with the Brown machine's gold-chained, shiny-suited, bouffant-coifed minions. Brown was an absolute tyrant over his musicians, so the sound check was an eye-opener. He'll stop song run-throughs ten times and scream at some horn player for missing a beat, then do it again with some other member of his band. And then again. But most disappointing and feather-ruffling for the Godfather of Soul was our apparently "crappy" soundboard and monitors, and our inept soundman at the dials. Brown's crew became argumentative. By contrast, most of the struggling rock bands we put on had four lads and four instruments: two guitars, a bass, and a drum kit, think Beatles or The Who. They could usually bang out a sound check in under an hour. Brown & Co. had at least sixteen backup musicians, maybe more, from backup singers to horns of every brass, and near as many hangers-on. The whole fiasco was a bust, and the sound check went into the early evening.

It was cold and blustery the night of the show, with rain spitting. The crowd for the first show started lining up at 7pm, with the sound check still raging. By the 8 o'clock opening, the band and Brown were still dicking around. How had it gotten so late so soon? The Godfather's tour manager and I even got into a verbal row when he overheard me say that Brown's perfectionism was the problem. He shot back that it was our "lame dick honky" soundman they had to work with who was the fuck-up, and so on, back and forth. So, with the Dr. Seuss dicta "so late so soon" in mind, the clock ticked inexorably to 8:15. The sold-out crowd was still on the sidewalk, of course, all down the block. There they huddled in a typical fine November Seattle drizzle. But this wasn't our regular crowd, this was Brown's crowd: hundreds of fancy-attired dudes in fine threads and fedoras, and ladies dressed to the hilt in heels, jewelry, furs, false eyelashes, and enough perfume to fell a truck driver. They were all standing out on the sidewalk like beaten dogs beneath the hail, waiting for the doors to open. By this time, Brown's crew were shouting invective at me, I was stressed to the max, and at least a thousand street dealers kept barging up to the ticket booth with some jivebo riff along these lines: "Say slim, I got what's happenin' fo' dah head! Nice fat ol' line of blow brothah, trade it fo' you let me in, man! Fine stuff, clean-o-clean, fine buzz, big ol' fat line!" and so on, yadda yadda. Finally, Brown's men gave the signal and in poured the sopping crowd. Fedoras! Furs! Silk scarves! More jewelry than the crown jewels. Spats. Fine coats. Wow, what a fabulous parade, all five hundred plus of them. And then all hell broke loose.

Twenty irate brothers, then forty, decked out and grumpy, immediately came flying up to me yelling: "Where's the seats, man? My lady ain't sittin' on no floor!" They were coming at me from every angle. Seats? Uh, excuse me sir, we don't put on shows with people seated in rows. You stand and bop in the mosh, got it?

But no, they didn't get it, and frankly they were right, we should have thought of seats. I mean, the Godfather himself musta been foolin' when he sang "Git Up Offa That Thang!" I kept thinking: you come to see James Brown and you want to sit on your bottom? Oy vey. Everyone suddenly had to have "seats." WTF now? Somehow Terry M. (the one African American manager at Modern Productions) got a call through to a joint called the Seaman's Chapel down in Pioneer Square which catered mostly to drunks, the homeless, and the AA crowd. PTL, it was open for Jesus till midnight, and yes, they apparently had several hundred metal folding chairs on wheeled carts they'd rent. Someone on our crew had a van, so down to First Avenue we flew, backed up to the rear door of the church, threw in the chairs, flew back up First Avenue, put on flashers, and wheeled in some 200 goddamn folding chairs. It was still not nearly enough but hey, we tried. What a fiasco! The upside was that James Brown was killer, and by the second show most of the first show's SNAFUs had been worked out. But that, in truth, was just another Showbox show; some were even more chaotic. Especially those where half the owners thought it a good idea to drop acid, looping around on Cloud 9 the day of, answering every question with "I don't remember!" like a rallying cry, leaving the details to everyone else. That's all I have to say on that. I loved those guys, even though one of them ultimately screwed me over big time.

Bands I loved working with were The Police (Sting and Copeland are smart men and pros), Television, The Damned, Delta 5, Bush Tetras, Echo and the Bunnymen, the Cure, and the Gang of Four. The latter were brilliant Brits who lost their bass player in SF due to strep throat, so they hired ace bass player Darryl Jones. He flew up from LA the morning of the show and danced around during sound check with a Walkman on, learning the Gang of Four set through headphones. By show time he was note-perfect amazing; no wonder the Stones hired him after Bill Wyman left the band. There were so many others as well; I even had a hoot out drinking with Huey Lewis and his band mates, ending up at the 24/7 Dog House Grill for breakfast at 4am. But the punky-pop group I had the most fun with was the B-52s. They were just so goofy, irreverent, and down-to-earth. They had a day off before the show, so I took some of them and their roadies out canoeing on Lake Washington for the afternoon. What a gentle, delightful time we all had, paddling about and feeding the ducklings. Thanks guys, I think we ducklings became fine swans by trip's end.

At about this time, a club called WREX was established by three enterprising guys in a funky part of grungeville Seattle called Belltown. Belltown was the original skid row back in 1880, because of all the logging skids that were sent sliding down to the mills on the wharfs and the waiting ships along Elliot Bay. As my apartment was right there, WREX became my hangout. Their first show, and the first I ever attended at WREX, was Grace Jones, who drew the gay leather crowd for a convivial evening. She was wonderful, and a great lady, doing this sort of snake-dance voodoo trance thang only Grace Jones can do. Oddly, it wasn't sold out, so I had a chance to chat with her at the bar for the better part of an hour. She was delightful, her deep-inflected Jamaican patois putting me at ease, and dressed to kill in some sort of shiny pole-dancer-from-space outfit. All the pictures of her in glossy magazines have her looking so serious, but in person she's all keyboard smiles and gay laughter.

I ended up working a number of shows there, doing whatever was needed, including shows with Joan Jett and Romeo Void. The stream of bands just kept coming in by the baker's dozen, week after week. Back in those days it seemed like anyone who could hold a drumstick or guitar started his or her own band. It's all a blur. But WREX, with its half sawed-up, tilted Cadillac seat stands, was, like all other Seattle juke joints, always broke. The building it was in had been a sailor's boarding house cum brothel, so the narrow three stories upstairs had these tiny dusty rooms, like withered grapes off a vine, each with the rusting remains of a well-thumped spring bed. One room at the top of the stairs became the office, with jury-rigged wiring and electricity. The place officially closed on my birthday, March 18, 1982. But it soon reopened as Club Vogue under new management, that being Michael V. of Modern Productions, myself (as room manager), and my then girlfriend, Annie M. (as stage manager). She was the sweetest woman, the one-time drummer for the all-girl band Children of Kellogg and a hard worker, but an alcoholic. Many a night we only had DJs, but we still managed great shows with regional acts on the weekends, and here and there some national bands not quite ready for the 1000-seat Showbox. What I am ashamed to say, though, is that despite signed "riders" (band contracts) vetted and initialed by club manager and partner Michael V., he still managed to stiff several national acts. This was particularly true if the door take (e.g., ticket sales) was woefully inadequate to cover paying them in full. Several times, Michael just skipped out, leaving me and Annie to shell out every last dollar we could scrounge, even from the bar till, to underpay these poor bands with abject apologies. Anyone who has toured with a struggling band in a van, as all these groups certainly were doing, and as I have, too, knows that it's all hand-to-mouth, show to show. To play a gig and not get paid can mean no gas money to slog on down the road to the next show. So, Michael and I parted company.

Here's the thing about memory: it's a fickle mistress. My last show at the Vogue was a line-up of great local bands, and Iggy Pop. Yes, the very Iggy of my Preface. It was a full house that night. Iggy Pop wasn't supposed to headline at the Vogue that night; he'd headlined at the Showbox four days before and was staying on in Seattle for some reason. I'd heard that he'd been at a party at a friend's house out in the U District where he purposefully dropped the eggs from the fridge one at a time to the floor, for no other reason than he was pissed at something. On what turned out to be my last night at the Vogue, Iggy arrived during the ongoing show at about 10pm, with a tall, beautiful friend of mine on his arm. In they waltzed, Iggy obviously smashed beyond recovery.

He asked me at the door if anyone had "blow" for sale, I vaguely remember. Nope, I would have said, no blow, sombrero Tony is in jail, so go drink a glass of water for crying out loud and sober up, you inebriated git. I don't recall all the details of that night, as I was doing the all-cash door register. The fact was, if I had let someone else man the register and stamp the wrists, they'd skim $100 off the take with no questions asked. It came with the territory.

I don't remember what band was playing their set that night (everyone I've asked names a different band.) But suddenly from the sweaty mosh-pit came a chorus of "Iggy! Iggy! Iggy!" So Iggy elbowed his way through the mosh pit, stumbled onstage, and proceeded to make a pathetic hash of it, "too drunk to fuck" as frontman Jello Biafra of the Dead Kennedys aptly put it in one of his songs. Whoever the damn band was, Iggy tried to leap on stage and missed, only to be hauled up, mid-song, by the band's lead guitarist. At that point he tried to grab the microphone from the singer, began singing off key, and then for reasons beyond comprehension, made a poor effort to flop back into the mosh pit. Maybe he was just too drunk to stand on his own two feet, poor idiot. The crowd was too drunk themselves to catch him, and so an inebriated Iggy Pop goes "plonk!" onto the floor, headfirst. Ouch, boink. In the end I was babysitting Iggy in the loo as he tried to retch his guts out, the gash on his head gushing out blood. So on this delightfully muddled high note, wherein somewhere lies the truth, it was nevertheless a fare-thee-well for me and the Vogue. Maybe Iggy wasn't even in Seattle—but here began the end of my erstwhile daft career in punk.

I began the preface of this memoir with the shaggy dog story of Iggy and the loo because it was a turning point in my life, literally a halfway point at age thirty-four to my current age of sixty-eight. Whatever a *coup de grace* is, this was mine. I had tried to skate on thin ice with my hands, feet in the air like a circus performer, only to find I couldn't skate worth beans and the ice was thinner than advertised. I promised myself that night, with Iggy's head in the bowl, that come what may, I had to find a different way to make a living. Returning to Alaska wasn't it, but what was? I had no idea, least of all that night as I walked home alone at 3am after locking up the club, so thoroughly exhausted and depressed that I think I spent the whole next day in bed.

There were, nevertheless, true high points in those hectic days. Perhaps the most rewarding was working with Seattle's most inventive and uncompromising, maybe its truly greatest band, the Blackouts. They were four incredibly talented and astute musicians, fiercely true to their artistry. I was both honored and thrilled to serve as their erstwhile manager for a couple of years, not that I did much to advance their careers. They've often been voted "Seattle's greatest band," even above Nirvana. In truth, as a manager, I just didn't have the relentless drive, the schmooze, possibly even the sleaze, still less the basic business chops, to put them on the map as they deserved. All four of these wonderful lads, two of them brothers, remain dear friends. Bass player Paul Barker went on to play fulltime with dark-metal band Ministry; Bill Rieflin, the drummer, also joined Ministry for a while, but later played with Nine Inch Nails, the Minus 5, R.E.M., and King Crimson; Roland Barker, Paul's brother, now runs an organic farm in Hawaii; and lead singer Eric Werner, arguably my closest friend of the four at that time, moved to San Francisco and entered the trades. They soon got better band managers (I believe Ric Ocasek of the Cars was one) and moved to Boston; they then toured west again to SF, where they broke up in late 1984.

I can recall one side trip I took, certainly with lead singer Eric, possibly also with drummer Bill, in a painfully slow VW bus from San Francisco to go camping at Pyramid Lake in the northern Nevada desert. It was a barren moonscape of dusty scrub and small cactus. Out in this blazing wasteland, the low hills are like copper piping buttressing the expanse of the fifteen-mile-long lake, shimmering in royal blues in the slanting light. There's barely a tree to break the alkaline stubble of the shoreline, such that one has a clear feeling of desolation seen straight through to the desert horizon. The lake gets its name from a distinctive set of rock formations at the north end that break its breadth here and there in steep pinnacle accretions. At the last lost end from the highway, some twenty miles down a dirt road, the pyramidal formations are close enough to shore to swim out to. The reason this area is considered a destination is because of the large natural hot springs found there, and it was to their rising steam and welcoming warmth that we headed over rutted roads.

I recall swimming out to one of the pinnacle islands a hundred yards off shore. I started to climb it, only to find that it was a rocky rookery for a small colony of barn owls (Tyto alba) roosting in the crags. Two of them, terrified as they burst away, could have scalped me with their claws I had so surprised them. The first afternoon at the lake, after setting camp, some of us took magic mushrooms. Eric and I became daring and climbed one of the steeper land pinnacles, rising like a crooked finger at a near vertical incline. It was maybe forty feet high and steep; the worn platform at its peak was maybe three feet across.

Here we made ourselves at home, gazing in dazed wonderment at the vast expanse of the desert stretching in all directions. Ingesting a hallucinogen brought out the sheer beauty of the barren landscape, how sunlight and shadow played upon the undulating hills in the east, how canyons wended off into mystery, how a sense of eerie solitude settled on the land. We both vaguely recalled hearing distant thunder from the west. By this time, though, we were engrossed in a duet we had undertaken. Eric was playing a metal penny-whistle and I was drumming on my thighs with my hands, but it wasn't until Eric pointed to a flock of American white pelicans (*Pelecanus erythrorhynchos*) half a mile off, gliding across the shimmering water like white-clad witches on brooms, that suddenly his metal flute started picking up some DJ's garble at a Reno gospel station. We were so startled by this that we looked at each other, only to howl at what we saw: both our scalps sported hairdos sticking straight up like we were alive with electricity. Eric stuck the penny whistle out again, and the same muffled static of a distant radio station whistled with the gathering wind. Then it dawned on us: we'd become lightning rods, with our bodies encased in static electricity. Finally, we heard the approaching thunder for what it was. Looking over our shoulders we saw an enormous wall of black clouds pushing a desert downpour our way over Tule Peak. The whole western skyline was a billowing banner of threatening storm clouds. Yikes, lightning! Never did two lads descend that vertical finger of alkaline rock as quickly as we did.

Howling with laughter, knowing we'd just dodged by a straight hair a lightning bolt out of the whirlwind, we decided to head to the hot springs for a soak as the great wall of dark clouds rolled in. We could see the limber lightning clearly now crackling through the atmosphere, and the first splotches of rain started coming down. We stripped and jumped into the hot water, luxuriating in its soothing warmth. About then the rain came down in earnest, as the brief thunderstorm thrashed across the heavens overhead, a seething downpour washing clean our dusty heads, earth and heaven wedded in the embrace of a deluge. In time, the thunderheads drifted east and the first evening stars began to appear between the racing clouds. Suddenly an enormous North American porcupine (*Erethizon dorsatum*) appeared out of the creosote bushes, rushing straight for us in the steaming pool.

I knew that several species of wild animals enjoy a hot soak in volcanic springs, the most famous perhaps being the Japanese macaques or snow monkeys (*Macaca fuscata*) of Shigakogen National Park. Were we now obliged to share the hot spring with a porcupine? It seemed so, as the big rustling bundle of angry quills came barreling over to the pool edge all the while chattering angrily at us. We huddled in the middle, terrified and laughing nervously at same time. The jostling beast came to a halt at the pool berm, then sniffed the air. Ascertaining that we weren't a threat, I guess, it eventually backed off. Despite the failing light, we could still see it amid the bony vegetation a way off, keeping its wary eye on us. We hopped out of the steamy pool, grabbed our wet clothes and shoes, and dashed for our campsite buck naked. The porcupine did not follow. So ridiculous is what followed that the word "folly" barely encompasses it. Having escaped the nasty armature of that prickly pincushion, I was so high on mushrooms that I didn't even realize that I was dashing in the fading light barefoot through every imaginable spiny plant in the Nevada desert. The rest of the night was spent yowling as each of dozens of spines was yanked out of my bleeding feet with a pair of Swiss Army knife tweezers.

This night of pinprick torture was no fault of our erstwhile attacker. I'm actually very fond of porcupines; here's a glimpse of how beautiful they can be:

Quill Scripture

Always in the wild
happiness has been
most mine when
the thorny porcupine
trundles into view
on Stillwater Lake
where the ducks tail
up in shallows
and the basket willows
trail their long leaves
upon the pond, food
our black pincushion
haphazardly
chews at waterline
a wreck of pick up
sticks stripped green
and white in ringlets
gnawed to bones
a beautiful economy
of tooth marks, pen strokes

You Call This a Career?

one could almost argue
that serve as writing quills
and she an eccentric
critic who daftly gnaws
and waddles, waddles
and gnaws leaving
always a rave review
of unused wooden nibs
in her wake, tonight's
theatrical play one of light
on the evening lake
our favorite reviewer
never scribbling
a word of ill will
toward anybody.

Chapter 7

Like the Golden Toad—
Sit and Do Nothing

Like an Ignorant Ox, I Grew in Impatience, Not in Wisdom

After nearly five years of a hectic lifestyle of managing clubs and putting on shows, in truth, I was a bit of an emotional wreck. I had stood so near the speaker stacks at so many shows that I was also now half deaf. I felt somehow bereft inside, knocking about the bright lights like a pinball. I yearned for solitude again, for evenings of contemplation and quiet nights.

That I should yearn for something else to fill my soul, something centered in quietude and contemplation, may seem strange given my recent career choice. I took counsel from mystic and Buddhist Alan Watts, who wrote: "Every explicit duality is an implicit unity." I even bought a beautiful first edition of his book *The Way of Zen* somewhere in Seattle, which he had inscribed to someone else. Years before, I had taken a weekend retreat with Watts when still a student at the University of Connecticut, Torrington. He came to lecture at a weekend workshop at the Yale Music Conservancy grounds in Norfolk, CT, where I was living in 1972. Old and frail but still clear-minded, this was just a year before he died in 1973. So yes, I yearned for some sort of inner peace despite the thrashing nights, searching for a deeper sense of purpose, isn't that the phrase, a sense of purpose to life? A more mytho-intellectual milieu, in any case, kept calling for me to grow up out of my puerile fantasies of the rock life, to embrace a richer inner life, one unlikely to be found bellying up to a bar and having another shot glass amid deafening cacophony. Counter-intuitive as it may seem, given my "day" job (which was actually a night job, of course), I nevertheless had the discipline to take up Tai Ch'i while putting on shows, practiced Transcendental Meditation (thumbs down) which morphed into Zen sitting (thumbs up), and sought out spiritual guidance wherever I could find it.

Recently I was reminded, after reading a news item about tribal whaling among the Makah tribe of the Olympic Peninsula, that I had actually studied under a Salish shaman for several years. He had a lodge of sorts out on the Olympic Peninsula, and once a month in the early eighties, I'd take the long trip by ferry and circuitous back roads to visit him. I say "lodge," but it was really just an old canoe rental shop tucked behind a Citgo Gas Station with a green stand of incense cedar (*Calocedrus decurrens*) to break the ugly view. His name was Michael Nilluka if my memory serves, though that may be a misspelling. I guess today you'd say he was meta-sexual, leaning gay, soft-spoken, good-humored, sincere. He had a long black braid of hair, big wondrous eyes, hand-sewn beaded vests, cowboy boots, and a ball cap. He smelled of sage and salt. He was a far cry from the "noble savage" photos of Sitting Bull and Quanah Parker. He had an odd assortment of plastic storage containers in which he kept his sacred objects, such as his eagle feather fan and seashells he'd imbued with spirit. I always thought it was odd that he kept his sacred objects in plastic, but I've noted over the years in working with many Native people that they are very practical about such matters, and don't spend unnecessarily on such things as rare wooden boxes from Bali that may look nice but cost a paycheck. Plastic containers cost a buck at the dollar store. When I asked about it, Michael said simply, "Plastic is cheap and waterproof." It made eminent sense. He would take us, a small group of, what's the word? Acolytes?

Followers? Pretend Indians? Anyway, he would take us seekers on guided meditations into mythical lands of coastal Salish mystery. He taught us plant lore, or wort cunning. He taught us the secret names of animals, and was absolutely delighted that I, this big strapping Anglo, took the lowly, though ubiquitous, western gray squirrel (*Sciurus griseus*) as my first spirit animal or totem. Explorers Lewis and Clark first described it in the early 1800s. It was chosen, in any case, because squirrels are remarkably adaptable survivors, sturdily thriving in every sort of habitat, with the added bonus that they are always curious, acrobatic, clever, and, despite their bad rap as being rats with bushy tails, truly beautiful little creatures, all things considered. Michael laughed uproariously and thought it brilliant. "Most white guys," he said impishly, "they all want to be Wolf, or Coyote, or Big Eagle Man. Woodchuck would fit 'em better. But you're my first Squirrel!" He rolled back on his haunches with a belly laugh, eyes twinkling.

I told him, in turn, that in the Norse mythic tradition, the squirrel was known as Rata'tskr, the messenger upon the world tree Yggdrasil. It carried messages from the deep roots of the tree where the great serpent Níðhöggr dwelled, up to the highest spire of the tree to the sentinel Veðrfölnir, the hawk-eyed eagle of Odin. Michael grew grave for a moment. "That makes sense," he said nodding thoughtfully. "The squirrel is the one mammal of the sunlight, unlike the rat of the dark, who bridges the world of nature and the world of man."

I doubt that Michael was a day over thirty; he was so childlike, yet so innocently unaffected, even wise, and I chose to believe he was blessed with Sight. I learned so much from him about how to create ritual in my hectic life, thereby bringing the Spirit of the natural world into my daily routines and being. I am eternally grateful for his wise guidance during the many months we worked together. As Francis Weller has said in his wonderful book *The Wild Edge of Sorrow: Rituals of Renewal and the Sacred Work of Grief* (North Atlantic Books, 2015): "Ritual is able to hold the long-discarded shards of our stories and make them whole again" providing "the elements necessary to help transform whatever it is we are carrying in our psyches into a unified soul." This was Michael's gift to me, transforming my psyche into a vessel, if I could but muster the spirit in a world gone crazy. This vessel contained my gratitude, my forgiveness such as it was, and my kindness to myself and to others. Not a bad analect to hang one's own hat on.

Sometime around 1982, in my apartment in Belltown, Seattle, I sat in mediation one morning, as I normally did upon arising, on a little cushion there in our quaint little living room. I recall listening in perfect stillness to the distant traffic. And then some sort of quantum curtain of all probabilities parted and with a whoosh of enveloping certitude my consciousness supernova'd into Oneness with the cosmos. If you're not careful describing such things, I realize, you can come off sounding like a tin pot guru off his meds. But it did come upon me, just like that. I'm aware in writing these words that squishy phrases like *oneness with the cosmos* sound corny enough and are likely to make any sensible reader groan, with eyes rolled heavenward. But the experience is well known to all Zen masters, and most long-time meditators as well. It is called *kensho*—"a tiny flash of the true nature of reality." I was blessed to join this select club of *kensho*-ites. I felt suddenly as if I were a conscious quark-like pinprick in a cosmos filled with living quarks, undifferentiated, at One and at peace. I was strangely cool, calm, and collected during this otherwise remarkable experience, this little window on *satori*[21] that shot through me like a bolt. Rather than get too woo-woo about it, let me quote the brilliant radical thinker and emphatically down-to-earth scientist with a Harvard Ph.D. and an M.D. from Columbia, Robert Lanza in his book, *Biocentrism* (BenBella Books, 2009, p. 34): "In 1976, the *New York Times Magazine* published an entire

---

21. Satori, from the Japanese Buddhist verb "satoru"—to know, to see clearly. It is considered a permanent state of full enlightment, whereas kensho is just a "flash" of insight.

article on the phenomenon of being taken 'out of oneself,' along with a survey showing that at least 25 percent of the population have at least one experience that they described as 'a sense of the unity of everything,' and 'a sense that all the universe is alive. With a feeling of deep and profound peace.'"

I quote Lanza to place my own experience in a stolidly mainstream context, to indicate no special accomplishment on my part. The great sages caution that this sort of sense of momentary "Oneness" is but a distraction from simply "Being" wholly in the present. But for me it transformed my life. In that instant I gained some sort of ineffable insight into how the universe and my physical sense/mind/consciousness actually entwines. It's not an insight you can ever "undo," still less put into words with any accuracy. The famous koan: "When a flag volleys in the wind, what moves?" The answer: Nothing. It is the Mind that moves. That instant of Oneness destroyed all of my book-read beliefs in "arrows of time," "pasts and futures," realities of an "out there" as opposed to an "in here" and so on. As the koan suggests, I also realized instantly that the entire world *out there* is really just a construct of my mind; that's how our consciousness works. As the Irish philosopher George Berkeley, for whom the university and city itself is named, once wrote: "The only thing we can ever perceive are our own perceptions." Exactly. This is not to say the universe "out there" doesn't exist. It does. It is just that the attributes of meaning, color, movement, sound, taste, and hearing are all 100% mediated by the mind; none exist outside of consciousness. Suffice it to say, these insights are the essence of Lanza's book, and they revealed themselves fully formed in my moment of *kensho*. But there are hundreds of books that describe kensho, from various Sutras as old as the hills to Berkeley physicist Fritjof Capra, with a lot of New Age claptrap between.

This is something that now fascinates me, so let me elucidate further. Take "visible light" as a starting point. Out in the cosmos there is actually no color, no objects, no shapes, no depth perception, nothing as we perceive it. "Out there" (itself a misnomer but bear with me) there's just a vast ever-changing interaction of quantum events made up of wave-like and/or particle-like phenomena, or as Princeton physicist John Wheeler put it, "naught but the quantum foam." What makes it all seem so real, of course, is that the rods and cones of our eyes pick up the frequencies of the "visible spectrum," send neural messages of those frequencies to our occipital lobe, which then turns this blank "foam" of frequencies into colorful, visible objects and movement. It's a neat trick of mammalian biology, admittedly. It's the same with sound. What we perceive as "sound" is also just a frequency that propagates a wave of pressure through a transmission medium such as a gas (air), liquid (water), or solid (earthquake rumbles). That "longitudinal wave of pressure" itself produces no sound. Ever. But the miracle of the ear is that it translates those (soundless) *waves of pressure* by funneling them into the ear canal, which in turn stimulates our ossicles, passes this plethora on to the cochlea with all sorts of wonderful nuances, which in turn fires bio-electrical pulses that then ignite neurons in the brain which *only then* tells the sentient creature (bloodhounds to humans) ah-ha, sound. It's also the same with smell; the molecules our noses pick up have no smell. The molecules simply have different chemical (atomic) structures, which the miracle of our olfactory organ differentiates into the scent of baking bread or the rot of maggoty road kill.

It was Einstein himself who said emphatically, "Reality is merely an illusion, albeit a very persistent one." One soon realizes that it is human consciousness that brings all these elements of our universe into being. Most people balk at this point since it seems to defy the "common sense" of our senses. I will forego further effort to convince the skeptics. Having been fascinated by the science of the *kensho* experience, which pries open how consciousness actually works, I have amassed a large library of books that explore this topic thoroughly. So, chin up, you are not alone in being flummoxed. As Sir Isaac Newton himself said in his classic book *Opticks* (1704): "The rays are not coloured." Sir Isaac knew that the "colour" resided in the human eye, not the "out there" of even a rainbow. The reader can ignore all this, of course. I am not proselytizing.

Back to terra firma. I do not suggest for a second that our universe as perceived does not actually exist "out there." What a miracle, though, that our minds have evolved such a magnificent sensory apparatus as the mammalian brain (called by physicists "the observer") to give us our sensual view of Reality. It's probably a good thing that the wide universe is mediated by this self-same mind, since if we could "see," "hear," "taste," and "feel" the entire panoply of frequencies of the quantum world, all those trillions and trillions of sub-atomic particles whizzing by us, saturating all space every second, we'd probably be so overwhelmed as to evolve biological barriers to filter out that quantum racket as being utterly useless for our survival. Guess what, that's precisely what happened to our lineage of mammalian evolution through natural selection.[22] It's the same for every other sentient creature out there. Their senses, like the bee's compound eyes that see in the ultraviolet, uniquely evolved to ensure their biological survival, fitness, adaptability, and in the case of humans, the ability to experience fully an "external" world to go forth into, to survive in, to propagate and thrive.

My experience of Brahmic splendor, my kensho, in any case, forever obliterated in me a belief in a "separate reality"—*out there*—in opposition to the perception of myself in the world—*in here*. *Kensho* tends to sweep that delusion from your mind instantly. My meditation that day simply blew all those misconceptions out of my soot-filled stack like a canon blast. Slowly, it's

---

22. Mirrored by the theory that evolution bred out of us these wider states of frequency observation as having no particular survival value, becoming thus entirely vestigial. See: Daniel Cossins, "The Time Paradox: How Your Brain Creates the Fourth Dimension," *New Scientist*, July 3, 2019.

true to say, over many months, the Oneness "high" of my *kensho* experience fell back into the habits of normal day-to-day mental chatter. The proverbial monkey of thought was back on my shoulder, screeching in my ear. It truly does all boil down to simply being in the quietude of the Now, and letting go of distracting thought chatter.[23] That's the essence of meditation, which I've practiced ever since in attentive walks several times a day. I stay centered in "no thought," bringing my mind back to silent attentiveness if it wanders. The health benefits of this practice are enormous.

To Bellingham and the Magical Realms of Random-Myrth

I had, by this time (late 1983 into early 1984), met a wonderful artist named Laurie whose milieu was visual arts, with an emphasis on murals. She was a remarkable woman, forever attired in a sort of hip Morticia Addams chic. She zoomed about town on a Triumph 450, often without a helmet, since the law did not require one back then, her dark hair flying. Striking and beautiful as she was—think Neil Young's "Unknown Legend"—she was also always somehow aloof from whatever surrounding scene she was in, art openings more so than music shows. I came to learn that her aloofness stemmed from an inherent wariness that expressed itself in an aversion of mundane chitchat. By the time I met her, I cannot recall where, she had been hired to paint two large murals in Bellingham, WA, where years before I had been an erstwhile fishmonger on its grimy docks, hawking whole salmon to anyone with a ten spot in hand. Bellingham back then was a fishing port

---

23 I admire Tony Parson, the calmly self-realized Englishman, who wrote the marvelous book *As It Is* (Inner Directions, 1995). As the blurb for the book says: "*As It Is* is a profound and radical work that points to the fundamental freedom that is independent of path, process, effort, or belief." I would say the works of the German-born Eckhart Tolle also express the same freedom from striving, guilt, anxiety, and fear that allow this Oneness to arise.

and a lumber town, and that was pretty much it. It's an hour's drive north of Seattle and shadowed by the magnificent volcano, Mount Baker. As we had become an item and saw a life together, I tagged along with her, heading north.

It was through Laurie, and by moving to Bellingham for a respite, that I met two of the most influential people I have had the pleasure to know in my life, Random Greene and Robin Myrth. They both went by one name, so everyone in Bellingham knew them simply as "Random" and "Myrth." They lived out of town in a magical, handcrafted castlelet of wood and glass, not large, but rising up at all angles out of a northern woodland forest. The two-acre property was entirely surrounded by alder, pinewoods, and woven brambles, a quarter mile down a hidden dirt road. In the center of their garden was an enormous vegetable patch in the shape of a maze, interspersed with blueberry shrubs and surrounded by Harry Lauder's walking sticks, which are remarkably contorted trees with twisted branches that spiral off in delightful corkscrews. This type of hazelnut tree is a little marvel, bursting into flowering color in the spring and in winter providing the most eye-catching whorls of snow-covered branches imaginable. To get to Random and Myrth's house, one had to park a hundred yards away and wend your way down a mossy path. It was, in short, an enchanted garden and a lovely, welcoming magical domicile.

Random was rail thin, tall, and sunken-cheeked, with long flowing hair and a pointed goatee. Robin was Rubenesque, sweet-faced, big-bosomed, and like Random, only wore handmade clothes of satin, velvet, flowing silks, and Egyptian cotton, all brought together with handcrafted leather and embossed metals. Their color schemes were invariably deep purples, royal blues, forest greens, hand-dyed ochres from herbs in their garden, blacks, reds, and gold trim. They drank wine out of brass goblets studded with jewels. Their home was a riot of crystals, tall feathers, satin cushions, candelabras, paintings of mythic scenes, tapestries, and any number of wonderful examples of the best in craft arts. They eschewed TV with a vengeance, and whereas too many families give this heinous electric rectangle pride of place in their living room, these two had a pagan alter laden with all the magical accoutrements of their Wiccan lives.

It was through them that I came to read the works of Aleister Crowley, Gary Zukav, Fritjof Capra, Lawrence Blair, Isreal Regardie, and tomes such as Carlos Fuentes' *Terra Nostra* and Hesse's *The Glass Bead Game*, known also as *Magister Ludi*. They were firmly rooted in the western Wiccan tradition, but were otherwise well-read in the world writings of Nikos Kazantzakis, Jorge Louis Borges, Mikhail Bulgakov, Gabriel García Márquez, and Haruki Murakami. Random studied Gaelic, wrote in runic alphabets, used the Enochian language in his rituals, and had his own Magus vocabulary handy for invocations. He was also forever making intricate drawings reminiscent of the heraldic beasts in medieval Celtic vellum manuscripts. Neither of them had more than a high school education, I'm guessing, but they were nonetheless brilliant, erudite and knowledgeable in their quirky ways. Random seemed to have a photographic memory. Myrth was the gardener and understood in her spirit the art of foraging for the proverbial wild asparagus. She would collect morels and chicken of the woods mushrooms from the surrounding woodlands. She picked all the blackberries from the brambles that encircled their property like some sort of thorny spell keeping the modern world out. Her vegetable garden was a riot of food provender studded with an odd assortment of frog statuary and sun-shot crystals. They kept a flock of tame ducks to eat the bane of slugs that are everywhere in the northwest.

What was so wonderful for me was that they broadened my understanding of earth-centered ritual. I came to understand how important it is to offer obeisance to the fey spirits in natural systems. What they taught me through example built on the work I had already done with my Salish shaman Michael and other spiritual teachers of my past. If a spider happened to weave its web over the front door of Myrth's home, you ducked down to enter until its birth sack released new gossamer spiders on the wind. Birds nested everywhere. Above all, they eschewed the petty politics and news headlines of the outside world. They did often enough listen to the Canadian Broadcast Corporation news on the radio to keep abreast of world affairs, but that was about it. No TV. No newspapers. No internet. Would you be surprised to hear they were into psychedelic drugs of every kind, too, with cannabis buds to die for?

Perhaps most remarkable of all was that the weirdest shit, for lack of a better expression, wove a warp and weft through all aspects of their lives. I have mentioned the works of South African cetolgist Lyall Watson and his exploratory books such as *Supernature* and *Lifetide* that delve into the science of the supernatural. Random and Myrth were the progenitors who Watson never met. I recall sitting in their home one early evening, when out of the blue Myrth says, "I think we should do the Ouija board!" Random and I looked at each other with quizzical expressions. We both considered the Ouija mostly a silly sort of parlor game. But when Myrth received a psychic hankering, Random never questioned it. Myrth herself never thought she was gifted, still less cared to call herself a sorceress, and was absolutely disinterested in New Age labels. Although dismissive of it, she still had "the gift"—of that I am certain.

But the Ouija board? That was a new twist. First introduced as a parlor game in the 1890s, it was promoted during World War I more as a get-rich-quick scheme for "occult divination"—a sort of DIY magical craze. It was hawked for sale by a popular American spiritualist (i.e., shyster) named Pearl Curran, a self-aggrandizing con artist who claimed the mysterious board could contact the spirits of the dead. Talk to Departed Daddy, but first pay Pearl her penny. Frankly, I have always thought it hokum and Random, too, was skeptical. But what the heck. Random found the board that lay hidden in some cupboard, blew off the layers of dust, and set it up on the floor. We asked Myrth why she wanted to use it. She just smiled that sweet smile of hers, gentle mirthful soul that she was (the words "calmly phlegmatic" come to mind), and said: "Because the board told me to." Fair enough. I then asked when had they last used it. Random and Myrth looked at one another. She turned to me, and said, "Probably five years ago for Random's thirty-fifth birthday, at a party we threw. The kids felt like playing."

All three of us put our finger on the sliding pointer or planchette and off we went. What little science actually lies behind the Ouija board is that it uses the term "ideomotor response" to describe the involuntary movement of the pointer by those participating in the divination. In any event, Myrth's first question to the board was to ask what spirit had summoned her to pull the board out of the cupboard. Our fingers immediately traced out: WolfBob. OK, that was weird. We next asked what WolfBob wanted. "To dig a hole" came the board's prompt reply, traced by our involuntary fingers. OK. Why dig a hole? There was a pause. "Best if 8 inches by 8 inches and 18 deep." OK. When should we dig this hole? "Now." Now? "Yes now." Where should we dig the hole? Pause. "Outside under white tree." That made some sort of sense, as there was indeed a lovely paper birch in the yard. OK. We all looked at each other with bemused shrugs. WolfBob? Yikes.

Ever enterprising, Random got to his feet, muttering that "now" actually meant now, so we followed him out to the garden shed in the gloaming of a lovely evening. We grabbed a shovel, while Myrth found a ruler, and we dug the damn hole as instructed. We then returned to the board. WolfBob, what now? Pause. "Thank you." After that, no matter what question we asked or whatever the entreaty, the board just offered up gibberish. We got bored and didn't give it, or the hole, any further thought.

I had offered to take Random and Myrth out to dinner at an establishment called The Black Cat (readers take note), where my paramour Laurie had painted one of her gothic-inspired murals, so off we went. It was late when we returned. We took the sharp turn off the arrow-straight back thoroughfare called Noon Road onto the curvy dirt lane where they lived, and it was then that it occurred. We hadn't even completed the turn when we saw in the headlights a black furry lump in the middle of the road. Calmly and with absolute certainty Myrth said, "My god, that's Hecate"—their cat. And indeed, the poor animal lay dead in the middle of the road. It was curled up in a ball as if asleep, showing no signs of any injury or having been hit by a car that we could see. Hecate seemed at peace, as if waiting at the end of the dirt road for Random and Myrth to return, deciding to curl up in a pose the better to give up her life force to the night. With loving care, Myrth carried her beautiful old longhaired black cat into the house. It wasn't until we saw the Ouija board on the floor again, that we instantly recoiled as if struck by a bolt, recalling at once the task that had been set upon us by WolfBob. With Hecate in Myrth's arms, we stood in silent, stunned, momentary paralysis. So, it had come to this. We buried Hecate in WolfBob's hole under the lovely birch tree and placed upon her grave a large amethyst crystal. Random and Myrth performed a loving ritual of farewell and we went back inside.

We decided not to contact WolfBob again. What can one do with such an experience? How do you process it, still less explain it? My hosts obviously grieved the loss of their old beloved cat, but WolfBob, who the F was WolfBob? By what remotest mechanism of precognition had this "whatever it was" asked us to dig a hole perfectly sized to accept the stiffening body of an aging cat that would die in the near future? Perhaps Hecate herself had known she was dying, and had somehow, through some quantum entanglement with Myrth, driven the planchette to ask that we dig her burial hole? It seemed far-fetched, even if Hecate was going on seventeen and a weirdly prescient pet. Had her feline mind created what Tibetan shamans call a tulpa, or powerful thought field to influence Myrth, or had Myrth subconsciously known her aged cat was dying but been in denial? Maybe, but that too seemed really hokey. The anthropologist Omar Kayyam Moore studied the Native tribes of Labrador who themselves used a similar form of divination with pointed bones. Those bones foretold where deer and seals lay dead, albeit at the hands of the Indians themselves—these foretold deaths would only occur after they'd gone hunting in the following days. In other words, where they envisioned dead animals lay was where to find them alive for the upcoming hunt. Moore found that this divination worked far more effectively than could be accounted for by chance. As he wrote: "Some practices which have been classified as magic may well be efficacious for attaining future ends envisioned by their practitioners."[24]

Then again, were the two events even connected? Perhaps they were just a strange coincidence? None of it made sense. We even picked apart the name WolfBob as well, consulting dictionaries and encyclopedias, even Kabalistic numbering systems such as Gematria, to see if there was some cognizant sounding or numerical word-counting or perchance a name with an entirely different phonetic meaning that might give us a clue as to who WolfBob may have been. Nothing. I mean, of all the ridiculous names for a preternatural uber-being to pick for themselves, WolfBob wouldn't be the first *nom de magique* to come to my mind. Maybe it came from the same creative corner of the universe as SpongeBob SquarePants.

But I do believe with Carl Jung that there is some sort of collective unconscious that somehow imprints in quantum probability (wherein Time ceases to have meaning), palpable remnants of human experience in consciousness. The stronger the experience the more palpable and enduring it is. I will not go into these ideas here, suffice to say that it's an example that may explain, partly, how a disembodied WolfBob "predicted" a future happenstance.

---

24. "Divination – A New Perspective," *American Anthropologist*, v.59, p.69, 1957.

Too many academic researchers, in my humble opinion, refuse to acknowledge the inexplicable or deny some phenomenon because they cannot explain it through logical experiment. But surely this is foolish. We are mixing up whether we understand how something happens (science) with the confusion over the question of whether it exists (human observation). As Christopher Ryan says: "When it comes to mystical experiences, the wisest course is to judge their results rather than be derailed by our current inability to understand their mechanism of action." In 1796, Dr. Edward Jenner had no idea how a cowpox prick given to a child conferred immunity to the far more grievous smallpox then in epidemic. By the Logic of Science, Jenner should have been cast out as a voodoo charlatan to suggest a pinprick could cause immunity. WolfBob's result was pretty clear: essentially, and wisely, dig Hecate's grave in a lovely spot to the correct dimensions. How WolfBob "did it" is immaterial when all is said and done. All that's actually needed is to thank WolfBob and move on.

In similar vein, I once attended a Dream Workshop in Seattle. There were about forty of us in the class. At some point the teacher asked us to pair up with someone and share a dream that had recurred in our lives more than three times. Without hesitation, what came to me was a dream I had had repeatedly as a boy in England on through to the age of about eighteen in the US. In the dream, I lay in bed at night when suddenly the drone of airplanes came upon me and, looking up with the ceiling suddenly stripped away, I saw the now famous nighttime formation of Luftwaffe bombers roaring over the British Isles with payloads, as ground-based searchlights combed the night sky. Those bolts of light showed roaring black outlines of the Junker 88s against the velvet blackness. I have no memory that their bombs ever rained down in my dream, but I do recall being utterly terrified, feeling naked and exposed to the coming horror. I decided to share this dream.

My partner was a young man of about my age, an American like me, notably gaunt, shy, and pimply. I let him go first. He shared that he had grown up in England as a child himself, overlapping my own years there. Then he told me his dream. I remained both speechless and stunned as he recounted his own terrifying nightmare of lying in bed as vast armadas of Luftwaffe bombers droned overhead. He had had this dream, as I had, almost two dozen times. I hardly knew what to say. When I finally shared that this was precisely my own dream, he at first thought I was making fun of him. But when we compared certain ineffable quirks about these dreams (e.g., feeling paralyzed and unable to crawl under the bed) he finally believed me. So how was such a synchronicity of experience possible between two utter strangers tasked to share a dream? What I am sure of now is that in this dream state as very young impressionable boys, we had picked up a collective memory of the English people themselves who had witnessed the bombing raids first-hand. The abject terror of these raids, occurring nights on end for months, had somehow imprinted itself as a "physical" meme in the palpable consciousness of a people at war, expressed somehow through unconscious avenues of collective neural resonance with the still-forming minds of us two boys. This was the very essence of the Tibetan *tulpa*. Who knows? Read Jung if this seems farfetched. He had many such experiences himself and recorded hundreds more from patients. If the past is so fluid in the present, is the future also now known in the present? Many models of quantum physics posit this.[25]

I don't know how many events such as the one with WolfBob seemed to follow Random and Myrth around like the dust cloud around the character Pigpen created by Charles M. Schulz in the daily comic *Peanuts*. But it was often enough. I experienced at

---

25. Some of how this neural resonance works, I have already explained in previous descriptions of my experience of *kensho*. Later, I'll describe a resonance with a housemate named Tom, in which we shared a moment of exquisite disolving of ego boundaries as we both experienced Oneness in tandem. Lee Smolin's book: *Time Reborn: From the Crisis in Physics to the Future of the Universe* (Houghton Mifflin, 2013) delves into all this thoroughly. But there's scores of sources for the curious.

least a half dozen similar happenstances of varying weirdness, and the two of them, Random and Myrth together, would laugh like whistlers in a graveyard telling me tales of a dozen more. It was uncanny. Yet they always remained fiercely earth-centered, ritual-intensive, seekers of trance-states knit by conscious invocations, in short doers of Magick but pretty level-headed all the same. They were in all things fiercely anti-establishmentarians.

To balance the unsettling entanglement of WolfBob and Hecate, let me share another experience of a far more upbeat note which I had with them. Random played the piccolo, rather well actually; he had in him something of the goat-footed god Pan whom he sometimes in fact evoked. He was masterful on half a dozen pipes of different shapes and sizes from around the world. Pan, too, was a piper, ergo the Pan pipes. One day, with our friend Denny S., we went out to a rugged peninsula overlooking Puget Sound, with the San Juan Islands to the west, and ingested psilocybin. Michael Pollan in his insightful book, *How to Change Your Mind: What the New Science of Psychedelics Teaches Us About Consciousness* (Penguin Press, 2018), quotes his spirit guide on his first guided psilocybin trip as follows: "The mushroom teacher helps us to see who we really are, brings us back to our soul's purpose for being here in this lifetime." For me, Pollan's summary is as good as any as to the "why" I take this wonderful psychotropic compound myself. It is always a companion and mind-sprite, my little mushroom cap of magic. Without fail, it reveals "my soul's purpose" every time.[26] I've found it growing all over the western hemisphere. It's a true treat.

By the time we got out to the high bluffs on that gloriously sunny day, with a salty breeze soughing in the gnarled pines above

---

26. To quote Christopher Ryan from, *Civilized to Death* (2019): "Roland Griffith, a psychopharmacologist at Johns Hopkins is mystified by our culture of panic around psychadelics. Griffith has studied how psilocybin occasions experiences of the mystical. In these studies, pasrticipants rank their experiences on muchrooms as being the most spiritually significant in their lives, equal to the birth of a child."

us and the gentle snore of the surf below, we were, as they say, flying. We had each brought sacred objects important to our own spiritual practices, so as to build for ourselves various makeshift alters to give thanks to Gaia, or our particular totems on that glorious day. I brought a deer toe rattle, my jasper spearpoint (as previously described), and a sage bundle. Denny brought his deer-hide drum, Myrth her cymbals and, of course, Random his piccolo. I don't know how long we all sat there looking out over the wave-tossed cove and the wide sky-reflected sea beyond, grinning in delight as the seagulls whirled overhead and the fine sun beat down. Suddenly the high clear notes of the piccolo pierced the air as Random began to play beautifully. I rattled my deer toes, Myrth tapped her cymbal with a stick, and Denny gently struck his drum. We were, all at once, a magical quartet. Suddenly, from a direction not one of us saw coming, a double-breasted cormorant (*Phalacrocorax auritus*), a large, goose-sized, black-feathered, orange-masked, long-necked seabird, flapped right into our midst onto the bluff and shook the seawater from its feathers. It was within six feet of us. After preening its wings for a moment, it finally raised its shiny eyes to each of us in turn, as if gifting us with an avian benediction. Beaming, Denny audibly intoned, "Io Pan!" (Praise the great god Pan!), to which the cormorant responded with a rattling squawk. Again, "Io Pan!" said Denny. The cormorant lifted its neck and, beak to the sky, gave the throatiest of rattles a second time. Random then picked up the pace with his piccolo, at which point the cormorant waddled over to him, seemed to stamp its webbed feet as if dancing in time, and throat up, stomped along but a foot-tromp away from his knees. And by gum, Random and the cormorant began an otherworldly duet, a dance like this: Throat rattle > piccolo high notes; squawk and instrument trills; guttural call > the breathy sound of the silver piccolo working in synchrony. The rest of us put down our musical instruments, enthralled.

The duet probably went on for no more than a minute or two, much as it seemed a magical eternity drawn out in the perfectly lucid languor of that day's psychedelic trip. Twice the cormorant squirted out a stream of white guano, absolutely unconcerned by any sense of impropriety. I only mention this because the next day I went out to the point again to retrieve a felt beret, a gift from my father that I had left on the rocks, and there in painterly white was the telltale guano—right where our avian maestro had perched on the rock next to where Random had so beautifully played his piccolo. So, the waterfowl had been there. In any event, with us in quiet reverence, Random finally brought his playing to a close, the notes fading on the breeze. There was a moment of spellbound stillness, as if in our collective state of wonder the cormorant had become for each of us the very center of our universe. It then did an odd bobbing weave, a fare-thee-well perhaps, followed by a final throaty rattle, then flew off into the wide shining glare of Puget Sound and disappeared. We all four burst into mirthful laughter, Denny thumping his drum as if to applaud the performance. Random took a bow as Myrth and I clapped joyously. Bravo!

Terrance McKenna, ethnobotanist and metaphysician, puts forth in his book *Food of the Gods* (Bantam Books, 1993) a tantalizing theory that what led *Homo erectus* (or other early hominins) to evolve into modern, if archaic, *H. sapiens*, and thus higher mental and analytical capacities, was the ingestion of *Psilocybe cubensis* mushrooms (and cognizant hallucinogens) in the hominin diet. Low doses of this edible fungus heighten visual acuity, attune the inner ear to deeper hearing, and increase a vibrational empathy with animals (as we witnessed that day with the cormorant and which I've observed many times first-hand since). I've taken mushrooms dozens of times and all these descriptions are spot on. Heightened sensory inputs would have made early hominins who took said fungus far more attuned, more psychically alert, and thus, in McKenna's telling, more effective hunters. He then posits that, at higher doses, *Psilocybin cubensis* activates "language-forming regions of the brain" (and studies show they do, ergo Michael Pollan) that involve latent, and probably innate, explorations of music (crude flutes, rattles, and drum gourds have been found across the globe, some dating to 50,000+ BCE), evoking deeper empathy with tribal kin, a more expansive sense of wonder, and thus nascent proto-religious understandings of cosmic oneness and so on. Certainly, all of this would have created a more visionary activation of the mind/body/cosmos emersion that shamans have in their trance states, leading to closer contact and sympathetic resonance with animal species in their local environment. Thus, more food for the tribal clan. Consider all the magnificent animals, aurochs, woolly rhinoceros, cave lions, and Irish elk, drawn by torchlight upon cave walls throughout Europe c. 35,000 BCE. They are magical evocations.

It's a fascinating hypothesis, all of it seemingly expressed to the hilt in this one instance with us, there on that windswept bluff long ago. The dancing cormorant, the piping piccolo, our unalloyed wonder + mushrooms creating our own fable above the shimmering sea. And what a miraculous dance it had been.[27] For the twenty-five years I knew Random and Myrth (both sadly dead now), I would return to Seattle/Bellingham on a pilgrimage

---

27. Laboratory studies with Australian white cockatiels have conclusively shown these playful birds can dance to a beat, with each separate bird exhibiting a unique set of break-dance moves, varying with the rhythm of whatever music is being played. Precisely because of this, Random and Myrth acquired two cockatiels themselves who were absolutely magnificent dancers. To Oingo Boingo's throbbing song "Dead Man's Party," these cute birds could synchronize their wild cockade weave and stomp to make any "Dancing with the Stars" wannabe green with envy. They'd egg each other on. Look out, Michael Jackson! And if you train them to talk, they'll even synchronize "Ooo Ooo I'm so sexy!" and so on. It's really quite something. Or consider B.F. Skinner's dancing pigeons. Birds that dance as lekking males prove this evolutionary ability every mating season. That cormorants, under right conditions, clearly also have the moves, well, that's hardly a stretch.

pretty much every other year through the intervening decades. And the times we had, each an exclamation mark of wonder!

One evening after leaving a souvlaki joint in Seattle, my on-again, off-again girlfriend Laurie and I found ourselves out on the sidewalk. To our annoyance we saw a familiar crazy homeless lady walking toward us. We'd seen her up and down University Avenue many times. Throughout the meal prior, Laurie had shared her angst about her future as an artist: what to do, where to go, how to survive, the usual twenty-something anxiety attack. So, there we were on the sidewalk with the crazy lady approaching. We were miffed when the old crone came right up to us. She wouldn't let Laurie pass, saying over and over: "What to do with your life? Eh, eh? What to do with your life? Eh? What to do with your life?" Then the old bat jabbed a finger into Laurie's chest and said: "Nothing to worry, your life's ordained!" We were flummoxed until I gained my wits and shoved the woman aside. One month later, Laurie was killed in a motorcycle accident. It was summer, 1985, and the crone's words came back with unwelcome insistence. My girlfriend died of a brain hemorrhage, in a coma at the hospital. I held her hand when they finally pulled the respirator plug. As the green screen pulse went flat, she became nothing more than the wailing lamentations of her mother and sisters. Think W.H. Auden's words at the death of W.B. Yeats: "The current of his feeling failed; he became his admirers." Strangely, both of her murals in Bellingham were subsequently to be destroyed under strange circumstances, the one at the Black Cat restaurant from a kitchen fire that got out of hand. Another in a gothic mansion on a hill above Fairhaven developed disfiguring cracks in the wall base and the plaster fell off, as if the gothic painting on it was too haunting for the wall itself. No one could say by whom or how each happened.

Laurie was a pagan at heart who clearly had her soul and spirit wedded to the passion of her creativity, all the while absolutely rejecting her Polish Catholic upbringing. She had joked with me that if she died, I should cremate her body and spread her ashes out at Shi Shi Beach on the rocky coast of the Olympic Peninsula. But her religiously conservative mother and equally staid sisters insisted on a church service and coffin burial. They dismissed my comments about Laurie's wishes out of hand. I sat alone in the back of the church. As the priest droned on with unctuous, well-practiced, oily prattle about Laurie's death and "dying in the arms of Jesus," with Laurie somewhere up in Heaven now with her father apparently, the emptiness I felt listening to that fakir was fathomless. It just seemed so wrong. It was as if, in death, the wild-haired, beautiful, wayward, wiccan-leaning, motorcycling woman I loved could somehow be reeled back into a box of conventional propriety, lying amid plush coffin satins, their little girl again made properly normal, if embalmed, in a casket. The words of Cicero, my favorite Roman author, hardly held comfort: "The life of the dead is placed in the memory of the living." I did not attend the burial.

At the time of her death, I was thirty-four years old, once again bereft and unsure of my future. Luckily, it was my brother who again offered a way forward. He is one of the world's experts on neotropical birds today, with a focus on a biological family of colorful little tropical passerines known as manakins, the *Pipridae*. Current exploratory research in the jungles of the Americas suggests that fifty-three species exist in all. At that time, bro Dave was doing his doctoral research. He invited me down to the cloud forest reserve at Monteverde, Costa Rica, where he had his research plots out in the jungle. It sounded idyllic and I said "Sure."

Into the Lands of the Golden Toad

In many ways my six months in Costa Rica were little more than a doomed effort to study myself, the choices I'd made, and the paths not taken, in some muddled hope of accepting that I had to find some sort of career path and get on the straight and narrow.

What a dreadful word "career" is. I've always balked at the notion as congruous with a conforming straight-jacket. But living the bohemian life into your forties and fifties only really works, as I've said, if you become somehow famous for being a bohemian, either through your art or your antics. Fame, still less notoriety, was never what I was after, as it held no allure for me. Turning now as I was toward my mid-thirties, it seemed that my options were narrowing in the manner of a Chinese finger basket. The harder I tugged to get out of myself, the harder my doubts held fast. Was it really time to choose a path to financial stability? Any meaningful path surely meant going back to school. My father certainly continued to snipe at my singular lack of direction. Coming home with odd hairdos didn't amount to much in his mind. Fair enough, the fact that I didn't own a comb spoke volumes. As for my music career, such as it was, I neither aspired to nor had the drive to attain the status of an arena rock promoter. I did briefly team up with an aspiring big-shot named Steve P. who was as tall as me; we briefly started Too Tall Guys Productions and even put on an Eric Clapton show. That was the time when I asked the guitar god if he remembered the stoners splashing about in his pool with Colin back in 1970 or the pub visit with Francis Ormsby-Gore. But though matched in height, Steve and I weren't matched in temperament or musical tastes, and our sortie into the big time soon fell apart. My uncle Jack (known to the world as John McDonald) was at that time University Librarian at the University of Connecticut. It was he who urged me on several occasions to consider library school. With that as an aspirational flag post along an advancing front of quiet panic, I flew with my brother to Costa Rica.

Anyone who has ever been to Monteverde, CR, knows just how beautiful and idyllic it is. The Monteverde Cloud Forest Biological Preserve covers some 1400 acres under agro-pasturage and pristine cloud forest above in the Tilarán Mountains of north-central Costa Rica. The preserve was created through an original purchase by the Society of Friends (Quakers) during the Korean War. The founding Friends were from Fairhope, Alabama. After WWII, a number of the congregation became war-tax resisters, seeing the military-industrial complex drift the nation into yet another war. At least four were arrested and soon convicted, and two were sent to prison. In order to flee the rising militarized oppression in the US under Senator Joe McCarthy, the Fairhope Friends pooled their resources and bought the Monteverde tract of tropical montane cloud forest. They've added to it since. The purchase was facilitated to protect a pristine upland watershed. Their prime acreage was slope pastureland below the cloud cover. The intention was never to buy a World Heritage biodiversity site, but out of foresight for the need for clean water they have preserved the cloud forest. They built a school, a meetinghouse, sewage and water treatment systems, and eventually a milk dairy, thus becoming (Monty Python jokes from *Life of Brian* aside) respected, if also blessed, cheese makers.

When my brother and I got there in the early spring of 1984, the population of the community was probably no more than forty-five. It is three times that today, or more. These wonderful Quakers were hospitable and levelheaded dairy families, kind and generous in all things, and had something of the Amish diffidence about them. Though it was not required, they expected researchers doing work in the cloud forest and living amongst them, like my brother and I were, to make an effort to attend weekly Quaker Meetings. Other than a few community announcements, Meetings were generally experienced in silence, with no preaching, no sermons, no proselytizing.[28] I admired the grace of that quietude. Occasionally a person would say some sort of

---

28. When I moved to NYC in 1987, I decided as a spiritual practice to attend Sunday Meetings at the Friend's House near Gramercy Park. Yikes, how dismal. Everyone attending seemed to have to go on about all their aches and pains and little problems through the entire service as if on a therapist's couch. I fled for good after my second visit.

personal benediction. I guess their hope was that Meetings would bring to the brainiac scientists who came there some sense of calm equanimity, perhaps even open up these Darwinistas to some sort of experience of God. I'm guessing, also, that I wasn't a particularly thoughtful guest because I skipped as many Meetings as I attended over the months I was there. No disrespect was meant, it was just that my temple was the cloud forest itself. I had the whole 1400 acres and beyond to myself during Meetings. In every moment of free time, that alluring cathedral of trees beckoned me. It was there I would go to give thanks to Gaia in a state of wide-eyed wonder.

I loved the surrounding jungle, with its howler monkeys (genus *Alouatta* subfamily *Alouattinae*) and towering strangler figs (*Ficus aurea*). Mammals included the afore-mentioned howlers and white-faced capuchin monkeys; ocelots and the related margay, oncilla, and jaguarundi forest felines; sloths, tapirs, peccaries, coatis, and several species of porcupine including the Mexican hairy dwarf. There was also a plentitude of birds, approaching 1,000 separate species, with over one hundred of them endemic. Alaska had made me a birder, following in my brother's footsteps, so it was no surprise that by the time I left Monteverde I had identified upwards of 250 species, with probably twice that many spotted on the wing but not firmly identified (I am sure my dear brother, the exacting scientist, will contest my numbers as way too high-falutin').

Monteverde was also the home of the famous golden toad (*Incilius periglenes*). Once abundant, they went extinct around 1989—simply vanished from the face of the earth. Small and brightly hued, they were a glowing gold in color, veritable dollops of radiant jewelry amid the verdant greens and flowering foliage of the deep moist forest. My brother and I once followed some herpetologists up into the clouds, to the montane habitats favored by the toad, and even in 1984, there were few to be found. In hindsight, what a sad end to such a beautiful bright little

Bufonidae, yet how blessed was I to be one of the last of a handful of researchers in the world to witness the little chap, alive and in the wild, this fleck of living aureate. Today their memory serves as the veritable poster-child for the worldwide crisis of amphibian decline. Through such encounters with extinction, I came to experience a deep and abiding grief that grows today with each passing year and each passing extinction. No, that's not right. It has become a smoldering anger as surely as I live and breathe. Humankind's wanton destruction of the natural world is a crime both heinous and suicidal and knows no terminus. I carry that grief and anger upon my neck like a yoke, as heavy as our third planet out from an indifferent and unforgiving sun.

The work my brother was doing for his Ph.D. dissertation focused on the mating habits of the long-tailed manakin (*Chiroxiphia linearis*), a diminutive black bird the size of a sparrow with a red skullcap, a robin's egg blue cape over its wing shoulders, and two thin black tail feathers about five inches long. Certain birds, including the fifty-three species of manakin and most species of grouse, as well as colorful tropical birds like the cock-of-the-rock, have what are known as leks, which are groomed breeding grounds that the male bird guards during mating season. Through unique sets of rituals all of these birds in their various ways lure females onto their leks to mate. All alpha male manakins create some sort of courtship space in the jungle, fiercely guarded against intruding males, where they perform elaborate dances, sometimes alone depending on species, sometimes choreographed with a beta, or non-breeding males. Other species of birds like grouse claim their lek by loud throat pouch calling, with tail feathers splayed and drumming throats engorged. The bowerbird does it by building a magnificent boudoir studded with every bit of shiny flotsam they can find. The long-tailed manakin claims its lek wherever there is a thin vertical branch in an open space in the forest. Alphas initiate their elaborate dance with buzzing and rapid wing beat sounds. They then launch into their famous

"Toledo" song. In fact, the Costa Ricans call the little bird *Toledo* in honor of their song. The alpha manakin is then joined by a beta male, essentially a courtier in training. When a drab little green female finally shows up, the alpha calls his beta partner down to the dancing stick and they then do an amazingly intricate series of leaps and flutters, jumping over each other in rapid succession all the while buzzing with guttural tweets. Zeee-yowhn! Zeee-yowhn!

Many of the long-tails in the Monteverde forest had been mist netted previously, and tagged with colorful little ankle bracelets. My job was to sit in a jungle blind and watch the alpha male manakin's lek. I was to identify which males were dancing by their anklet colors, and record the number of toledos and the nature and number of each dance step with a long roster of check marks. It was dull work because you could sit in the blind for hours, bored to tears, while the manakins were off feeding. It's hard to sit still in a jungle blind anyway; there's so much going on outside the canvas flaps that you get antsy as hell. Skwonks, squawks, roars, screeching hissyfits, and bell-clear sounds ring through the cloud forest and there you are, unable to look about because you're stuck in a bleedin' blind. Besides that, after viewing one's fiftieth courtship dance and recording it with hatch marks on a clipboard, the amazement of these fierce little dancers wears thin, to be blunt. There was some excitement one time when I was in a blind and heard a growing pitter-patter behind me, which I at first thought was an approaching rainsquall. But looking over my shoulder I saw no rain, just a wave of leaf-litter disturbance coming right at me as if a giant of the forest were shaking the jungle floor like a rippled carpet. I got up to take a look. It was a raid of army ants (*Eciton burchelli*) coming, with my bird blind dead to sights.

This swathe of swarming ants is a stark reminder that tropical rainforests are habitats utterly indifferent to the life of individual denizens. The phalanx was probably no more than twenty feet across and eight feet long, medium-sized as it happens. In any case, it was doing what army ants do, marching with fearless resolution on, through, around, into, up, and over everything in their path. Locals call these swarming swathes *marabunta*. Everything in their path is swarmed and killed by fierce mandibles, either out of sheer ornery pugnacity or to be carried forward as provender when they bivouac for the night in the trees. Instantly the world in their immediate path becomes utterly panicked, as beetles, centipedes, scorpions, tarantulas, frogs, lizards, and snakes all flee for their lives. In their headlong escape, this wave of shaking leaf litter moved across the forest floor. It's a myth that these fierce little black-hued myrmidon warriors march in vast mats hundreds of yards wide, though it makes for great B movies.[29] Legends of their ferocity, though, are certainly warranted. They swarm over everything, relentlessly. Even in the Friends' village they'll swarm a cottage floor to roof, with a methodical and relentless search and seizure. Every nook and cranny empties of its terrified inhabitants, racing out of the cottage at speed. As a rule, locals quite liked these short bouts of inconvenience since the ants soldier on, leaving their houses spic and span, free of all scorpions, biting spiders, centipedes, and nesting bats.

So, there I was, watching the army ants marching through the blind with amused amazement. I was disconcerted by how many nasty creepy crawlies fled out of the blind with the advance. After about twenty minutes, the ants had marched on into the forest and things grew quiet again. One bird surely does profit from this march; indeed, it considers a swarm of ants its moveable feast. This is the collared forest-falcon (*Micrastur semitorquatus*), an accipiter with long yellow legs, a barred tail, a dark black back, and white breast. It stays ahead of the approaching ants, but hops back and forth on the margins, feasting on the fleeing morsels and shaking off the ants from its leathery legs. All the while it

---

29. For the best over-the-top B role melodrama on army ants, watch Charlton Heston in *The Naked Jungle*, where he single-handedly flushes a vast horde or ants, the dreaded "marabunta" by blowing up a timber dam on a Brazilan cocoa plantation and sending them to kingdom come on a floodtide.

calls happily like a carnival clown with a sound that mimics a deranged laugh.

I mentioned that the resident Quakers raised dairy cows, from whom they made various excellent cheeses for sale.[30] It was a major source of income for them. Surrounding their far-flung cottages, large communal cow pastures stretch down the valley slopes. The cud-munching cows, as cows do, pooped a whole lot of poop. And cow poop is one of the most fecund soil sources for psilocybin mushrooms, the little liberty caps. Walk in any field and you can fill a ball cap up of the little 'shrooms after a rain in no time. No need to harvest really, just pick as you go and eat when you want. On several of my days off, I'd find myself a little cluster, pop them into my mouth, chew them raw, and await the dawning of the day. Then for the next several hours, as if blessed by the jaguar mysteries of the forest's verdant pathways, I'd wander through the tropical cloud forest in a state of blissed-out curiosity. Howler monkeys would follow me from the canopies; sometimes they'd even throw their own feces down from on high as a simian insult. Bellbirds with their odd wattles, stark against the canopy with their striking ochre and white bodies, would send out their brass-toned calls and toucans clattered their rainbow beaks. Curious brown jays (*Psilorhinus morio*) followed me everywhere.

Strangler fig vines (sometimes called a banyan tree) are the towering lords of these forests. At maturity, they can reach 150 feet and counting. They seem like massive hollow sculptures with flying buttress roots, the latter often tall as a man. Strangler vines start out small, no more than a single thin runner that begins in the canopy tops of large tropical hardwoods. Seeds deposited in small crannies by frugivore birds take root and slowly snake down the larger tree onto the forest floor, where runners find a foothold in the soil. Once the vine tendril is established top to bottom, it

---

30. You will have noticed I use the human "who," "whom," etc for describing all animals in this text. That is intentional. They deserve equal status with the naked ape.

begins to send up nutrients to its runners, and it climbs back up the host tree, forever sending out more of its tendrils. No matter how large or hardy the host, the poor tree's days are numbered. The vine grows, and grows, then grows some more, like a slow-motion python, eventually encircling the entire host right back up to the canopy. At that point, the vine literally strangles the life out of the center tree. By such means, the strangler fig finds both sunlight high in the foliage and roots below in the mycelium of the soils. Squeezed to death, the host tree withers slowly as the fig encircles it. Within a decade, the tree that served as the vine's center rots inside the fig, collapsing into mulch to feed the vine's insatiable root system. Two decades on, the entire massive fig tree grows to be a hollow lattice all the way up to the tippy-top, high as heaven in the tropical air. And along the way, epiphytes like bromeliads, pitcher plants, toupees of longhaired moss, and lovely orchids find a home, as do many creatures. On this account, the colloquial name for the accommodating fig is *Ficus condominium*.

Strangler figs are easy to climb up the insides, all the way to the canopy. While I was on mushrooms one day, I climbed one of the larger fig trees I had often walked under on my way to the manakin blinds in the jungle. Up, up, and up—to the tippy top. As I was maneuvering to find a ledge for my bum in order to look around and enjoy the view, I realized I had entered someone else's living room. A Mexican hairy dwarf porcupine (*Sphiggurus mexicanus*) was sharing the space with me, curled into a sleeping ball. I was not too alarmed at first, even if it was a hundred plus vertical feet down the latticed trunk tube if she decided I was not welcome. She roused herself long enough to look at me, bared her teeth, and let out a hoarse warning squeak. My quilly-dopey companion apparently saw in me no usual predator like the nimble jaguarondi, so she just skooched around so that the more prominent quills on her back formed a semi-circle of trouble and seemed to go back to sleep. I decided that this was her way of saying that this half of the canopy platform was hers, go find your own.

Like a chuffed spouse turning her backside in bed, she was done with me. Together high in the canopy, my friend the porcupine and I enjoyed the haunting mists as racing clouds rose up from the warm valleys below to bathe us in cool, soothing particles of moisture. The mushroom gods granted me many visions.

Costa Rica then, as now, was an oasis of national sanity amid the morass of rightist regimes armed to the teeth elsewhere in Latin America. Not a dime is spent on any sort of army. Almost a fifth of its land mass is under protection as some sort of parkland or conservation trust. It has one of the highest per capita living standards in the New World, good health care, and an upbeat body politic. It stands in stark contrast to the endless civil wars north and south, where death squads and vicious insurgencies carry on under the tutelage of the behemoth to the north. On the international happiness scale, it ranks several dozen slots above the US.

During the time my brother and I lived there in our small wood-frame cottage, on any given week maybe a half-dozen tourists would pay a modest fee in a slot at the entrance of the preserve, and wend up into the misty forest. Once a month, a tour guide might bring a group of ten. Other weeks, there were no visitors at all. Today it's two hundred trekkers on up a day, an endless stream of eco-warriors and thrill seekers. There are even entire eco-outfitters now, who rope you up, stick a plastic helmet on your head, and guide you up some worn strangler fig for a hefty fee. Any porcupine is a mile off under this racket of intrusion. Back when we were there, the entire thirty miles of road up into the mountains to the preserve was just a torturous dirt rut, winding like a lariat all the way. A packed bus ride to the Inter-Americas Highway, near sea level below, could take several hours, what with all the passengers getting on and off, the grinding backups on narrow stretches for some lumbering lorry itself grinding up, then a breakdown, and what have you. Everything in the tropics is a patient adventure.

At night I would lie in bed and hear the jungle orchestra of cicadas, tree frogs, and singing katydids, and sometimes even the strange haunting cries of a peccary being caught by a jaguar. Some nights, if the wind was right, I could faintly hear above it all the fierce firefights and bombardments twenty miles north over the border in Nicaragua, between the Contra militias and the Sandinista army. These intermittent firefights would rend the night asunder, not only with sounds of struggle, but a gut-wrenching sense of disbelief and foreboding in me. As our cottage was perched on a mountainside, the sound of battle carried south on the wind. I'd often think of Matthew Arnold's "Dover Beach": "And we are here as on a darkling plain/ Swept with confused alarms of struggle and flight/ Where ignorant armies clash by night." We had no current news in Monteverde. But since the twentieth century began, the story of American imperialist ambitions has been a reprehensible screed of conquest, invasion, and depravity even if there were no newspapers to report it. Howard Zinn's masterful work, *A People's History of the United States* (Harper & Row, 1980), had laid it bare for me some years before.

After I had lived in Monteverde a good five months, I came down off the mountain to explore the wonderful climes of Costa Rica for several weeks on my own. When I finally headed back to the US, departing from the airport in the capital of San José, our rickety jet stopped in San Salvador, the capital of El Salvador which was then a US-backed junta dictatorship. This country, too, was in a civil war between the Farabundo Martí Liberation Front and the country's repressive army, backed by extra-judicial death squads sponsored by US counter-insurgency personnel. Paramilitary goons literally roamed the streets dispensing totalitarian justice at the end of a gun. This is no exaggeration, as three American Catholic nuns were shot in the head point blank and had their bodies riddled with practice bullets in El Salvador in 1980. Their only crime was steadfastly aiding the poor, vocal in their sympathy with the oppressed Indios in the beaten countryside. There was no point in fooling yourself, an American passport meant absolutely nothing if these paramilitary squads thought you an insurgency sympathizer.

On the flight back, through-passengers like myself to Mexico City were not allowed to disembark at the San Salvador airport even to stretch our legs. Boarding passengers trickled onto the plane, practicing the time-honored ritual of storing their luggage in overhead compartments and taking their seats. Suddenly, four heavily-armed soldiers came into the cabin, sauntering up the aisle with a swagger. The flight attendants seemed terrified. They were asked to hand over the passenger manifest. At two rows of seats occupied by the newly arrived, the cocky soldiers, AK-47s slung over their shoulders, exchanged brusque words with the poor souls who'd just buckled up. These soon turned into heated exchanges. Without warning, one soldier cold-cocked a male passenger with his rifle butt right in the face, then simply dragged him off the plane in a gush of blood. The other person interrogated was a young woman. Out of the corner of my eye, I saw her leap to her feet as if to run to the lavatory in the rear and lock herself in. What protection that may have afforded her is hard to tell—not much I am sure, as they would have kicked open the door anyway. But the closest soldier caught her by her braided ponytail and with it twisted in his fist, yanked her off the plane, too. She left screaming for her life. I just hunkered down, terrified, as the elderly Latina beside me clutched my arm for dear life, crossing her breast as she muttered a prayer to the Virgin Mary. The casual brutality of this terrifying drama left me a wreck. I realized that all constitutional protections in totalitarian states are paper thin, and the fist of any murderous regime can punch right through that veneer and haul you off to be disappeared, no questions asked. Can't happen in the US? Guess you didn't grow up poor, Black, and male. If the Maryknoll Sisters Maura Clarke, Ita Ford, and Dorothy Kazel, and lay missionary Jean Donovan, each a US citizen, could be brutally raped and then slaughtered by US-funded counter-insurgency goons, what chance would I have? I'd be battered blue, then bayoneted and tossed in a ditch.

But hey, this was American tax dollars hard at work, funding the depravities of the Salvadoran dictatorship, as well as the rightwing Contras in Nicaragua to the south. As if in disgust similar to mine, Henry Miller wrote in 1939, with the world rolling toward world war: "Do we fall back and writhe with the evolutionary worms? The game is played out, these figures melt away, the lines are frazzled, and life's playing board is mildewed. Everything has become barbarous again" (*Colossus of Maroussi*, Colt Press, 1941). Once back in America, on good old Yankee terra firma, I took a breath and sighed with relief at my good fortune to have been born an American citizen, even as I took stock of what a shit world it was under the Morning in America pabulum and the exported brutalities of the Reagan years.

And Now for Something Completely Different: With Feeling

At this midpoint in my life, perhaps like Dante in the guise of Virgil, who served as guide to the *Inferno*, I shall let the Roman poet also serve as my own brief amanuensis: "Mid-way upon this journey of my life, I found myself in a forest dark, for the straight pathway had been lost." And lost I was when I arrived in Costa Rica at age thirty-four, and when I left at thirty-five, precisely halfway through my life to date. Indeed, my sojourn in Monteverde only partially brought Dante's "panther light" into the darkness of my vexed misgivings about what to do with my messy life. I had thought of library school as perhaps the safest harbor ahead, a bookmark to put order back into my life. "Grow up, Pete, get ahead, and strive toward some sort of outlier conformity, even if it's but a gesture," I told myself.

And yet in reading this memoir back to myself, I realize in hindsight that I have revealed little of my emotional life. Unlike many memoirs, I haven't delved much into the whirlwinds of my love life or the ups and downs of my emotional states. Indeed, I almost recoil with horror at the thought of revealing the intimacies of my relationships. These sorts of revelations feel too much like I am being flushed from concealment like a terrified fox, forced onto an open plain without immunity from the barking hounds of my own anxieties, and just as nakedly alone as that sad fox. There is also this: when my mother was age seven and a day, her own mother Irene was committed against her will to an insane asylum. Bereft, my mother fell under the jurisdiction of her father who was always aloof and coolly undemonstrative, a stickler who committed his own "annoying" wife to the madhouse for being too emotional, too fraught with angst and perceived despondency to remain his lawful wife. He soon remarried, and my poor mother came under the spell of an equally aloof and undemonstrative stepmother; it was a Dickensian childhood to be sure. Like young Pip in Dickens's *Great Expectations*, my mother lived with few expectations. In her case, however, there was no exiled benefactor in the outback like Abel Magwitch of Dickens's tome. At the age of fifteen, my mother caught pneumonia and was sent to a New York hospital, where her father came to visit. Before my mother even recovered from her own illness, her father unhappily contracted the disease from her and died with a lung full of fluid one floor above. Throughout her life, my mother would claim on occasions of quiet despondency that she had killed her own father—her exact words. Her bereaved stepmother promptly shipped the annoying teenager off to a boarding home in Vermont, blessedly run by a kindly soul whom my mother ever after called Aunt Edith. Mom at last found some sort of sanctuary and began to make what sense she could of her lonely childhood.

I make this digression to say that those deep insecurities and guilts harbored lifelong by my mother imbued her with a regretful melancholia fixed in her soul like a dark crystal. These protective attributes of remorseful concealment were in turn passed down from her to me, her middle child, denied both the unspoken status of a glowing first-born or the delight expressed by my father in a blonde and adorable younger sister. At the age of six, I too bore my own sense of being exiled to an orphanage, into a dark world of boarding schools, always the last to take refuge in affections that were in any case denied me. Sent unprepared into the night shadows at Papplewick, I learned soon enough that the key to my survival was to toss any possible latchkey of human warmth into the deepest well of desperate loneliness, turn my back, and soldier on, the wounded if stoic lad. Ever since those lonely days, try as I might, I have been quite unable to fish that latchkey back out into daylight. I've had girlfriends tell me on separate occasions that they felt I was sometimes far more verbally demonstrative invoking the moon on an evening walk than I was likely to show in our living room as a couple. There's some truth in that. As a child at Papplewick, my bed was directly beneath a window in one of my dorm rooms. When night came, the beauty of the moon's rays often lay over my cot like a comforting blanket. Embraced by the light, I talked to the moon as if the white orb were an older sibling, sharing my lonely woes. That the moon is a lifeless rock never entered my mind. And so, I have often found in the pure glow of moonlight a deep sense of my belonging at last in the shadow lands as Selene, the moon goddess, parts the darkness. A case for the loves in my life, I suppose, of living with me, yet somehow also seemingly living alone in my company. Here is D.H. Lawrence, in his poem "Moonrise": "And who has seen the moon, who has not seen/ Her rise from out the chamber of the deep/ Flushed and grand and naked, as from the chamber/ Of finished bridegroom, seen her rise and throw/ Confession of delight upon the wave/ Littering the waves with her own superscription/ Of bliss, till all her lambent beauty shakes toward us."

Emotions are in any case messy. To survive at Papplewick, I became inordinately fastidious about what little order I could exert over my life, folding my clothes at night, for example, or the precision of contents placed inside my school desk. That sense of needed order also imprinted itself on my emotions. Paths through varied love interests in my life seem always by day's end to skirt a precipice of anxious uncertainties, nagging distrust, or feelings of hushed inadequacy. So, I withdraw. With any sense of accomplishment I might harbor in life, too often also comes a corresponding thought of being unworthy. With these fears comes a stoic façade of chipper denial. And so on, as the sting of these hurts in my imagination knows well their endless repetitions. The antidote has been to assume an attitude of quiet aloofness in most interactions through all the roil, unruliness, and tumult of my obdurate inner sanctuary of feelings. This sort of detachment has served me well for the most part. Indeed, I am most content when quite alone, as this memoir perhaps make plain. Being alone, in wild lands and barren places, is for me a recognizable homecoming to whatever I might claim as my true self, unburdened by self-whelmed feelings. I have browsed innumerable memoirs and recoiled from the naked revelations made therein of shameless emotional states exposed like soiled underwear: the petty jealousies, the unrequited loves, and the naked unhappiness of loss, from a child's death, perhaps, or from a lover spurned, a cruel parent, or just icky relationships. I clap these books shut with a shudder. If at the memoir's end there is some sort of radical and embracing redemption, it seems so willfully to transgress the proper boundaries of privacy that I hold dear. Glib talk of "Discovering the Deepest Language of My Soul" by last pages strikes me as a sort of jiggery-pokery piled high with last week's baloney. I therefore confess to an acknowledged gloss where what may pass as emotional candor has of it the quality of that lost, haunting rowboat I once witnessed hurtling by on the White River in the Yukon wilderness. Flailing wildly upon huge waves of icy water, but instead of diving into the terrifyingly murk of those deeper currents beneath, as many do in their memoirs, I reveal only surface anecdotes as my barque slips mysteriously by.

Knowing this about myself, I have thus striven to cherish kindness as a virtue, even as anger, too, has been my friend. The secret to a better world, the Dalai Lama said to me once in a small gathering, is simply "Be Kind." Saying this, he rolled back impishly on his haunches, chuckling at the simplicity of it all like a child, his bright eyes twinkling behind his nerdy square glasses. The innocence of that sort of childishness is not one of my virtues, alas. But this choice of mine to actively cultivate kindness in my dealings, even if I sometimes fail, is itself a sort of armor to protect my inner feelings from prying inquiry. Otherwise, I might come across as too dour, too much the misanthrope, too cynical and irreverent for "polite society," which is perhaps closer to the mark. Kindness serves as a buffer from further inquiries about the whys and wherefores of my latent melancholy.

So, in fairness to the girlfriends and sweethearts of my romance days, since none have given me permission to expose the intimacies of our lives together, I remain steadfastly mum on this throughout, as in so much else about my emotional life. I will say in my defense that there is not a woman of those I have loved, inside the boudoir or in the borderlands, who is not either an abiding friend or someone I wouldn't be absolutely delighted to bump into again by happenstance. There must surely be some sort of decency of habitude in that. Many in fact suddenly popped back into my life, like gifts from the past, when I finally joined Facebook around 2016. They began to gather on my home page on the addictive platform as my so-called "Friends." Ugh, we collect these like kids collect marbles. So before Virgil takes me further down into ever lower circles of hell, here ends today's lesson on relationships, feelings, and the inner emotional life of your author. The next memoir over will have plenty of that, I am sure.

Chapter 8
Real Career Daze

Hey Good Lookin', What You Got Cookin'? Between the Covers of a Good Book

The University of Washington (UW) is a splendid institution of higher education, with one of the most dramatic campuses in the country. What other academic institution can boast a view of Mount Rainier down the central avenue of campus? Somehow this august institution of higher learning thought my tuition check worthy of being cashed. With a letter of support from my uncle, John McDonald at UConn in Storrs, plus high GRE scores, I entered the Master of Library Science program at UW upon my return from Costa Rica. I had a lovely two-room suite in a shared house on 19th Avenue near Ravenna Park, an easy walking distance to the university district and campus. My digs even had a small porch with a view of the Cascade Mountains and, to the south through the trees, the peak of snowcapped Mt. Rainier. The library school was situated on the ground floor of Suzzallo Research Library, itself opposite the Allen Undergraduate Library, across the main open quad of the university grounds. During my two years there, I was happy and pleasantly surprised by the intellectual challenge. I won't spend much time describing my library school experiences. To 98% of any reading audience, it would be a sure snore, cataloging rules being what they are.

I'm not sure that the professors at library school knew quite what to make of me. I had a very long shank of hair as a forelock that reached well below my chin when it wasn't tucked behind my left ear. Perhaps it resembled a turkey wattle. I had a gold loop in my left ear. I wore tight black jeans and Keds sneakers a la Joey Ramone. I wore a leather coat when it was cold, black T-shirts in summer, and occasionally daubed kohl round my eyes, doubtless left over from some show the night before that a friend had put on. In short, I didn't look like the rest of the students. But I did well. I enjoyed writing essays and exploring First Amendment arguments, and loved how large libraries came together as institutions. Yet my inner Velcro cottoned not at all to cataloging rules. Be that as it may, card catalogs were nevertheless the keys to the arcanum in my school days. I still have a deep fondness for these stolid cabinets full of 3x5 cards. They were the source code to the kingdom of knowledge, their marvelous marginalia a sort of secret script for the initiated. I knew, in any case, that I wanted the intellectual challenge of a career in academic librarianship like my uncle had at UConn, so I took courses with that focus.

I continued my shamanic trainings with Michael, my Salish friend, throughout my time in library school. I visited Random and Myrth often enough and honed my Wiccan skills. I took tai chi classes under the tutelage of a jolly Jewish instructor named Aaron. I learned from him that my beanpole posture was hopeless, and now, thirty years on, with two cracked vertebrae welded together from various tumbles, one on the sloshing deck of that ferro cement boat to Yakut, I have mild sclerosis. Aaron, to his credit, never gave up on me. It was hardly a surprise that, during this time of intellectual and spiritual ferment, I came by turns to a uniquely personal form of ceremonial devotional practice. I realize in hindsight that my spirituality remains to this day an odd assortment of practices: an amalgam, if you will, of Zazen, pagan ritual, Wiccan magick, shamanic explorations, Native tribal sensibilities, readings in symbolic literature, psychedelic explorations, nature worship, spiritual totems, visions, and so on. Some of us carry these stone gods of our yearnings with us wherever we go even as we place these lodestones on our alters hoping, I can only assume, for some sort of salvation from ourselves. It is an odd mulligatawny to be sure, but it is my spiritual mulligatawny; that's what matters. I've been at it ever since.

One day, months into the school year, I was sitting in the kitchen of our shared rooming house with an ascetic lad named Tom. He reminded me a bit of actor Harry Dean Stanton. Tom had about him the severe countenance of a Zen abbot. He was a rigorous meditator, eschewed chit-chat, delved into Krishnamurti and Dogen daily, ate sparingly, didn't drink, and seemed to have no friends beside our housemates; in short, he was a man to whom humor was an alien artifice. His room was spare: mattress on the floor, a lamp, one chair, a few books, bare walls. He kept his clothes in cardboard boxes. That January day, however, we were reading poems from Pulitzer Prize-winning poet W.S. Merwin's book, *The Compass Flower* (Athenaeum, 1977). Tom came to what is now my favorite of all of old acquaintance William's (Merwin's W.) poems, called simply, "A Contemporary" (p.15). It's a lovely little verse about a poet living as a tree in the mountains. I had never heard this poem before. It ends with these lines: "I would be green with white roots/ feel worms touch my feet as bounty/ have no name and no fear/ turn naturally to the light/ know how to spend the day and night/ climbing out of myself/ all my life." As Tom read the last line, the whole universe shifted but an inch, yet shift it did in my open mind with a profound insistence. It was as if I had been looking at our dim kitchen as a flat two-dimensional picture one minute, and then out of the blue an invisible hand descended to plop a vibrant stereoscope before my eyes, a visionary panoply in multi-dimensions, transforming in that instant the little grungy cooking room into shimmering aliveness. All was as before, yet how radically different all the same, as if seen for the first time with a deep inner stillness.

The experience came very quietly, but was exquisitely profound. At once, everything became luminous, the "I" that I thought I was melted away. I had had another *kensho* experience. It seems to me now in retrospect that in times such as these, pure Being unfolds in the manner of one of those store-bought dry-pressed sponges that fulfills its purpose when watered—expanding into pure utility and unity of purpose. That little room with the refrigerator humming, tap dripping, the out-and-out mundanity of it *as it is*—I realized *this* in itself was enough. A deep affiliation with its utter mundanity was the key. This was the totality of living free. This moment. This kitchen. This Now. As Ralph Waldo Emerson once wrote in his essay, "The Poet":

> Here we find ourselves, suddenly, not in critical speculation, but in a holy place, and should go very warily and reverently. We stand before the secret of the world, here where Being passes into Appearance, and Unity into Variety.

Allow, though, an amendment. Emerson has it inverse, for it is the universe of appearances that coalesces into Being, just as in variety, those "ten thousand things" that we see as separate, in truth these pass quietly into Unity. We become no more than Consciousness itself observing the entire Universe as, surprise, simply a manifestation of Consciousness. I looked over at Tom. Wide were his eyes. He was looking straight into mine with a little Mona Lisa smile. Clear as day, the "separateness" of the dendrites and neurons within our "split" brains were somehow firing in mysterious fashion together as if in perfect harmony. It felt as if we were two tuning forks in sympathetic vibration. Nobel laureate Francis Crick and Christof Koch, the German-American chief neuroscientist at the Allen Institute for Brain Science in Seattle, worked together on a number of studies on the deepest roots of consciousness. Reductionist they may have been, but in several studies they proposed that the neural correlates of consciousness arise through a synchronization of cells in brain waves.[31] Their papers describe this type of tuning fork synchronous vibration. In our case, obviously, what was occurring by mechanisms widely explored but as yet not defined by hard evidence, Tom and I, literally and physically, got on the "same wavelength," or in the parlance of Crick and Koch's research, we were in "gamma oscillations," those powerful vibrations at 40-Hz.

We acknowledged what had just happened to both of us, but did not speak about it. Neither of us felt any need whatsoever to say a thing, in fact. He too had opened up to the hushed splendor of *what is* with no effort, no striving, just some switch going "poof"— and all thinking disappears and clarity of Being arises. That's the totality of it. As twined oscillators, if you will, words between us just seemed superfluous. It was the vitality of duende, that quality of ineffable inspiration pulsing through our bodies sung in a key silent to the ears, that infuses reality. Experiences such as this may sound silly, but they aren't. The science is extensive: electrodes and MRIs have captured the oscillations of this state repeatedly. Very matter-of-factly, Tom said he had to get to work at the bakery where he kneaded dough into every imaginable shape and texture. The day-old elderberry muffins he'd bring home were little sugary loaves of delight. With a nod he walked out, as untalkative as ever. Several months later he was institutionalized for a while. Apparently, the severity of his inherent asceticism and overall *contemptus mundi* seemed to make his mind go off the rails into realms of quasi-schizophrenia. It was tough to see him finally being led out of the house by a medic to a waiting ambulance. He had become a danger to himself.

Even a rapscallion as drunk and unapologetic as Jack Kerouac had his moments of *satori* or *kensho* enlightenment. In fact, he

---

31. See for example Crick, F.C., Koch, C. (1990). "Towards a Neurobiological Theory of Consciousness," *Seminars Neuroscience*. 2: 263–275—but all of their co-authored work hangs together as a whole.

wrote a whole book about it, *Satori in Paris* (Grove Press, 1966). With his usual insouciance, he could hardly be droller about what he experienced. "Somewhere during my ten days in Paris I received an illumination of some kind that seems to've changed me again, towards what I suppose'll be my pattern for another seven years or more...but as I say I don't know how I got that satori." And so on for 118 pages. I add this aside with Kerouac as protagonist, first to say that if Jack could get *satori*,[32] then anyone could and can. Secondly, his humdrum description puts the brilliance of the experience into modern vernacular, bringing it down to a streetwise parlance of the everyday. That's probably a good thing. When it gets all swami'd up, you have to wade through Vedas of verbiage to get to the truth of it. It is a state of clear contentment, well described by mystics such as Rumi and Rilke, of embracing the Beloved. For an atheist like me, I can sometimes squint through the curtains a t that wisdom.

For several months thereafter, as if I'd been reborn to embrace my lackluster academic studies, I found even the dullest courses taught by pedant professors suddenly piquing my interest. That's the good thing about the plebian sort of *kensho* I seemed destined to have: everything is suddenly wonderful, even the mundane unwonderful. Embracing strangers in your enthusiasm, however, is not advised. You can bet as well that no mystical angels will lift you up if you blithely wander into traffic. I lived, ardent atheist that I am, in a sort of state of Grace; but these states too must pass, I knew, as they did for Jack K. In time, whatever *satori* was, it melted away like ice in a forgotten cocktail glass. With the sheen dulled, back to the street you go, stuck in traffic with the rest. I've never had such an experience again, though out in wilderness I can touch it with my mind when surrounded by the complete stillness of an ancient forest. Just breathing the mountain air is to

---

32. *Satori* is the "sudden enlightment of seeing into your true nature." While *kensho* is a momentary glimpse, *satori* is a lifelong immersion in the true quietude of your pure Being.

step through a portal of no thought, no effort, into the stillness like the eye of a violet, just so. I am convinced that at the cellular level, with regards to how neural byways in the brain actually function, some trace imprint of the satori state remains in our consciousness forever.[33] Yet as day tumbles after mundane day, as bodily aches and pains intrude, as everyday assholes annoy as they will, doubtless the layers of our roiling and fallible personality silt up the enlightenment experience with the muddy runoff of our noisy egos. Am I to accept that it is my aging body and constipation that has closed that door? Years at a job? Harried responsibilities? Or maybe a cat's mad curiosity that keeps my mind filled with useless factoids and inconsequential worries? Who knows? Somewhere during this time, in any case, I sought out my geology professor who had studied, nay admired, wide-eyed, my jasper spearpoint. If you ever read this, dear sir, truly, my radiant thanks.

Most of us who have ever felt the stirrings of spirit rise up pass through a period of mystical dabbling in our lives as we seek some sort of external validation from Buddha, Jesus, Allah, name your guru. Meanwhile, it's hard to figure just how we are so able in our misspent youth to give that bent penny such a sleeve-sheen of self-regard. In truth I was too often conflicted and unsure of any path forward, as it branched into a thousand tributaries like a river through an estuary before it reaches the sea. I may have chosen a career path in seeking to be a librarian, but my heart and mind still found it slow going through a thicket of doubts.

---

33. There's a fascinating book about a self-realized Algerian woman known as The Mother, (born Mirra Alfassa) who became the consort to Indian holy man Sri Aurobindo c1914. The exploration in the book, *The Mother v.2 The New Species* (Institute for Evolutionary Research, 1976) by a Frenchman named Satprem (Bernard Enginger), records how this remarkable woman came to directly experience the "lives of her own cells." A French Resistance fighter during WWII, Enginger was caught and sent to a Gestapo concerntration camp in 1943 and survived. After the war (1953) he moved to India to live at the Pondicherry Ashram where he met Alfassa, The Mother, and became her amanuensis. In terms of how humans might biologically evolve as a species, within the sphere of our self-consciousness, no book is more fascinating.

One big nudge to become more involved in social justice at this time came during my second year in graduate school. I picked up a copy of Barry Lopez's harrowing tale of the wholesale slaughter of wolves in America, *Of Wolves and Men* (Scribners, 1978). Having seen wolves in the wild in Alaska, so beautifully fierce and majestic, to think of them so senselessly slaughtered filled me with such burning indignation I think it honestly seared my soul. When Lopez's book came out, Vietnam was still a raw wound, so reading that upwards of a million and a half wolves were ruthlessly and relentlessly slaughtered from coast to coast, indeed in many places simply eradicated from the face of the earth, filled me with an abiding rage. It wasn't just the outright cruelty, but the arrogance and spiritual vacuity in this mindset of carnage—a carnage that seems to be such a peculiarly American trait. Perhaps most societies have it, but only in America is this cult of death elevated to a patriotic duty, like the carpet-bombing visited upon innocent Vietnamese peasants but a decade before. How can one excuse it? Not in my book. Yet Lopez, to his credit, remains ever the reserved narrator throughout his unstinting book, and checks his disgust at the door. More power to you, Barry. That ain't me, I realized as the earth crusader in me was rattled awake. Truthfully, I chafed reading the book: where's your outrage, dude? Since those days of bookish reflection, as I awoke to an innate sense of responsibility owed to our wild lands, my headlong plunge into the *dharma* was to find its deepest roots in an unapologetic Earth First! sort of crusading environmental activism. It all began in earnest in library school, that deep urge to fight like a cornered wild cat for the remnants of intact ecosystems that remain. And yet like Lopez, I have always had to "tame my hurricane mind, filled with esoteric information" to channel my anger into more socially acceptable channels, not just febrile pratfalls of mouthing off like an orotund crank. It's no small task, as I'm pretty cranky at the dirt-dumb world much of the time. From the time of reading this book, I have been an ardent and active environmentalist.

Missing New York City during my second and final year in library school, I decided to do a capstone internship at the Metropolitan Museum of Art in the Thomas J. Watson Library. Though small compared to many university libraries, this fine art library is one of the finest of its kind in America. I found the menial tasks assigned to me rather dull, but having the magical lanyard that all Met employees get in order to show their affiliation allowed me to explore the bowels of that vast mausoleum of forgotten artifacts like a cat burglar. I could even head to the museum's upper reaches where the grandees and money-grubbers worked in gilded cages. There is beneath those 2,000,000 square feet of marble and limestone a vast subterranean underground, think the Ark of the Covenant being carted off for storage to be lost forever in the last scene of the film *Raiders of the Lost Ark*. There were various Curatorial Departments, each with their adjoining conservation rooms, for every imaginable type of artwork, from marble statuary to chips on Chippendale furniture. But the true dark storage rooms, good grief! You want works by Kandinsky that have never been seen? Over here, by gum, there's a room full of them. Picasso? Ten enormous flat storage shelves just for his drawings, and fifteen racks of paintings, now apparently lost to the world of human appreciation. Armies of medieval armor march mutely, precisely nowhere in dark barracks; tribal dances worth of African masks gather dust in the next room; then more Renaissance paintings of the Virgin Mary and baby Jesus than in the rest of Christendom combined, on and on. Frankly, it's utterly obscene when wonderful art museums by the hundreds in small cities across the U.S. would die for a single Rothko or Calder mobile. The Met has so many of these unseen artifacts that they have whole card catalogs just to inventory them, the vast majority never once having been displayed to the public, ever. "Languishing" is the operative word.

    Almost as entertaining as these explorations into the cavernous basements and their hidden byways was delving deeply into my favorite wings of the Met with a leisure the harried day-tripper can never afford. I loved the Arts of Africa. Oceania and the Americas beckoned. I got lost for hours in Egyptian Art and the Temple of Dendorah. Musical Instruments were always a draw. Then up to visit all the permanent contemporary art collections and the half dozen great halls which at any given time had special shows.

One day, I was on the second-floor balcony of the Grand Hall through which, below, you enter the museum off 5th Avenue. Here on the balcony, they have Babylonian and ancient Middle Eastern artifacts in the Ancient and Near Eastern Art Hall. I came to one display case and saw a cylindrical seal covered in cuneiform writing. I suddenly began to feel very woozy. I swayed forward, concentrating to read the label, growing light-headed. I felt nauseous. Squinting, I saw that the card said the object was a 1800BCE "curse wheel" that would have been attached to a wooden handle and spun for efficacy. I suddenly felt a deeper flush. I loosened my tie. I began to sweat profusely, becoming increasingly unsteady and disoriented. I leaned over, placing my hands on my knees, gasping for breath. Then the world spun round, I lost my legs and promptly fainted.

When I came to, I don't know how much later, I found myself suddenly surrounded by a little crowd that had gathered around. A security guard and a kind elderly docent were fanning me with brochures. After ascertaining that I had simply fainted and wasn't having a heart attack, they helped me to my feet and asked if I wanted to go to the infirmary. No, I said, I'm fine. But I wasn't fine—it was damn frikkin' spooky, if you ask me. On three subsequent visits to check and re-check if by accident alone I had just happened to faint upon seeing a Sumerian curse cylinder, I can say that without a shadow of a doubt every visit caused a noticeable sweat, no exceptions. I will concede that my mind could have induced a fight-or-flight response in my heart beat, turning nascent fear into subconscious alarm. That's probably the half-truth of it. Could I have induced sweaty palms to assuage my embarrassment at fainting? Maybe, but I don't think so; that sounds too much like the performance of a drama queen. I like to think that isn't my forte. It was a conundrum worthy of Sherlock Holmes, surely, who said to Watson in *The Sign of the Four*: "Eliminate all other factors, and the one which remains must be the truth." Eliminate other factors? Let's see: In peak health. Had eaten lunch, so no reactive hypoglycemic low blood sugar lightheadedness. Have never otherwise fainted in my life. Did not have a single prior obsession with Sumerian artifacts or curses. Felt woozy *before* I read the damn label about the curse, in fact that's why I read the label. I will let the reader judge. It sure beats me. But pity the poor fool, 3600 years ago, at whom the curse was originally directed. May we meet on the other side of the grass someday, amigo, and compare notes. At the end of my internship in New York, I returned to Seattle for my graduation.

Lieberry-an It is Then as Books Burn from Within

My parents came to my MLS diploma ceremony in the UW football stadium in May of 1987, prompting a tour of all my old rock'n'roll haunts and, to pretend academic diligence, all my favorite carrels in the library. A few of my rockin' friends may even have combed their hair to be introduced. Several professors, who thought highly of me in the MLS program for reasons unbeknownst, shared that a brand-new career path had opened up in librarianship, especially in academic libraries, in the area of "preservation." The library world was aghast that their shelved tomes, which were supposed to last the millennium, were suddenly found to be burning from the inside out right there on those miles of library aisles. Tens of millions of books were under threat, so said the claim, of turning literally to ashen flakes. The fire, of course, was the acidic nature of western paper making over the past hundred and fifty years.

The earliest paper (not vellum) that we know came from China c100BCE. It spread to the Islamic world during the European

Middle Ages, back when Vikings still raided the coasts of the British Isles. Only during the era of high chivalry in Europe c1300 did paper finally find a home in kingdoms throughout Europe. All of this papermaking, on up to the early 19th century, was from pulp slurry made either of pH neutral hemp (slightly poorer paper) on up to those made of linen rags (the better paper). These long fibers are "soaked, cooked, rinsed and traditionally hand-beaten to form the paper pulp," then smoothed on screens to dry and, voila, paper. These two types of fiber do indeed make fine paper, carrying in their very durable sheets a singular characteristic: the fact that they are generally chemically neutral, providing a long-lasting level of balanced pH. In short, they endure. But with the rise of coal-fired industrialism in early 19th-century Europe, with powered steam, we moved into the era of industrial papermaking. The new techniques of mass production in those early years, combined with the rise of capitalism and its cost-cutting imperatives, took linen rags out of the production process as they were too costly. Instead, the factories used acidic pulped pinewood chips to make "modern" paper. More importantly, as uniformity of product output became paramount, the wood chip slurry was summarily bleached, first with a chlorine mixture, and later more cheaply with alkaline hydrogen peroxide, to create in bulk an even whiteness in the paper. These twin innovations were to lock into the bookmaking paper itself the fires within. Acidic paper inevitably turns brittle, becoming increasing brown and flaky over time. Newsprint is perhaps the worst example, as none of those "products" were intended to last. Sadly, millions of books published from about 1830 through to the Second World War were printed on vast rolls of acidic paper just a step up from newsprint.

 I was urged to apply to the Rare Book School at Columbia University, for their new "Master's Certificate in Preservation" program to save the History of Mankind (sic) from dissolution. To my surprise, but wide grin of delight, I got a scholarship to attend. So back to NYC it was. A good six weeks before start of fall semester at the great Ivy, there I was once again, almost penniless. As to where to live in Gotham, there seemed no one to ask for advice, and anyway I was doubtless too stubborn to take any. Somehow, I found temporary berths in crummy walk-up flats belonging to women I had known from my promoter days, brave souls who had moved east from Seattle like myself to the big bad city of Broadway and Times Square. They'd found digs down in Alphabet City, in the far reaches of the East Village around Tompkins Square, that even in 1988 was still full on anti-establishment with a permanent punk scowl. It was emphatically a neighborhood with an Attitude, capital A for Avenue A eastward to Avenue D, where you could actually still find free squats in more than a few wrecked tenements. While living in this vibrant, swaggering, in-your-face, anarchic part of town, first with my wonderful friend Kayla for a few weeks and then with lovely Robin for a few more up on 13th, Tompkins Square Park erupted into full-on riots that August when the NYPD arrived to evict the youthful homeless camped under the park's canopy of sheltering trees. The surrounding neighborhood, my own street included, joined in the street battles that ensued, as civil disobedience ran amok and skirmishes flared up for days. The stench of burning trashcans filled the streets with smoke, wafting through the smashed windows of fancy cars and looted gentrifying storefronts for blocks around. Alright! I was smack-dab back in good old crazy Gotham. Jeepers, Robin, where's Batman when you need him?

Another pal from my Bellingham days, Alan H. came to live in the city at this time, and we agreed to find a sublet together near the university. I hauled my modest boxes of stuff up from smoldering Alphabet City to south Harlem and a six-floor walk-up sublet on the corner of W 110th and Central Park West. This street corner is the northeastern terminus of that vast swathe of verdure and green space today known as Central Park, which was designed by Frederick Law Olmstead back in the carriage-and-top-hat days of the robber barons. At that time, squalid tenements sprawled with grimy clotheslines down on Hester Street and beyond. Most white-folk Manhattanites know this wonderful park from about the 97th Street Transverse south—you know, the big Onassis Reservoir with its two-way running track, The Meer, The Oval, funky Naumberg Bandshell, Sheep Meadow, and so on. The north end, not so much. But that is where Manhattan's wildlife comes to roost, stopping to find brief migratory respite. I have seen great egrets (*Ardea alba*), in flocks of several hundreds, resting up near the North Woods and the Blockhouse. In addition to egrets, I've seen on my many walks through the park both mute and tundra swans (*Cygnus o.* and *c.*), flocking brant geese (*Branta bernicla*), northern pintails (*Anas acuta*), blue-winged teals (*A. discors*), canvasback (*Aythya valisineria*), glossy ibis (*Plegadis falcinellus*), and dozens of other wading birds. Flocks of migrating birds came through all that fall. I even saw a short-eared owl (*Asio flammeus*) once in a little pine tree. Raccoons, possums, and coyotes seemed to thrive there, as confirmed by the city park service. Walking through the park at dusk, I confirmed these sightings when ethereal shapes became familiar ghost animals filling the evening with copper-hued mystery. This is where Dominican families and Black folk down from Harlem come to picnic and stroll on weekends.

Two things made our apartment uptown less than ideal. One was the six floors you had to stagger up, lugging groceries and stuff. The other was the crack addicts, who were endemic during the Dinkins mayoral years, and could be found pretty much everywhere north of 96th and below 14th around Greenwich Village. Walking to school and back, almost every day, I literally stepped over crackheads conked out on the pavement. It was a proverbial stepping over the dead, as it happened; so much for my Buddhistic vows of kindness. I just turned away, stepping over these supine bodies as if they were nothing more than tossed cigarette butts on their stoops.

The Columbia library school occupied the top floor of the Butler Library, Columbia's main book repository. The dean of the library school at the time was Robert Wedgeworth, Ph.D. The professors were uniformly knowledgeable, especially Terry Bellinger, the Rare Book program director, and Paul Banks, my mentor on the Preservation side. The preservation program was wonderful in some respects and, as with all things, less so in others. I particularly loved the hands-on classes on book making and mending, with all their lovely tools, the smell of glue, and learning the toolcraft. On the other hand, identifying which decade during the reign of HRH Queen Victoria certain gold embossing or marbled endpapers date from, nah, who cared? I mean, for heaven's sake, just open the goddamn book and find the MDCCCXCVII date on the obverse of the title page and there you go. We are memorizing this stuff, why? Alas, it was not an attitude that endeared me to either the preservation zealots or the antiquarian deacons who taught at Columbia's Rare Book School with missionary zeal. An Ivy League university education demanded the highest cram of knowledge that one can possibly stuff into one ear and not have it come out the other. If you're a bit full of yourself already, the laws of physics apply.

My professors, it's fair to say, were almost all wonderful people, especially one favorite who worked for my decanal uncle at UConn. Her name was Jan Merrill Oldham, a true preservation pioneer. When it came to the crusade to "save the history of the world in books" from the certain fire from within, she like the rest took it as a humorless fight to the end. Even turning down the smallest page corner of a book brought gasps of approbation. Time has shown that much of the hype (which we all admittedly bought into at the time) was largely overblown. Paper was certainly acidic, and it does get more brittle over time, but the world's collections of old and dusty books still sit on library shelves the world over. Their internal fires may still cook the paper, but so slowly that most "old books" are still perfectly usable.

Largely to augment my scholarship at Columbia, you know for pocket money and rent, I took a job at the Grolier Club as a lowly shelver and sorter, working up to modest cataloging by the time of my departure. Here's how the club describes itself on its website: "Founded in 1884, the Grolier Club is America's oldest and largest society for bibliophiles and enthusiasts in the graphic arts. Named for Jean Grolier (1489 or 90-1565), the Renaissance collector renowned for sharing his library with friends, the Club's objective is to promote the study, collecting, and appreciation of books and works on paper." Precisely, even as this description sidesteps just how gloriously stuffy the place is. Only the antiquarian crème de la crème ever gets in. The Club, with its magnificent library, its several reading rooms (one with a cocktail bar with bottles of Scotch and bourbon for members), and its exhibition spaces, is housed in a charming old row house at 47 East 60th Street, between Park and Madison in the city's Silk Stocking District. There are at least four public floors (if memory serves, or maybe three?), with the building manager and housekeeper's digs above. It is arguably the finest library of books on books in the world. The director at the time was Robert Nikirk, a charming man and ardent bibliophile, whom I was able to persuade to hire my roommate Alan as a secondary scrivener. I think we both worked twenty-hour weeks. It was such a trip to have free access to the place, and dive headlong into tasks of arrangement and pre-cataloging amid a wonderland of all sorts of arcana and bookish stuff. In all, it is a bibliophile's paradise

I also got a job cataloging "the world's finest collection of Graham Greene first editions," as the owner of this personal library claimed. He even had a little stack of the author's manuscripts, collected by a Wall Street banker known for his conservative fundraiser aplomb, as I saw from poking through his papers. I spent months sitting at a cramped computer in the owner's opulent apartment, cataloging the books. As an aside, let me say that my favorite book of Greene's is a little-known oddball, *Journey Without Maps* (Heinman, 1936), describing his 350-mile 1935 trek across Liberia on foot and by camel, horse, car, and lorry flatbed. He relied solely on local porters to guide him through the trackless desert lands. Greene travelled with his cousin Barbara Greene, who produced her own travelogue, *Land Benighted* (1938). I make this aside because British travel writer, critic, and novelist Jonathan Raban has said about Ms. Greene's account (as opposed to Mr. Graham's): "She contradicts Greene's memoir on almost every point... neither narrator agrees with the other as to anything at all, where they were, who they saw, what they met, the condition of his illness, whatever. There is just no consonance between these two accounts."[34]

In writing this memoir, I have made an honest effort to contact family, friends, and acquaintances to ask for jogs of foggy memory or for their take on this or that escapade. Putting aside those who didn't or wouldn't respond, I find in review that two remembrances rarely seem to line up particularly well. Some recollections are polar opposites, others circle separate solar systems altogether. Some even defy the laws of physics; I mean, how could I have been in two different places at the same time? The past, it would therefore seem, mirrors the experiences of the protagonists in Kurosawa's film, *Rashomon* (1962), in which the four key characters each hold some strand of truth in their separate recesses of mind, telling four distinct and varying stories of "what happened" to the investigating officials. None believe they are lying, yet all are steeped in some sort of self-deception. Obviously, the same drama of dueling recollections plays out in this Underground tome. But to be on the safe side, if I say I took Princess Diana to bed on a dare, or jelly-brained aliens flew me to Pluto, I would caution skepticism.

---

34. Michael Shapiro, *A Sense of Place: Great Travel Writers Talk about Their Craft, Lives, and Inspiration*, (San Francisco: Travelers' Tales, 2004), p.55.

Tally-Ho! Getting a Real Job

When I got my preservation certificate from Columbia, I applied for, and got, an Andrew W. Mellon Preservation Internship at the New York Public Library (NYPL), the big one with the heraldic lions on 5th Avenue and 42nd Street. The Mellon Foundation had given money to this vaunted program to pay for the internship salaries of five or so preservation graduates a year, to be distributed among a handful of major academic research libraries with preservation programs up and running. As one of the largest libraries in the world, NYPL already had a robust preservation program long before the "fires within" concerns surfaced in the early 1980s. Of all the actual libraries I've worked in, NYPL (known colloquially to employees as "nipple") ranks first. There's really no institution like it anywhere. There are three magnificent research libraries today: the main one on 42nd, (with its sister buildings, both on 5th, the Schwarzman and the Science & Business Library—SIBL), the second one for performing arts at Lincoln Center, and finally the Schomberg Center for Research in Black Culture up in Harlem. The system also has dozens of truly worthy non-academic public libraries of the "regular" sort all over Manhattan, serving the general population.

It was as an intern at NYPL working under the director for preservation, John Baker, that I came to realize just how woefully unprepared for a "real" job I was, irrespective of my native intelligence or burgeoning sense of professional self-worth. Up to this point in my life, I had lived and worked variously as a hermit, an Alaska bar maven, a deck hand on fishing boats, a waiter here and there, a cook or dishwasher in various dives, a cannery worker, a plumber's assistant, a house painter, a porno-palace projectionist (yes, I'll get to that hiatus in a minute), and as the ever popular, if dubious, top resume stuffer: Punk Rock Promoter (whatever that actually is). Throw in my tennis court gig in DC, or mining for iron ore in the arctic, and even driving a cab in Seattle for a while, and not one position would you ever put forward to indicate that you deserved serious consideration, still less employ, at a job the workaday world might actually consider a career move. All of these haphazard jobs can be accomplished with a sort of elbow-in-the-ribs bonhomie, follow the chop-chop-chop routine, where just showing up for work even if you look like a fashion disaster, are all just fine as long as you do the drudgery assigned and don't screw up. Employment at the main research establishment of the New York Public Library, however, did not particularly cotton to these sorts of rakish survival skills of past employ. The imperious twin visages of the two stone lions out front more readily captures the sort of quiet hauteur of the place. So, from day one it was a steep learning curve for me.

I moved from uptown to a loft on 6th Avenue and 26th Street above a redolent pizza parlor. They were great digs and, as a sublet, had manageable rent despite inducing a 24/7 yearning for a slice. At this time, I did take to wearing tweed sports coats and a silk bow tie to work each day—partly as a mental tick to bend my wild ways into a more decorous and appropriate haberdashery. It was as much an act of rebellion as anything, to cast aside my former predilections for hipster attire and conform now with dweebdom apparel. But a fancy suit doth not make the man. Once it happened that we were invited to a meeting with legendary publisher of the *New York Times*, Arthur Ochs Sulzberger Sr., at his palatial suite at the NYT's building on 229 W. 43rd. We were to discuss a contract between the newspaper and NYPL to microfilm every edition of the paper as it came out each day, sometimes as many as four separate editions in a heavy news cycle, each with different headlines and other variations. My boss, John Baker, his assistant, and I walked over to the *Times* tower, took the elevator up, and were ushered into the grand board room by elegantly clad minions. Everything seemed so plush, not the roil of a great newspaper that I had expected. I'm not sure exactly what that may have been, but at least vast rooms of busy reporters tapping out stories on typewriters, pencils behind a hundred ears. But then again, we were in the publisher's suite, at the top of the heap. This provides an example of my utter ineptitude in office etiquette in those early days of my professional maturation.

Left on our own, we three librarians briefly wandered round the storied room, looking at dozens of Pulitzer Prize-winning framed photographs, when in walks Sulzberger Sr.'s assistant, announcing that the great man is but a step behind. In my wanderings about the room, I had ended up at the first seat to the right of the head of the table and without a thought I sat down in this "preferred in pecking order" swivel chair—not a care in the world, look at me, meeting the fabled publisher! This of course left my boss, Mr. Baker, to find a seat further down the table in the cheap seats. In walked grand NY patrician A.O. Sulzberger Sr.; we all rose, and since I was in the preferred seat, he just assumed I was preservation director John Baker. I had to stammer awkwardly that I was just a fly-on-the-wall intern and turned to John, the actual director. Well, duh, any employee with an ounce of sense offers the top seat to their boss. I was later told that Baker was affronted by this thoughtless indiscretion which, coupled with other mildly unprofessional infractions, culminated by the time of my departure in the blunt fact that he thought me a bit of an arrogant twat. Perhaps rightly so, though it was never arrogance, I can assure you. Rather it was a sort of brash cluelessness, which may amount to the same thing. It doesn't feel like it though, because arrogance demands you take yourself seriously and in truth I rarely do. Arrogance, quote, is "an attitude of superiority manifested in an overbearing manner or in presumptuous claims or assumptions." I never presumptuously assumed the good seat was mine, it just happened to be the one nearest.

Alas, from that day forth at NYPL, John Baker and I had a bit of a frosty relationship, to the extent that word of my impudence got out into the small world of library preservation. I never got a job in this field of our profession; despite my Columbia pedigree and three "polite" interviews at major research libraries, it all came to naught. But it is with such faux pas as these, surely, that you learn your place in the everyday world of office etiquette.

As my time as a Mellon intern drew to a close, and as interview after interview for positions as a preservation officer went nowhere, I began to panic. What now? Enter the very nice woman who ran the Reference Department up in the grand rotunda outside the famous high-ceilinged grand Rose reading room. This perspicacious supervisor mentioned casually she was short a reference librarian; might I be interested in applying? With few other prospects, I said "Sure!" Unlike decent John Baker, who was nevertheless fastidious and somewhat aloof, this woman was a lovely charmer, with an easy manner and a curious mind. I quite fancied her, but being the consummate professional, she was quick to say in the weeks ahead, in that sweet way of hers, that she never dated her employees. Chalk up another tip of office etiquette. And so, by hook and by crook, I became a reference librarian at one of the Greatest Libraries on Earth.

At the desk one day, a thoroughly unpleasant patron came up like a swaggert elbowing his way to the front of the bar for a whiskey. Who of all people stood before me but Norman Mailer, arriving like a rumpled satchel, hair uncombed, gruffly asking me what the hell the library had on some *obscurum* on American intelligence agencies? He was impatient and rude, perhaps expecting me to pull this datum rabbit out of a hat right there and he'd be off. Ever self-obsessed, uni-focused, crotchety, and insistent, I could have been a talking robot for all he seemed to care. He peppered me with questions about this, then that, and then the other, all related to his quest. When I finally unearthed several points of data that proved useful, he looked up as if surprised that I, a human being after all, even existed in the flesh, and drawled in his gruff New Jersey-ese: "Damn I love this place. You guys are great. Thanks." He vanished from whence he came like a golum. I guess he was doing research for *Harlot's Ghost* (Random House, 1991).

Another time, a street prostitute (I guessed by attire a practitioner of the oldest profession, or else an excellent drag queen), teeter-tottered in on seven-inch platform boots, hot pants to here, maybe a brazen wig teased blonde as Carmen's ripe banana on top, boobs out to there, white fake fur ruff around half jacket, fingernail attachments as long as scimitars, the works, came up and in a Minnie Mouse voice, asked me: "Hi there, mister. Got anything I could read on Aphro-die-tee?" Ah, the goddess in Olympus must have perked up at this fine utterance, awakened from her many centuries of slumber by a Queens borough accent. "Yes ma'am! Lots on Aphrodite!" The lass just marveled, "Lookit all these books!" She blew me a kiss upon her satisfied departure. I knew perfectly well our Library Code of Ethics demands our vigilant protection of the transactions between patron and reference staff, but allow me this thrice to bend the rules. We're talking thirty years ago and counting.

For my next highlight, some weeks later, of all wonderful accomplished women, in came author Barbara Tuchman, one of my favorite historical authors. How I love her work; a cracking good read, as they say. In her matter-of-fact manner she came quietly to the desk with no hesitation, as if she knew the ropes. My, oh my, what a difference between her humanity and Mailer's grumpy disdain. I recognized her because I had read most of her books by that time and had followed her changing appearance over the years from book jacket photos, PBS interviews, and just as a general news junkie. She seemed so very frail, and complained straight off that our reference phone seemed always to be busy, so she had come round in person, all the way from Connecticut by train, sounding miffed by the inconvenience. With that complaint behind her, she delved into her research conundrum with great detail and eloquence, engaging me as an equal, trusting my intelligence. I don't recall today what it was she wanted exactly, but for the forty minutes we spent together, I vividly recall it as an engaging, even intimate, dare I say magical encounter. Honestly,

I don't believe that's too strong a word. She treated me like a fellow being of intelligence on an equal quest for hidden knowledge, asked questions about where I was from, and was politely talkative, curious, and engaged. I was absolutely broken-hearted when, seven months later, I read in the *New York Times* that she had died.

We had a busy phone line in reference as Tuchman's experience testified; generally, only one dedicated librarian manned the old rotary telephone at a time. One day when I was on phone reference, a very nice chap began to ask a single, pointed, very obscure question related to an even more obscure 20th-century British author named John Hodgkins. Apparently, he had written a book titled *Proper Nouns*, which had been published in the UK in an edition of only one hundred copies. My phone caller's research concerned one single missing datum, to be found only in the pages of that singular edition. My interlocutor was stumped as to how he might find a copy. This was all pre-Google of course, even pre-online catalogs of any inter-connected robustness. I managed in some reference work or other (probably the National Union Catalog, amid its 754 volumes), to track down the mysterious author and locate a copy of the exact edition needed, held at the Wilson Library of the University of Minnesota, the only library in the US to have that very edition, apparently. So pleased was my interrogator on the phone, that he said his name was James Lipton and he was working on a new edition of his famous book, *An Exaltation of Larks*. I was stunned, for when the book first came out in 1968, it was for a time one of my father's favorite books. He'd even read aloud from it to us kids at the dinner table, the whole family giggling at all those "aggregate nouns." Lipton's work does indeed list all those peculiar names for groups of things of which most of us know only a few, such as, well, an exaltation of larks, a pride of lions, a troop of whores, a murder of crows, and so on. There are several thousand entries now and most will delight any reader. No disrespect, but it's a great book for the loo. I, too, shared my father's delight in Lipton's book. Since I had been so helpful, he promised me over the phone that in the introduction to the next edition, he would mention my great assistance. Sure enough, when his book came out, a copy duly arrived with a kind inscription scrawled across a blank opening page. This is the third edition,[35] and on page 33 my name is in lights, bracketed in gratitude by Mr. Lipton himself.

Lest people be fooled by this, reference work, while noble in theory, can be dull as nails in practice. We helpful librarians might stand there for an hour as the riff-raff of the world wanders by, with not a one in need of assistance, still less acknowledging us. Then someone at last comes up! And—wants to know the location of the restroom. The joy, nevertheless, is that humankind really does need assistance finding their way through the world's thicket of information overload, meaning for the tens of thousands of reference interviews we actually do in the course of a year, many can be a delightful challenge in the hunt for that right citation or exact article spot on topic. Our successful bibliographic dig, in turn, more often than not delights our patrons, so the work can be a joy in return. The whole purpose of our noble profession comes into focus at these times. I can no longer count the number of distinguished people, of all professions and races, regardless of their ethnic backgrounds, young and old, who say straight up that their local library put them on the path to success. I can think of no other profession whose practitioners so freely serve the public every day and ask for nothing in return. It's one of the last bastions of civic service in its purest essence in this mad world, providing a welcoming space open to all. That's worth its weight in gold. "Whatever the cost of our libraries, the price is cheap compared to that of an ignorant nation," said Walter Cronkite. Fifty million Trump voters who form the vanguard in the cult of

---

35. James Lipton, *An Exaltation of Larks: The Ultimate Edition*, (New York: Viking, 1991).

ignorance might well heed these words. Sadly, in the hinterlands, libraries close all the time for lack of support.

I moved nine times in my two and a half years in NYC. Jeez, Louise. Always pinching a penny drove me to find short-term sublets at low rents. From south Harlem, to Brooklyn's Carol Gardens, to lofts in Soho, south to Leonard St., back over the Williamsburg Bridge to the borderline between Queens and Brooklyn, and in rough-hewn Williamsburg itself with its gauntlet of hawking prostitutes along the underpass at Roebling. Man, I been everywhere. I even occupied a magnificent penthouse, my last digs in NYC in fact, on Bleecker Street—and for free, hallelujah—barely one hundred yards from CBGB, across the street on Bowery. Truth be told, as the dweeb librarian I'd morphed into, from black swan to aspiring duckling, I don't think I ever visited the old haunt while staying there. Sitting in the penthouse roof garden in the evening, sipping a Manhattan, holy moley, the racket! No wonder I'm deaf.

One evening I got a call from an old friend from my Seattle days. She said she'd just arrived in town, and might she crash at Sally's, the penthouse's absent owner and an old friend. I said sure, but the attractive friend of yore I held in my mind had been transformed into a Raggedy Ann, clearly strung out on drugs and disheveled to the point of being unrecognizable. No fool, I didn't beat around the bush and laid down the rule: no addicting drugs at Sally's, not while I was the one responsible to keep it in beautiful shape. Sure, she said. Uh-huh. Within forty-eight hours, little things of Sally's and a few of mine had gone missing. After a week of this, and burnt tinfoil everywhere, I chucked the friend out. I mention this to say that from this time on into the 1990s, word would trickle my way occasionally that so-and-so had died of an overdose, or from AIDS. I don't know how many wonderful acquaintances and friends I lost to those twin scourges. Certainly, many friends from the riotous gay leather bar scenes I had experienced in Seattle dropped one after the other to AIDS, felled by an assassin in the guise of the slightest touch of pneumonia or flu. On the drug side, even well-known rock musicians like Joy Division's Ian Curtis, the Germs' Darby Crash, Sid Vicious, Kurt Cobain, and Chris Cornell of Soundgarden, all of whom I'd known briefly or worked on their shows, died from their messed-up lives, needles on the floor, or from suicide—and a dozen good friends besides. A lucky few, like my dear friend Jim, who co-managed the Showbox and owned Time Traveler Comics in Seattle, somehow managed to claw their way back from full-on heroin addiction to what passes for normalcy. For me, some prophylactic in my psychic profile, or perhaps in my physiology, has emphatically stopped cold all cravings for this sort of "euphoric" high, and even more so its lifestyle.

The great grimy thoroughfare of 42nd Street back in the late eighties had little to recommend it, least of all the endless rows of porn palaces and sex shops. I suppose for drunken tourists from Omaha it may have been a titillating experience, but for New Yorkers it was just one long seedy eyesore. 42nd Street did provide me with two wonderful memories, nonetheless. The first was Mort's Barbershop, situated on the main concourse of the great subway station at Times Square and 42nd. There were all kinds of small shops on the concourse, magazine and candy stands mostly, but also a flower shop, a shoe repair place, another that sold and fixed watches, but always set apart was Mort's. I have never been particularly fastidious about my appearance, exemplified by the fact that I have never visited a "hair stylist" in my life. I happen to like my head as is; it needs no further "style." Other than costing quintuple the price, how does a stylist differ from just a regular barber? Truth be told, for twenty-five years of my life, I cut my own hair with shears, leading to me as often as not skulking out with hat on head to cover the disaster. Ah, but Mort's! I probably walked by his shop a half dozen times, a harried commuter among myriad others, rushing somewhere, when one day his fine sign finally caught my eye. It was nothing fancy: "Haircuts $4. Buck a side. Real deal!" Buck a side! Oh! How one might ascend into heaven from the grimy innards of the Times Square concourse escapes me, but that sign got me halfway there with shoes still on the ground. Yes, my kind of barber. So what can an honest sinner do but enter said establishment with a fiver in hand, the extra buck being the tip of course.

I have no doubt Mort knew that a thousand and one schmiels traipsed by every day through the labyrinthine miasma of that purgatorial station, each mope thinking "hmmm, maybe my mop needs a buzz," and in they go. So in goes me, this tall Episcopalian with a bow tie, 100% goy. When Mort heard I was a librarian at the big heap down the street, oh, did he open up. Might they be interested in his father's papers, may he suffer no more! He survived Buchenwald, this I know, sez he. Would I give him a tour? Sure, I said, and I did. So, sez he, my niece Deborah, never Debbie, she don't like Debbie, no, it's Deborah, she just finished City College, see, no idea what to do, so my sister sez to me, what we gonna do about Deborah? Oi vey, just a party girl she is. She sez someone sez to her, be a librarian! Maybe she go to library school up there at Columbia? You think? Sure, sez I, have her give me a call; I handed him my card. The odd thing about Mort being a barber, though, was that the man was mostly bald by the time I came into his life, with just a hint of tufts over the ears. "God—He cuts my hair!" was his conceit. I always came by at Hanukkah and gave Mort a big tip as a gift. Up until I left the city for upstate two years later, four bucks a side it was. Ah, Mort. I am sure he's dead now, but if there is a place in heaven for Jews like you, let me buy the Shabbat candles.

So, what does the term "Porn Run" conjure in your mind? Naughty business, I am sure. But let me assure you, chastity was our shield. The Porn Run was an annual event at NYPL, when the library would fork over something like $200 to four enterprising reference librarians, me always first in line to volunteer, to go buy a heaping printed pile of the most disgusting smut imaginable from the sex shops up and down 42nd. No, seriously. Higher ups deemed it essential that Manhattan's greatest research library must also include in its collections all the lowlife smut that the city that never sleeps had to offer. It made sense—hell, 42nd Street was thronged a good parson's mile with the stuff. So it came to pass that one of us would be appointed "treasurer," the keeper of the wad of cash, and off we went, lady librarians welcome, to buy heaps of porn. The instructions were explicit. We couldn't just buy thumbed mags of buxom babes revealing their Edenic lack of runway fashion and lust for life. No, we must buy guy on guy, guy and guy on girl, girl on girl, black girls on white guy, black/white guys on Asian guy, and so on, though the Rolodex. In short, we must acquire a research-worthy sampling of the goods. My first time out, cross my heart, it was my inaugural run into one of these, ahem, establishments. How depressing it was to realize that shop after shop after shop had miles of racks of this sordid stuff. But, cataloging librarians, do take note—the bin labels were a fine metadata record of a sort: Gays, Fatties, Thinnies, Bondage, Anal, Blondes, Blacks, Brunettes, Lesbians, Asians, Oral, Teens, Cunnilingus, Blow Jobs, Hags on Home Boys, Black&White, and even publications of full-throttle boffing in costumes like (not fooling, sorry Walt, cover your eyes) Mickey and Minnie like you've never seen them before. Who knew pleasure had so many forbidden flavors?

The first time I went we forgot to take along tote bags, so as we sampled the establishments for that 42nd mile, each one of us, like cartoon dishwashers tottering with slippery piles of plates, had to lug around our growing stacks of porn that, being slick covered, shot out from under our arms like wet soap bars. We then had to pick up the icky stuff from the icky sidewalk, amid sidelong glances from sniffy passersby. Ah, but the research value of such true-to-life erotica! As to acquiring a fair sample, we gave it our best shot, pardon the pun. Sadly, it all went straight to the processing guillotine when we returned: spines cut, contents microfilmed, and originals tossed in the trash. Agree with me please on this point: research value notwithstanding, it's not quite the same thing as letting your fingers doing the walking, with the excitement of sheer serendipity, through Ahmed's Sexpot Emporium, when instead you have to ask a librarian at the desk for the microfilm reel of *Bouncing Bung Boys* v. 2, then sneak off to huddle under the hood of a mechanical micro-reader with some hope of capturing the zeitgeist.

All of this, of course, puts me in mind of my own brush with porno palaces. I know you've been waiting for this penny to drop. There was a spell of about three or four months back in my Seattle days when Ian Copeland, the grand national promoter of hotshot New Wave acts, must have been on hiatus. Half of the punk promoters in town, Modern Productions included, were broke and just scraping by with hackneyed local acts. But suddenly, our enterprising association of reprobates seemed to hear all at the same time that the porno palace on First Avenue just north of the Pike Street Market was under new management and looking for projectionists. The next day there we were, sober as ten empty beer cans on the wall. Let me say that these are peculiar establishments of a certain kind, catering to "gentlemen" (mostly) of a certain kind, providing as it were entertainment of a certain kind, to do what in the dark bowels of these establishments I really don't want to know. But if you have four bucks, you're in—the management is not discerning. The job of porno palace projectionist only had three moving parts. One: sell tickets. Two: keep the two projectors and corresponding platens of 35mm film running constantly—one with the film being shown on Projector A, as the other platen on Projector B awaited the re-coiled celluloid so that when A was done, you flipped over the celluloid with a sort of Rube Goldberg re-spool, ran it over to the B platen which would then start rolling, and voila the endless reels of dreck barely had time to go limp. Maybe the lights would go on long enough for a quick trip to the men's room (there was no ladies' room) for the bladder-busted clientele. Well anyway that was how it was supposed to go, in theory. In practice, not so much. Then there was the small matter of the *third* duty of a porno projectionist: splice together the ratty, flickering, beaten-to-shit, often partly melted, well-thumbed reels whenever the sagging celluloid decided to give up the ghost for all the endless humping. Each reel seemed to have a thousand splices. Did guys take home clips? Depending on the night's offering, a torn spool could split three times in a six-hour shift. You'd have to shave at least two frames off each end to resplice the damn thing, so every one of these fine lessons in human anatomy had the feel of a jerky 1920s Buster Keaton film.

I was blessed in this employment with visitations from my lovely, wonderful, dear friend Frankie. She is dead now, alas, but she was arguably the most perfectly attired woman I have ever spent time with. She was in all things a whirl of immaculate fashion, mostly acquired at thrift stores, but all put together as if Anna Wintour herself tied the secondhand bows. Beautiful, intelligent, inquisitive, talented, Frankie was in all things an adventurous trooper in my day. She played bass guitar in several of Seattle's most storied alt-bands and became in her own right one of the northwest's great visual artists, eventually teaching canvas painting at Cornish College of the Arts. Why this magnificent human being came to visit me at the porno palace escapes me to this day. Yet many a night that I worked there, Frankie came by, elegantly attired in stylish retro, jumped over the ticket counter and climbed the little ladder up through the ceiling hole that led, like Jack and the Beanstalk, to my small projectionist's aerie. It was madness, for celluloid is so flammable, but in that hot little enclave she smoked like a chimney, a habit that eventually killed her.

There we would sit on low stools, discussing Kierkegaard, Kandinsky, and our favorite band at the time, Killing Joke, as all the while "Little Often Annie," "Tale of Two Titties," or "Malcolm's X's" scrolled through their dreary routine. One might readily assume, given the fare, that projectionists partook. Nope. From the projectionist's perch there was only one eight-by-eight-inch window to look through, which stood about chest high. This served exclusively to allow one to focus the projector properly, your head close to the projector knob irrespective of the grunting carryings on. But watch it? I have to say, the utter lack of imagination, B-quality camera work, dumb plots, spliced jumps every minute, absurd dialogue, tedious close-ups of stretched anatomy, and lack of any sign of humor or lick of intelligence at all (excellent titles notwithstanding), all proved in the end staggeringly disgusting and believe me, I'm no prude. I doubt on any given night there were more than fifteen customers, but that apparently paid the rent for both the owner and myself.

Two of these customers were regulars, but always got in for free. Let's call them Bubba and Jeff. Bubba and Jeff were the two flat-foot Seattle street cops assigned to the Farmer's Market District beat and, oh lucky sods, Porno Palace Numero Uno was smack in the middle of it. Hefty duo they were, too, with girths approaching barrels. In they'd waddle every night, cop accoutrements clanging from their ample girths, with the usual drill: "Uh, hi, we need to see if there's any of that, you know, perverted stuff going on." Perverted stuff, sure. In a porno palace? Since the gate counter had to match the gate cash, over the counter they had to huff like two grunting walruses. Plonk, they made it! Half an hour later, I was sure I knew who the pervs were. They seemed particularly fond of the meaty gems with handcuffs. That said, the only perv they actually ever arrested while hard at work watching "The Penetrator (I'll Come Again)," was some poor homeless guy who panhandled $4 to use the porn palace as his nightly boudoir, snoring up a storm behind the rear seats in the back row. Someone complained that his snores were so damn loud they were "ruining my experience." Hmm...OK. Actually, I'd have joined the homeless guy myself for a good nap, so bored was I with "Anus and Andy," if the thought of that floor hadn't been even more disgusting.

Flattered as I was that someone of Frankie's panache and caliber thought fit to visit me in my den of decadence, and recall it was to discuss Kierkegaard, the problem for me was that I would get easily distracted so deep was I in philosophical discourse with my siren muse. One time, the film coming through Projector A, that was showing the night's gymnastics, broke on its way to rewind on Platen B, such that after an hour of gab, Frankie said: "Is that supposed to be happening?" I turned. To my horror, about 1000 yards of celluloid lay in coiled gorgon heaps three feet deep on the floor. What a mess. You had to stop the presses at mid-stroke on the screen, turn on the house lights so the poor sods in the pit below weren't entirely thrown into stygian darkness, from which pit of Hades came muffled cries, shouts, hoots, boos, bellows of disenchantment, consternation, and SOS distress calls, arising as if from a ghoulish crypt in the enveloping gloom below. There was something just so dreadfully "ewwww-ick" when thinking about the front of the house, so I didn't even care when the poor clientele were $4 short on their bang for a splice. More than a few would storm out to the tiny foyer to complain. Oh, but then, like a Botticelli's blonde Venus upon a half shell, Frankie would descend the little aerie ladder to sooth the wrinkled trousers of the huffed, while up the ladder I frantically spliced the ends and re-spooled the damn footage. She was masterful, if that's the right word, for such a Magnificent Mistress of the Night. Catullus, Martial, and other fine Roman writers of smut would have been smitten, agreeing that *Lasciva est nobis pagina, vita proba.*

Another minor problem was getting the twist wrong. I mean, turning the film over to rewind it onto the second platen, so that all would be right side up when you ran it again on the other projector. It would sometimes happen that after the entire ceaseless three hours of "The Best Rears of Our Lives" followed by "Titty Titty Bang Bang" plus who knows what else, you'd be spooling the film to the other platen, but with the wrong twist—once in a blue moon, numbed by the boredom, you'd spool it wrong-side up. Then, as you sat back to enjoy another three uninterrupted hours reading Kierkegaard (OK, it was usually borrowed comics from Time Travelers Comics across the street), suddenly from the crypt below those same muffled cries, shouts, hoots, boos, bellows of disenchantment, consternation, and SOS distress calls would arise from the dead-like darkness. Dashing to the eight-by-eight hole, egads, there was "Rear Admiral" doing it *upside down*. To my mind, let it be said for posterity, this was a vast improvement to the usual. Hilarious, but alas funny to only one seer amidst the distraught horde: me, though surely worthy of some sort of Dada-Surrealist film experiment accolade.

Several years later, when I was visiting my parents in Connecticut, Frankie stopped by with the Blackouts, a band I'd managed for several years, all crammed in their tour van. Frankie and the boys stayed for the night; at the time, Frankie was dating the lead singer, Eric. Unbeknownst to me, Frankie and my mom stayed up half the night, drinking tea and talking art. Frankie and the band continued on their tour the next day. Once they'd left, my mother said, "Now there's the sort of nice young girl you might consider marrying one day!" She added, in sweet maternal words ruinous to the reputation of any hip alt-rock band trying to craft an aloof New Wave pose, "How nice and polite those boys were, too." She was apparently realizing with relief that not everyone in my rock world was Alice Cooper with a headless chicken or Megadeth. Frankie's gone now. I do so miss you, girl.

So, there you have a glimpse of my life in what Dylan Thomas might have described as my *Adventures in the Skin Trade* (1955), full of salubrious and salacious perversion, or as the Welshman himself wrote: "... might lure off his buttons with their dangerous, fringed violet eyes, under the bedclothes where all the company is grand and vile by a flick of the cinema eye." Close enough. Surely small potatoes by the horrific standards of today's #MeToo movement, yet just risqué enough never to appear on my resume. I've always wondered if anyone ever actually asked to see any of those microfilms of porn at NYPL. Why? They were dreadful in the original, but on a spool?

From Porno to Progressive Politics

New York City doesn't lack for liberals, but as with too many other American cities, then as now, it could use far more hard-core activists. While at NYPL, I volunteered after work two days a week at Fairness & Accuracy in Reporting (FAIR), a national media watchdog dot.org. They were only two years old when I came by to offer my services, and from their perspective, having a mole as it were at NYPL to do research was a major plus. FAIR's focus back then was mostly on calling out local city media, both print and TV, for bias, including any obfuscated reportage, outright blarney, hidden agendas, or conflicts of interest and attendant skullduggery between reporter and topic. The *Times*' neoliberal gloss often got our fiercest broadside. It was a great group to work with, and I even published a few pieces in their monthly magazine. One was on the shoddy treatment given by the *Times* on the destruction of waterfowl habitat out in Jamaica Bay due to runway extensions being planned for Kennedy Airport. Another concerned the bilge dumping of container ships along the Arthur Kill waterway that divides Staten Island from New Jersey. I was conversant on these topics since I'd also joined the city's Sierra Club sub-committees dealing with water issues around the docks, canals, and extensive shorelines out to city limits on Long Island Sound-Fire Island beachfronts and beyond. Often as not we'd take field trips to odd city locations to verify the damage being done. As usual, it was a depressing litany to see so much inadequate city oversight.

When the ACT-UP (AIDS Coalition to Unleash Power) Movement sprang to life in Manhattan in the late eighties, I was quick to join, especially in their protests on Wall Street in 1989. One successful demonstration blocked the Stock Exchange for several hours. I called in sick to NYPL and headed down. As one of the people who refused to "vacate the premises," I was arrested, quickly cuffed, hauled off in a paddy wagon with a dozen others, and taken to a holding pen at the city jail. I recall the woman sitting beside me in the police van as we trundled along: her face was oddly beautiful in an exotic way against the hard struts of the paddy wagon. She wore overalls, a grungy T-shirt, and heavy black boots, and she had her hair up and wore no makeup, Obviously, she was someone who had intended to get arrested since she'd dressed for it. She didn't seem inclined to talk, though she said curtly that her younger brother had AIDS, and since most of the others in the van didn't know each other, either, a cautious silence hung in the air. Within the hour I was booked and sent packing.

The next day, I was leafing through the *New York Times*, looking for coverage of the action, when I came to a full-page fashion spread and there, in a perfectly styled Dior advertisement, was none other than my co-conspirator on the Group W Bench—so alluringly attractive, down to the same mole on her cheek, I was taken aback. Same person? Seeing her photographed this way, it was a lesson in how I so often judge a person by their looks. In this case, I had a received bias that attractive models weren't likely to be the first to volunteer for a political action lest they break a nail. That's clearly bunkum, but this is how you grow into seeing your own prejudices, I suppose. New York City is a marvelous crucible this way. The majority of people travel by bus or subway and the city by default simply instills tolerance, teaches acceptance, and asks, nay, demands that you respect diversity. Anything short of getting along with others means that every day you're elbow-to-elbow with the discomfort of your own small-mindedness. We are obliged to be taught by these gifts of insight. It's a lifelong trial and error and we all do it.

I am not sure who at NYPL told me that a group of "progressive librarians" had started to meet to form a radical organization to champion essential first amendment, social justice, and labor issues related broadly to the profession of librarianship, but I was glad to know about it. On December 9, 1989, I showed up at a classroom at Empire State College (I believe) where Elaine

Harger, newly minted Columbia librarian herself, had her first job and served as host. About twenty librarians of varying persuasions showed up, but all held in common the belief that a radical perspective on the profession needed to have an independent organized outlet of expression. Moreover, it needed to not be beholden to the rules, strictures, or control of our national library association. These were the retrogressive Reagan years after all, with proxy CIA wars flaring everywhere.

That night was the group's second meeting and the main discussion topics were how such a collective might be organized, what sort of membership might it expect, and what name should the assembled chose for the radical organization they envisioned. That name would need to be one that would stand up boldly to the mushy, middle-of-the-road soft liberalism all too evident in libraries and librarians everywhere. Thus was born the Progressive Librarian's Guild (PLG). Out of that first meeting I attended, I was to make many lifelong friends, comrades in arms in the struggle to voice a radical social justice agenda within the profession, and especially within the American Library Association (ALA) itself. I was honored to attend those inaugural meetings where the name, mission, structure, membership, and intended actions the group might engage in were hammered out. They were heady times. I've been an ardent member of PLG ever since, served on the editorial board of its long-running, one-of-a-kind, journal *Progressive Librarian: A Journal for Critical Studies & Progressive Politics in Librarianship*, and served as a member-at-large on its steering committee on and off for the past thirty years.

In his seminal work, *Progressive Library Organizations: A World History* (MacFarland, 2015), Al Kagan, long-time African-American bibliographer and research librarian at Illinois University Library, gives a masterful history of PLG that is forty pages long (pp. 241-282). I need hardly recap all that this scrappy, hard-hitting, too often embattled, sometimes chaotic, always true to its radical roots organization did for the profession, for ALA, and the world sphere it struggled within. Al's book is a magnificent history of how groups of dedicated people, especially in libraries throughout the world, fought through the twentieth century into the twenty-first for social justice, equity, labor unions, and indeed for justice in most all progressive arenas. Al does this entire history, including PLG, fair dealing.[36] He describes the struggles we engaged in related to South Africa, Israel, disinvestments, boycotts, unions, war mongering, racism, censorship, even the seemingly headlong embrace by libraries of every new-fangled technology without a considered analysis of the precautionary principle. I will not recap what Kagan covers so well, but will only touch on those times through the years when the critical work done by PLG (and other progressive groups within librarianship), in turn, impacted my own life. Suffice it to say, no other organization has influenced me as much professionally, ethically, intellectually, and certainly politically as this guild of brilliant thinkers and activists. I can honestly say it was PLG more than any place of work that infused in me a passion for our wonderful profession. It gave me the critical thinking skills to see just what a noble calling I had chosen and that I could be proud of it. In the end I came to see how profoundly we librarians stand at the very heart of civic society and a functioning democracy in America. For that I am truly grateful.

Turtle Dreams and Roebling's Tomb

Chicago's independent Newberry Library prides itself on being one of the strongest collections on American Indians in the world. But in its quiet way, the collection of Native Americana at the New York Public Library is its rival. For lack of anyone else stepping up, within two months of joining the reference staff, I was assigned the duty of "Native American Bibliographer" whose tasks were

---

36. Though why Al put my mug in his book, p.250, escapes me. Many others have been far more often on the front lines than me.

varied but included buying all worthy monographs (books) on related topics. The historic collection of lexicons dating back to the sixteenth century, wherein Native words and phrases from all known tribes at the time were translated into corresponding Romance languages, is itself perhaps second to none. What was disheartening, though, was that this rich trove of materials seemed forever woefully underutilized. One patron group who did know about it were curators from the National Museum of the American Indian down in the grand old Beaux Arts Alexander Hamilton U.S. Custom House in southern Manhattan on Bowling Green. In 1989, it was the premiere museum for Native tribe collections in the United States. The Smithsonian's grand new National Museum of the American Indian on the Washington Mall hadn't yet been built. While the latter has all the "wow" factor of a specially designed cultural center amid the plethora in Washington, DC, the old location in the city on Bowling Green was by far my favorite.

It was my favorite because of the old school funk vibe of the place, fifty years past its former glory, the quirky nineteenth-century architecture of the repurposed custom's house, its lost location south of Wall Street, and the easy access to its curatorial staff. In short, it seemed cozy. As the appointed NYPL bibliographer, I would often get calls from their curators about some American Indian arcana or historic spelling of an artifact in a particular tribal language. To build better relationships, I went to visit and got to know the staff. What a marvelous bunch of people, so fearlessly advocating for and working hands-on with the artifacts related to the history of Native America. The customs house museum is today known as the George Gustav Heye Center that houses, as it did back in 1989, exhibitions, research, educational activities, and performing arts programs. The best gems in its collections went to the museum in DC on the mall.

Through this connection, I became particularly close with a Potawatomi clan mother named Sharon who was an assistant curator. The Potawatomi are from the Great Plains, originally from lands stretching from Canada in the north, south to the territories on the underbelly of the Great Lakes. They fall within the larger cultural designation of Algonquian Tribes, and called themselves *Neshnabé* or "original people"—and have strong historic ties to the Ojibwe and Odawa. Today the entire tribe numbers less than 2,500 individuals. My friend was of the *Mshike'* or Turtle Clan. With braided hair and a stout, strong figure, she stood about 5'3" with the most remarkably clear skin shining from an always-smiling round face. For reasons unknown but surely appreciated, Sharon took me under her wing, giving me in-depth tours of the conservation rooms and other warrens of the museum's inner bowels until it seemed I was a regular. At the time I got to know her, she was working on rehabilitating the ceremonial robe from a named warrior of the northern Cheyenne, dated from around 1870, thus pre-Little Big Horn. It was magnificent, made of scraped and softened deer and buffalo hide, with beautiful beadwork around the collar and wrists, and various medallion-like tin bells, cowries, animal claws, and even a little ornate silver teaspoon all dangling like medals from the chest, where slats of porcupine quills created a ceremonial bib of body armor. There were also fading star-shaped images painted in ochre-colored stains directly on the hide. I coveted it immediately for it conjured in its beauty a lost world I would never be part of—but I dared not ask if I could put it on.

One time Sharon took me to her little office to fetch some notes for me to take back to the library to see if we had information she was looking for. On the window sill of her office lay a brightly-colored silk scarf, upon which was placed a beautiful rattle made from a turtle shell. Beside it was a sage bundle and a few other beautiful artifacts, an altar of sorts where the wan sunlight slipped through the grimy window like a fading benediction. She said the turtle shell had come from an ornate box turtle (*Terrapene ornata ornata*), which are common in Wisconsin where she had gone to college. The favored shell, though, before the white man took their lands, was the northern map turtle (*Graptemys geographica*), those with the yellowiest fringe around the shell's edge being especially prized. With her permission, I picked up the rattle reverently, feeling a rush of good feeling resonate in me and the room as I gently gave it a shake. She said the handle was made from a river willow branch. That night I dreamt of an ornate box turtle.

The next time we met, I recounted my dream to her. She said perhaps I was destined to find my own turtle, who knew? I asked how the turtles were harvested. She replied that historically, the turtles of a variety of preferred species were caught along waterways through tribal lands, boiled in their shell, eaten with proper gratitude to the turtle spirit, then cleaned out and made into rattles. I recall thinking this couldn't have been much fun for the turtles roasted alive for the evening meal. Today most of these turtle species are protected, she said, so supplies for new ceremonial rattles were limited, especially for species not raised as pets. Besides, she added disdainfully, pet turtles were nothing more than spirit-broken, tamed and sold. That was her opinion: they had no wild magic in them and should never be used for ceremony. I asked if she knew of any place where I might find a wild-caught or found shell. She chuckled.

"Call upon the spirit of the turtle, Peter. If turtle wants you to have a shell, it will join you and your turtle." It was then she told me her clan name. From that day forth, on many treks into the wild, I secretly thought that maybe Turtle Spirit would look kindly on me. And for many years, Turtle Spirit was deaf to my entreaties. You see, from that day on I fancied making a rattle myself. Unhurried by my impatience as turtles doubtless should be, Turtle Spirit took many years to find me.

When I was next out in Seattle, I drove up to a funky, old-school, enormous leather emporium in Everson WA, called Akers Pelts and Leather, that per its name sold every type of leather and pelt under the sun, in bulk. I had with me a trace paper outline of the skins needed to make a ceremonial robe, that had been given to me by Sharon. By reputation, Akers made the finest Indian handheld drums in the country. I have one with the richest sound, whose skin has a dancing figure on it made entirely of natural sinew. With help from a knowledgeable clerk, I bought two beautiful soft Columbian white-tailed deer (*Odocoileus virginianus leucurus*) tanned hides, and a strip of mountain goat (*Oreamnos americanus*) for the shoulders. Over a number of years and three visits back to see Sharon, she walked me through every step of the creative process of robe-making: correct sinew thread, type of stitch, how to cut the fringe so it all would hang properly when worn. She even let me borrow her little bead loom. This robe hangs behind me in my office as I type this. Even down to the cowries, all the ornamental things that hang from it, each and every one has a personal connection and meaning for me. On a copper disk at its sternum, the claw of my spirit animal is attached, a Mount Wilson squirrel (*S. g. anthonyi*), a sub-species of the California western silver-gray squirrel (*Sciurus griseus*). When visiting the Mount Wilson Astronomical Observatory one time, as an early snowfall lay deep amid the conifers, I found the poor little guy dead by the side of the road. I took him home for proper burial, snipping his forepaw for the robe. When I go, I'd love to be cremated on a pyre wearing this lovely robe, but that won't happen. Death in America is a vast corporate enterprise that not a living person can escape with any hope of returning their constituent molecules back into the ecosystem without first paying through the nose for the privilege.

 I am sure that now, to the great relief of vegans everywhere, half of Akers' inventory would be banned under international treaty. Their original ramshackle warehouse out on a back road is gone now. In place of the funky old warehouse of animal pelts to the rafters, a production line of "Indian drums" is being made at a mail order outfit named Akers Drums. They are still probably the best handmade drums in the country and still in Everson, but none of the warehouse funky feel remains. In America, in the age of Amazon, this is called progress as we drift into the blender of bland homogeneity.

Speaking of music, the following vignette is for my dad, now dead, who was so tickled by it. I never met Paul Simon in New York, but I did meet his yoga teacher at a party somewhere. I found this gentleman inordinately self-whelmed, a polite way of saying he was full of himself, quick to tell anybody within earshot he was the yoga teacher to the rich and famous. Somehow, we were thrown together at that shindig, chatting about this and that, when he mentioned that he worked with Paul Simon who was furiously writing songs for a new album with an Afro-Brazilian-samba-beat twist. I mentioned, with nothing more in mind than small talk, that I had about fifteen old 1950s EPs and LPs from Brazil, with amazing music you'd never find in any record store in New York. I told him my dad had picked them up on his travels through South America. Suddenly Mr. Yoga Pants, till then looking bored, his wandering attention eyeing all the comely women at the party, snapped back to me. Hey, he said, maybe I'd be willing to lend those EPs to Paul; he'd guarantee their safe return. I didn't have a turntable at the time so had little to lose, and I felt certain Mr. Yoga Pants was sincere. We exchanged phone numbers, and a week later we met at a nearby bar and I handed over a bag of really cool old Brazilian LPs for "Paul" (was I now also on first name terms?) via Mr. Yoga Pants. This was the same stack of wonderful records that had belonged to my father, who had passed them on to me, the rock promoter, hence to the rock star. I appended a little note "to Paul" saying I wanted the stack back, happy listening.

Truthfully, I forgot all about Mr. Yoga Pants, Paul Simon, and the records until one day a few months later when I got a call at the library reference desk (yoga pants had since lost my number), and was told that Paul had finished listening—would I mind coming 'round and picking up the stack? The same bag thus circled through time and space, 'round Paul's record needle, back to me. Simon had dashed off a kind note, singling out half a dozen songs he found particularly interesting for their complex rhythms. Later in 1990, *Rhythm of the Saints* came out, one of my favorite albums of Simon's, though it was not at first a commercial success. Who knows, maybe some riffs were inspired by Dad's records, though none sounded quite similar to my musical ear. I gave my father the note as a sort of thank you for passing the records on to me. Dad didn't really have a clue who Paul Simon was. It was simply that something he'd picked up (as with all the quirky, offbeat, folk artifacts he hauled home like lost treasure over the years) had proved useful to someone who was apparently famous at my assurance. Scrap of paper in hand, Dad launched into a story of how he'd found the records in a San Paulo cantina bin.

Then came the night of the sad solitary cricket atop Roebling's massif. Let me explain. How odd it was that my girlfriend at the time, Kate (who was a good friend of SAMO's back in the day), and I should find ourselves of a sudden in the dark defile of Pearl Street in the rain. We'd had a big row and were walking off our separate hurts toward the weighted cable curves and monolithic towers of the iconic bridge at the southern tip of Gotham. In the distance the Broadway local clattered over the black East River. To the north, and across the river to the south, we saw Walt Whitman's city glimmering like a jewel box, drawing us on in silence toward the dark mirror of the river at night. In halting steps, we made our way to Park Row, thence to the footpath where few were walking that night, in the slanting mist, over the deserted bridge.

The great towers loomed above us, ringed by a cast of scaffolding which workers had erected to paint the giant suspension cables, as big around as Leviathan. Turning up my collar, I reached out with conciliation and kindly put my arm around Kate's shoulder. The reconciled smiles we shared in that moment melted the awkward acrimony. "Come!" she said jumping the wire fence the workmen had erected, and I nimbly jumped as well. Laughing now, we began on a dare to climb the scaffolding together. We scrambled, hand over hand, to a high iron opening half way up the granite massif. Gleefully we reached the odd hole in the massive masonry and tumbled in.

Bowled over, we found ourselves in an enormous chamber lit by one bare bulb, with workman's gear strewn in piles upon a bare floor. Paint buckets were everywhere. With a single look about, we established in a second where we must go from there. With our hearts racing, a bolted ladder upon the far wall enticed us up to a black hole gaping in the ceiling. In a truant flash we were clambering again, me first, Kate two rungs behind. The climb from there on up was in perfect tomb-like darkness, as the faint light from the hole below faded with each ascending rung, into a pitch-black cavern that blazed for what seemed eternity in our fevered imaginations. Forever we seemed to climb into the gloom, one rung at a time, in darkness, until the familiar rungs ceased abruptly. Startled, I grasped nothing save sepulchral air.

Cautiously, I hauled himself up like a tomb robber into the black sky crypt of the tower, saying, "Be careful," as I flicked Kate's plastic butane lighter to give her some light. She then emerged up the ladder herself, batting round owl eyes. At last together, we stood in silence in the inner sanctum of Roebling's tetanus-beset genius. One hopes in moments such as this to find the mask of Tutankhamen afloat in gold and jewels, or a bank sack filled with $100 bills. Instead, we found a crumpled six-pack and the wrinkled skins of two spent condoms in the dirt—ah, well. All else was bare in that awful chamber, save for some cobwebs. Yet hope, like a dream ascending against the far wall, beckoned us on to one last ladder leading to a small trap door in the dank mausoleum ceiling above.

By the lighter's frail flame, we climbed again one last time. I creaked the trap door open on a rusty hinge, and like divers too long beneath the waves, the cold night air of New York washed over us in a thrice, and we stood atop the world like mountaineers.

All at once we felt the blessed rain spit upon our sooty skin, and the salty wind calling from beyond Sheepshead Bay, out where the Ferris wheels of Coney Island turn. Oh, more miraculous than the billion-dollar view, more thrilling than the Hong Kong steamer sailing out to sea hundreds of feet below, or the strange exhilaration we felt at our dare-devil feat, was the utterly incongruous, plaintive sound we heard above the distant din, a sad siren song rasped by a lonely cricket pining for love amid the glistening grasses wavering in the cold wind atop the west tower of the Brooklyn Bridge.

So, the great city provided highpoints of joy and days of brackish heartache, the same as I might have found in any other burg, I suppose, in this great land of ours that was made, so one singer had it, for you and me. Yet for much of 1989 into 1990, I was wearying of the endless, unceasing, incessant, unremitting, nonstop, continuous, sky-high, gung-ho, 24/7 roil and racket of New York City. Oh, city that never sleeps, much you gave me but wanderlust beckoned. I had loved hearing the amazing Bhundu Boys at the Band Shell in Central Park; listening to Philip Roth read at the 96th Street YMCA; seeing the Van Gogh retrospective at the Met; and climbing into the skyline awning of NYPL's grand reading room with two delightful gay guys and their favorite model at the Yves Saint Laurent fashion show. I even got to flash VP Dan Quayle on Halloween as his motorcade zoomed by City Hall Park, me dressed in nothing more than boots, a trench coat, and a G-string made of a silk fried egg, dangling over me freezin' nethers—Flash in the Pan this, Danny Boy! Yet my yearning for the natural world was left to feeding pigeons in Bryant Park at lunch and tossing grey squirrels a peanut or two. Neither Union Square, nor Washington Square, nor even Central Park, not Madison Square Park, nor Riverside has the remotest feel of a wild walk in the autumnal woods, far from the madding crowd. I had found a retreat in The Cloister, it is true, high atop Tryon Park, so far north on Manhattan the city runs out of numbered streets from 191st Street to 204th on the

A line subway. The A line, in any case, comes to an abrupt end here at the north tip of Manhattan, leaving the poor southwest borough of the Bronx to simmer riderless over Spuyten Duyvil Creek with no subway connection.

Hence to the Land of Hippies, Where Nobel Laureates Stalk the Halls

Are readers familiar with this college song?

> Far above Cayuga's waters,
> With its waves blue,
> Stands our noble Alma Mater,
> Glorious to view.

Would that were true of the first dive I moved into when, in 1990, I left New York City for good, heading for Ithaca, NY in the upstate Finger Lakes region, to take up a job at the Albert R. Mann Library at Cornell University. As their website says, their mission is: "Supporting learning and research in the life sciences, agriculture, human ecology and applied social sciences." What is it about great research libraries that says more is better? And lots more, better still. The halls of Cornell, far above those waters, have twenty-two separate libraries, which granted is a pittance compared to Harvard's seventy separate libraries. But in retrospect who was I, a lowly new librarian, to raise a ruckus over such largesse. My job interview at the Mann Library, in any case, was bizarre even by the odd arcs of my life to this point. The position was listed as a three-year stint on Ford Foundation grant funds for a Core Agricultural Literature Project (CALP) to create and place stand-alone CD libraries of full-text research articles into all major developing world ag-centers in Africa, Asia, South America, and undeveloped lands between. It sounded interesting. Certainly, the mission and aspiration for this enterprise sounded noble, so I applied and was invited to interview. After I'd done the usual rounds of "meet with staff" and search committee interviews, the Mann Library Director, Jan Olsen, arguably the most dynamic library director ever to lead libraries at Harvard, Berkeley, and the Library of Congress (to name three), sat me down and asked: "So, you want the job?" Uh ...yeah, sure. Hired on the spot, imagine that.

So I moved upstate to Ithaca, and what's not to like about Ithaca? OK, the winters suck, but besides those drifting snow banks high as your car hood with temperatures two below at daybreak, is there anything else? This offer to return to a countryside homecoming seemed as close to a gift of grace as I would find anywhere else. America is blessed with lovely college towns from Pomona College in the west to Williams College in the east, sharing in common that they all form the nucleus of marvelously well-educated liberal municipalities that in turn sprout around them like bastions of sanity. The reason I had even interviewed for this job was that by this time I was dating an architect who had been accepted as a graduate student in Cornell's excellent architecture program. Liliana was born in China, but was a New Yorker to her core. We had met in the city after being introduced by a mutual friend (at the Mr. Yoga Pants party, in fact), and down the wide avenues we briefly dated, enjoying a shared love of crossword puzzles and Latin American authors such as Gabriel García Márquez, Mario Vargas Llosa, and Carlos Fuentes. Like me, she had grown up to the age of twelve south of the border, in Peru, where her father had dragged the family in 1950 when they escaped by a hair's breadth Mao's communist takeover of mainland China. Apparently, you can spend your entire life in the grand sweep of NYC's Chinatown along Canal Street, and never learn more than two words of the King's English. "Hello. Goodbye." That would be Lili's mother, who spoke to me haltingly through her English-speaking children. When we moved to Ithaca, I asked Liliana how, at the age of thirty-two, it was possible for a grown-up like her not to have a driver's license. She simply raised her hand, as one can see on every street corner in Gotham, and cried out: "Taxi!" Ah, got it. In the city, we'd lived in separate apartments. But when I was given the job at Cornell, we threw our lots in together. The fall leaves were turning in hillside palettes of color when we arrived upstate, refugees from the city that never sleeps.

Our first living quarters were a rather cramped and damp basement apartment in college town. I hated these unprepossessing digs, which I considered barely a step up from a dump. I imagined us living in a cottage by the lake or in some small farmhouse near the woods, but that was not to be in those first months in the "centrally isolated" middle of nowhere as Eleanor Roosevelt had dubbed Ithaca. And yet we survived that first year just fine, squeezed into that dank basement apartment with a futon on the floor shared with daddy-long-legs and a view of clammy stains on the ceiling. Every morning, I would slog up the hill to the great university high above Cayuga's waters and go to work at Mann Library, Core Agricultural Literature Project, College of Agriculture and Life Sciences, Cornell University. How grand it all sounded. As lake breezes shook the autumn leaves, as Nobel laureates slogged uphill with me, and a thousand fit coeds too, sure enough, I came to realize in those early days, that despite the cramped flat, our move to Ithaca was a good one for me. The years of shuttered life in Gotham peeled away like a layer of old paint.

The Core Agricultural Literature Project that I worked for, as first conceived by the Ford Foundation funders in concert with Jan Olsen of the Mann Library, was arguably one of the noblest academic enterprises I have ever partnered with firsthand. Two strands of endeavor braided together our work. The first was identifying the core (i.e., the highest cited) agricultural literature in the world, with an emphasis on research in tropical countries. From this arduous work of analysis, we then created comprehensive bibliographies of the research cited. These identified works, in turn, would be systematically digitized, in full text, onto CD-ROMs. Then these disc libraries, plus the CD-reader technologies to read them, would be shipped all over the developing world to the top tropical agricultural research centers on every continent. We dealt with copyrights, agreeing to strict restrictions that the read-only content would not bleed beyond the research centers themselves. Most of these humid ag-stations, in any case, had no hint of the Internet at that time, but did have electricity to spin stand-alone CD libraries of digital content. My task was to identify, through interminable, pain-staking citation analysis, which journals and which articles stood out as worthy of digitization and inclusion in the CD libraries. The second strand of our work was to put together scholarly monographs on the seven distinct areas of related agricultural sciences. Working on CALP, I came to deeply appreciate the depth and the tedium, as well as the ultimate fulfillment, of science scholarship. It's hard work. But let's be honest here: though I have been surrounded by the scholarly enterprise of the academy for thirty-odd years now, I have never considered myself any sort of scholar. I just don't have that relentlessness or the aptitude to fuss about an exacting datum, as scholars must. My scattershot sampling of scholarship is more the improvisation of jazz rather than the classical fugues of Bach.

Working every day in the agricultural sciences, I came to meet many, if not most, of the greatest scientists in the world working in crop science, soil science, forestry, food science, animal husbandry, agricultural engineering, and human nutrition. Out of this magnificent project, I was to write extensive chapters in three out of the seven books in the series that were finally published by Cornell University Press. On two of the tomes, I served as senior editor: soil science and agro-forestry. In 1997, the seven-volume set, under the leadership of Wally Olsen, senior editor and husband of Mann Library Director Jan Olsen, won the Oberly Prize for Best Bibliography in the Agricultural or Natural Sciences at the American Library Association annual meeting in San Francisco. I give Wally Olsen full credit for this accomplishment; the man was a relentless go-getter, an exemplary evidence-based researcher who, with his equally tenacious wife, was able to pull off this enormous project from an unprepossessing second-story office above the Ag Quad at Cornell, with little more than dogged persistence.

You will have noticed that when I name an animal or plant species, I append the Latin name. To some this may seem a rather precious conceit or a just a tedious pain in the ass one must skim over with a sigh of forbearance. Cornell University taught me the importance of Latin nomenclature. The head of Collection Development at Mann Library at that time was Samuel Demas, arguably the most insightful, decent, fully-engaged, academically astute, relentlessly cheerful librarian I have ever met. I was honored the more to call him a dear friend. He and I started taking noontime courses in identifying the enormous plethora of worldwide plants which grew across every corner of campus, from weeds to arching trees. If, on our walks of identification, we identified a red oak as a mere red oak we would receive scowls from our professors. Latin names please! OK—*Quercus rubrus*. No! *Quercus rufous*? No! *Quercus rubra*? Yes, well done. Weeping willow—*Salis babylonica*. English hornbeam—*Carpinus betulus*. Etc. These Latin terms were hammered into us, because North America has dozens of types of willow and almost forty species of hornbeam, from the shrub-like to giants. Even the ubiquitous "goldenrod" of late September growing along a roadside has 120 separate species. Or, take the blue florets of "lupines" in mountain meadows—is it really true they have 200 varieties, each distinct? Yes, all only identified definitively by a unique Latin name thanks to progenitor Carl Linnaeus, who first devised the two-part name in the mid-eighteenth century. Only with Latin nomenclature can you exactly identify the plant (frog, mouse, leopard, or little brown bird) down to specific species, further to varietal strains, or else you are at best just somewhere in the ballpark. But "somewhere in the ballpark" when foraging for edible mushrooms, for example, can poison you all the way to the emergency room. Sam was always far better at Latin names than I was, but the Latin habit stuck. I offer no apologies.

Something in the rough-hewn farm country of upstate New York, and the long beautiful Finger Lakes in their splayed hand, awoke in me again the song of the wild woods I had so missed living in the roiling city. It was in Ithaca that I finished sewing my Native warrior robe based on a pattern from the *Wičhíyena* Sioux garment in the museum collection. It was in Ithaca, too, that I returned to my own mythos of pagan spiritual practices. On weekends, I would explore every state forest within fifty miles of home, all the way up the Iroquois lands to the Adirondacks. I was forever seeking what I've come to call my personal "power spots" in the state forests of the region, sacred sites such as they became for me, where my restless spirit might find surcease beneath towering trees shading the flowing waters of streams where trout hid in the broken pools. Quiet places, in an unnamed country that still felt like home, where I could stand alone, leaning toward sunset, feeling underfoot the ancient mycelium that feeds green life, where the wood thrush sings and where all life thrives.

I am not sure how I stumbled upon it, but Cornell has one of the most impressive, if small, quasi-independent libraries in the country, with strong eclectic holdings in radical, environmental, labor, and other progressive activism topics, with an emphasis on alternative communities and lifestyles, to rival anything anywhere in the country, possibly the world. The Durland Alternatives Library (DAL) is nestled in Anabel Taylor Hall, itself a stone heap on the western edge of campus above the bluffs from which you can gaze down into the town proper far below. When I was introduced to this gem, I immediately volunteered to join the DAL board, soon serving as board chair for six years and counting. This wonderful library fought valiantly to keep from being subsumed into the maw of the university library system proper. We felt it critical to guard its independence through fierce meetings of advocacy with higher ups. Under the board's guidance, the wonderful DAL librarian, Lynn Andersen, instead led us in joining with the Finger Lakes Public Library System. Access to our radical materials added immeasurably to their collections, and in return they gave our DAL patrons access to thirty regional public libraries. It was a perfect synergistic fit.

One important contribution I made was to generate a joint partnership between the DAL and the Progressive Librarians Guild, in order to publish the latter's *Progressive Librarian Journal* under the publishing umbrella of the Durland's not-for-profit status at Cornell. DAL had connections with union print houses, so the link-up aligned. The Durland had already published a number of poetry books by incarcerated youth at a nearby juvenile detention facility. This partnership between DAL and PLG served both well for almost two decades, cutting costs for PLG and providing DAL with a joint publication for articles championed by them. The DAL also had a burgeoning Prisoner Express program, connecting over 3500 incarcerated persons with access to progressive literature, donated books, distance learning, writing and poetry workshops, and other opportunities. Honestly, I can't think of a more amazing library for its size and budget, championing such easy access to radical information as the Durland. My highpoint in working with that wonderfully scrappy library for so many years was helping to bring poet Denise Levertov to Cornell. Denise is arguably one of the finest American poets of the past fifty years. I had met her several times and had heard her read at Elliott Bay Bookstore when I lived in Seattle. She spent a wonderful day in Ithaca, coming to campus to read at Anabel Taylor Hall on a blustery fall evening, reading so beautifully by a log fire inside. "You have come to the shore. There are no instructions," she told us. "How will your life reply when you are old?" To sit by her, and listen with a sort of childlike rapture to her sibilant, slightly London-inflected voice, what a delight. "Have Courage Always" she wrote when she signed my first-edition copy of *Oblique Prayers: New*

Poems (New Directions Publishing, 1984). I've sought always to live by that inscription, with varying degrees of success, despite my share of wayward failings. Suffice it to say, I came to know her well enough in her fading years of health, when I visited my old haunts in Seattle. My deepest appreciation Denise, especially for that wonderful morning we spent together walking head-to-head around the peninsula of Discovery Park. She taught creative writing at my alma mater, the University of Washington, while I was a student there. Her readings were always packed.

When 1992 rolled round, I joined the Counter-Quincentennial protests of the 500-year commemorative festivities that marked Christopher Columbus's disastrous "discovery" of the New World. In Ithaca, I became by default a lead organizer. I joined with the amazingly erudite and insightful leaders of the Onondaga Nation, such as Oren Lyons and Chief Irving Powless, to build momentum for a program we envisioned for October of that year at the Riverside Church in New York City. We roped great writers and Native American activists such as John Mohawk and Vine DeLoria into meetings. The then wife of Ward Churchill was a writer in residence at Cornell in 1992. She kindly introduced me to Ward, a fierce Native scholar, political activist, and professor of Ethnic Studies at the University of Colorado, Boulder. Ward and I hit it off, to the extent that with shades on, we actually looked surprisingly alike: tall, square-jawed, and big-voiced. Unlike me though, Ward Churchill is no pacifist. His books and many journal articles delve headlong into the injustices visited on Native tribes the continent over, with fierce invective. As I came to realize, Ward honestly believed that only some sort of armed struggle would ever dislodge the imperialist rule of western powers which had subjugated the Indigene since Columbus. He was definitely a polarizing speaker. He said what was on his mind, fearlessly and without equivocation; words came out of him like an uncensored blast furnace. His book *Fantasies of the Master Race* (1992) was published that spring, available in a City Lights edition now. I read it in two sittings. It is a powerful indictment of how Native Americans have been co-opted into clownish football team names, lines of automobiles, or two-dimensional portrayals like Tonto (in Italian = "dumb person") on the TV series *The Lone Ranger*. Author and political commentator Rebecca Solnit, in her book *Whose Story Is This? Old Conflicts, New Chapters* (Haymarket, 2019) describes the Quincentennial counter-celebration beautifully:

> My formative intellectual experience was, in the early 1990s, watching reactions against the celebration of the quincentennial of Columbus's arrival in the Americas and the rise in visibility and audibility of Native Americans that radically redefined this hemisphere's history and ideas about nature and culture. That was how I learned that culture matters, that it's the substructure of beliefs that shape politics, that change begins on the margins and in the shadows and grows toward the center, that center is a place of arrival and rarely one of real generation, and that even the most foundational stories can be changed.

I'm not sure what we changed in 1992, but with a small group of ardent Indian activists from a number of tribes and a band of disparate supporters, we traveled together through much of that year to all manner of counter-Quincentennial programs, events, conferences, and protests up and down the eastern seaboard. I also helped publish an authoritative *Counter-Quincentennial Directory*[37] with Mohawk activist Joseph Brandt, a distant descendent of the Joseph Brandt, and Dr. Gabrielle Tayac, an historian and curator with the National Museum of the American Indian. Through Ward, I met Russell Means, a featured speaker at some of our public programs. Despite being "a person of interest" wanted for questioning by the FBI, the gumshoes always managed to be three steps behind, unable to arrest him even as his name featured prominently on our posted fliers. Means has a wickedly wry, dark sense of humor, as does Churchill. Means called Columbus Day

---

37. McDonald, P., J. Brandt, and G. Tayac. *1992 Directory: American Indian and Related Resources for the Columbus Quincentennial*. Ithaca, NY: Akwekon Press, 1992.

nothing but a "celebration of genocide," a sentiment I had held myself pretty much since my days in Mexico during the 1968 riots. I had even written author Peter Matthiessen (*Indian Country, In the Spirit of Crazy Horse*) to ask if he'd care to join in our small coalition in some fashion. Somewhere in my epistle I wrote the phrase "let's roll up our sleeves and have at it" or some such thing. I was surprised at how quickly came his reply, by return post and written in longhand on the back of my typed letter. Almost his first words after salutation were: "Roll up my sleeves? I've damn well been rolling them up for forty years, thank you!" Ouch. But he obviously took a Tums to steady his agitation because he went on to offer a number of useful suggestions, not least of which was to contact Abenaki Indian activist Joseph Bruchac, who is a fine author, storyteller, poet, and publisher of children's books. Matthiessen himself begged off.

I knew Joe Bruchac from his visits to Cornell, so I called him up and found him as ever a delightful man bubbling with enthusiasm, veritably a wealth of ideas and information. I forget now if he was at our program that October, telling one of his entrancing stories. I want to say yes, but who knows? I did not keep copies of the program. Oddly enough, according to folks I worked with at the American Indian Community House in New York, a center with a year-round suite of support services and cultural events for Native peoples, I was surprised to hear that Gotham had more American Indians on any given day than the largest of the reservations out west. It was through these wonderful co-sponsors that we got the original referral to the Union Theological Seminary on West 122nd Street, where the Riverside Church is located. Even Noam Chomsky's wife, Carol, helped us with the planning of our October event. I had booked the Riverside Church back in April when New York basked in beautiful, blustery fifty-degree days. For the actual evening's three-hour program held in an unusually hot October, the temperature in New York rose well into the 90s, such that the church, lacking air-conditioning, was a whole hell of a lot hotter than Hades. I served as MC and the line-up we put together was sterling, even as we all dripped perspiration as if in a sweat lodge. The sensibilities of Native tribes everywhere, as they reclaim their cultural heritage, seem to me as good a path forward as any for the rest of us to find a deeper earth-wisdom that we might be advised to live by. Under their wise counsel, maybe we can even transcend the yoke of our neoliberal consumerist civilization. Wouldn't that be something?

Hardly a surprise, I soon got involved in city politics during my time in Ithaca and was appointed within a year by our city's mayor to the quasi-governmental Environmental Conservation Committee. My whole time in Ithaca had a quality of tribalism to it, in the best sense of the word: it had a sort of cultural cohesion born of small-town communal purpose. With an avowed socialist mayor at the helm when I arrived, there was a richer political dialog among residents than I had experienced anywhere else in my peregrinations. I felt in many ways that I had come home.

One airy apartment that I loved living in with Liliana stood on the corner of Falls Street and N. Tioga. One block to the north ran Fall Creek, which upstream carved out one of the deep gorges for which Cornell is famous. Out of the maw of the gorge, the creek cascades down in an enormous waterfall known as Ithaca Falls. Just above this magnificent cascade, high above the gorge, sits a rectangular white house that has all the appearance of a royal mausoleum. This was Dr. Carl Sagan's home for most of the years he taught at Cornell. Kitty-corner across the steep gorge above the falls, on the other side of the creek, stood the vacated ruins of the Ithaca Gun Company Factory. Through the end of the nineteenth century into the twentieth, Ithaca Gun was respected as a maker of fine shotguns, especially its Flues double barrel 12-gauge. Landlocked freshwater salmon come up Fall Creek every summer and spawn in the large pool beneath the falls. For me, living nearby, it was an easy walk to fly cast for a salmon after work.

Perhaps we who toil in the arena of environmental justice are granted some sort of inner compass to point to the labors ahead. Each fight seems to engender another; the iniquities of the world stretch far. I mention this, for I do not know what drove me one summer day to climb the steep bluff beside the rugged face of the falls up to the gun factory. I guess I wanted to enjoy the coming sunset from a perch above the town. So, off I set climbing. It was miserable going, literally hand over foot, using trees as a foot rest below and an arm pull above. I reckon it was a 65-degree incline, even steeper in places. There was also poison ivy and a good share of brambles. Still, I persevered. Unfortunately, the higher I climbed, the more unstable the soft soil became, until I almost lost myself in a miserable tumble. I was literally clawing with my hands into rooty soil, hoping to pull myself up, when I noticed something very odd. The soil seemed inordinately slick, as if greased, and exceedingly heavy. Looking more closely, I was stunned to see that every handful was half full of lead buckshot. Everywhere I dug into the soil, it was the same. In a flash I realized the entire bluff-side was a toxic waste dump of old lead buckshot. There were literally tons of the stuff coating the entire 90-foot bluff up to the abandoned gun factory ruins above. One would have thought the weight of the lead would have sheered the bluff to bedrock.

As I was on the city's Department of Environmental Conservation (DEC) steering committee at the time, I immediately reported my findings to chair Betsy Darlington, one of Ithaca's storied and fearless eco-warriors, who never saw a fight with a developer or dumb city councilor she didn't take on with relish. From her I learned so much, such as to never kowtow to the troglodytes. You might have to let the trolls bluster on for a bit—but when it's your turn, it's all about the evidence and sticking to the facts. I don't recall all of the machinations that followed after I reported the mess. I seem to recall that it went from denial, to shrugged dismissal, to a "clean up" that would cost too much, slap to forehead, to finally some sort of state and federal EPA mandates. As is so often true with environmental fights like this, the process of wending from revelation to litigation can take years. The city finally removed the entire gun factory and hauled out the tons of lead.

But as the first news of this broke in the daily paper, and more extensively in the weekly *Ithaca Times*, Dr. Sagan, who by this time was seriously ill with a rare bone cancer, came to join our pushback to have it all cleaned up. Any smart person living in the vicinity might well wonder if the misty spray from the dramatic falls wasn't itself laced with lead residue. As for Sagan, he had to ask himself if he had been breathing a carcinogen in the moist air about his home for decades. It was at one of the earliest public meetings that I met him and his wife; he was gaunt as a ghost, walking painfully with a cane. It was his wife who spoke for him during public comments at that first meeting before council. Afterwards, I introduced myself to them as a member of the DEC and the erstwhile whistle-blower to the toxic site. We chatted, and I said I was an avid amateur astronomer and a great admirer of the "billions and billions and billions" Cosmos TV series that he had hosted, and other usual niceties. I described how I had come upon my find. At some point I mentioned that I was going to a conference at the University of Virginia, and it was then that Sagan mentioned the Robert E. Byrd astronomical telescope in Virginia, which I've previously described. He said he'd be honored to set up a tour via his colleagues there if I was interested. Why not? Though it was his wife who later followed through with a return call on the details, I was given a fascinating tour of the facility on the astronomer's behalf. Years later, in 1996, Sagan died of complications from a nasty cancer called Myelodysplastic syndrome. Organic forms of lead are very dangerous—it's easy to conjecture the "why" of his cancer.

By the usual standards of environmental advocacy and litigation, the lead waste of the Ithaca gun factory was a laborious but straightforward win. In this case, no existing corporate behemoth stood athwart our calls for cleanup. It was simply bureaucratic inertia coupled with the huge task of demolishing a whole factory, and literally scraping a hillside away and carting off the toxic gunk by the dump truck-load. I wish all such "wins" were as "easy" as this one! The unrelenting brutality with which corporate capitalism and its proxy abettors in government heap upon any and all kinds of environmental stewardship is a staggering indictment. One is so often left speechless at the level of willful ignorance and kneejerk ideology that drives this systematic denial and distraction. And then there's the rage one feels when the troglodytes win a ruling. If you're not feeling the rage about now, best get thee to a doctor to check your pulse. As to my own health in the spray plume of the falls, I'll bet all those salmon and trout I pulled out of Fall Creek for supper were laced with lead traces as well. How could they not be?

I have never shied away from monkey wrenching, and have been a lifelong admirer of Edward Abbey—I own most of his books in fine editions, some signed for me by Ed himself. There is a state forest southwest of Ithaca called the Connecticut Hill Wildlife Management Area (CHWMA). It has 11,000 acres of mixed hardwood forest hilltop habitat dotted with a few untilled fields. Several creeks run through this forestland, which is logged of the biggest trees selectively on a rotational basis, mostly in areas about two football fields in size at a time. One of my ritual power spots in these fine woods was located in a grove of mature red maples (*Acer rubrum*) rooted about an ancient moss-covered granite outcrop. At least three times I saw beautiful barred owls (*Strix varia*) in the trees, two of whom seemed to be a breeding pair, always seen together. I never found their nest, though. One weekend, heading out to enjoy the late November woods there, I saw that two small NYSDEC—Forestry Division signs had been posted saying that the area would be logged that winter, sometime in January or February when sled skids make hauling out the felled trunks easier. Many large trees in the woods itself were ringed with the dreaded orange cut paint. I was stunned.

That following week, I took a ratty old piece of plywood about four-by-three feet in measurement, painted it white, and in bold green letters wrote: THIS AREA SPIKED THOROUGHOUT WITH 4" NAILS. NESTING BARRED OWLS. Rising one cold morn at 5am, I went out to the CHWMA while it was still dark. A light snow had come down overnight, along with a hard frost, and by the time I arrived to the spot where the NYSDEC-FD signs were posted it was just getting light. I saw three coyotes in my headlights on the way up plus innumerable deer, which were reason enough to love this sliver of upstate wilderness. The headlights then caught some sort of owl-blur gliding across the dirt road at shoulder height, heading left to right, although by its size I guessed it wasn't my barred owls but a smaller eastern screech owl (*Megascops asio*). Any fool can look for omens when embarking on nefarious activities, but I did take this as a sign from Hecate, goddess of owls, that all was aright with the world. In the back of my Honda Civic I had tossed a ladder, a box of 4" nails, a large head hammer, and gloves to avoid fingerprints. In the leaden daybreak of that winter dawn, I leaned my ladder against a large bare tree at a prominent turn in the road, struggled up with my heavy sign, nails lined up in clenched teeth, and hammered the damn thing to a big old bare tree. What a cold and bitter daybreak it was, cheerless with no sun, under a tin-hammered sky. But in truth this Abbey-esque act of quiet sabotage warmed my soul. Coming down, I admired my handiwork from the gravel road. You could see the lettering from fifty paces, even in the half-light. Perfect. Did I ever actually spike the hardwoods themselves? Of course not. Two weeks later, I returned to find the sign gone, but thankfully, too, the state logging permit notices had also been removed. Three thousand miles away now in California, and twenty-five years later, I can still see on Google maps that the west side of Todd Road for about a mile at the curve has never been logged. Notch one for monkey wrenching.

Hecate, the goddess of owls, witchcraft, and the night moon, has in return blessed me a thousand-fold since that time by letting me sleep beneath her arching skies at midnight, to see the heavens sparkling with stars and a gibbous moon. I will praise the nocturnal mind of her witchcraft, as coyotes in me howl thanks. She also gave me the gift of sighting every one of the fourteen known species of owl in North America over the years. The tiny dark-eyed flammulated owl (*Psiloscops flammeolus*) is my all-time fave, seen but once amid a grove of ponderosa pines high in the Sierra. Looking over me still, apparently, Hecate has sent a great horned owl (*Bubo virginianus*) to roost in the enormous camphor tree (*Cinnamomum camphora*) in my shady backyard right here in Fresno, CA where I live now. I have christened him Owlbert. Wide-eyed he may be, but Owlbert is always utterly unconcerned by the impertinence of my coming and going in his yard. I won't quibble about whose yard it is. If you question my emulation of Abbey's tactics, let it be said that I've never poured sugar into a Logging-Cat gas tank, nor fought the hard-hats in single combat. I think all logging equipment these days have locks on their gas tanks since Ed let on how just one cup of sugar gums up the engine for good. I avoid destruction as a valid act of resistance, but the sign I tacked up in that cold dawn to that bare tree was a fool's ruse. Not a single tree suffered a nail, but how were the foresters to know? After all, a chainsaw hitting a large 4" nail can send sharp metal chinks flailing off, which could really hurt someone. Do I think that monkey wrenching is a valid call to action? Generally, yes, as I'll get into in a bit, but laying your own life on the line as Julia Butterfly Hill did for 738 days, a hundred and eighty feet up in a coastal redwood (*Sequoia sempervirens*) seems a stronger sort of statement.

Once again in my life, around 1996, Nature blessed me with another marvel, in Florida of all places. I absolutely loathe coastal southern Florida. It's not Florida's fault. I am sure that these shores were spectacular in their pristine abundance before Juan Ponce de León (c1513) tromped around like a clanking tin man. Now, of course, it has become the blue-haired dreadfulness of retiree St. Petersburg. Turn around and it's the bimbo debauchery of Daytona Beach at spring break, or the hideousity of Mar-a-Lago and its rancid proprietor chintzing and cheating at golf on its manicured lawns. It's all such a spreading miasma of horrid. I am sure the homeland of the Seminole Indians, the only tribe never to cede their lands by treaty to the US government, was at one time doubtless a slice of Paradise.[38] Today, not so much. But interior Florida? From the Everglades to the lake-pocked pine barren scrublands of the north, I just love interior Florida, where not a single bikini-clad lady or cap-backwards college dude will ever be found. If one could expunge from this fascinating terrain the extruding excrement of Orlando smack in its middle, all the better. With its soulless Sea World, the sprawling mange of Epcot Center, ugly ICON Park, the bogus Holy Land Experience, Ripley's Believe It or Not Museum, Pirate's Cove Miniature Golf Extravaganza, thousand-and-one shopping mall outlets, and, not least, Walt Disney World Resort, all offensively shouting Conrad's "The horror!"—it's just hell on earth, were you to ask me for a definition. If Tinker Bell could give a little wave to her magic wand so that it all went "poof!" I'd be first in line to buy a ticket and watch it crumble.

Gainesville is another matter, as it is a livable college town, streets of sanity amid the Florida Sunshine effluent. I flew there one time, while winter still howled in Ithaca, in order to go birding in the pine barrens of north-central Florida. I went to Gainesville

---

38. There is no better panegyric on this destruction of Florida and its adjacent archipelagoes in the Caribbean than Kirkpatrick Sale's *The Conquest of Paradise: Christopher Columbus and the Columbian Legacy* (Knopf, 1990). Says Sale: "The conquest enabled (Europeans) to achieve, and sanctify, the transformation of nature with unprecedented efficiency and thoroughness, to multiply, thrive, and dominate the New World as no species ever has."

specifically because my brother was doing his post-doc work there at the University of Florida (UF), and thus lodgings would be free of charge in an area where I'd never birded. I also wanted to spend time with some Seminole Indian activists whom I'd met touring on the Counter-Quincentennial circuit. Their funky house, with indoor pet miniature pigs, of all things, barging in and out like four-legged fire hydrants and just as immovable, abutted the Sweetwater Wetlands Reserve near Newmans Lake. They threw a little dinner party for me where all the guests seemed to come from families named Osceola or Cypress. I have been around a lot of American Indians in my life, or at least those who claim heritage. I'm always surprised at how light-complected and Anglo so many appear, think "Pocahontas" Elizabeth Warren or even Ward Churchill, who is only 1/16 Cherokee and so on. But the two wonderful gentlemen and one striking woman who joined us for dinner that evening were full-blood Seminole with the most beautiful faces of ruddy burnished copper imaginable. They seemed sculpted of beautiful amber. You immediately sensed a deep resoluteness in them, a posture of calm dignity that shone forth in their smiles, etched in the wrinkles about their bright eyes. One man wore a tan cowboy hat, the other gent had long braided hair, and the woman had straight black hair handsomely adorned with handcrafted Native jewelry. All were college educated; the woman was teaching as an adjunct and one man was an administrator, both at the University of Florida. The other man was visiting from Miami, where he worked in county government. Each in their own way was active with Seminole tribal social justice causes. It was a thoroughly enjoyable evening as they spoke freely about the upcoming Green Corn Dance ceremonies.

 Gainesville is where I had my first ambles along canals laden with so many alligators that they seemed like plastic replicas stacked to the rafters in some Disney display gone awry. On land, gators generally consider you, the human interloper, as the top predator, so are a bit fidgety and wary as you walk by. The rule of thumb is that you're safe to walk by them, even lots of them as they bask in the panhandle sun, at a distance of about fifteen feet. And so, keeping a fifteen-foot distance, I felt quite safe. I'm not sure why exactly, because it wasn't as if a wall stood between their malignant teeth and me. Why was I there? I wanted to bag a life-lister, which is bird-watching lingo for sighting a bird species you have never seen before in your life. I particularly wanted to see the diminutive brown-headed nuthatch (*Sitta pusilla*). This tiny bird is adorable, with a brown cap, gray back and wings, and a white underside. Like all nuthatches and creepers, it wanders up and down tree bark, looking for insects. The Cornell Lab of Ornithology claims it has "a fearsomely hard beak." I'll take their word. This small species of nuthatch often hops along a branch upside-down, punctuated by a characteristic arching of their necks backwards to spy for their next hop, a move which reveals their lovely white throat patch. You can sometimes identify them first by sound, as they emit a constant squeak-like chatter as they go. This species of nuthatch is endemic to the deep southeast, interior Florida especially, as they prefer scrub pine habitats.

The birding was indeed worthwhile in Gainesville; throughout its surrounding pine scrub habitats, I saw many subtropical species but never the brown-headed nuthatch. Even my brother, an ace birder and avian biologist, couldn't scare one up for me. I spent a magnificent day at a state park where the Santa Fe River roars up out of a thirty-foot-wide hole in the limestone bedrock at Ginnie Springs. With a dramatic onrush of clear groundwater, this fountain of youth, as I'll call it, starts a small river which wends its journey west, a full-on gin-clear river tumbling to the far-off sea. The aquifer caverns, which source the river, spout up from an aquamarine hole six-hundred feet deep. Today there's a raging backlash against Nestlé Waters' proposal to take 1.1 million gallons per day from Ginnie Spring for its nearby bottling plant. To see an entire river just gush up out of a deep blue translucent hole in the earth to begin a crystalline surge to the arms of the sea is a marvel. On the day I went, with ambient temperature of about 50F, there was not another soul about. There was also still no brown-headed nuthatch, which was proving to be a real disappointment.

On the day I was to fly back to Ithaca, my brother and his girlfriend said their goodbyes as they had to dash off to work. With about four hours to kill before my flight, I decided to drive out to the University of Florida's Austin Cary Forest, a thousand-acre training plantation created in 1939 under the federal Work Progress Administration (WPA) to develop a forestry facility for "the purposes of academic teaching, research, extension education, and demonstration." Only one 150-acre patch of the forest property is considered original pine and cypress woodland. My brother thought this sector might harbor the illusive nuthatch. The rest of the vast teaching forest is used as a research site for graduate students to grow commercial twenty-acre test plots, trying different methods for faster growth and higher yields. I could not find any sort of way into the old growth section, so I parked on the side of Route 24 and hopped the wire fence. I entered a silent wonderland.

The natural habitat of a scrub forest in central Florida is hummocky, which is to say that mounds of soil and vegetation rise out of the shell fossil bedrock everywhere. It's as if giant moles lived there. The habitat is largely xeromorphic, mostly dry land with poor soil. Sand pines (*Pinus clausa*) compromise the canopy, with a few scrawnier types of sub-canopy sand oaks, all interspersed with scrub and saw palmetto fronds. Occasionally a lone cypress shoots up as an interloper. The canopy is dense and the understory dark. The grassy hummocks that poke up everywhere are about six-to-eight feet high with fourteen-to-sixteen-foot diameters, studded often enough with small yucca and a type of Florida prickly pear (*Opuntia humifusa*). As I entered, I soon found mossy paths through the forest, all haphazardly crisscrossing one another. I had no fear of getting lost, because the sun was by now in the south and the straight road where I'd parked was due west, so I could take any path with the sun to my left and come out eventually somewhere along the highway where my car was parked. Besides, I have an uncanny geographic compass inside my head from living so many years in trackless wilderness. I have never become lost in any terrain, even when wandering miles off trail. Upon entering the dark wood, I immediately felt a haunting disease evoked by the gloomy place which I at first could not quite identify. Then it came to me: the forest stood in dead sub-tropical silence. There was no chur of insects, no chatter of birds, not even the rumble of a distant truck on Route 24. It was dead silent with not a breath of wind, as if I were lost in a world suddenly gone deaf. There also seemed to be no evidence whatsoever of other human visitation, nor even of animals. There were no footworn paths, no bits of human flotsam like gum wrappers or cigarette butts, nothing. Just the random meanderings of pristine mossy pathways, themselves without any sign of animal excrement. Thus, there were no raccoons, and no deer either. Bereft it was.

I must have walked all through that forest in a serpentine amble. At one point my path led me out to a clear-cut patch where, at last, and with relief at having living companionship, I saw several crows cawing on some distant stumps. Life at last. Plunging back into the gloom, the same evocative silence enveloped me, as if I'd stumbled into a dark forest lifted from a fairytale penned by the Grimm brothers. After well over an hour of fruitless wandering, I decided to head back to the road to my car, then to the rental depot and the airport. With the sun to my left now, I came to a mossy fork amid the pathway choices: 'round a hummock to my left or along a swampy depression to my right? Thinking the swampy bit might more likely harbor at least some sort of life form, I headed straight westward to the right.

But with each step I took upon the path I'd chosen, something like a tug of disquiet slowed my footsteps, until I came to a halt. For a moment I wondered if the brackish waters in the depression might be exuding sulfur gas. So I turned and went back to the fork. The other path curved around a big hummock. The sense of physical foreboding immediately subsided, so I started to pick up my pace around the hummock. It was then I came upon what I can only describe as the most symbolic gift ever entrusted to me in my many wanderings across the Earth. For there, lying perfectly at peace, dead center on a moss cushion in the middle of the path, lay something very peculiar. It took several seconds for my eyes to register what it was, for what I saw, as if laid out in a museum display case, was the immaculate shell and perfectly preserved skeleton of a humped turtle many years dead, picked perfectly clean. Every tiny bone, the small skull, and even the tiny reptile toes were all splayed out in absolutely perfect symmetry on a cushion of moss. I gasped with startled surprise. Peering down, I could literally count each miniscule vertebra, toe bones, and little femurs, see the scalloped curve of the shoulder blades and the perfect remains of its skull.

I dared not touch it. In awe, I simply collapsed back against the hummock to admire my find. I was utterly disoriented by this revelatory gift—how was I to fathom the miracle of the dead turtle? And then, as if there were still magic left on this battered Earth, as if sent by some unseen woodland elf of the understory, a little flock of cheeping brown-headed nuthatches, of all damn things, came bouncing through the air like playful tykes, landing in the pine boughs overhead. There were probably twenty of them, twittering, inquisitive, hopping about, right above me! To this point in my ramble, I had not heard a single sound of any animal, bird, or insect save for the crows in the far clear-cut. I leaned back against the hummock, palms under my head, eyes wide with wonder, and just burst into glad laughter at the sight of my illusive quarry. "Hi, little guys," I said aloud with unalloyed joy at the happy garland of little birds—a flitting flock, so cute.

The little tree climbers were there for barely thirty seconds, then off they flitted into the forest. Sitting up, I immediately did a ritual of offering, tapping at heart, head, and sky, giving my sincerest thanks to Mother Earth. There were obviously silent spirits in that haunted forest after all. The gift of the turtle differed in kind from finding my spear point in that the stone-age tool had not been willed to me by invocation. It just appeared one spring day like some mythic talisman out of the depths of a cold glacial lake. But to stumble on a lost turtle shell in the wild, after years of invocation, to finally come upon such a find, I wager that's something else entirely. I gazed back down at the turtle, half expecting it to have vanished since last I looked. But there the poor reptile lay in absolute repose, like a strange gift from the unknown. Giving thanks to Gaia again, with a deep nod of appreciation to my Potawatomi clan mother back in the city who had first sent me on this quest, I lifted up the shell, cupping it in my trembling hands like the most precious artifact in the world. It was then I realized, with a start, that the poor reptile was a sort of mutant, a beast burdened to drag its shell its entire life with no back legs. Nor did it have a tail. The shell casing, where the hind legs of the turtle should normally have protruded in the rear with a plastron flap, was entirely shut closed, clamshell tight, sealed. Nor were there any rear leg bones or tail cartilage on the mossy cushion where it had lain. Right here, at this spot, it had decided to die, giving up its long life's haul. It must have been years ago, because the whole carcass was now picked clean by ants through the intervening seasons to a perfect skeleton. Looking again, to be sure, yes, there was no hole at all in the rear of the shell for the legs. I pondered this anomaly all the while marveling that this creature, who had finally beckoned me to find it, had spent its entire life of possibly forty-odd years as a cripple with only front legs for locomotion.

I placed the shell and all the bones, skull included, into my backpack compartment and headed back to my car. On my flight home I thought deeply on what had occurred there in that silent forest. Having worked on, and by then published, an entire book on agro-forestry, I realized that with trees grown for fast yield crop, pesticides were often used on the small seedlings and young trees, especially against certain species of boring beetles. There were even certain tar-sprays dropped from crop dusters to saturate the tender pine "candles" (new branch tips) with bitter oils so they would also be unappetizing to deer and other herbivores. I could only assume that these toxic substances had drifted over this old growth forest habitat and had caused in vitro the mutation I had seen. What else could explain it? Having experienced more than a few wonders in my life to that point in my journeys, I was not entirely flummoxed by the find. I had learned from Michael, my Salish shaman in Seattle, that if you want Spirit to hear a request from your own being, you must do a ritual whereby you invoke your request in a conscious act of calling upon Spirit to listen. Once your request is released into the aethyr, you then must let it go completely. Cease all wishing and wanting for it, else these new yearnings override the gift you have already offered Spirit in the form of your original supplication. Spirit, said Michael, will see this latter yearning as an arrogant form of nagging, a sign, in short, of your mistrust. Just let it go. There is no quid pro quo.

So yes, years before when I had first arrived in Ithaca, I had made such a request, with my Potawatomi clan mother in mind, for Spirit to bestow a turtle or tortoise shell into my life in order to make my rattle. From that day forth I had tried to let the invocation go. I am rarely as steadfast as I like to think I am. The nagging thought that I might find a turtle shell in some visited habitat would come over me through the years. But not in a million years was a turtle rattle on my mind my entire time in Florida. Yet there I sat on an airplane, tongue-tied, with an entire preserved turtle in my backpack. I do feel that some sort of "energy"—I'll call it "Spirit"—connects my Being to a greater whole. I don't measure or figure it lest the reasoning mind stifle it, but that Spirit, whatever it may be, doubtless gifted me the turtle shell, of that I am certain. This thought did not entirely surprise me. Perhaps the best way I can describe it is to say it is a form of Gratitude for all Gaia gives us on this beautiful blue water planet, this one and only Earth. As we open to Gratitude, the varied phenomena of the "world out there" synchronize with our own humble humanity "in here," and the Gift is revealed. I can live with this myth.

Amazing as this find was, what actually stumped me far more was the sudden arrival of the sought-after brown-headed nuthatches within seconds of my discovery. That's the piece of this experience that seems more miraculous by half. Stumbling on an old turtle shell in untrodden woods is serendipitous enough, but I have a whole collection of animal skulls. Tromp around in the woods long enough and you're bound to find your share. Granted, each find can be tinged with a certain macabre wonder but there is nothing particularly miraculous about such finds. But a blessed halo of twittering tiny birds you've been looking for, for years, at the exact moment you stumble on a turtle shell you've also been looking for, for years? That's the corker for me. Coincidence? Sure, obviously, but to my inquiring mind I am inclined to say when too many moving parts decide suddenly to pile on like a synchronous scrum, coincidence seems a bit of a lame dodge. I now subscribe to a different viewpoint backed, I'll confess, by scant scientific evidence. How can you measure the uncertainties that we chose to follow as human beings in our quest to understand a labyrinthine reality?

But here's the thing: if our mind is in resonance with the Earth in its pristine state, and by that I do not mean devoid of humans, but devoid of human civilization, in such a world I am certain, as all Indigenous tribes well know, Spirit abides. The Irish call these wild spirits of place Leprechauns and watery Selkies, the Norwegians their Elves, Scots their Pixies, the Brits their fairies, sylphs, nymphs, sprites, and the Greeks their sirens—all over the world we find forest guardians, sylvan deities, fauns, satyrs, and so on. Common to all of them is the here and now of Spirit of Place. I am inclined to believe they are nothing more than subconscious avatars, but we still imbue them with mythic and corporeal qualities as a means to explain why certain places at certain times seem to have an indelible magic. Take my nuthatches, for example. A stone age human who felt one day he had experienced a miracle (such as my turtle) at the exact same moment as a halo of well-loved little birds appeared, would, I am sure, imbue the little birds with a cohered consciousness of Spirit. It is thus a small step in retelling the story to rapt children to call the birds "winged sprites"—to give them a magical name, and the myth is born from a real happenstance.

Sit alone in Chaco Canyon in New Mexico as the sun goes down over the desert lands, watching the shadows lengthen in purple hues over the open kivas and you will know what I mean. As a lone coyote appears to capture your attention, you call her Trickster in the telling. These experiences are a cohered element of all sacred sites, which the human mind experiences viscerally as we become the subterranean smithies of our own inner alchemy of transformation. The bare facts of the land suddenly become landslides of the phantasmagoric, creations of our creative minds. To ancient peoples the world over, all of these spirits of place were quite real, clearly still residing in the last remaining wild tracts hidden in plain sight to this day. You just need to open up somehow, anyhow, to experience them.[39] The shamans tell us these spirits do indeed see and hear us as fellow travelers in spirit if we but open our own strength of mind to their possibility. I am convinced that Nature unsullied by the heavy footprint of civilization is full of such strange and miraculous wonders. I do so pray you've had these experiences too.

---

39. I once sat on a bluff above the Pacific Ocean on a summer day and watched the kelp fronds below sway back and forth with the action of the gentle waves. I was soon in a tance state, and I swear it was not long before the swaying fronds came to appear like flowing lovers entwining themselves in the sea. Thus were Selkies born to four thousand years of imaginative bardic minds on the coasts of Ireland.

Today, with the wanton destruction of the planet, with our forests on every continent shorn for lumber, rivers dammed and polluted everywhere, wild lands gouged with open pit mining, and the oceans dying, there is no longer "the peace of wild things" as Wendell Berry so aptly called it in his poem of that name, "where the wood drake rests in his beauty on the water, and the great heron feeds." These sacred places are mostly gone today, I'll grant, as that peace gets loudly snuffed out by ORVs racing over fragile terrain. Gone with the corn snake and the soft-eared marten, the frosty eyes of the northern lynx, all "gone under earth's lid." One is left to lament with the Lakota song, "The earth is weeping, weeping, Grandfather, all the sacred things, are weeping, weeping." I am left today with a bitter gratitude that I have seen the world firsthand in its peace of wild things, only to mourn today its passing.

It turned out that my crippled turtle was a Florida box turtle (*Terrapene carolina bauri*), with its rounded dome shell, a beautiful chocolate brown color with bright yellow radiating stripes. Its plastron or bottom flaps can be closed tight to cover both front and hind legs, plus its head, so it's as impregnable as a coconut. But the rear plastron flap of the shell I'd found was sealed shut, as if fused. Perhaps the vestigial hind legs got encased in the shell as the little reptile grew, hauling itself haplessly about by its forelegs. A tough life that, to wander through the decades down those mossy paths of that desolate forest dragging your home along on two legs. A look with a flashlight confirmed a jumble of fused bones at the back of the shell. How I grieved for the poor cripple.

To fill the rattle that I made from my find, I used all the reptile's own bones, setting aside a humerus bone for my left pocket of treasures and the skull. I tossed in several small gemstones, a ruby, a cut emerald, a tiny shell, and other small items from bowls full to overflowing with a bower hoard collected over the years. Then I drove up to the Onondaga Nation south of Syracuse to ask a grower friend on the reservation if he'd give me a small pouch of ancient sacred corn seed for the rattle I was making. He said sure, so home I went with a handful of red corn kernels. For the handle of the rattle, I waited until the Winter Solstice that year when the witch hazel (*Hamamelis mollis*) was in first bloom, with long-petaled little blossoms that seemed to wave like deformed pale-yellow hands in the winter moonlight. I cut my branch and left it to dry by the woodstove. Eventually, using the skull for size and shape, and with pictures of Florida box turtles as guide, I stripped the bark and at the tip end I carved a replica of the turtle's head exactly to size. I attached the handle through a hole in the front plastron with wood glue, all secured by a tiny brass nail. I have the beautiful rattle still; it has the loveliest sound, I must say.

Ithaca was a good fit for me for the sixteen years I lived there. It's a fiercely liberal town, laid back, with secondhand bookshops aplenty. When I first arrived, it lacked a single big box store. By some oversight in the relentless apparatus of capitalist progress, the geography of nowhere that blights towns everywhere in America today had failed to bring its sclerotic mange to Ithaca. I made many dear friends in that time, could get to world-class fly-fishing waters most any free afternoon, was only a morning's drive to the Adirondacks, and summers had wonderful outdoor concerts and festivals. Ithaca had arguably the best farmer's market in America, two artsy film houses, and a socialist-leaning city government, all surrounded by the intriguing offerings of a world-class Ivy League university.

My last six years there were spent in a sort of tree house right on Salmon Creek in the hamlet of Ludlowville, twelve miles north of the university. The tree house had been built by the fashion designer Eileen Fisher and her husband David on forty acres of land with three 35-foot waterfalls cascading through private gorges down two good-sized wooded tributaries feeding into the main stem of the larger creek. Home here was a five-minute peddle by bicycle to swimming holes on Cayuga Lake. Eileen and David moved to New York to start a fashion house juggernaut, while the house they left behind was entrusted to me. I was in heaven there, falling asleep every night to the quiet rush of the creek below, and eastern whip-poor-wills (*Antrostomus vociferous*) calling the night forth into the darkening woods. Any time the mood moved me I could amble the quiet gorges to the waterfalls for daily contemplation in what was essentially my domain. Yet beneath it all, as the warnings of climate change first hit the news, as I witnessed firsthand the encroachment of big box stores into the sleepy town, as I saw everywhere the fast-fading beauty of the green holism of Earth, I grieved.

Since I don't believe humans *as a species* are in fact redeemable, often enough I have been called misanthropic. But this description fits like a jacket that's a good size too small; the label becomes an epithet used by those who want to continue to believe in the civilized enterprise, insisting against all evidence that we are progressing to some grand omega point where perhaps AI and biology merge to create the deathless uber-human of the future. I never know where progress boosters think we're going. It sounds dreadful to me: the soulless dead. At best, it's a chimera. In any case, I'm inclined to agree with anthropologist Marvin Harris that "in most ways the rise of nation states was the descent of the world from freedom into slavery." Or as Franz Kafka said: "There is hope; though not for us." We are the hapless slaves to our fascination with the mirage of civilization delivering us unto the promised land. Yet when I look at our vaunted industrial civilization, with its addiction to every techno-advancement of progress it can wring out of a precious metal, all I see is that it begins to consume itself voraciously by borrowing from the future and feeding like a maggot off the past. I see the whole apparatus as an entropy trap, a necrophilic feeding frenzy, with a grim terminus. How could it not be? But I am also tugged by a feeling, indeed a responsibility, that I must do even more "to save the world," whatever the hell that means. If humanity is irredeemable, to what end is the saving? Yet how can one not join the struggle, whatever the odds, when there's so much suffering in the world? At one point in my life, I realized that in addition to delivering the radical alternative paper about town, I was sitting on approximately fifteen boards for do-good organizations, all with their separate missions to save or ameliorate some piece of the world's woes. There I was in the middle of it all, like Balaam's ass, braying, "What's all this struggle for?"

To this end, I can hear the words of Henry Miller in *The Cosmological Eye*, a book of wonderful essays, published by New Directions in 1939 just before the war. "There can be no doubt about it," said the Big Sur satyr, "the plight of civilized man is a foul plight. He is forever singing his swan song without the joy of being a swan. He has been sold by his intellect, manacled, strangled and mangled by his own symbology. He is mired in his art, suffocated by his religion, swamped by his work, paralyzed by too much knowledge." The inimitable screed goes on for several dense pages that a castaway truculence in me too often reads with an unseemly relish. Henry's cacodemon-inspired rants aside, I am inclined to say in my defense that my cynicism aligns in the classic sense with Diogenes, the Greek philosopher who expounded on these topics as the first Cynic. From the vantage of the hermit, he chastised the excesses of opulent Greek society. I, too, live a relatively simple lifestyle, as he did, and in like manner rail against the miasma of our civilized consumerism, which drives the juggernaut, the corrupt, confused, indeed neo-Hobbesian, society of cellphone gizmo-addicts we have become. As I've shared before, Francis Weller's *The Wild Edge of Sorrow*, is as good as place as any to embrace the deep mourning you may feel at our lost planet. It undoubtedly helped me to come to grips with my own deep sense of grief at a world gone mad. Here's a poem I wrote that describes my quiet terror of what humankind has in store in the decades ahead. I penned it in pencil on an envelope while I sat on the tree house porch one evening, as the fireflies came out. The creek murmured below as the day fell shut about me. Darkness came on.

Ragnarok[40]

In the slow smoldering heat of this June evening
strange sparks rise out of darkness
into crowns of walnut trees, higher against the sky
they fall like spent fireworks into jewelweed,
are lost in blackberry brambles, guide pond minnows
with luminescent lanterns into ooze,
swing out again from shallows into sumac, into scented pines
up into the hemlock where the heron sleeps
on the edges of the world calling the night
to tell us the first fireflies have returned
flashing in moist cloisters of the black wood.

If only we could read the code-language
of these pricks of light winking on and off
in the humid night, we would know that all
the ghosts of our forbearers are set
upon the hierophantic task of telling us
in the mute music of the firefly
that great cities are falling
the clocks have all struck twelve
no tower will be left standing
steeples shall fall to dust while
waste and refuse become our heritage
then only the names of these ruined places
will remain in the margins
of the lost maps of the dead.

Here in Salmon Creek valley
all the lordly sycamore wither of anthracnose
the beech are blighted by fungal nectria
gas companies, in our back yards, sink iron into the earth,
while the once quiet corners sprout golden arches,

---

40. Ragnorak is the final battle at the end of the world in Norse mythology when all the great gods die in world catastrophe.

and our rivers carry poisons to the sea.
Twenty years ago, bob whites, woodcock and cuckoos
called this wild understory home. And landlocked
salmon plied the runs. Today they are gone,
they have vanished with the corn snake and the river mink.
I hear Cassandra squawking from the grackle's throat,
fierce and beady eyed, she croaks strange runes
of longing and despair, spells to raise the crestfallen
but she does not wake these sleepwalkers
oblivious to the spells of fireflies in their coven
as in the dusk, kids play softball on summer lawns.

Progressive Policy Wonk

During my years at Cornell and then at Syracuse University from 1999 on, I took up the cudgel to become an active member of the Progressive Librarians Guild (PLG). I also got involved in the politics of the American Libraries Association (ALA), of which I was an active member. ALA is one of the largest professional organizations in the country. I ran for a position on the steering committee of the association's Social Responsibilities Roundtable (SRRT), serving for many years. I also ran to sit on the governing Council of the entire association, and for six years served there too as an at-large member. Those were heady days in our profession. I became good friends with Mark Rosenzweig, fellow graduate of Columbia, who held numerous positions through the years, for a while at Mid-Manhattan Library while I worked across the street at the research division. He moved on to run the library-archive of the Communist Party of America in the city and much else. A core group of progressive librarians, like Mark, all of a sudden exerted considerable influence in the profession of librarianship, quite out of proportion to our numbers. I credit PLG with being the catalyst.

The better part of these stories of struggle in national library policies can be found in Al Kagan's book, previously described, and also in Elaine Harger's wonderful book, *Which Side Are You*

On: Seven Social Responsibility Debates in American Librarianship, 1990-2015 (MacFarland, 2016). Further reading to which I might steer you can be found in the insightful works of scholar John Buschman, such as *Libraries, Classrooms, and the Interests of Democracy: Marking the Limits of Neoliberalism* (Scarecrow Press, 2012), and Alison Lewis' handsomely edited *Questioning Library Neutrality: Essays from Progressive Librarian* (Library Juice Press, 2008); all are good places to understand how radical librarianship works.[41] I said in the Preface that I would avoid delving into the specific politics and tactics of these efforts at bringing a more radical agenda into the soothing suburban hot tubs of mainstream get-along liberalism evinced too often in our library profession. Suffice it to say, the oral battles brought to debate on the floor of ALA's Council and other forums took heroic efforts of planning, clear strategies and tactics, attendance at the right committee meetings to voice our emphatic positions, working through sectors of the bureaucracy, preparing the floor plan for debate, followed by yet more meetings—often late into the night—and then, dammit, showing up, speaking forcefully, and never being cowed by bland calls for compromised consensus or paeans to professional neutrality. On questions like South Africa's apartheid, where does one compromise? The effort was very much to rock the boat, and if some folk got tipped from their deck chairs, so be it.

All through this ardent advocacy, the *Progressive Librarian Journal* published powerful articles on radical aspects of our profession, on First Amendment and free speech rights, the dangers of information technologies, issues related to education and the environment, and the whole power structure of corporate incitement to complacency amongst the voting public. Authors as diverse as

---

41. I have a chapter in the latter book. It also appeared: McDonald, P. "Corporate Inroads & Librarianship: The Fight for the Soul of the Profession in the New Millennium" *Progressive Librarian*, v.12/13. Summer 1997. Selected for: *Best of the Alternative Library Literature*, ed. by Sanford Berman. McFarland & Company: Jefferson, NC, 1998. 280 pp.

Naomi Klein (#23) and Theodore Roszak (#6/7) wrote compelling articles for PLJ. In 1999, we put out *Anarchism & Libraries*, a Supplement to Issue #16. I wrote several essays myself, including "Corporate Inroads & Librarianship: The Fight for the Soul of the Profession in the New Millennium" (v.12/13, 1997), which was subsequently selected for inclusion in: *Best of the Alternative Library Literature*, ed. by Sanford Berman (McFarland, 1998). For a number of years, I served as an editor of the journal.

Several "actions" by PLG are worthy of a shout out. We led boycotts of conference lodgings such as Marriott International for their corporate ethos of anti-unionizing; called for boycotts of the government of Israel's unconscionable treatment of Palestinians; excoriated the all-white government of South Africa during apartheid; took various actions in support of Cuba's inherent national right to exist as CIA-backed shills in US-backed anti-government propaganda cells called for overthrow; protested the tepid award (later called a citation) given to (librarian) Laura Bush for her advocacy on behalf of US libraries as her husband, the POTUS, actively destroyed libraries and archives in Iraq and Afghanistan; vociferously fought against the USA PATRIOT Act with its green light assault on libraries under the bogus guise of "national security;" and so on. We brought in nationally-known speakers such as the Green Party VP candidate Native activist Winona LaDuke, a powerful Ojibwe voice for Native rights and social justice; author Nicholson Baker, who denounced the ubiquitous destruction of the nation's print newspapers in libraries everywhere as they turned instead to microfilm; and journalists from radical news media, such as Amy Goodman. PLG members also surged onto the stage, protest signs held high, when keynote speaker Al Gore came to ALA and we publicly yelled our criticism of his war-monger vote (*An Inconvenient Truth* aside) to invade the sovereign country of Iraq on absolutely spurious, saber-rattling, bogus WMD intel.

Later, when the ALA invited "war hero" General Colin Powell to speak as keynote at the annual conference in New Orleans, complete with a six-figure speaking fee (!)—once again, there was PLG crying out 'Shame!" and waving signs in the entrance hall of the New Orleans Convention Center. All that wasted money spent on a wealthy warmonger could have been better spent on ALA library school scholarships, for heaven's sake. The New Orleans police quickly threatened us all with jail. One oddly reasonable officer was quick to add, "Seriously, you don't want to end up in a Louisiana jail, trust us." True enough, a Louisiana jail with dodgy bail and all those opportunities for "a failure to communicate" a la *Cool Hand Luke*? Not so much.

Being chased out of the New Orleans convention center by the NOLA-PD for protesting Colin Powell is one thing, but to be shown a dank jail cell out in the bayou country of Louisiana a few days later by a true southern swamp State Trooper is another. Having packed up my protest tent at the Crescent City convention center, I decided to skip the rest of the conference, rented a car, and headed south out of New Orleans to go birding on Grand Isle, LA, several leisurely hours south of the Big Easy. Birding there, I was told, is apparently some of the best on the Louisiana coast. What I love about New Orleans is that it is the only large city in America (with the possible exception of Charleston, SC) that has kept its 19th-century charm throughout, resolutely turning its back on the bland progress traps of strip malls and miles of soul-numbing Jiffy Lubes. Everywhere you go in NOLA there is a palpable sense of pride in the human-scale life of real people in their home-styles of yesteryear under shrouds of Spanish moss. But I loved the quirky, rundown, hard-scrabble bayou country even more. I drove down the back roads with their idled shrimp boats, rust-bucket hamlets hit by hard times, heck just the deep south mangrove swampy vegetation was in itself fascinating. For the life of me, though, I can't fathom why the Audubon Society recommended Grand Isle on the Gulf Coast as a birding destination, but they gave it four stars. It's just a long spit of land facing the Gulf with one gigantic oil refinery dominating the landscape. Seaward it's just a vast sea forest of oil derricks as far as the eye can see. In short, it's a shithole. But true to the stars, the birds don't seem to mind. I had my second only clapper rail (*Rallus crepitans*) sighting, a handsome, largely illusive bird, that was just putzing around in a brackish puddle at the gargantuan entrance to the oil refinery without a care in the world. "Yo darlin'!" I cried, alarmed by her taste in habitat, "get a life!"

I didn't stay long to go birding. It was just too depressing a visual every-which-way you looked, even if clapper rails were in the foreground. In heading back to N'Awlins, having so enjoyed the ambience of the bayou country coming down, I mapped out on my gazetteer a new route back, along even more remote back roads. Pretty soon I was on pot-holed back tracks that seemed destined to get me nowhere. I stopped in one desolate spot to admire a huge flock of roosting roseate spoonbills (*Platalea ajaja*), arguably North America's most adorable though utterly ridiculous bird, with its peculiar head and bill that looks like an alien vacuum nozzle attached to a slender neck with a fluff of pink below. It was a glorious day; I had the windows down and my elbow out on one desolate stretch of road, when suddenly the ragged little one-and-a-half lane back road turned into a wide four-lane highway. I pull over to look at the map. Am I on the right road? No highway was indicated. I decided that I was still heading north, so I pulled back out and picked up speed on the four-lane. The road being wide and free of traffic, with a grassy meridian, I thought heck, might as well hit sixty and make some time, right? Oh, lordy, bad plan, Pete.

I was not a quarter of a mile down the raceway when, out of who knows where, I'm suddenly being tagged by a Louisiana cop car, with flashers and sirens blaring. I dutifully pulled over. Shit. While I rummaged for my license and rental agreement, I also saw this good ol' boy cop, right out of *Cool Hand Luke*, shades and all, hitch his pants up over his pot belly and stride right up to me like he owns the world. The dialogue that follows is all in the thickest of Louisiana drawls.

"Lookee here if it ain't a yohng hoss!" he chortled, coming up to my window. "So, tell me young hoss, this here's God's country, why you be drivin' thru it like hell? Hmm?"

Flummoxed, I thought…uh…hmmm…what the fuck do you say to this opener?

"Know the speed limit, hoss, on this patch o' highway?" he continued.

"Uh, no sir, it wasn't posted."

"Wasn't posted. That's a good one, hoss. Speed limit is thirty-five miles per hour. Yessir, on account of all the gators crossin'. Gotta keep ever one safe, don't we now? And runnin' over a gator out of season is also a crime. So, tell me young hoss, what yuh think I clock yuh at?"

I hadn't a clue, but I ventured, "Uh, fifty-five?"

"Fifty-five!' he repeated my words with an awful grin. "Another good one, hoss. Ever-body sez fifty-five. Shit, no. Yuh was doin' sixty-three! Imagine that, sixty-three, that bein' let's see…" He pretended to count. "Oh my. That's near thirty miles over the speed limit, young hoss. Now ain't that a might shame, son. Cuz we don't like no law breakers down here in Jefferson Parish, do we now, know what I mean, yohng hoss?"

"Uh…yeah," I said slowly, hedging my bets against where this was all going.

"Now, son, yuh look like yer edercated and all. You might be thinkin' this Parish named after that Virginia Jefferson president guy. No, siree. Named after Jefferson Davis, yes, sir, Jefferson Davis, President of the Confederate States of America. See, young hoss, yuh larnin' something about Jefferson Parish already, ain't ya now? So yuh happen to have a driver's license? Some sort of ID?"

"Yes, sir, right here." I handed him my New York state driver's license.

"Well, lookee here! Our yohng hoss, he's from that good old libral Yankee state of Noo York! Ain't that something now? Yuh're a loooong way from home, yohng hoss, ain't yuh now? Long way."

"Uh…yes sir."

"So, yohng hoss, here's how it works. I'm gonna be a real nice guy and let yuh off without a ticket. How about that?"

I shrugged. "Sure!"

"Good, good. Thing is, to save me the whole bother of not writin' that damn ticket, I think yuh should be payin' the goin' non-signage fee, and that's a hunnerd cash." His big fat grin says it all. Non-signage fee? WTF.

"A hundred bucks in cash?" I said, incredulous.

"Ain't that something! Boy's got ears. Yes, yohng hoss, that's right. A hunnred bucks."

I thought for a moment—this ain't right, but calculating at the same time that I'm out in the middle of butt fuck nowhere, Bayou Somewhere, Redneck Parish, Louisiana. Yet some sort of gritty sense of what's "Right and Proper!" rose up in me. A peeve, if you will, at this whole charade of graft.

Then, like an "idjit," I said: "First off, sir, I don't have $100 cash, and even if I did, I kinda think I have rights here. Can I talk to your boss?" But I was fishing in an empty barrel. The good ol' boy howled with false laughter.

"Oh, that's just dandy, yohng hoss. My boss, huh. My boss? Yuh want my boss?"

"Uh, yes, sir, actually I do." No, no, no! Pete, way, WAY wrong answer!

The cop rocked back on his black boot heels, looked up at the sky, and pondered a minute. Then he came right back down to the car window with an evil grin.

"Well, young hoss, yuh in luck. My boss just happens to be in. So, here's how it works, see. Listen good now, son. Yuh gonna follow me. My car's gonna lead. Whole way I want yuhr two headlights in my rearview mirror. Understand what I'm sayin' son? Rearview mirror, both lights, just like Dolly Parton's eyelashes, right in my mirror." With his right hand he split his fore and middle fingers and did the "my eyes—your eyes" gesture. "Got that, young hoss? Both headlights. Then we gonna see my boss. We understand ourselves heah, son?"

"Yes, sir, I understand."

Off he waddled to his cruiser, and I started up my rental. I tailed him with a twenty-foot gap the whole way. So intent was I on staying glued to his rear end, I didn't really see where we were going, what with all the twists and turns we took. At last, I saw a tiny bayou hamlet coming up ahead with some fish warehouses, runty homes, racks of crab pots, and a general sense of southern white trash poverty everywhere. We finally came to a tiny drab dull-yellow one-story dump of a building that had a sign saying "POLICE" at a cockeyed angle. Had the Coen brothers written this script? He pulled into the small parking lot filled with potholes of beaten dirt, and I pulled in next to him. It did NOT look promising.

"This way, son," he said, walking over to the paint-peeling front door. He kicked it open and walked in, with me a few paces behind. What I immediately saw was a ramshackle office, big old lazy ceiling fan squeaking overhead, drab file cabinets, the usual office bric-a-brac, a counter with a coffee maker, and a disorganized desk. I saw a doorway leading off to another room to my left, but it was barely ajar, so I couldn't really see in. The big ol' cop plopped himself down behind the one cluttered desk, heaved his big ol' boots up onto the papers, spread hands over belly, and said in a tone dripping with condescension that obviously amused him to no end, "Here's where we find ourselves."

Then: "Close the door, hoss! Don't want no stray dogs wanderin' in!" I closed the door obediently. "OK, yohng hoss. Go ahead. What yuh got t' say t' my boss? Fire away, yuh lookin at him."

Well, shit, so much for being from a state where the rule of law actually means something, at least for well-heeled white males who can afford a lawyer. Being no dummy, I got the drill. But just for the hell of it I said, "And if I want a real ticket, day in court, and can't pay the $100?"

"That ain't no problem t'all, yohng hoss." The man heaved himself up and waddled over to the other door and threw it open. I peered in. There was a jail cell right out of some western TV show, with big iron bars on three sides, a hard plank bunk, and a shit bucket. The cop was grinning ear to ear. "Don't your jowl muscles hurt from all that," I was thinking.

"Might fine accommodations, son. Best in town, in fact. And guess wut, it's free!"

I sighed, whupped, just shaking my head that this sort of open graft could be happening in the US of A in the late 20th century. Had I been a black man, of course, I'd have experienced this brazen police lawlessness two dozen times by now, in every damn town I'd passed through. Rather than keep the charade going and knowing his boss wouldn't think twice about throwing me into that miserable hole, I rifled in my pocket and pulled out a wad of cash in different bills. I counted it.

"All I've got is $67, down to the penny. Here." I held it out.

The good ol' boy kept on grinning his evil grin. "Why, lookee here. Sixty-seven dollahs. Praise the Good Lord! Guess I'd kinda thought fancy Noo Yokah fella like yuh'd have a big fat ol' roll. But guess wut, son? The speedin' fine done jus'been reduced by my boss to $67!" And out came his greasy fat mitt to take my last dollars from me.

It took me forty-five minutes to find my way back out to the four-lane speed trap, after getting lost on dead ends a half-dozen times. You can be sure I was doing thirty-five mph the whole rest of the way. In fact, for the next ten miles, I was doing thirty-five mph no matter what the speed limit signs said. But here's the rub: my gas gauge by now said "Empty." Finally, I came to another run-down hamlet and found a beat-up shamble of a gas station. There was one pump, but no slot for credit cards. Of course. No wonder Louisiana is such a mess—bad cops and still in the 19th century, sez the privileged white Noo Yokah with disdain. No one was in the station office, so I walked over to the auto mechanic's garage and found two feet sticking out from underneath a muddy pickup truck.

"Excuse me…" I said. Nothing.

"Excuse me," I said again, louder.

"Hold y'damn horses. I done h'ard yuh the first time!" Out scooted the mechanic on a rolling platform. He grabbed a rag from his belt and wiped his hands, then sat up. I explained that I have no money, a cop up the road took it, poor me, yadda yadda. Might his office have a card reader? I really needed some gas.

The mechanic was dressed in overalls and every inch the grease monkey, his mouth just a busted picket fence of no solid teeth. He looked me up and down, and the only thing he asked was: "Ya didn akchooly pay thayat shit fo' brains shay-riff nuttin didjya?"

"The cop?"

"Yes, the fuckin' cop! Who else we talkin' 'bout? That wo'thless piece of shit…" And for a good two minutes the mechanic went off, calling the "wo'thless shit fo' brains shay-riff" every dad-burn epithet known to a boy with a certain Anglo-Saxon eloquence from Bayouville, Louisiana. He too had been shaken down by shit fo' brains. Finally, he got to his feet.

"Well, since yuh done bin robbed, guess I'll give yuh three gallons free. Should git ya far as Larose on highway one. That OK? Ain't got no credit card reader heah."

OK? Wow! "Sure. That's great! I really appreciate it." Three gallons of gas and another big "thank you," and there I was, headin' back to the Big Easy, feeling, surprisingly, like a million bucks—well, minus the $67 of course.

I had a good friend in Ithaca at the time, who was an African-American lawyer who had taken on a number of civil cases in New Orleans. He made a major bundle in one court case concerning rank corruption, came north, and lawyered now as he pleased. When I told him my story, all he could muster, with a wry chuckle, was: "And your point is? Hell, Peter, I've seen graft in the Big Easy that would make your $100 just the match to light those god damn good old boys' fat cigars." OK, got it. I wasn't too miffed anymore, actually. In fact, it was almost comforting to know that out yonder the lawless wild west was still at its shenanigans.

Learning to Manage Out of Paper Bags

I returned from my trip to NOLA to move from Cornell to a job at Syracuse University, fifty miles up the road. I was to take up reins as the Associate University Librarian (AUL) for Collection Development, a job that entailed several essential duties. The first was to manage a big budget for purchasing scholarly journals and monographs. The second was to endlessly negotiate contracts for online databases and e-journal packages. The third was to supervise several dozen librarians, "selectors," whose job it was to comb the literature in their respective disciplines for new books and journals. They also doubled as the reference contacts for the subjects they managed. Finally, I was to build consortial relationships with other university libraries, in order to strengthen the purchasing power of the library in the increasingly corporatized world of "scholarly publishing." As we all have in our job descriptions, there was the perennial, "other duties as assigned" as well. These turned out to be supervising the Rare Book Department and the university's Belfer Audio Archive. In any case, it was there, at the Byrd Library at Syracuse University, that I was finally tested as a manager, and eventually learned the ropes of what passes for my leadership skills. With a budget approaching $6,000,000 for materials, with upwards of twenty-five staff reporting to me, and with both campus and national representative duties, I was thrown into a whirlwind at this new job the likes of which I'd not experienced before. Yet I thoroughly enjoyed it.

I had been thrilled that my future boss, University Librarian Peter Graham, had actually had the chutzpah to join PLG at our protest at ALA-NOLA, crying foul at paying over a hundred thousand dollars for a one-hour stump speech to the architect of going into the quagmire war in Iraq, General Colin Powell. Yet there he was in the fray with a sign. Peter and I hit it off immediately. He was a good man who cared deeply about our profession, and was kindly in mentoring me in my first position as a top manager at a major research library. I was blessed that every single one of the staff and librarians who I worked with during my six years at Syracuse never created any intractable personnel issues that can dog many managers. To the last, they were wonderful colleagues. Yet purposefully, I did not make real friends there, partly because I felt it unwise to manage a person at work and then be their friend off-duty. I could see the inherent conflict in that, and this doesn't mix if problems arise. Besides, my beautiful tree house with the waterfalls in Ithaca beckoned me home after work and it was a fifty-mile drive each way. There was never any traffic on that long slog, but it was brutal in winter.

I recall a quip by President Harry Truman, to the effect that "I sit here all day trying to persuade people to do the things they ought to have sense enough to do without my persuading them." I know you are not supposed to pass undue judgment on those whom you supervise, but in many ways our former president sums up people management pretty close to the mark. And truth be told, it isn't far off from my own style of managing employees in that I believe firmly in self-motivation as the key to a good performance review. In this regard, I have always sought to give everyone who reported to me wide leeway to succeed their way forward, only stepping in when work flags or they suddenly shoot off in aberrant directions at odds with the expectations of higher rungs of management. I have also been a fierce advocate in all my library positions that it is my job to provide sufficient funds for the professional development of both staff and librarians. I am also a firm believer that every employee (and by extension every library patron as well) needs the best technology to do their work, whether it's office computers, digital cameras for special collections, or iMac workstations for our students.

My biggest weak spot as an AUL, and subsequently in my work as dean at Fresno State, was in my inability to attend to endless small details. I attribute this failing entirely to genetics. It's an unfortunate mutation, as you can well imagine, as our profession loves its details. But I'm here to tell that it's a fallacy that if you shut your eyes tight, those details miraculously go away. So, you do the next best thing and assign the nagging details to someone else far more competent at deciphering how to manipulate, well, complex spreadsheets than you are. I am convinced there's an entire division at Microsoft whose sole duty is to create byzantine Excel rules out of nothing more than ersatz sadism. I can't be alone in thinking this, can I? Then comes the dreaded "upgrade" and further ersatz rules run rampant. Overnight all the little tricks you so diligently learned by rote, thinking yourself ever so clever, all suddenly vanish into cyber obsolescence. Only the certifiably insane look forward to that little prompt on their mobile device that says with robotic aggression, "You need to upgrade your software to 12.2.4.7! Would you like to upgrade now?" I mean, how lucky were the stiffs in the perpetual war state of Orwell's *1984* that Big Brother didn't know about "software upgrades"? Gripes aside, while it was tough for me in some ways, that first year at Syracuse still afforded me the opportunity to move my division forward. I enjoyed the creative roil of working with great librarians, smart people all. Recall, these were the golden years of the early aughts when search engine design and wrap-around websites blossomed with potential. I'm proud that, with my help, we were slowly able to move the library at Syracuse into the vanguard despite the limitations of not having enough tech staff or the bottomless pockets of the libraries at the big Ivies. I like to think, as well, that these improvements really served the patrons for whom we came to work each day.

One of the most enjoyable aspects of the job was working as the supervisor of staff at the Belfer Audio Archive, arguably one of the finest historical collections of recorded sound in America, second only to the Library of Congress. Every physical type of recording is held in that collection, in all musical genres, including spoken word and sound effects. The cylinder collection itself is perhaps second to none, with items going right back to the earliest wax recordings by Edison. What vexed me, as it did many of the professors in the recording industry program in the College of Visual and Performing Arts, was the problem of making the splendor of such an archive more readily available, anywhere, anytime. The technologies required to make an analog recording into a digital one were well known, since music CDs were by this time fifteen years old. Recording studios were slowly moving away from 16-track tape to digital DAT forms. By the time Apple came out with its third generation iPod in 2003 and the iTunes model of music sales had largely taken off like a bottle rocket, a wonderful professor named David Rezak and I began to explore ways to get the archive itself into some sort of digital database akin to iTunes. What stumped us was always the intractable and thorny question of copyright.

Musical recordings have a plethora of rights holders: the composers, the musicians, the engineers and producers, the sheet music composition companies, the record companies, and everyone in-between. In the case of historical recordings, the question was "where in hell were all these folks now?" Was there possibly one last rights holder still alive from Shirley Temple's first recording in the 1930s? But the iTunes model at least gave us an opening. What if, instead of asking permission for historical copyright up front, we instead asked forgiveness and made a payment down the line? What if a multimillionaire like David Packard (of Hewlett-Packard), who was a huge fan of historical recordings, gave Belfer a matching $10M grant, as he'd given the Library of Congress for their recordings, and we digitized 100,000 old records? There would be no cost to the rights holders or the record companies. On the back end of this digital archive, universities and schools could negotiate open access licenses by campus IP addresses, giving educational institutions *streaming-only* access to all the content. With streaming there would be scant incentive to digitally dub the old songs, thus no student theft of master-level recordings a la Napster, LimeWire, or Kazaa. On the front end, for the public, all the identified rights holders could come together as they now do with iTunes, and offer songs for $1.29 a pop through some agreed-upon middle man: say, consortial not-for-profits. With these "honest brokers" in place, there would be some sort of escrow account and revenue stream for rights holders who might pop up out of nowhere asking for their dividend. This idea of mine began to get traction amongst music industry types both in NY and LA. I even sat down with the financial manager of the Rolling Stones through his old buddy David Rezak, who helped us hash out some of the early drafts of my idea.

It wasn't long before David and I were sitting in a 60th floor meeting room of VPs for Music Recordings at Sony Entertainment. With us in the million-dollar-view office were his counterparts at Warner Music Group and Universal Music Group, in short, the honchos who controlled 80% of the music business in the western world. There was even some mucky-muck from AOL (then a giant corporation tied to Warner) in the room. In opening the discussion, the big wig at Sony (and all present but David and I shall remain nameless) made it clear that what was happening in that very room could be seen as a breach of the Sherman Antitrust Act, which prohibits separate corporations from colluding to price-fix, still less cook up other "monopolistic" practices. He mentioned a couple of other laws we might be breaking, partly in jest, and everyone chuckled nervously. These high and mighty men in the room all seemed to know each other; they oozed New York moxie and entitlement. So, everything was off the record. The upshot was that there were two key issues seen as stumbling blocks. One, the seed money sufficient to digitize thousands of recordings; two, creating or finding a legal, business-savvy third party (but not Apple, who all the execs excoriated as underselling their music) to manage the payouts, preferably a not-for-profit university consortium of some sort. We on the academic side would have to create this financial umbrella since the music corporations, at a stroke, might be investigated for conflicts of interest. David and I came away highly encouraged, and I even got a free stack of the latest Sony CD releases that just happened to be lying around the CEO suite floor; the staff handed them out like breath mints.

Soon after, I booked a meeting in Palo Alto with David Packard and the head of his philanthropy operations. On the back of the napkin, Packard thought the cost would be $3-$5M. The amount was eye-popping to me, but his nonchalant look and "not so bad" shrug, along with his donor dude quietly nodding back, spoke volumes. They seemed intrigued by the idea and suggested I write up a proposal. They'd shop it around to other tech heavyweights in Silicon Valley and see if it got legs with other investors. Once again, I came away highly encouraged. I talked to folks at the National Recording Preservation Board at the Library of Congress, Yale, and other holders of large historical recording collections. Again, I met with encouragement. David Rezak set up meetings with copyright brokers ASCAP and BMI, plus some sheet music companies who also had a hand in older music copyrights. Then all came to a screeching halt. In the middle of all this exciting exploration, word came via the university provost that my dear boss, Peter Graham, would be taking an extensive leave of absence to deal with therapies related to his sudden battle with cancer. The provost immediately iced all projects, including ours, at the Belfer until the future of the library itself became clearer. Months later, on August 11, 2004, Peter died of complications from his illness. What a sad day.

Over the next two years, various interim people served as temporary university librarian, and one at least was rather good, but over time our truly innovative historical recording idea just melted away for lack of university backing. Neither the provost nor the interims would give a green light for such a massive enterprise until a new library leader was chosen. In Fall 2005, the university finally began interviewing for a new university librarian. I won't go into all of my own opinions here, just suffice it to say that the pool of candidates was weak and the weakest, in my opinion, was offered the position, reportedly due to internal connections. Time would tell that the decision to hire this new university librarian was not a good fit for the Syracuse University Library. My new boss, as I had intuited during the interview, was clearly not the decent human being that Peter Graham had been. We each bring our own management chops to every new task at hand, but in the case of my new boss, this seemed to mean leaning heavily on making peremptory decisions with scant consultation with senior staff. This riled me to no end, and I said so as politely as I knew how, in private. Clearly, we were at an impasse. Through unnecessarily convoluted channels, she suggested I find other employment if that's how I felt. I was essentially given six months to find another job. It's fair to say that new top managers should be given the opportunity to surround themselves with people they feel most comfortable with. I've had to remove some employees myself from positions of responsibility when their M.O. and mine as supervisor didn't jibe. In this case, the new university librarian was sweeping house her way and I accepted that as her right. I felt no personal failing on my part; we just weren't a good fit. I began to look for employment elsewhere.

It was all for the best, because in moving on, I came to finish my career as Dean of Library Services at the Henry Madden Library, California State University, Fresno, serving from February 1, 2007 to May 31, 2017. The provost there didn't so much as blink as to the "why" of my leaving Syracuse. "That isn't relevant for this position," she said at my interview, with no explanation. She'd obviously done her homework, though. Whatever rumors swirled, given my sterling references, my exemplary work experience, my grant-writing and fundraising acumen, my wide contacts in the industry, and my proven engagement with the community at both Cornell and Syracuse, any concerns about me, she said, didn't add up. So I was to have, with her blessing, a truly wonderful ten-year run at Fresno State. But before I go on to that part of my career, first a word, or actually several thousand words, about poets, poetry, and poems in my life that have arguably been my greatest extra-curricular passion for the past fifty years

Chapter 9

Westward with the Joads

Sam Hamill in the Land of "Almost Paradise"

On a long day's drive down to New York City from Ithaca, all the bridges over the highway bore disturbing signs of national rage and stunned disbelief: "Kill the Bastards!" "The Only Good Arab is a Dead Arab!" "America the Strong!" It was the first week of October, 2001. Down in the city, the Twin Towers lay in a smoldering heap and search dogs continued sniffing for the dead. But finally, all the bridges, subways, and ashen thoroughfares were open again to traffic and commerce.

With me in the car that day were poet, publisher, and fine hand-press printer Sam Hamill, and a delightful chanteuse and fine musician Kathy Z., a neighbor of mine from Ithaca. Sam and I, being by nature cynics, made a running commentary on the world's mad xenophobia and ethnic hatreds as we drove down, excoriating the knee-jerk prejudices that seethed so suddenly across a riled nation. Optimist Kathy, bless her, finally told us grumpy and disparaging older crocks to change the subject, jeez-louise, talk about something else, please. So. we all sat in glum silence for the rest of the trip, our thoughts as leaden as the gray day.

Sam, in more ways than I can count, was arguably the most influential friend and mentor in my life. Brilliant, caustic, steeped in the traditions of poetry across the globe, he was also generous to a fault, heuristic in his approach to prosody, and an irascible

Buddhist in the mold of the beloved abbot Ikkyu of 15th-century Japan, whom Sam admired. Like abbot Ikkyu, Sam was a fierce iconoclast, intolerant of bullshit, and dismissive of pomposity. Both were eccentrics in extremis, Ikkyu going so far as to live contentedly with a blind brothel courtesan even as he served as a Zen abbot at one of Japan's most storied monasteries. "I would rather meditate in a brothel than amid the false pieties of priestly Zen," he is purported to have said. It was a quote that Sam would have made quite happily himself had he not found his own muse in his delightful artist wife, Gray Foster.

Sam Hamill: who knows of him today? Has anyone read his wonderful collection, *Almost Paradise* (Shambhala, 2005)? Or his magnificent collected works, *Habitations* (Lost Horse Press, 2014)? Yet he was the founder and editor of Copper Canyon Press (CCP) for forty-five years, which published its first books of poetry in 1972 and is considered by many to be the finest small poetry press in America. Renowned the world over as a great poet, Sam was largely ignored at home by the establishment critics in America. Doubtless his fierce criticism of that same establishment won him no friends in the rarified world of eastern belle lettres. Refusing an invite to the White House in the winter of 2003, Hamill publicly renounced the invitation extended by then First Lady Laura Bush. Instead, he founded the organization Poets Against War (PAW) to fight the sword with mightier words, or so he hoped. PAW in any case sought to use poetry as a platform of lyric rage to oppose the Iraq War. Within a year, many thousands of poets had published anti-war poems on the PAW website, and a bestseller of selected poems was put out by The Nation Press. In our voluminous email correspondence through this period, and again when we met in person over sake and boiled eel, Sam expressed his fear that he had let loose a ravenous worms ouroboros in PAW, a beast that was suddenly consuming all his time and energy. Amidst the outpouring of grief and anger, his life as a writer and poet, his lifetime dedication to the care and craft of poetry, and all his publishing and printing work seemed suddenly to have been subsumed by the maw of PAW. Scratching his head, he bemoaned that this work had led his life many miles astray from the spare path of prosody of those Japanese (Basho, Buson) and Chinese (Wang Wei, Du Fu) poets whom he loved and had translated. He felt exiled into a world of other people's expectations.

Another author and irascible poet, Jim Harrison (*Legends of the Fall*), once said of Sam: "Hamill has reached the category of a National Treasure though I'd doubt he'd like the idea." Sam didn't like the idea of being a national treasure, but was prescient enough to edit and publish the most beautiful edition of collected poems by Harrison, *The Shape of the Journey* (CCP, 1998). Both Sam and Jim signed my rare hand-bound copy of this lovely book, and I recall several banquets of wine and fine food we three shared in Seattle when Jim came out for a visit. As PAW became a national phenomenon, by his own admission, Sam got shunted to an outsider role of cantankerous trouble-maker even among the board members of Copper Canyon Press. In the high-status world of Pulitzer Prizes and academic accolades, he became *persona non grata*.

Copper Canyon, in its heyday, published some of the finest poets in any language, in books crafted with care and exquisite design elements. Sam was also a renowned letterpress printer, whose beautiful broadsides, hand letter pressed on the finest Japanese paper, are simply exquisite. It can be said truthfully that no one did more for the art of poetry in all its manifestations in the latter half of the 20th and the early 21st centuries than my dear friend Sam, now deceased. Here's one of Sam's last poems:

> And what am I but its solitary
> pilgrim—lost, found, lost again—
> on the long journey whose only end
> is silence before the burning
> of my body, one last moment
> of flame, a whiff of smoke

> washed clean
> and gone with the rain.

My own fifty-year love affair with poetry came to maturity through Sam. "Can't stand all this clever MFA crap being published today," he'd say out of the blue over a third bottle of sake. "Every damn little newly minted poet with their cookie cutter first books must have their little literary prize. Ech." He'd then spit out a bit of ash from the joint of pot he smoked every evening. "Poetry must start in the ear, dammit," he'd go on. "In the ear! Before they write a damn line, all these wannabe poets under the age of thirty should damn well memorize twenty of the great poems of the canon, and learn through the arduous work of memorization to put their soul's expression into reciting them. Maybe then, and only then, should these punks be allowed take up a pencil and write their trite posey." He'd scratch his head, downing another little glass of sake as if to wash away the bad taste. Sam often quoted the Cuban poet Dulce Maria Loynaz, who said "Leer más escriber menos" ('Read more, write less') as a way to make his point. Lawrence Ferlinghetti, owner of City Lights Books in San Francisco and a grand poet himself, had this to say about recent American poetry fads, which was also a favorite quote of Sam's:[42]

> Time now to open your mouths
>   with a new speech
> All you dead language poets and deconstructionists,
> All you poetry workshop poets
>   in the boondock heart of America
> All you house-broken Ezra Pounds
> All you pre-pressed Concrete poets
> All you pay-toilet poets groaning with graffiti
> All you eyeless unrealists....

[and delightfully on for three whole pages, thanks Larry!]

---

42. Lawrence Ferlinghetti, "Populist Manifesto," in *These Are My Rivers: New and Selected Poems 1955-1993* (New Directions Press, 1993), p. 205.

Of course, the "boondock heart of America" is the Iowa Writers Workshop franchise, where half of this mischief emanates—Sam's bane, Larry's, and mine. I remember when I happened to be visiting the Bay Area when Sam was giving a packed reading at City Lights. Ferlinghetti took Sam and me, along with a few other hangers-on, to dinner in nearby Chinatown where Sam got into a drunken row with the proprietor. The contention was whether the Chinese T'ang poet (c800 BCE) Du Fu, Sam's claim, was twice the poet as his contemporary Li Po (the proprietor's claim). We all laughed at this absurd fracas, as two stubborn curmudgeons gnawed on a thousand-year-old bone through half the repast. Larry proposed a toast to both.

In any event, I take this detour into my apprenticeship under Sam, to simply say that every wall of my home today has a bookcase lined with fine books of the great poets of the 20th century. Most are first editions, many signed, many more again gifts from the poets themselves, whom I've befriended over the years. Banished from my shelves are the tepid cocktail-hour Eastern establishment poets such as Lowell, Merrill, Jorie Graham, Paul Muldoon, Archie Ammons (whom I knew at Cornell), and Robert Pinsky to name a few. I recall an evening with the wonderful poet Hayden Carruth, a compatriot of mine at Syracuse University, sitting in his cramped kitchen in the no-wheres-Munnsville upstate NY boondocks where he'd made a hermit's home with his lovely poet wife, Joe-Anne McLaughlin. Somewhere on the kitchen table was a review of A.R. Ammon's new book, *Bosh and Flapdoodle: Poems* (Norton, 2005). Hayden, who by this time looked like a demented Walt Whitman in overalls and wool cap, and was probably well over eighty, said with a howl: "Well, good for you, Archie, fucker finally got a title right!" Miss ya Hayden, lord you were funny. The first book of poetry I ever bought, right after high school, was one edited by Hayden, a fat little paperback put out in 1970 called *The Voice That is Great Within Us: American Poetry of the Twentieth Century* (Bantam Books Poetry, 1970). I still have the same little book with marginalia throughout, thumbed but still tight in a frail binding. If there is such a thing as a gateway drug to addiction, for me this diminutive tome was my gateway to poetry obsession. *Northwest Review* published my elegiac poem to Hayden when he died in the fall of 2008.

As for Sam, his earliest selected works, *Destination Zero 1970-1995* (White Pine Press, 1995), garnered sincerest praise from such luminaries as W.S. Merwin, Donald Hall, and Denise Levertov. This is testament enough of his craftsmanship. I'd have to say that the opening poem, "Lover's Quarrel," is as fine a poem in the English language as ever was writ, sonnets of the Bard included. Few wrote as lyrically or with such elegiac clarity as Sam, though poets such as John Haines, Robert Sund, Robert Fulton MacPhereson, Lisl Mueller, Louise Gluck, Denise Levertov, James Wright, Hayden himself, Thomas McGrath. and Kenneth Rexroth come close. I knew, and loved, some of these folks as drinking companions; many of these poets were gentle mentors as well. What I admired in Sam's poetry, although I failed too often to imbue my own work with the same sensibilities, was his ability to unfold his soul, with each stanza and line break unfurling like a petalled flower or some strange origami. His turns of phrase seemed to flow so effortlessly from his pen, all offered to the reader in the most direct language of the spoken word, with a clear eye to the natural world and grounded in the seasons, the sea, the sky, the silent woods. Stripped of artifice or academic embellishment, his poems have been acknowledged as some of the finest in the American literary canon.

Among the many poets I've known, perhaps the oddest was James Laughlin, founder and senior editor of New Directions Press (ND). His last wife was a dear friend of my mother's. J, as he was known, was close to my father's age, born in 1914 (Dad in 1916) with a silver spoon in his mouth half the size of Manhattan, the son of America's top steel tycoon. In other words, he was loaded from birth till the daisies did come up. In the 1930s,

Laughlin travelled to Europe and lived near Gertrude Stein and Alice B. Toklas' gathering place for artists and writers, as a sort of breathless acolyte. J brought his rather wretched early poetry to see if some folks in Paris, like Sylvia Beach of Shakespeare & Co., might publish it. His manuscripts went nowhere, so upon Gertrude's suggestion, he went to visit Ezra Pound in Italy, who was no more kind toward his poesy. Sez Ez: "You're never going to be any good as a poet. Why don't you take up something useful?" Pound then suggested, since Laughlin was a millionaire's son, that he go into publishing. The J I knew was no dummy. Thus was born New Directions Publishing house in 1936, arguably the most avant-garde press in America throughout the 20th century. Their books had a signature look and feel—every cover a monochrome, arty in abstract design, distinctive. Their stable of poets and writers was the most existentially "out there" from the war years through the aughts, unmatched by any other publishing house anywhere. J poured his fortune into publishing.

I'd visit Laughlin whenever I came home to my parents throughout my years of itinerant travels, until he died in 1997. At his sprawling compound in Norfolk, CT, up on a hilltop in bucolic surroundings, with a lily pond far below, the Berkshire Mountains beyond, and the gardens manicured, we'd delve together into poetry and the craziness of the gone world. His library, I am guessing at this time, held both the finest collection of ND poetry first editions anywhere, and of every other publishing house, too. It all burned down in 1995, two years before he died. Like so many poets, and J wasn't a bad poet at all in my opinion, he was a disorderly drunk. We'd sit in his living room, three cocktails to the wind, and for the umpteenth time I'd hear about his escapades in Barcelona, Paris, Florence, Lisbon, even Constantinople, and each conquest in the retelling, apparently, had boobs "like the Matterhorn"—which always had me thinking, rock hard and ice cold, hmmm, where's that at? Doubtless in the mad men days of the 1950s and 60s those push-up bras did wonders for the libido.

I came to care for the old geezer, draped in his silk bathrobe, in his declining years when apparently no one else came to visit him in his exile of convalescence. He gave me some of the most wonderful and rare ND books out there, and signed them all. Pound loved him, and so did I. Here's to you, J.

I am particularly proud of being the founding editor of the only scholarly journal in English dealing with world haiku, senryu, haibun, and haiga: *Juxtapositions: The Haiku Journal of Research and Scholarship*. Some of the finest scholars of haiku sit on the editorial board with me. It is an annual monographic series of edited essays, book reviews, and pictorial haiga with both an online presence and a print volume. We are in our sixth year of publication. Our essays range widely, from medical research into how writing haiku has been effectively used in brain research as a prophylactic tool related to depression, PTSD, and other forms of mental disorders, to essays on historical poets from 17th-century Japan.

At Cornell (sometimes in conjunction with Ithaca College), then even more so at Syracuse, and perhaps in the end most effectively at Fresno State when I became the director of the Fresno Poets Association, I certainly tried to enlighten the eager minds of students by inviting some of the finest poets to read. These included Denise Levertov, W.S. Merwin, Donald Hall, Joseph Stroud, Dorianne Laux, Eleanor Wilner, Tomas Tranströmer, Tess Gallagher, Louise Gluck, Sharon Olds, and the list goes on. Sam, on his second invite to read in upstate New York, five years after our grim trip south by car with Kathy, was the last poet I brought to Syracuse University, in the spring of 2006. By year's end, I had pulled up stakes, said a sad farewell to my Ithaca tree house amid the waterfalls, and moved to Fresno, California.

Vagabond with the Joads: California's Central Valley

To go from bucolic, beautiful, leafy, rain-soaked, liberal, small town Ithaca, from a tree house above Salmon Creek with its three waterfalls, to the bone dry, 110F summer days lasting seven months on end without rain, yes, to land boots to the ground in the deeply conservative, culturally challenged Central Valley of California where Fresno sits like a lynch pin smack in the middle of the state, was a real eye opener to say the least. Luckily, I came west with my future wife, so as a couple we had each other to lean on through the early months of adjustment.

While still at Syracuse, I met and fell in love with a lovely woman who worked as a campus videographer for Cornell University. Her name is Joy Quigley. We met at a summer beach party on Cayuga Lake. We dated. Joy is only too happy to tell anyone that throughout our courtship, I regaled her to no end with erudite reams of verbosity. In her telling, half the tales of this memoir arrived in her inbox via long emails. I remain skeptical. She might further tell you that my tendency to name drop in these excessive exegeses was not sufficiently puerile or annoying as to upend our courtship. Because apparently, despite my loquacity, I somehow succeeded in winning her hand.

Joy is now my wonderful wife. She is an Emmy-award-winning videographer. When we first met, she had a fabulous job, it seemed to me, as she filmed Nobel laureates, famous faculty, fascinating projects, and grand lecture series, all going on at Cornell. It might be that on one day she was off to Texas to film rabies inoculation of coyotes for an animal scientist; on another shoot it might be an expert in high Andes Peruvian native cultures, or Bill Nye the Science Guy, one of the frequent talking heads in her viewfinder. She even got to go to Paris for two weeks to film French law professors, interviewed with Notre Dame as a backdrop. It all seemed so glamorous compared to my humdrum life as a librarian. This talented videographer was so intelligent, involved, and fun to be with that I was smitten. We immediately hit it off. Honestly, I am still not sure to this day why she gave up such a great job at Cornell to come west with me to an unknown future in the less than desirable zip codes of Fresno, but come she did in January of 2007. Having given up her job at Cornell, she came west without health insurance which can bankrupt you overnight in America, I well knew. So when I started work at Fresno State on February 1, 2007, we decided to get Joy on my generous benefits. Our wedding rings were bought on the fly the day before the ceremony, as we headed to see Michael Moore's new film Sicko at a nearby Cineplex. This was an appropriate dénouement as it happened, because we were marrying for health insurance reasons ourselves. So in a small goofy ceremony in a mountaintop home in Auberry, CA, an aging agnostic officiant named Bill Young and his even older but sweeter artist wife, maid Miriam, presided over our secret marriage ceremony in their living room overlooking the San Joaquin River gorge, 4000 feet below. A twenty-something neighbor we had just met served as witness. Somehow we managed to convince the poor lad, a Korean whose English wasn't particularly good, to hop in our car and troop into the mountains for this oddball ceremony. I think the "I Dos" lasted about a minute, which even at that length produced little more than bafflement in our poor witness, but he was a good sport. First to last, our impromptu wedding was delightfully seat-of-the-pants. The following August in Ithaca we had a proper wedding with ceremony and feast, but it was legally a redundant, if wonderful, ceremony.

Fresno has always been an odd fit for us. Joy and I come from East Coast backgrounds, coming of age in or around great cultural cities like New York and Philadelphia. Fresno, by contrast, is a large agricultural commodities center that happens to have a city haphazardly growing up around it. When a year later the financial crash of 2008 came, this one-trick region was hit particularly hard. The last extensive film work that Joy was able to get was serving as a second camera on a national film tour of the Barack Obama 2008 presidential campaign, which opened in California with a speech he gave at the former Black Panther center in Oakland. We've always felt a bit out of place in Fresno, despite meeting new friends and enjoying the nearby Sierra Mountains. My library at the university suffered massive budget cuts itself when the crash came. Poverty and homelessness in the town soared. The promise of the Obama years, in short, began as a mixed blessing for us.

Fresno, last I looked, is the thirty-fourth largest city in the US and the fifth biggest in California; bigger in short than Miami, Minneapolis, Atlanta, Cleveland, and New Orleans, to name a few. Yet on the *New York Times* weather page, of the thirty top cities where temperatures are given, including all the cities above, Fresno alone is absent—the butt of many a Jay Leno joke back in the day that we're just a bunch of pumpkin-growin' bumpkins. I confess, after fourteen years in this baking, small-town-mentality city, I sometimes find it hard to be a Fresno fan myself. Heaven knows I've tried, but as a Scotsman who prefers the cold damp drizzle of a boggy highland moor to living under a cloudless sunny sky for months on end, Fresno can too often be sheer and downright purgatory.

The city is rock bottom in air quality, also in green space as a city, worst for "quality of life" for African-Americans in California, worst gang violence per capita, highest disparity of wealth to poverty in the state, abysmal in health, education, and quality of life markers, and crime and life expectancy are no better—all with one of the largest undocumented immigrant populations in the US, which in the age of Trump and ICE is an unenviable statistic. And that's just the city of Fresno. In the wider Central Valley, out in the agricultural flatlands, the statistics of poverty, lack of educational attainment, abysmal health services, toxic air and water, and all other environmental challenges are worse by far than Appalachia. It's heartbreaking.

Fresno and its Central Valley remain a uniquely curious and haunted part of North America. For one, it is arguably the most productive agricultural land in the world. The magnificent Sierra Mountains, which form the eastern boundary of the city, are home to Yosemite, Kings, and Sequoia national parks, all within two hours of downtown. Within an hour and change of leaving home, I can stand absolutely alone and transfixed amid the largest stand of giant sequoia (*Sequoiadendron giganteum*) anywhere, and not see a soul all day. Yet this is also the land John Steinbeck wrote of in *Grapes of Wrath* (1939). His protagonists, the Joad family, flee the Dust Bowl of the central plains states and move to California, only to find little but misery in the Golden State. Ostracized, they make pittance pay for day labor in lugubrious work camps, picking grapes and cotton through the unending years of the Great Depression. Here's Steinbeck in his own words describing their plight: "There is a crime here that goes beyond denunciation. There is a sorrow here that weeping cannot symbolize. There is a failure here that topples all our success. The fertile earth, the straight tree rows, the sturdy trunks, and the ripe fruit. And children dying of pellagra must die because a profit cannot be taken from an orange. And coroners must fill in the certificate—died of malnutrition—because the food must rot, must be forced to rot. The people come with nets to fish for potatoes in the river, and the guards hold them back." To my mind, Steinbeck was a true socialist of the proletariat in so much of his work. Grapes of Wrath is spot on. It seems that little has changed for the farm workers since the grinding destitution of the 1930s dust bowl. California is blisteringly dry as a semi-desert seven to eight months of the year, so you survive with drought tolerance or your garden withers brown and dies. And of course, the hottest, driest lands on the continent are just a half day's drive away in Death Valley.

Yet I will assert to anyone that this beleaguered valley still has much to be proud of. This is not to sweep aside the challenges we face: the overdraft of well waters for thirsty export crops, the destitution of the immigrant field worker camps, the small run-down towns turned to busted dreams as most kids flee their dusty streets after high school for a better life elsewhere. These shortcomings are as "deep and wide" as Job's travails, one might say without exaggeration. As someone in the activist trenches pretty much every day, I know this landscape only too well. Cesar Chavez and Delores Huerta, co-founders of the United Farm Workers who organized the Delano grape strike in 1965, did not risk arrest and banishment from these thriving vineyards of produce because things were alright in the fields. They fought because migrant workers broke their backs picking grapes ten hours each day as the orchard owners drove by in Lincolns, uncaring that pesticides drifted over the pickers. Certainly, they did not risk all because the valley's plenty belonged to the people.[43] It never has. They fought because poverty and injustice are rife, then as now, because pickers face oppression and brutal conditions every day. Because ICE is having its day in the brutal sun in this age of post-Trump and rampant xenophobia. I crib the words of Charles Bukowski as my own here: "If I suffer at this typewriter, think how I'd feel among the lettuce-pickers of Salinas?"[44] Exactly.

This schizophrenic landscape may be baffling, but there is something about this valley that grows on you. Perhaps it's precisely because of the poverty and awful air; perhaps because Fresno regularly appears on lists of "worsts" in any given year by news organizations across the country; perhaps because we suffer every manner of chronic social problems; and despite all of this, there is by turns a corresponding fierce camaraderie among local progressives and the left-leaning Latino majority, a collective sense of fighting the good fight here among peoples of all backgrounds, all races, labor and academia, poverty advocates and environmentalists, that one doesn't find in most primarily-white upper-class college towns like Ithaca. Perhaps nowhere else in America is the potential for transformation occurring as much as here as the Latino majority finds its voice, its power, and its vote. Yet the wealth divide is particularly bad in California, as we rank near the top nationally. The further north you go in the city of

---

43. One of Peter Mattheissen's lesser-known books, *Sal Si Puedes: Cesar Chavez and the New American Revolution* (Random House, 1969), is an excellent place to start if one wishes to understand the valley's history of struggle in the picking fields.

44. From Charles Bukowski's *Love Is a Dog from Hell* (Ecco, 1977), p.139.

Fresno, the whiter and richer it becomes, as these politely racist folks fled the influx of people of color from Mexico and Guatemala moving into neighborhoods in the south. So by conscious choice we bought our lovely home in the south, and have Black, Asian, and Latino neighbors and even one back-door drug dealer on our block instead. We revel in this diversity even as the dumb drug dealer and his stupid girlfriend argue into the wee hours. It's still a step up from living on the outskirts of Harlem.

The student population at Fresno State is majority minority. Anglos or whites make up barely 20%, Hispanics close to 50%. Seventy-five percent are first-generation college attendees, as are our president, three VPs, and the provost. The largest graduation ceremony at the university each May is the Latino Graduation Celebration, which fills the indoor arena of 15,000 seats to the rafters replete with mariachi bands, dancers in colorful skirts, and Hispanic faculty in sombreros. It's a fiesta like no other that is gloriously deafening from beginning to end. And everything is bilingual. Welcome to our Central Valley.

The library I inherited as dean was nothing but a huge hole in the ground when I arrived. What passed for our remaining services was squeezed into the "old" library building, built in all its Stalinesque ugliness in 1981. Our entire collection of print books and journals was warehoused seven miles away as the crow flies, nine by car, in a huge hangar out by a busy freight highway. One might assume that this would not look promising to a job interviewee such as myself. Quite the opposite. To me, that big hole, and the plans to completely refurbish Stalin's wing, were pregnant with opportunities to reinvent our role as "information specialists" in the new century, to become the true "home" for our struggling students. What was eventually built with a $100,000,000 state bond that passed handily was a magnificent library which opened February 9, 2009. As a married but childless male of sixty-eight, I honestly don't think I'm a crowing parent here. But the new Madden Library that rose up, steel girder by steel girder, is arguably one of the most striking and dramatic academic libraries in the state, possibly the country. At 340,000 square feet, it is not the largest even in the California State University (CSU) system (San Diego State holds that laurel), nor does it hold the most books and rare items (Berkeley and UCLA share that honor), but for sheer eye-popping beauty show me something more amazing, please. The entire north wall of the building is glass, looking out on a beautiful Peace Garden at the heart of campus. Yokut design motifs are threaded throughout the building, and the colored granite, creating designs on the floors, were locally quarried from the Sierra foothills. While not a LEED certified building (the cost for that was prohibitive), features throughout were designed and installed for reasons of green sustainability. Oddest of all, a sixty-foot video screen on the exterior of the glass north wall shows a film on a loop of a renowned Yokut basket weaver named Lois Connor (now a friend) as she meticulously weaves an enormous gaming basket, a contemplative, mesmerizingly slow, year-long task. There she sits, basket in lap, as month after month the coils grow out into a magnificent basket almost four feet across when completed. Then the film begins again; it's quite Dada in a way.

For this feature and many others, the library has won a string of design awards over the years, and was featured in our trade's professional publication, *Library Journal* in its annual recap of "The Best in New Library Buildings" (2009). Institutions of higher education in California fall into three tiers. First are the eleven major research universities such as UCLA and Berkeley. Then there are the twenty-three campuses of the CSU, of which Fresno State is but one in the upper tier of size. As an aside, the CSU is the largest state university system in the US (near the top in the world outside China) serving something like 450,000 students every year. Finally, you have the more accessible system of local two-year community colleges. In aggregate, combine the three, and California serves more students in state-run institutions of high learning than the bottom thirty-five states combined. So many of our students begin in community college, transfer to Fresno State as juniors, and then go on to get Master's degrees or PhDs at the UCs.

I felt a deep sense of honor and responsibility leading this library through two challenging years of construction and diaspora. At one point, all of my staff was housed in large trailers on a patch of grass in the quad halfway across campus. Yet we persevered. Then came the financial crash of late 2008-2009, just as the magnificent building was beginning to rise up gloriously from its former hole. There was even talk between myself, the president, the provost, and the VP for Finance that maybe we should hold off on the ribbon cutting ceremony. As economies everywhere began to tank, CA Governor Arnold Schwarzenegger put a statewide moratorium on all major purchases in state-run agencies, including universities. So we couldn't purchase the beautiful tables and chairs we had chosen for the students. The provost, bless her, trusted my pluck and determination, and convinced the other administrators that we could open if we ordered hundreds of plastic folding tables from Costco, and thousands of folding chairs on contingency funds. And that's precisely what we did. The "Wow!" factor of the architecture won the students over. The books were finally back in the building, my staff had far better offices than they'd ever had before, and there was a great Reference Desk—all in a building that in every facet, despite the ugly tables, was a big hit with everyone right through to the city's mayor. Over the next eighteen months, through channels of creative accounting, all of the beautiful furnishings on order arrived one truckload at a time. Many years later, the students still consider the library the veritable heart of the campus, with over a million plus of them coming through the doors each year and the website databases garnering upwards of two million hits a year.

So how did a pot-smoking, punk rock-hustling, deadbeat, porno palace projectionist, and ardent political subversive attain to the position of Dean of Library Services at a major university in

California? Well, with luck, pluck, and ducking out of some bad career choices at just the right time, apparently. Doubtless these all played their part. I was also always willing to take risks in my life. *Per ardua ad astra*, as they say. I had never yearned for the biggest, still less the most prestigious positions in academia, so I never applied. I am actually not particularly ambitious that way, and for me, such a single-minded drive would have been a fool's errand. I remain too much the iconoclast to fit into a major role at one of the top ten. I took it as a compliment, when a fellow academic dean at Fresno State said to me once, over wine and cheese at a function: "You have this zany energy about you. You make meetings fun." Who knew?

All this said, my years as dean at Fresno State obviously had their own challenges. Dealing with unhappy employees can be the bane of any administrator, people being what they are. Sometimes it felt like I had more grievances and gripes than all the other administrators on campus combined. But every administrator is convinced that is their lot. Yet for each grievance came a dozen wins; it evens out. Most of the troubles actually had absolutely nothing to do with me as a supervisor, even though twice in ten years a fractious group of library faculty became disenchanted by my leadership and huffed up to the provost's office in a peeve. They certainly raised a loud ruckus! Some of their concerns were valid, I have to admit. Yes, I didn't much care to consult with the grumpiest of them, score one for them. Honestly, I forget the rest. Too many of the loud complaints, in any case, seemed like personal peeves to the provost, and as such they did not strike him as actionable. I have always been willing to discuss what was happening in the library during these travails with other administrators and key staff when it seemed appropriate. Even with faculty I'd talk it out, the best along with the less-than-good. On the positive side, I always focused on making the Madden Library the best it could be with those willing to roll up their sleeves and join in the work. As for the criticisms: honestly and in fairness, stand back, step into those employees' shoes, and try to understand the issues from their opposing point of view. If the view looks nonsensical, abort. If not, listen and learn. My advice in hindsight is to always let your umbrage go; you'll get a much better night's rest if you do.

At the end of the day, all that mattered was that we remained Number One with our students. They loved the library. The provost loved the library, as did the president. The Starbucks in the library became the busiest in Fresno, hands down. Our services got high praise from a swathe of patrons that included farmers in the valley, and not least from the central Office of the Chancellor of the CSU itself. Often as not they turned to our exceptional tech staff for support and leadership. Here's a datum I'm particularly proud of: we were deemed hands-down the best employer of student assistants in the whole CSU system. The campus-wide graduation rate at Fresno State was somewhere around seven years to commencement for upward of 68% of our student population when I arrived. By contrast, for those student assistants (SAs) who worked in the library, to the last, they got their cap and gown in four years, quickly enough to actually impact the university stats several percentage points for the better. Working in the library proved to be that much of a motivator for our SAs. I know at least four who graduated from Fresno State loving librarianship so much that they went on to get their MLS degrees. One such student even rose to become my associate dean after six years, an amazing trajectory for someone so young, yet so talented. Pretty cool if you ask me. In short, we were acknowledged by one and all as the very hub of campus life and with the stats, the kudos, and the student accolades to give us that well-deserved edge. I also raised more donor dollars (not gifts in kind) every one of my ten years there than all of the twenty-two other CSU library deans, combined. The wonderful dean at San Diego out-matched me one year, though it was a gift in kind. It must be said, maybe I excelled in this one arena, but CSU's Council of Library Deans was the most invigorating harbor of fine minds you can find anywhere in librarianship.

I want to stay with these lead librarians a moment, as their work as collegial deans too often goes unrecognized. They are an exemplary assembly of leaders with whom I shared a common bond of "in-the-trenches" camaraderie. From them, as both dynamic individuals and as a group, I learned so much, saw how they carried on with dogged perseverance themselves in the face of adversities, and built with them shared ideas of purpose, consortial innovations, and strategies to improve graduation rates. I came to understand that my role as dean, in so many ways, was simply to step aside, give my best librarians and staff the support and tools they needed, and watch them succeed. Time and time again, they knocked it right out of the park.

Interestingly, there was one time as dean when my long-forgotten days of punk rock came in handy. In the early fall of 2012, I invited an old acquaintance of mine to come to Fresno and talk to the students about "Participatory Democracy" and how the US should move from a winner-take-all electoral system to one of proportional vote counts as seen in European parliamentary systems. The speaker was none other than Krist Novoselic, the bass player of Nirvana. For years, Krist had been active in electoral reform and proportional representation, writing op-eds and serving as a spokesman for various non-profits. I thought he'd be perfect to talk about the upcoming 2012 election with my students. I'd lost touch with Krist over the years, but through my friend Susan M.—Seattle's top music maven—I called him up and asked if he'd be willing to come to Fresno to talk to the students. He was hesitant, but my pleading finally won him over. The big beautiful lunk (heavens, he's 6'8", with four inches on me) flew his own plane down to Fresno with his wife. The evening of his talk, while sitting in the green room shooting the breeze, I noticed Krist seemed unduly agitated. Outside in the auditorium some five hundred students and townies were shouting "Nirvana! Krist! Nirvana!"

"Man, I'm nervous," he admitted looking at me like a five-year-old about to get spanked.

"Jeepers, Krist, I've seen you play before 50,000 people, what's up?"

He gave me a hard look. "You don't understand, dude. With my bass in hand, I have a wall of sound between me and the crowd, plus I had Kurt and Dave to run interference. But tonight, aagh, I'm a solo act with no guitar..." He gulped, admitting he'd never actually spoken just one-on-a-thousand to a crowd before in any depth, about anything. The big galoot was actually shaking he was so nervous. So OK, the first few minutes of Krist alone up there on the empty stage were painful and his nervousness was palpable. But slowly he warmed to a topic dear to his heart and lo! By the end we had a rockin' hit single. Perhaps I should have known ahead of time that whatever educational benefits I thought might accrue from a rock star talking about democracy to my students, these hopes were dashed during Q&A when 95% of the questions were all about Nirvana and how did Krist play certain bass riffs on certain songs. I finally had to intervene and say we'd keep questions to democracy, thank you very much. Krist would welcome chatting out in the lobby afterwards. If you wanted to know how he pounded the bass lines on "Mr. Moustache" (album *Bleach*) here's your chance, but outside afterwards. There you have it, deadbeat to dean in one showstopper.

The secret to my success as a dean, from working out of office trailers during construction on to managing one of the best libraries in the state was simple: identify great faculty and staff to lead all efforts, inculcate support from a wonderfully supportive university across the board, and give your people full funding to succeed. These colleagues deserve the kudos.

So Which Side Are You On?

Emma Goldman, the great 19th-century anarchist who was often imprisoned for her convictions, once said: "Idealists foolish enough to throw caution to the winds, have advanced mankind and have enriched the world." I've never aspired to her stature nor ever emulated her unbending conviction, much as I admire her whole-heartedly. But I do believe she was right. Goldman's letters to Helen Keller, and from Keller back, are in any case some of the most endearing correspondences in the English language, steeped in radical feminist-socialist rhetoric. So how do we live up to Goldman's exacting standards, or to such thinkers as Bill McKibben of 350.org, or Paul Hawken the author of *Drawdown*, or Native warriors such as Casey Camp-Horinek, Councilwoman of the Ponca Tribe of Oklahoma, or Oren Lyons, a great leader of the Onondaga Nation? Heck, throw in Greta Thunberg.

Throughout my time as dean, I took up a variety of positions on not-for-profit boards in our region. Clearly my position at the university, the largest regional employer in the Central Valley, seemed to lend some sort of gravitas to my serving these ever-struggling organizations. Some were civic in nature, some based in social justice work, and others fiercely for the environment. I share this disquisition of my work outside the academy simply to say it is possible, perhaps increasingly a requirement, for top administrators at large universities to become active in social and environmental causes even while executing our duties to the academy. Universities, above all, should be leading the fray. The coming chaos of the climate crisis will demand that all citizens vote with their feet in any case. Obviously, it's a balancing act—to be active enough to have a real impact, but restrained to the extent that you don't bring needless notoriety to your employer. Most academic administrators, in any case, are what is known as "at will" employees: you serve at the pleasure of the president. For "just cause," s/he can fire you "at will" and you have scant recourse. Smartly, in my letter of hire, I had negotiated retreat rights so if fired for any reason I would immediately "retreat to faculty" and take up a position as a professor, with full tenure and union membership.

Yet all activists must act by the dictates of their conscience, even university administrators. When on my first trip up to Sequoia and Kings Canyon national parks as a new Fresno resident, I came to a foothill pastureland just then in magnificent spring bloom. The wildflowers were riotous, blues and yellows in undulating waves. The California poppies were especially magnificent, covering the steep hillside of a singular mountain on the winding road up to the parks. It was a beautiful sunny day, and the poppies, my word, how glorious! As John Steinbeck put it: "If gold could raise a cream, such is the color of the California poppy." Suddenly to the side of the road, I saw a series of alarming signs warning that the steep foothill to my left was under threat of mountaintop mining. I was stunned. Mountaintop mining, in California? You mean here, literally at the gateway to two of our most spectacular national parks, both World Heritage sites? *Wha'?* Looking up as I drove, the lovely 2,400-foot foothill identified seemed to rise up in majesty, with a cloak of golden cream gently shimmering in the spring wind. Thus began my first fiercely fought environmental campaign in Fresno, against the largest gravel and cement company in the world.

The company in question was a multinational conglomerate headquartered in San Pedro, Mexico. Its corporate name is Cemex. Its original CEO, Mexican national Lorenzo Zambrano, now thankfully deceased, was at one time the richest billionaire in all of Mexico, possibly in all of Latin America. I soon found that Cemex's record of abusing and breaking US environmental laws was shockingly abyssal, garnering the highest ever EPA corporate fine by 2006 for its wanton disregard of federal laws. It thrived solely by a hell-bent ethos of ecocide in its mining operations. It was nothing better than a legal Sinaloa cartel for blasting stone to gravel, half of which was used in various types of cement. The rest was construction fill. The bean-counting reprobates at Cemex, with paid armies of engineers in tow, came up with a brainstorm to mountaintop blast-mine, West Virginia-style, the most beautiful foothill on the only road up to both Sequoia and Kings Canyon national parks? How could this be? This was literally the gateway to the Sierra Mountains. And this travesty, just below the majestic stands of giant sequoias (*Sequoiadendron giganteum*, the sole living species in the genus *Sequoiadendron*) towering into the empyreum but a few miles up the road? Here they planned to situate their mine. This foothill is known as Jesse Morrow Mountain, or in the language of the Choinumni, the local Indian tribe, "Wa-ha-lish" (pronounced by them with a quick guttural pause where the dashes are given). After returning that first day from seeing the magnificent twenty-five-hundred-year-old tree lords of the realm, with a little digging online, I was horrified by what I found. I joined the fight in late 2009, in its earliest rounds of duking it out with the Mexican Cyclops. We came to call ourselves the Friends of Jesse Morrow Mountain.

My first foray into the twin national parks of Sequoia and Kings Canyon was a soul-searing revelation. To stand beneath living beings two thousand years old, soaring with thick ruddy bark to green crowns almost four hundred feet in the mountain air was to be transfixed by astonishment, with the deepest feeling of humility. In a few giant sequoia groves you can wander as a pilgrim before the majesty of life on earth, willing in this instance to kneel in fealty. There's nothing like it, because the experience is of being confronted with your own insignificance. Grand as the Grand Canyon is, it is still the experience of the "superior" naked ape looking down into the cavernous majesty of the earth's epochs. Whereas to stand beneath a nearly four-hundred-foot tree bigger around than your living room is to be made small as a bipedal mammal. It is impossible to feel hubris, still less a sense of self-important entitlement.

In joining the fighting Friends of Wa-ha-lish under threat, I made a commitment to see it through to the end. Our band of eco-warriors was less than a dozen when I came on the scene, though over the next two years it grew to maybe thirty-five active participants, a hundred more in the bleachers, thousands of Lay-Z-Boy supporters at home, and general support throughout, outside of the Tea Party development boosters. If the mine were approved, we were all alarmed to panic that we would be blasted out of bed every morning as the beautiful 2400-foot mountain was carved to a nub every hour of daylight for thirty years (or when the gravel ran out—whichever came first). It would take upwards of 8,000 to 10,000 dump truck trips a week, spewing diesel smoke, clogging the two-lane road up to the parks, raking up the macadam day and night, to haul that mounding heap of rubble to gravel grinding facilities down on the valley floor. Vehemently opposed to this proposed wreckage was also the small band of the federally unrecognized Choinumni Indians, one of the many Yokut tribes in California whose ancestral homes were originally the Sierra foothills and high river valleys. The ancestral home of the Choinumni band was Kings River itself, flowing now through the Pine Flat reservoir and dam just to the north of Wa-ha-lish. The mountain was considered sacred to their cultural heritage, indeed it served as their traditional marker where the great Kings River finally tumbled out of the Sierra Mountains to flow leisurely through flat grasslands into Tulare Lake. The clan mother of this small tribe of Indians was a wonderful human being, a tower of strength and wisdom, ever stalwart, by the name of Aubrey Osborne.

What I brought to our group, as a longtime activist with time in the trenches, was a logical administrative mindset, hence structure. Meetings now had agendas. The multiform tasks were divvied up between the core members rather than everyone trying to sort out each piece collectively. We explored getting a lawyer. The permit Cemex required had to pass a majority vote from the five-member county Board of Supervisors (Supes) and all but one were in the "Rednecks, White Sox, and Blue Ribbon Beer" column as staunch humorless libertarian Republicans. The outlier was a blue dog Latino Democrat, who had shown scant willingness to walk out on a limb on our behalf. I met with three of the Supes several times. Just trying to find some sort of common language, let alone understanding, was so hard; it was as if we spoke different languages.

Throughout all this, it never surprised me that some of the university's biggest conservative donors took our president aside, asking what the hell the library dean was up to. The president talked to the provost; the provost talked to me. I made it absolutely clear that I was in it for the long haul, but I would not do anything that would otherwise put my standing as dean in jeopardy, nor attack any of the bigwig Republicans who apparently were heavily invested in Cemex. I asked the provost point blank, "Tell me truthfully, if only in spirit, what side are you on? Do you want a mountaintop mine as our gateway to the parks?" He chuckled (nice guy) and said: "I like mountains." And left it at that. It was a politically astute reply befitting a man of his stature. But it was clear that he wasn't going to fire me as long as "I walked the line." Fair enough. He gave me his tacit support and the president dropped it.

When all was said *and done, after* interminable meetings, hearings, lawyer affidavits, more meetings, endless messaging of our public outreach, on to fighting at every turn the sad pabulum of Cemex, the Supes voted maybe 4-1 to withdraw county support for their application. We had won. It was one of the few cases anywhere in the US where community plaintiffs stopped Cemex's environmental havoc ahead of time. I think everyone, Republicans and Democrats alike, could see by the end what a boondoggle the mine would have been. In celebration, we had a great feast out at Choinumni Park, adjacent to the home of the Osborne family, which became a sort of pow-wow celebration. I even had my first taste of dishes whose main ingredient was pounded valley acorns. I am so grateful to the Choinumni for their unwavering support and patient storytelling about Wa-ha-lish, their beautiful foothill mountain, with its golden fleece of California poppies thick on its hillside every spring. To this day, it endures unscathed.[45]

I share this story, in part, to say that other like-minded administrators in large bureaucratic enterprises such as mine can themselves explore ways to follow their own conscience as exigencies arise. First find out the boundaries your boss expects you to work within, and then act. Always be honest. Do the activism respectfully. In the end realize the First Amendment grants you the right of free speech. These rules of thumb worked for me. But it's always a gamble within the work environment to stand out as a rebel. I have one dear friend who has been an ardent member of the Progressive Librarians Guild from its inception, an ardent Marxist and outspoken activist in fact, who has lost several library jobs because of his politics, had contracts not renewed, and was given financial excuses for being let go. He finally had to go all the way to China to find meaningful professional employment. Weigh the risk, but having the tacit support of your supervisor is advised.

---

45. As a sad footnote, Cemex is back in the news, seeking a new permit to blast mine 600 feet into the ground adjacent to the San Joaquin River near Lost Lake Park, one of my favorite birding sites locally. As with all ravenous cancers, once again local residents must band together to stanch this disease of greed and environmental havoc. But it won't be me leading the effort this time.

Chapter 10
The Grief of the World

> I am at peace at last, with my own company.
> I have crawled through a labyrinth of worm tunnels
> and come out in an immense place to be free.
> ~Susan Zwinger, Yukon Territory[46]

In Wilderness is Preservation of the World

I fear each day for the health of our planetary biosphere. I fear that Gaia in her beauty and plentitude will grow barren with heat stroke. I fear also for humankind itself. The ravages of our climate crisis heighten all my fears that the everyday certainties of our Western lives may soon be rent from us. Above all, that which we experience as Nature in her golden plentitude, everyday seems more blighted by searing heat, continents on fire, extinctions, floods, drought, cyclone bombs, pollution, seas rising, and the eventual death of ecosystems at mass scale. It now seems likely that calamitous weather may well make our connection with Nature not one of joyous outings into the woods, but treks under an unforgiving sun fraught with unrelenting oppression. As temperatures soar, will our children, and their children after them, ever experience the beauty of the wild lands we have so loved?

---

46. From *Stalking the Ice Dragon: An Alaskan Journey* by Susan Zwinger (University of Arizona Press, 1991).

Am I young enough still at sixty-nine to witness a time when it is literally too hot to go outside? I grieve even as our generation leaves a broken and ravaged legacy.

Being alone in wilderness has always been the most important and restorative delight of my life. No other activity has brought me such solace or filled me with such wonder. It is here where the harried vagaries of modern life are put aside, where I can enter the old growth magic of an intact forest and restore my soul with a magic that most often emerges in deep solitude far from the madding crowd. Yet each day as the news grows grimmer, I fear that my generation will, in the end, be the last for a very long time indeed to see in Nature a friend, see its true grandeur, its uplifting majesty woven with verdure and gentle fecundity. All generations to come will be bequeathed a legacy of something that grows unforgiving in a world of precipitous decline. Gaia herself will not much care, evolution and catastrophe are her geologic signposts, but this ongoing collapse of the web of life might well kill off all that we now value in the natural world. Who among us does not harbor some quiet fear that a very angry planet may well become all that remains of our true inheritance? For me, grief and dread are entwined.

I begin this last section of my memoir purposefully on this very topic, so dear to my heart yet one that also fills me with anger and a sort of spiritual exhaustion. How I wish it weren't such a grim slog.[47] I speak, of course, of environmental stewardship and the burgeoning climate crisis that engulfs the planet. Yet as I approach

---

47. My relentless criticisms against "industrial civilization" that follow are not put on paper to convince anyone that I'm right or that you should agree. We all have access to the same facts; this is how I read and interpret them. You must read them in your way. Nor is my criticism hypocritical since I recognize I'm mired in the same civilizational miasma as the rest. All I suggest in this book is that we talk about this with a serious sense of immediacy, deeply, critically, and with honesty, and meet our fears head on. It starts with a radically new conversation about how humanity might reconstitute itself outside the dominant paradigm of industrial civilization. Beyond that, each to his/her own.

old age, I feel compelled to examine every angle of what I see as the coming chaos over the next thirty to fifty years. Its exigencies will inform how I might best approach the rest of my life. I want to make sure that my choices going forward give my wife and me the most holistic and wholesome chance for social and regional cohesion, as a radically changing climate unravels.

As of today, we think our future will be a return to Ithaca and the beautiful Finger Lakes region. Ideally what we want in moving back East is upwards of five acres of land, some distance from neighbors, and an old farmhouse. I like to think a corresponding beckoning from the Earth herself might draw us toward that future homestead. For us, it is emphatically not just about our preconceptions of what constitutes a "suitable" place to live, like ticking off a checklist of livability. That beckoning must have in it some possibility for us to enjoin a true community of resilience into the fabric of our future lives. Here's how D.H. Lawrence put it: "It is no use trying merely to modify present forms. The whole great form of our era will have to go. One can do nothing but fight tooth and nail to defend the new shoots of Life from being crushed out, and so let them grow."[48] Were I asked to describe what that community of resilience might look like, I would use words and phrases such as self-organizing, self-adapting, egalitarian, clear-eyed, cohesive, outsider to the dominant paradigm, and finally, truly communal in some fashion. There is no single blueprint, but these descriptors pertain. These sorts of communitarian efforts can be found in pockets all over the globe.

So I share my concerns and my grief as an exploration to better understand my own thinking on the matter of what lies ahead and how we will all be asked to deal with it. There is no more critical examination for Western individuals to undertake than how we plan to deal with the coming chaos. And I use the word

---

48. D.H. Lawrence, from the magazine *The Signature* v.1 (London, 1915). Lawrence and John Middleton Murry were the editors.

chaos deliberately. How does one find, if at all possible, one's true homeland today, those shires of honest humanity in close cohesive proximity amid an unprepared civilization whose industrial ravages it now sows?[49] English author Paul Kingsnorth asked how we can reimagine a new life in the Anthropocene "properly, deeply, even as I'm still embedded [in civilization] because I can't work out where to jump off, or what to land on, or whether you can ever get away by jumping, or simply because I'm frightened to close my eyes and walk over the edge."[50] I, too, share Kingsnorth's fears.

To some, what follows may be tough going through a litany of bad news regarding what I believe is in store as our climate crises gain momentum.[51] By choice, in any case, in this critical year of 2021, when humankind must summon everything that's in us to deal with this worldwide crisis as a species, as nations, and as individuals—surely, we must make this our life's work in the time remaining before all tipping points topple over. It is easy for any reasonable person to doubt that the worst of climate chaos has us in sights, but it's coming. Even Bill McKibben has admitted that we're not dodging this bullet. Truth be told, we are likely to reach 4°C warming by 2100+, which means that upwards of 75% of the world's landmass will be largely uninhabitable.[52] So why not start planning at the hyper-local level now?

---

49. Cognizant to shires, which I'll explain more fully later, are domus, rus, and humus. They all relate to an extended self-sustaining cohesive domicile (domus) connected to its surrounding fields (rus), and thus to the soil (humus).

50. Paul Kingsnorth, *Confessions of a Recovering Environmentalist and Other Essays* (Greywolf Press, 2017) ch. "Dark Ecology."

51. The best book out there that describes in detail what's in store for humanity is the hard-hitting *The Unthinkable Earth: Life After Warming* (Dougan Books, 2019) by David Wallace-Wells. He offers the most clear-eyed, albeit grimmest, list of likely calamities. It almost reads like disaster porn. To date, in a dozen reviews that I've read of this book, I have found not one salient criticism of Wallace-Wells' findings, other than ad hominen swipes at his gloom and doom. But no rebutting facts are forthcoming.

52. See Frank Jacob's article: "What the World Will Look Like 4°C Warmer" (BigThink.com 22.05.2017). Also see Robert Hunziker "Earth 4C Hotter" (CounterPunch.org 23.8.2019).

The years when we might have "solved" the climate crisis receded long ago in the rear-view mirror to vanishing regrets at actions not taken. In my wide work in environmental advocacy, one thing is absolutely certain: the most striking feature of the harsh social disorder we are facing in the years ahead is that its extremes are fundamentally non-negligible. There's no Gaian World Court to turn to, no UN uber-agency to whom we may appeal for a reprieve. Once the inexorable slide to unimaginable global heat waves gathers speed, it's a landslide all the way down, no matter what humans do or don't do. The planet's atmosphere itself will be 100% in the driver's seat, not us. And it'll be driving like a bat out of hell. We need to let that sink in. What happens then in our blighted human history is what fascinates me, and also worries me to no end.

Furthermore, the days of techno-geo-engineering solutions are passing into fantasy, it seems to me. Recently, it was Bill Gates' ludicrous Heliogen Energy Corporation making waves.[53] The minute you corporatize the "solution" as with Gates' new venture, you inevitably create new pollution downstream. It's not that people can't stop the mayhem, since the huge apparatus of our capitalist corporate consumerist dilemma is a human construction, and what we have made we can unmake. It's just that we have simply run out of time to take the hammers to it and build much of anything new at national levels with the time allotted. Full-on worldwide climate exigencies already sideswipe us. Where do we find the several decades for sound forethought and planning needed to respond intelligently and raise the proverbial levees to the coming floods? Not on planet Earth. The bumbling

---

53. As CNN reported: "A secretive startup backed by Bill Gates has achieved a solar breakthrough aimed at saving the planet" (11.19.2019). But it can't "save the planet." We would need upwards of 30,000 of these Heliogen gizmos up and running in the US alone no later than 2030 to so much as make a dent in emissions. But climate is global, so add another 500,000 worldwide. Even Bill doesn't have that sort of disposable cash.

governmental responses ahead will be, at best, little more than rear guard, reactive and inadequate.

I am hardly the town crier with this news. But here's the sad part. As a longtime environmentalist, I have become disenchanted with the overall environmental movement as a whole. It seems to have become a Green Industrial Complex unto itself, touting eco-tourism and "green" consumerism for earth-friendly stuff galore. The whole "going green" juggernaut suddenly seems a capitalist corporate hoodwink with scant paths forward to a livable planet at garden scale. "Going green" still seems predicated on keeping the massive system of civilization itself chugging along with the "good" bits (renewables/Green New Deal) replacing the "bad" bits (fossil fuels/plastic) as long as none of the changes demand we actually chuck our corporate task masters aside and step out of industrial civilization altogether. The nabobs of "progress at all cost" claim that these behemoths must endure to keep providing jobs, medicine, foodstuff, and all those marvelous consumerist juggernauts of modern society. But all solutions discussed today remain mired within the overarching structure of our industrial civilization itself, which clearly is a self-consuming and ravenous beast that's globally out of control. There's a disconnect, in any case, that we can somehow keep it all chugging along just as long as there's better attainment of CO2 reduction targets, coupled with carbon capture and sequestration, and some caring "going green" around the edges. Yes, if only we expand renewables, get better governmental oversight and "green" investments cracking, and so on. But hold on. Didn't corporate-consumerist civilization and its abetting governments get us into this mess in the first place? I just cannot fathom how we can put "green" lipstick on these porcine monstrosities at this late date and hope we'll somehow get ourselves saved. With more wind turbines? Really? You mean those turbines mass produced at huge environmental cost over in "coal is king" China?

I attended the 2018 Bioneers conference in Marin County, CA. Bioneers is an organization that puts Spirit, Earth Reverence, and the Rights of Women and Indigenous Voices at the center of their work. Bill McKibben, Winona LaDuke, Paul Hawken, Kenny Ausubel, Terry Tempest Williams, and all the grandees of climate action were there to speak eloquently from the dais at that year's Bioneers confab. It's a wonderfully celebratory event, don't get me wrong. But my most memorable and disturbing recollection of being there was standing in line for the gent's restroom beside Bill McKibben and John Powell (director of the Haas Institute for a Fair and Inclusive Society) and overhearing their hushed conversation. McKibben conceded quietly to a question Powell posed, to the effect that the world had pretty much run out of time to find meaningful solutions to the climate crisis, at least at scale to thwart it. We must now, he said, figuratively sandbag what's best of our civil society as the sea levels rise and the climate bakes us into an uncertain future. It's time to start marshalling rearguard actions to preserve what can be saved of humanity's future and the earth's biodiversity. Heady stuff. Needless to say, when on the dais as a keynote speaker later in the day, McKibben gave a rote talk, to my mind, as a distracted and clearly deflated firebrand going through the motions. He tried to rally us with as much upbeat chutzpah as he could muster, but his shoulders were so slumped it was plain as day to those with clear eyes that he hardly believed a word of his own talk. He'd given it a thousand times to a world grown worse each time. In fact, during a panel Q&A, Bill sat there and held his head in both hands most of the time, never once looked at the audience, and seemed like he just wanted to get the hell "outta here." When John Powell himself spoke from the stage, he made clear that what he had heard at dinner and throughout the conference from Mr. McKibben had left him "profoundly shaken." As an African-American activist, Powell conceded that if the worst came it would obviously affect communities of color and the poor disproportionately. Spot on, heaven help the equatorial and developing world—and all speakers agreed with that sentiment. Publicly at least, Powell did not share what had been so harrowing in talking to McKibben in private, but my bladder had obviously placed me at the right place at the right time to hear at least some of it unvarnished.

As described in his marvelous masterpiece *The Road to Wigan Pier* (1937), George Orwell went north in the 1930s to live with industrial workers and miners in midlands England, sharing their daily grind, their shabby tenement lodgings, their cheerless diet, and their dank lives in the mines three miles underground. It is a remarkable, if depressing, account of human suffering and arguably my favorite book of his. Nevertheless, he perfectly captures how the brutal conditions of 19th-century coal mining begin, by the 1930s, to change as if for the better as the technological marvels of the 20th century brought a few modest improvements to the lives of workers. Sez he: "And then there is the queer spectacle of modern electrical science showering miracles upon people with empty bellies. Twenty million people are underfed but literally everyone in England has access to a radio. What we have lost in food we have gained in electricity. Whole sections of the working class who have been plundered of what they really need are being compensated by cheap luxuries which mitigate the surface life." The surface life, exactly! The genius of emergent capitalism was that it offered then, and continues to offer today, so much mesmerizing glitter and attention-grabbing baubles of crap for *the surface life* so we working stiffs have at least something to hold on to, from iPhones to fetching eyewear. With the burgeoning plethora of consumer goods in the 20th century, roaring into the 21st, we in the West are constantly showered with miracles of cheap surface-life luxuries. Even with the meager wages too many working stiffs get today, they can still shop till they drop for the veneer of surface-life luxury, even if it's with unaffordable credit cards. We all acquiesce, to a greater or lesser extent, to the ongoing depravities of industrial civilization for fear of losing what kit and caboodle of the surface life we have horded or are addicted to.

But in truth what planet exactly are we saving with our surface lives? And from what? Oh, that's right, you've seen the social media posts decrying "The 100 Top Corporations Responsible for Climate Change!" Naturally, we all want a pass on being called hypocrites for the next little bit as we still shovel our shekels into the maw of these companies for more surface life stuff. I certainly do. You know, that "get out of jail free" card to keep all our kit and gadgetry chugging along. Don't get me wrong, I know perfectly well that the lion's share of the planetary mayhem we face today was cynically and actively foisted on us by the industrial, extractive, manipulative, dishonest capitalist models of Big Oil and all the other venial biggies. What scant thought these corporations give to caring for our biosphere, they monetize and commodify as a public larder for plunder, all to produce those sultanic piles of plastic gizmos we haul in our bulging luggage to the climate march.

My point is not to cast blame at us consumers per se, but to suggest that our consumptive industrial civilization, soup to nuts, top to bottom feeders, even the so-called *good* bits (e.g., *my* stereo, *my* fridge, *my* mobile phone, etc.) is itself the contagion. By way of example, take the solar panels on my roof here in sunny California. I put them up thinking renewable solar was somehow a good thing, going green to do my bit in saving planet Earth. The panels installed by my solar company came from China. So, let's pop over to China and see what's up with "going solar"—everyone says it's one of *the* solutions. In the Dragon Lands across the Pacific some of the most ravaged environments on earth are pocked like cancer sores throughout central China, where the panel components are mined and manufactured. No surprise. The environmental laws governing production there are laughable. The fact that half the major cities in China have absolutely unbreathable air is precisely because lax laws rule supreme. Yet we blithely believe that with these nice "clean" solar panels attached to our roof, we are doing our part to "save the Earth." There's a zero-sum game going on here. We have to get that. If you're OK with that, install away; I have. But let's not fool ourselves that there isn't an enormous global trade-off, essentially shunting off production pollutions to NIMBY. Climate chaos is global, it doesn't stop at China's borders any more than the coronavirus has.

When all is said and done, though, it's really all about keeping our kit and caboodle chugging along. Besides, if you think driving an electric car is "going green," remember that child miners aged four are "living a hell on Earth so you can drive that electric car."[54] Have you ever actually stood right under a 350-foot wind turbine? Yikes, it's terrifying. In *A Short History of Progress*, Ronald Wright explores how most innovations, like wind and solar, eventually come back to reveal themselves as "progress traps": "a short-term social or technological improvement that turns out to be a backward step." Better than coal? Sure, why ask? But as I look to where to move to, these are the questions I keep asking myself. I don't want to buy a lovely little farm plot on a hilltop somewhere and suddenly be surrounded by wind turbines; you'd see the environmentalist in me going full-on NIMBY. So I ask myself, can I try to live within the bounds of true local sustainability wherever it is I move to? I have no ready answer; it seems pretty damn difficult if you ask me. I know this much: climate chaos will demand an answer before too long, so we may as well start asking now. Our civilization is in universal moral failure, buffeted by climatological models of worldwide havoc. Is a Green New Deal enough? Who will be dealing by day's end? You can bet that stepping up first at the federal spigot will be "green-washed" corporations. Don't get me wrong, I'm all for the GND, but it's decades too late to "stop" or

---

54. For a quick primer, see journalist Barbara Jones' article in the *UK Daily Mail*: "Child miners aged four living a hell on Earth so YOU can drive an electric car" (08.05.2017, https://www.dailymail.co.uk/...).

"solve" the climate crisis. That's like hoping to "solve" the weather. The chaos is here, now.

Yet we keep believing that the "solution" to the climate crisis is a technological one—more wind, more solar, more geo-techno-heliogens—when it seems so patently obvious that we need to start addressing the climate crisis as an *adaptive challenge* requiring a profound inner shift in our human psyche. Our values, beliefs, social norms, the soothing myths we live by with the surface life so thoroughly embedded in a ravenous civilization is now the mimetic contagion. At scale, for eight billion people, wind and solar produce just a different set of deleterious impacts on Earth's frayed ecosystems than reliance on coal and gas, and to get there we are twenty or thirty years off, at best. Playwright Eve Ensler (*Vagina Monologues*), whom I've had the pleasure to meet, recently wrote in a wonderful piece entitled "Letter of Apology to Mother Earth": "Mother, I am the reason the birds are missing. I am the cause of salmon who cannot spawn and the butterflies unable to take their journey home. I am the coral reef bleached death white and the sea boiling with methane. I am the millions running from lands that have dried, forests that are burning or islands drowned in water."[55] Her honesty in owning her role in this havoc, as an affluent white woman immersed in civilization, is a welcome breath of fresh air.

But here's the hard part. Let's make no mistake, our rocky planet Mother Earth *does not care* about "being saved" or the "environmental movement" or whether this species or that habitat exists or is wiped away. What's to save? For four billion years our home planet was nothing more than a boiling toxic hell of intolerable heat and poisonous gases, without a single bacterium making a go of it. It was as lifeless as the moon, just 1000 degrees hotter. Yet over millennia, Gaia became the magnificent biosphere of

---

55. Posted on Maria Popova's wonderful blog, *Brain Pickings* (10.2019 - http://tiny.cc/xl7rgz).

intact living organisms and flourishing earth systems our forbearers once knew. What people seem to mean when they talk about saving the planet, of course, isn't the messy world out there, you know, where the tamed industrialized-suburban-farmland ends and an utterly indifferent "natural order" begins its riotous dance of life and death at the end of the road. Yes, what we mean is we want to save *civilization* (at least the "good" bits) and the lifestyles we've grown accustomed to, a civilization moreover which to our superior human minds must have pockets of Nature here and there for us to find some semblance of spiritual, psychic, or emotional sustenance. Elegiac 19th-century poet Gerard Manley Hopkins said it best in 1881: "What would the world be, once bereft of wet and wildness?"[56] That's what is at stake, our missing the wet and wildness. Environmentalism fights to preserve this wet and wildness with all it's got, but turns a blind eye to the jet trails it offers its membership as it touts a hundred and one eco-tourism destinations in its dot.org's membership magazines.

Our panic with all this is a sort of psychic fear of losing the last elbowroom for harried 9-to-5 stiffs like you and me to go birding, mountaineering, or canoeing amid the last tidbits we label Nature. Let me ask you: if you went to visit the Louvre, only to find that two-thirds of the paintings had been removed for good from the walls, surely you'd gripe and want your money back. How could they take down so many of the grand masters' works? Splendid as the Louvre architecture may look from the outside, all those empty walls in gallery after gallery on the inside: a travesty, I say! But enter a so-called wilderness, crisscrossed with jet plane vapor trails above, minus two thirds of its endemic species, that's precisely the description of Alaska today, let alone our nearby Sierra Nevada Mountains. Heck, we don't even notice the wall gaps in Nature, the paucity of species, all the while glowing about

---

56. From his poem "Inversnaid."

our wilderness experience on Facebook. Most of the eco-trekkers I've met forget that what they're actually doing is passing through government-manicured scenery where the grizzly bears and wolverines that discomfit us have been extirpated. "It is no longer a wilderness. It is no longer a place of natural life. It appeals to the wheelchair ethos of the wealthy, upper-middle class American," said Edward Abbey in his essay "The Damnation of a Canyon."[57] No argument from me.

As I ponder all this, my disenchantment grows in proportion. More and more I find that just sitting still and looking inward to expunge the delusions I've told myself about civilization seems to be more useful time spent. As long as industrial civilization is our societal benefactor, any expectation that we'll actually save much of anything unto the seventh generation is just a comforting illusion. There's no easy off-ramp, probably not even a very difficult off-ramp, from this highway to who knows where.[58] For now, there's just the Knowing that Industrial Civilization has always been an evolutionary dead end. Not when, always. And Gaia doesn't care. It's just you and me alone amid the sparkling stars, *mis queridos amigos*, gazing with grief at the dying embers of Earth. Our real fight should be to refashion the very soul-sense of our species. It was Whitman, after all, in penning his magnificent poem "When I Heard the Learn'd Astronomer" who understood that all this to-ing and fro-ing to define where we stand in the universe simply sets us apart from the very cosmos we are trying to define. Here's Walt at his finest in his poem from *Leaves of Grass*. The first line is the poem's title.

---

57. Edward Abbey, *The Serpents of Paradise: A Reader* (Henry Holt, 1995).

58. Oddly, Unabomber Theodore Kaczynski's book, *Technological Slavery* (Fitch & Madison Publishers, revised 2019) is as lucid a critique of our industrial society as you might read. The man himself gives me the creeps, but he does not try to justify his senseless murders or those he wounded. Even Bill Joy, founder of Sun Microsystems, said in *Wired Magazine*, "there is ... merit in his reasoning."

> When I heard the learn'd astronomer,
> When the proofs, the figures, were ranged in columns before me,
> When I was shown the charts and diagrams, to add, divide, and measure them,
> When I sitting heard the astronomer where he lectured with much applause in the lecture-room,
> How soon unaccountable I became tired and sick,
> Till rising and gliding out I wander'd off by myself,
> In the mystical moist night-air, and from time to time,
> Look'd up in perfect silence at the stars.

The perfect silence of the stars. We will have reason to return to that very act of actually doing something truly meaningful for our sense of place on this Earth when we get to the end. So, look up quietly at these sky-fires burning fiercely in the firmament with Walt and me. They don't care either, but they sure are beautiful. See, there's Sirius the Dog Star at the hunter's feet in the south. And over there, the beautiful swan Cygnus spiraling down the spilled diamonds of the Milky Way, her wings outstretched. Breathe. From this silence, we can begin an entirely new dialogue in a mythic language as yet unknown.

Pessimism, Hope, and Giving the Bastards a Black Eye

So, am I a pessimist? Unapologetically, yes, and, well, no, not exactly. Doubtless such an admission needs a more nuanced explanation. By saying *yes* to being a pessimist, I mean I see absolutely no off-ramp from the tentacled chaos we're in. The *no* to being a pessimist is that I chose to be chipper almost every day, and being chipper is a choice not a personality default. In any case, I use the term "pessimist" here in the philosophical sense, in the manner of the Greek Cynics, whose philosophy called us to live simply, offering the possibility of accepting suffering in any age of uncertainty—lived in their day without ever pretending the nostrums of [Greek] civilization were based on anything but exploitation, slavery, and war. I'm practical enough to realize, even to accept, that the macro-institutions of civilization have a role to play in the decades ahead, but we are fools to rely on them to lead us out of anything. Their failures are so manifest as to be laughable. If there's any "hope" for changing the external world's juggernaut, then I'd say a radically new shift in *hyper-local* self-governance is required, untethered to municipal vote counts. Let us turn the flaccid notion of "hope" into the active verb "to heal"—a Hippocratic oath we can invoke to heal the very Earth, our home. This isn't about ballot boxes, but tines and hands into the soil. These self-organizing communities can work within any environment, be it urban, suburban, countryside, the wild lands. But to make these self-adapting entities work, taking ownership of our own living and survival strategies through the morass ahead seems vitally critical. And that time is now. Remember, we are likely to reach 4°C warming by 2100+. Why not start planning at the hyper-local level now?

In his essay "Dark Ecology," Paul Kingsnorth writes: "It is far too late to think about dismantling the machine in a rational manner—and in any case who wants to? We can't deny that it brings benefits to us, even as it chokes us and our world by degrees."[59] So yes, obviously we can still rely on outside governments for rule of law, water and sewage, selected social services, regulations, forms of regional commerce and planning, and so on. But at the micro-level, I believe the only sane opportunity left to us is to take ownership of our own communal response to what's coming, to figuratively "weatherize" our lives against the chaos. Governments won't do it. Environmentalism fighting governments won't do it. It is this burgeoning realization that guides me now as I look to where I want to put down my roots in the months and years ahead.

All we may have in the end is a commitment to our own communal resilience: small-scale communities that are self-organizing, self-sufficient (to the extent possible), practical, and literally

---

59. From *Confessions of a Recovering Environmentalist* (Graywolf Press, 2017).

down-to-earth, with hands in the dirt, seeds in the soil. Lacking a better word, let's call them *shires*[60]—reorganizing society around a collective, people-centered means of smaller-scale emergency planning, food production, exchange of goods and services, fierce commitments to the good of the whole, and joint home-making and community garden-tending. Owning arable land, per se, is not a prerequisite for these shires; your shire might be a condo-complex, a city apartment building, or even a suburban housing block. That it intentionally coheres with forethought and egalitarian *jus publicum* is the key prerequisite. Consider that in China during the coronavirus outbreak in the spring of 2020, food production and access in several provinces simply collapsed. To prevent starvation among many millions of people, thousands of semi-trucks of food had to be imported in from less contaminated regions of China. This collapse due to food scarcity occurred within a few weeks, not months or years. America also experienced facing shortages of some goods. Perhaps the best place to explore the whole spectrum of these self-sustaining communities is at the Foundation for Intentional Communities website (www.ic.org). I truly respect the FIC's efforts and leadership, although I am not fond of the term "intentional community." There is no richness to the language, no correlation to the soil and local food, no historical context; it's a term too easily co-opted by mainstream corporate entities like retirement homes and so on. The Kendall Quaker-based, not-for-profit model is perhaps the best of the intentional living mainstream elder-hostels.

Do such communities of common aspirations exist, even in a rural college town such as Ithaca? Yes, there are many efforts in

---

60. A wonderful old British term which meant a small, self-regulating municipality or extended incorporation of farmlands. No wonder J.R.R. Tolkien used it to describe the homeland of his Hobbits, an integrated agricultural pastureland that was non-industrialized, and "that was a small but beautiful, idyllic and fruitful land, beloved by its inhabitants."

place.[61] By contrast, Fresno where I live now is just too scattered to cohere in this sort of intended communal preparation. There's no shared intellectual framework to deal holistically with the deleterious climate pressures building in the years and decades ahead. Hopefully that will soon change for the better. Ithaca is different, with a proven history of making a go of it. No generation in human history agonizes so deeply about how, where, and with whom to weather what's coming as do the people alive on Earth today. A growing sense of quiet panic seems to pervade us all, especially among Millennials—heck, even Young Republicans feel it. Things aren't normal, and the vast fires in eastern Australia during January 2020, with dozens of people incinerated, towns burnt down, and a billion animals burned to a crisp seems a close approximation of what our children, in fact all of us, will face. Something is coming.

The shire ideal, in any case, can certainly fortify us to be more resilient, more self-organizing and responsive than any other model I see out there. The geo-locale of our shires is immaterial. Each in their unique way must call upon human will to collectivize at small scale, that's what matters. And if alliances of such shires grow to support and learn from one another, as the FIC seeks to encourage, so much the better. This is emphatically not about survivalist Balkanization, since the shires I envision understand there is no getting away from the dominant system, and no point in fighting it. These aren't "drop out" hippie communes, either.

Furthermore, nothing in the shire concept remotely suggests that massive collective action at scale, nationwide civil resistance to "biznezazuzul" such as marching against the world's laissez-faire capitalist economic system, isn't still needed as well. It is.

---

61. As far back as 1987, author and poet Wendell Berry covered much of this in his book *Home Economics* (North Point Press, 1987). Perhaps no other thinker in America has so thoroughly practiced what he preaches as Berry, who eschews most all technology in running his farmstead.

But a million people marching in every national capital on Earth doesn't necessarily correlate to providing our own hearth back home with the protections needed to find solidarity of purpose in our immediate geographic region. Shires, by contrast, are intentionally hyper-local and self-sufficient, even within that dominant paradigm. These nuclei of lifestyle change, at day's end, are about having a more powerful and cohesive voice in (or against) the decisions that regional and state governments may undertake on "security," "preemptive," or "corporate personhood" grounds in over-reaction to the coming climate crises. Or conversely, to provide our shires with a more powerful voice cohesively demanding that local governments act in our interests. Even in the US, consider that a million people lost electrical power in California for days on end in 2019, as the largest power company in the state, Pacific Gas & Electric, shut off electrical generation north to south as a precautionary measure against catastrophic forest fires. The sick and elderly were terribly impacted. Hundreds of thousands of freezers full of food thawed to mush. Might a shire such as I am describing have had its own generators at the ready? Shires can certainly have something of the spirit of egalitarian union organizing to them as well, but still exist outside the corporate paradigm, a bulwark against cooption.

There are many communities of practice we could turn to as bellwethers. All are uniquely different, all shoulder on with varying levels of success. There's the global Transition Network, the Zapatistas in Mexico, Sweden's Viable Cities Initiative, and the international La Via Campesina. Or what about Cuba's Urban Farming initiatives, or the Amish (minus the rampant sexism), or even the Practical Farmers of Iowa or the Community Environmental Legal Defense Fund, which helps caring communities disentangle from the talons of corporate profit and ignorant policies. In Russia and Croatia, with the catastrophic failure of the communist regimes, new collectives called "zadrougas" arose as self-sufficient forms of social organization in traditional villages. Consider the Native tribal Havasupai on the rim of the Grand Canyon. "Havasupai" means "people of the blue-green waters," named after the beautiful pools, waterfalls, and natural flows of the Havasu River which carved out the canyon where they live. Their homes in this canyon are *ten miles* from the nearest serviceable road. Only packhorses can bring in provender to the people. The Havasupai have lived there for 800 years, retaining much of their Native culture in isolation, with only a few essential consumer goods of industrial civilization to sustain them. 800 years! It can be done, even in the 21st century. There are also the geographically isolated villages of Greenland, another 800-year-old example, with innate cohesion and self-reliance, living off the arctic sea's bounty. Or take the transformations happening in the most deprived boroughs of London, Barking and Dagenham, with their Participatory Cities program. It opened "shops" called Every One Every Day. These storefronts don't "sell" anything but are instead places for people to meet, discuss ideas, swap stuff, and launch projects.[62] Or consider the emerging barter economies and proliferating communal gardens in the "failed city" of Detroit, to entire small nations like Bhutan, with its Gross National Happiness index. "Small" is the operative word, as such efforts consciously step outside the corporate-driven paradigm. National struggles are increasingly beside the point because even the concept of nationhood is a failed model, both in practice and in theory.[63] For

---

62. George Monbiot, "Could this local experiment be the start of a national transformation?" in *The Guardian* (24 January, 2019).

63. In his eloquent book, *Dangerous Years: Climate Change, the Long Emergency, and the Way Forward* (Yale University Press, 2016), David Orr writes: "Rapid climatic change is more likely in a competing world of short-sighted nation-states inept in the arts of compromise and foresight." Spot on. He discusses a number of small efforts in building resilience at the community level, where affordable and sustainable modern marvels of innovation can be had reasonably cheaply to build unitary energy grids, water purification and sewage systems, food production, domiciles, and so on.

one thing, they have failed us entirely as climate chaos rages, their patchwork regulations grow more useless by the day in staving off the worst that's coming.

To me, the struggle to build self-regulating communities of common interest, in the end, may be the sum of its own incentive, the rewards uncertain. Our shires, in any case, can't hope to build walls high enough to keep the proverbial flood from seeping in. But if built literally today, on the bedrock of egalitarian principles of non-violence and inclusiveness, maybe these are the seedlings that will take root for our species and lead us into newer pastures. Calls to arm, in any case, won't work. The 1916 Easter Rebellion in Ireland is an exemplar of a misguided belief that armed struggle against empire can succeed. That May 1st, the city of Dublin lay in ruins, the first city in the modern era to be largely destroyed by modern military bombardment. The rebellion failed spectacularly. Today's neoliberal military capacity is simply too ubiquitous and overwhelming. Instead, our resilience and resistance must surely leaf out under their radar, our fists in the soil not in the troglodytes' faces, thus to ask forgiveness if we must, but not permission before we get to work. Some may call this hyper-local (fragmented?) path forward a "cop out" or some sort of effete and idealistic pipedream. So be it; frankly, I just don't much care. The success stories listed on the FIC website are their own proof. In any case, when the chaos finally arrives in our respective 'hoods, it's a no-brainer to suggest that the more cohesive and resilient our intentional social structures are, the more likely we are to make it through.

The take-away is this: How can we peer into our rampant civilization and see it at last for what it truly is? It's *all* of modern civilization we have to face, not its "bad" bits, as if the comforts of *our* homes are somehow the good bits. Right now, that piercing examination is all that's needed: truthfully, fully, no bullshit, no hope. If we seek communalism, the rest will follow. Our human-made world is in universal moral failure. To this end, in measured steps, my own creative, social, and political struggles move inward now and away from untenable macro-solutions promulgated by the techno-boosters in the interests of their empires and illusory techno-solutions. Surely it is time to germinate a new mythos to live by. Today it seems that thumb-tapped emojis on tiny screens are the new weapons of choice against "the man." I don't fool myself that weaning ourselves from all this is easy; it's difficult to put a stake into the backlit screen and the techno-absorption of our vampiric addictions.[64]

Here's a thought: What if we let earth-wisdom-women lead for a change? I mean us men letting go, and women stepping up? What if males learned the skill of deep listening? These won't change or stop climate chaos, still less save the planet, but if resilience is entwined into our beloved communities, into these our shires, women I am certain have the moxie, innate Earth knowledge, and hearth-centered management skills to give us the leadership we will all need to act nimbly enough, respond holistically enough, and be hard-headed enough to prepare for the worst, with a foundation of cooperation and resilience that is based on matriarchical systems. Here is as good a place as any to seek a safer harbor as our lives go forward into uncertainty.

I heard recently from a clan mother of the Ponca Tribe of Oklahoma. She asked if we might not turn the pervading darkness of the tomb we live in today to the darkness of the womb, birthing something new entirely? There's nothing new in what I am saying, but it's certainly worth pondering. It starts not with solutions, plans, or engineering blueprints, but with new myths to live by.[65]

---

64. Jenny Odell, of Stanford University, has written a witty book on this addictive weaning called *How to Do Nothing: Resisting the Attention Economy* (Melville House Publishing, 2019).

65. In his insightful book, *Pandora's Seed: The Unforseen Cost of Civilization* (Random House, 2010), Spencer Wells has a remarkably prescient chapter titled: "Toward a New Mythos" that delves into ancient soul-centers of mind to unearth new memes for humanity to live by, well outside the paralyzing paradigm of grinding consumerist civilization.

We need new stories of who and what we are as human beings, shorn of the neo-Hobbesian pablum of progress, of the exceptionalism of industrial civilization. Imagine instead with author and master of our myths, Joseph Campbell, who said: "People say that what we're all seeking is a meaning for life. I don't think that's what we're really seeking. I think that what we're seeking is an experience of being alive, so that our life experiences on the purely physical plane will have resonances with our own innermost being and reality, so that we actually feel the rapture of being alive."[66] Who can doubt that the known is inexorably coming to an end, whatever we individuals do. If we understand this profoundly, we then approach Mother Earth with a new realization of reverence, one that calls us to give Gaia our hard-won gifts of wisdom, with wind and stars in the high rigging, gifts that regenerate the living soil. Meaning is not intrinsic to Mother Earth. She only abides, without caring to manufacture meaning about herself, nor cares really what we do or don't do to her, as she's seen worse. It is we who bestow the meaning, we who must care. Start here, by knowing that we all live by the wrong parables of behavior in the West.[67] Maybe rectifying this complicity asks us to inquire what Gaia's own natural language of sustenance is, and by what mythos her ecosystems thrive. Indeed, what is Gaia's native language?[68] This author claims, with no hard-won evidence, I'll grant, that a true

---

66. *The Power of Myth*, 1988 documentary.

. Another good place to delve into this is with Jeremy Lent's book *The Patterning Instinct: A Cultural History of Humanity's Search for Meaning* (Prometheus Books, 2017).

68. To reaquaint yourself with the lost language of nature terms, I recommend British author Robert MacFarlane's delightfully lyric book, *Landmarks* (Hamish Hamilton, 2015) wherein he gives extensive glossaries of words long fallen out of common usage in English, words with loamy resonance, like "gallitrop," "barothy," "eawl-leet," and "copsy cyllog." He calls it "a word-hoard of the astonishing lexis of landscape and natural life." Robert Graves posits in *The White Goddess* (Faber & Faber, 1952), written over a period of only days, that Norse, Runic, and Gaelic alphabets (among other European scripts) were in fact references originally to specific trees, which in turn related to the ancient names of the gods and goddesses.

shire is best suited to language forth such a reverence, putting literal roots into the soil of Persephone's journey up from the underworld (seeds) and then harvest, in the autumn, her mother Demeter's fecundity (fruits, grains, squash, legumes, herbs) before Demeter's daughter must return to the underworld as hoarfrost grips the land. If done as a native tribe, there is powerful medicine and strength in this. Given half a chance, Gaia will respond. She always does.

What we're left with, when all is said and done, is to talk through all this honestly amongst ourselves. Begin at the dinner table. With our loved ones. At school. At church. With friends. Even at the checkout counter. Discuss. Ponder. Examine. Question. Probe. What might a holistic future entirely unbeholden to civilization actually look like? Then look in perfect silence at the stars with Walt Whitman. When was the last time we really did this? True wonder restores our holistic faith in a giving Earth, more than any climate march can, anywhere, at any time, with half the crowd checking their cell phones. The stars. Look, there's a beauty: Regulus sparkling in the breast of Leo, so prominent in the winter sky. And Rigel in Orion. Our modern electrified civilization doesn't know anything about the stars any more, except what the experts tell us. Instead, whiz-bang star apps supplant what the night sky was before it was reduced to digital pixels and light-pollution squinting. But tonight in silence just breathe it in. Be OK with how that loss of starlight (and all the rest) feels. Just breathe. Let us acknowledge in this silence our profoundest grief. Again, Francis Weller's *The Wild Edge of Sorrow: Rituals of Renewal and the Sacred Work of Grief*, is a marvelous tonic. Put your ear to that crying wound beyond all reckoning as we linger as a species in our solitary confinement, caged by our hubris as the world's apex predator paces the prison bars of our exceptionalism. Somewhere your shire awaits your leadership, if you but have the courage to start building it in a communion of discussion and dedication. You will discover the best blueprint for your shire, as my tribe will discover ours—with each budding sprout of new seedlings that emerge serving as the most wholesome answer.

So How Do We Make Sense of Our Own Senescence?

Here at last, after this long slog, we come to the final quiz. Chin up.

> Question: When is a retiree's bedtime?
> [Hint]: Three hours after he falls asleep on the couch.

While you're busting a gut on that, here's what I'm doing in my own retirement. After being Dean of Library Services for ten generally wonderful years, I stepped down in May 2016, with balloons and a farewell party attended by acolytes, acquaintances, academic deans, awkward allies, and even some antagonists among the library faculty and beyond. I may have gotten some sort of acrylic headstone to cap my illustrious career, memorializing years of service. In any event, I retreated thence to faculty, becoming a proud member of the California Faculty Association union, teaching critical thinking skills and information literacy to callow youths of whom I can only hope that one in five actually got any of it. Yet it's those one or two, let's call them diamonds in the rough, who made all the preparation, syllabi, and class scheduling worth it. Truly, I was just floored by the best of them, many juggling two jobs, three kids, broken homes, and sixteen credits. Hats off to youthful fortitude.

I never carried past regrets with me into my new work in library public services as a faculty member. I wanted to leave the profession, figuratively and in practice, embracing our students in the crucible of the classroom. I can think of no more noble profession than that of librarianship, whose entire credo is: May I Help You? How odd that in America today this ethic of active public service is so contentious and, in some circles, reviled. Retirement in any case is grand. But nothing could ever beat librarianship as a profession for someone like myself, so clearly once a deadbeat, to have come this far with such a sense of fulfillment.

One might well ask: how does one profitably spend one's time in retirement? Well, for one, I don't play golf so I've spared myself that dead end. And in any given year, I watch less than an hour of TV, maybe just the Oscars with my wife, so I've spared myself another waste of time. I don't do Twitter, Instagram, Snapchat, or Tik-Tok. And so on. Always an activist and no longer working nine-to-five, now with every hour of every day my own, so to speak, I do what I've always done: soldier on for environmental and social justice. The world doesn't seem to be improving any, so what else to do? I still dream of a bucket list I'll doubtless never fulfill as they all entail air travel. I'm inclined not to hop on planes anymore for my own pleasure. My bucket list is an odd assortment down offbeat tracks: I'd still love to quaff a frothy Mackeson stout at Durty Nelly's Pub, County Clare, Ireland; visit the South Sandwich Islands on a bitterly cold day; join a shamanic drum circle amid the remote Altai Mountains where the borders of Russia, China, Mongolia and Kazakhstan meet; see the Mount Klyuchevskya volcano on Kamchatka Peninsula above the boreal plain; see a Baobab tree forest (species *Adansonia*) anywhere; and perchance spend a week on the peculiar Isle of Socotra following the goats and looking out over the shimmering Gulf of Aden. I've never seen the Mediterranean, but the crumbling city of Venice and the dry hills of Orthodox Greece don't much draw me in. Though to set out across the Ahaggar desert by Bedouin camel train hence to sit alone on Mount Tahat and its haunting environs in the wastelands of the northern Sahara, that appeals.

As long as I remain in Fresno where the need for continued activism is so great, I have promised my colleagues in the trenches to soldier on with them pretty much as before, even as my wife and I plan a move back east. As an emeritus faculty I still serve as a coordinator with the university's "Sustainability Club"— what a great bunch of smart young adults! Fresno State ranks twenty-third (the bottom) out of all California State Universities in actionable sustainability programs, services, and infrastructure. Because of the inherent conservatism of our region and because the Democratic majority in the city is so poor and under-educated, the two combine to make the complexities of supporting a sustainable future for Fresno and environs a secondary priority. The students running the Sustainability Club have nevertheless done wonders to put before campus administration the dire need for our university to lead the Central Valley on sustainability issues in a region that will soon be hard hit by the exigencies of the climate crisis. What a welcome turn around.

Sometime in 2008, I started a men's gathering of five to seven gents of a certain age and inclination, who meet on a Monday evening every month, rotating as hosts, to drink whiskey and discuss topics loosely attached to a literary take on the day's news. In such camaraderie, we discover how we all deal with our own grief at a world gone utterly bonkers under the slash-and-burn idiocy of Trumpistan. For ten years we've been at it. We explore what intellectual pursuits lift us up, what battles we are fighting out in the streets. We discuss films watched, books read, pursuits followed that bring meaning to our varied lives. I have to say, this cadre of endearing reprobates, who would gladly admit they come for the whiskey as much as the gab, seem to be a modern mirror of those famous evenings of drinking and witty discussion held in the Turk's Head Tavern in 18th-century London when Joshua Reynolds, Adam Smith, Edmund Burke, Edward Gibbon, and Samuel Johnson and his biographer James Boswell met for scintillating conviviality. As Boswell recorded, they all met in a "constellation of talent that has rarely if ever been equaled."[69] I'd have to say our literary repartee is without doubt an (almost) equal. As each of us faces his own uncertain future, and creaky joints, one key to

---

69. Leo Damrosch's marvelous account, *The Club: Johnson, Boswell and the Friends Who Shaped an Age* (Doubleday, 2019) is a cracking good read.

keeping our sanity and spirits is to find in this gathering a sense of tribal communion, a covenant to be ruthlessly honest, dedicated to listening to each in turn, to the tales of our lives fully lived. Our communion is unapologetically male, but it won't be found online by paying for an Iron Man retreat with Robert Bly. Surely men in the West need something like this if only to fashion an abiding spiritual bond with other male cohorts, miles outside the sports arena or squash courts at the gym.

My deepest activist passion, as must be clear by now, lies in the realm of environmental work, with the climate crisis, earth justice advocacy, and natural resource oversight prioritized. While my disenchantment with the "environmental movement" grows apace, largely because it refuses to cut through the dominant "go green" consumerist myths of our destructive civilization, I have nevertheless found wonderful kindred spirits amongst its practitioners. My own hardwired dystopian misanthropy toward our collective futures is accepted by my comrades with amused forbearance. I'm OK with that. Surely, it's time for all of us to be grouchy and unreasonable with the status quo. Yet I've no mission to convert anyone. I have found the Sierra Club (SC) at the local level perhaps best suited to these mixed emotions of mine, given it has the broadest purview of environmental working groups statewide. So I sit on our local, active Executive Committee of the Tehipite Chapter of the SC as their liaison on air quality. I am also deeply involved, as a key representative of Earth Day Fresno, in creating a regional umbrella organization for all the thirty-five-or-so environmental groups in our region of the Central Valley. This scrappy faction of dogged activists seeks to bring an Earth Day Every Day ethos to the work that all the environmental orgs are doing. As an aside, my favorite environmental group today is the Center for Biological Diversity, arguably the hardest hitting and most litigious environmental group in the US at the moment. I serve as their Fresno liaison. Actually, I am active in too many arenas to touch on them all here; perhaps that participation will be, in the end, my parting gift and legacy for Fresno.

Today as I write, our very own *Fresno Bee* has a front-page article on homelessness in California, decried by Trump as if he even cares. It's a fair criticism, even coming from that grotesque blowhard. We're the wealthiest state in the country, fifth largest economy in the world, yet we have arguably the worst homeless crisis in America. In response, it was the vision of Fresno's most respected and prestigious architect, Art Dyson, to build an Eco-Village for the homeless. Here these troubled people could be given the simple comfort of a tiny home in an environment verdant as a garden. Rather than flimsy canvas barracks with bunk beds as proposed by the city, his Eco-Village Project seeks to provide a holistic approach to getting people without a home up and out and on their feet. I am a board member of this project myself. We now have a prototype property with a central home (the former domicile of a family) and a number of residential pods of different design in various stages of completion in the rear, where a large vegetable garden is planted. This demonstration village is known familiarly for the street it is located on, Dakota Eco-Garden, serving anywhere from nine to twelve residents. I like to think this is important work.

The language of science and political posturing which I've enjoined over the years now seems largely stale to me, both antiquated and inadequate to the tasks of survival ahead. Maybe the brave Native peoples I've worked with over the years are the true moral exemplars, from whom I might glean spiritual sustenance. I am fully aware that so-called doom-saying (which I am accused of), has beset alarmist Chicken Littles throughout history, from the Christian apocalypse, to Malthusian over-population, to moral perfidy during Prohibition, to peak oil, to limits on growth, to the ridiculous Y2K panic, and so on. Doomsaying is a veritable cottage industry. It's fair to say that scant evidence of any of these were remotely true. But these false prophecies all share one thing in common. They are based on misplaced *human* beliefs, fears, and prejudices, today stoked 24/7 by hyperbolic news cycles or from nut job pulpits. Climate chaos is not like these febrile claims at all. It is a chemical-physical-climatological phenomenon at a planetary scale. Humans may have triggered these physical developments through their rampant smoke-belching excesses, but the processes are now governed by strict thermodynamic laws of nature. Denial seems a sort of desperate act of avoidance. It's not so hard to fathom. How do we wrap our heads around something so vast, terrifying, and unwieldy when we know in our hearts civilization itself is first in line as a suspect? Here's the thing: our blue planet is now her own doomsayer, the raging heat storm has arrived, and she drives the schedule of disasters. Gaia has become Kali, the Goddess of Death and Destruction.

Extinction of humanity? I very much doubt it. But the end of our blithe bougie western lifestyles—for sure. So to stay sane I read a lot, mostly non-fiction and poetry. I play guitar, revel in music. I also spend as much time in the high Sierra as I can, exploring the last lost end of Forest Service roads where deer tracks take over into the pale hues of green manzanita. As the proud owner of a used pop-up Eurocamper van, the ease of camping now has me heading out into the wild blue yonder any time I choose. I work several hours most mornings in our garden, proud that wherever I have lived long enough to pot a plant, people have complimented me on how beautiful and relaxing my revered natural surroundings are, be they ever so humble. I've befriended all the squirrels in my immediate 'hood, who make their home in the camphor trees shading my yard. One young squirrel, while not quite brave enough to feed out of my hand, will happily eats nuts from a platter at my elbow. Then there's my favorite avian visitor (don't take offense Owlbert), a handsome little bird known as a black phoebe (*Sayornis nigricans*)—an insectivore who loves any spot above a fresh water pool where insects hover in the air on diaphanous wings, an easy meal. He's a black little chap, as his name would suggest, with a handsome white breast and tufted coal-colored crest. As flycatchers go, they're almost tame.

My wife and I also cook from scratch every day: fresh, organic, Mediterranean flexitarian cuisine. I am convinced that the contact of deep human relationships, regularly shared over healthy home-cooked meals, is without question the most direct path to a contented life that I know of. We have two other couples, dearest friends all, and once a month we rotate a dinner party that each couple hosts in turn. Our shared meals are a conscious effort to enjoy a home-cooked gourmet repast every month with deep companionship. This camaraderie has a tribal quality both deep and delightful, a small spark of how all humans lived ages ago as hunter-gatherers and sat around the campfire before civilization arrived to lock us all into separate electrified domiciles. Only being in the high outback, far above the alpine woods, beyond even the last wheel track, only those experiences in wilderness rival this communion.

Grandfather, Tell Me About Death

"If it weren't for your mother, and how it would embarrass her, I'd tie a plastic bag over my head tonight and have done with it," said my father with a forthright calmness that was, in retrospect, stoic. I have no doubt he meant it. Even at ninety-six, my father was always clear-eyed and unsentimental. By this time, he was bed-ridden and fed up with living a non-life in a hospice suite.

When he said this to me, I was sitting on a chair at his hospital bedside. It was 2012, and Dad was by this time entirely lame, his hands so weak he could hardly hold a spoon. Until the age of ninety, he had managed to walk with cane or walker, his mind ever alert, his heart strong, his humor intact. But finally, into his tenth decade, the curse of his neuropathy (a disease known as Charcot-Marie-Tooth for the three 18th-century doctors who identified it as "foot dropsy"), had gotten so bad he could not walk, dress himself, or even make it to the toilet on his own. I certainly felt his pain acutely for I, too, have Charcot-Marie-Tooth. Two aberrant peas in a mutated pod. To quote Jim Harrison, "After six decades, I've only recently understood the degree to which I'm my father's son."

It was not for me to supply my own father with a plastic bag to kill himself, much as I probably would have absent my mother, who at eighty-seven was still vigorous. The family doctor taking care of my father was also a WWII veteran, a medical colonel in the 80th Division of the European theatre, same as my dad. I was frank with this kind and elderly doctor about my father's sincere wish to end his life. We were sitting in the doctor's office at the time. He was certainly sympathetic, but…Connecticut is not a right-to-die state. Piss on them, I thought. My own dying, for one, will have nothing whatsoever to do with what the damn "state" does or doesn't say. Anyway, my rancor was hardly germane to my father's predicament. The doctor asked, "Can we speak frankly?" "Of course," I replied. "And it stays in this room?" "Of course."

He leaned forward and said in his plain Yankee diction, "From everything I've read and known firsthand about your dad, it's clear the man is a true war hero. His medals and citations speak volumes, and I was there myself treating wounded soldiers just like him, maybe your dad was even one of 'em, who knows. They were all faceless in their agony. He's also a damn fine human being. So yes, I'm damn well resolved I will cease [not ease] his pain with an increase in his medications." He left it at that. With tears of thanks, but no acknowledgement that he'd just committed to ending my father's suffering, I shook his hand and left. A few days later, after I'd flown back to Fresno, my dad was thankfully dead and out of his misery. He had led as amazing a life as anyone I know, equal to any of those I've read about such T.E. Lawrence (of Arabia) or even Marco Polo. My Dad's twenty passports that we found going through his things were stamped by countries from around the globe, twice over.

Who else but my father would have a tale of arriving in Winston-Salem one evening straight from Lima, Peru, when his DC10, headed for Idyllwild (now Kennedy) airport, was diverted by the northeast blackout of 1965? All passengers were given a berth at a cheap hotel near the Winston-Salem airport until the blackout sorted itself out. My father's seatmates were a frocked Catholic priest from Buenos Aires, and a black Brazilian circus performer, headed for Barnum & Baileys, who had a chained Capuchin monkey on his shoulder (allowed on the airplane, can you imagine!). Thirsty and grumpy, these musketeers struck out from the airport hotel by foot to have a drink. But this was the south in 1965. Winston Salem was locked up tight and uptight, though it was only eight o'clock. They found, at last, a lit diner and stumbled in. Asked Dad: "Where might we find a drink around here, ma'am?" Said the waitress sizing up my 6'5" Anglo father, the frocked priest with his cappello romano hat, and then, good grief, this black man with a monkey on his shoulder in Jim Crow south. "Winston-Salem is a dry county, thank the Lord. Y'all best get back from where ya come." This then is for my dad.

Blind Consolation

The sins of the father
pass on to son
or so it is assumed,
but none mention virtues
as a legacy, and so
each generation must find
its own blind consolation.
He is stooped now
at ninety-three, the fine
blue eyes seem milky white,
and from his wobbly shower
'tis I who must dress
his dear and wrinkled
now paltry stick-like bones.
Yet never once in all my years

of hapless vicissitudes
have I heard him
complain of any one thing.

For in this act
of strange contrition,
something I could never
have done when he was strong
and young as I am now,
I see in his wasting
lesions of the fading war,
scars of shrapnel from 1944,
bleeding near to death
in a snow drift full of terrified men,
more died of bitter cold at the Bulge,
than in battle, ragged sutures in slack folds,
in sagging skin and curled toes,
my own bent senescence
as I grow old.
I have inherited
his quick temper,
his restless mind,
but honestly, I lack
the nobility that exalts
his generous heart,
the balm of his undiminished
egalitarian charm.
I fetch the walker
and together, father
and son, we go out
to count the shooting stars
and walk the star strewn yard.

So where does our consciousness come from, I often wonder, and where do we go when we die? Not even Shakespeare, still less the Bible, is able to plumb that one. Talk of heaven and reincarnation just seems like so much blarney. I must say that 2012 certainly seemed to be the year of death, for a few months later my mom died also. She fell and broke her hip that fall after Dad passed and was rushed to a hospital for surgery. But even as she came out of anesthesia with high prospects of being ambulatory again, she made it clear as she lay in her recovery bed that she, too, didn't have it in her to carry on. She was in her late eighties and just didn't have the *umph* to go through with wheelchairs and months of rigorous therapy. My dear sister Carey called me one evening and said I should fly back east ASAP, as Mom was fading fast. I caught the next flight.

My wonderful mother's dearest friends had a limousine waiting to meet me at Newark Airport, and I was quickly whisked up into the quiet back roads of the Berkshires to the Sharon Hospital. It was probably close to seven pm when the driver dropped me off. In the dark room where my mother lay attached to her tubes, I saw my sister sleeping in the armchair beside her bed. Mom was largely out of it, heavily sedated with morphine. Carey awoke, saying that all day Mom had asked in an anemic voice: "Is Pete here? Is Pete here?" Finally, I was. Mom weakly clenched my hand when I finally bent over to stroke her head, telling her how much I loved her and that she'd been the most caring and wonderful mother, all true. There was always something deeply melancholic about my mother, as I've said. But to lose her quiet charm and wit in my life seemed unfathomably sad.

My sister had been at the hospital for hours. Since it would be she who drove us back to our parent's forlornly empty home, Carey said she was beat and had to get out into the evening air. Kissing Mom gently on the forehead, I said goodbye and we left. When we arrived back at my parent's home, glum and dejected in the gloaming, a nurse called and said Mom had died before we had even reached the parking lot, but twenty minutes before. She had hung on, obviously, to hear my voice one last time, to feel the depth of my outpouring of love and my enduring appreciation for what a truly remarkable woman she was. She was the kindest and most supportive woman I have ever known. Oddly, in the years since, it's Mom I miss more than my father, though he was the family charmer. She and I shared a deep melancholy about the world, unspoken as it may have been for us. Like so many women of her era, all her dreams had been thwarted under the prevailing patriarchy of the 1930s-1970s. Throughout her formative years, with the exception of the Rosy the Riveter excitement of WWII, all of my mother's desires—to become a classical pianist or to teach as a college professor—were nipped in the bud by the dominant miasma of Western misogyny. Instead, this marvelous woman was thrust into the narrowing cattle corral of being a housewife and a bearer of children for a booming economy and a gung-ho husband. One has to wonder how many magnificent female minds and creative geniuses were squelched under the regime of male dominance and hubris going all the way back to Eve. My mother certainly had been. Her IQ was 168.[70]

An Otter Came into Our Lives

When my wife Joy and I bought our home in Fresno from a delightful professorial couple from Fresno State, empty-nesters ready to downsize, in late fall of 2008 at the height of the recession, we both wanted to get a dog as our family companion. My wife and I are by choice childless. Why anyone with an ounce of sense would bring children into a world of climate chaos escapes me, but pop 'em out they do by the baker's dozen. It just seems so self-centered and cavalier. Anyway, Joy and I were barely unpacked in our new home when we went down to the local pound out on Rte. 99 to see if they had a pup we might take home. As we drove into the dirt-packed parking lot, we saw at least forty people in a line outside the shelter entrance, as if waiting for the doors to open. We parked and got out. But none of these poor people were there to find a loving pet.

Every single person in the line was there because they had lost their job, their livelihood, even their homes, in the 2008

---

70. Doubtless how I managed to edge into the triple digits myself.

crash. Two-thirds were crying without shame, each stroking their beloved pet, bereft at this further ignominy. These pets would now suffer an uncertain future at the pound because their cash-strapped owners had fallen so suddenly on hard times. Each and every one was returning to the pound their beautiful family pets on leash or in arms: mewling cats, sad-eyed dogs, ferrets, turtles, even a pet pig—the world's menagerie of loved critters being returned back to hell because their owners had been ground into the dirt by the rapacious collapse of our grotesque banking system. The people we saw that day obviously could no longer afford to feed a family pet, simple as that. It was heartbreaking, and as clear a snapshot of how venal and utterly vile the Wall Street world of greed and indifference is as you can imagine. For me, the entire financial crash was summed up in this single brutally depressing vignette played out in the SPCA parking lot in Fresno, California. We were all in tears, and the children! O heaven, such sadness in them as their confused, frightened pets remembered, through smell and sound, the grim fate from which their loving owners had once rescued them. The pound kill machine was on autopilot for about three straight years after the crash; they just couldn't keep up with the abandoned pets. We were one of but a handful in six months to want a new one.

 We walked in, unable to look anyone in their tear-streaked eye. It was just too painful. No, that's a dodge, it was just goddam fucking awful. Yet through that sad gauntlet, that's how we found Otter. His was the first cage we came to after instructions on how one is to identify the cage of a pet you might want. A kindly volunteer (bless them all with all my heart) opened the horrible piss-stained concrete cage and handed us this mangy, flea-bitten, scrawny runt of the litter into our arms. How utterly adorable he seemed nonetheless. Holding this wee pup in our cradled arms, we both knew: why look further? Joy was crying. I was trying to be more manly by holding back my tears as all about us young children wept aloud as their beloved pets were taken from them at the intake desk.

Joy and I had agreed beforehand we would name this sweet dog, whatever the sex, Otter. Otter was as sweet and beautiful a creature as could be found anywhere on Gaia's green Earth. Even with the mange, and the fleas he was only too happy to share with us, Otter was our prince. Apparently, you can't just take a pet home right away; the shelter has to neuter them, insert some sort of chip in them, and whatever else. But by week's end, cradled in Joy's arms, we brought our wonderful Otter home. I was a terrible parent at doggie school seeing how difficult it was for Otter to go through the paces of being a "trained dog"—whatever that is. I basically said to hell with it, since I didn't much care if he dropped out as a deadbeat like me or not. Joy struggled on, but I am glad to report that while Otter may not have learned all his Ps and Qs, he did learn by day's end to "Sit!" which IMHO is all a dog really needs.

It was for his anarchic spirit that I came in the end to love him so dearly. He grew into a medium-sized mutt, handsome in the truest sense of the word. He had a beautiful face, with deep brown eyes, and four paws each streaked with a touch of white. We guessed he was a black lab/border collie mix, with a lab's gentle nature but a border collie's enthusiasm. He was maybe three months old when we got him. He had the most perfectly proportioned body of any dog I've seen; even the vet admired his physique. I don't know if it's true of other dog owners' experiences, but I'd have to say that 90% of the people we met on the sidewalk while out walking him complimented us on how handsome he was, most often with, "Love your dog!" They would ask after his name, bending down and playing with him. If they stopped to engage, he was a big waggy love mutt, as most dogs are. In truth, Otter loved everyone and everyone loved Otter, even when I had my boss over to dinner and Otter shot his head right up her skirt and had a gander. "Bad dog," I said loudly, as inwardly I howled with mirth. My boss was not amused. The walks I took with him were always fiercely his walks. Wherever he wanted to go, we went. If he was eager, we walked fast; if he dawdled with endless sniffs, we dawdled. I was committed to making these times on the leash entirely his quality time. He was the prince of our 'hood, following his nose to his heart's content.

The love we share with humans, especially partners, spouses, and children, is always a compromise, involving concessions, negotiations, and a devil's bargain fraught with emotional roller coasters, wonderful highs, many lows, and inevitable stretches of stress through the middle ground. But a dog's love is the polar opposite. There is no compromise, no quid pro quo on their part, no devil's bargain. If we are kind enough to a dog, it will love us in return with all it's got, each and every day of its doggie life, no questions asked. Obviously that big-eyed adoration is precisely what gave early campfire wolf-mix hangers-on that edge to thrive among early hunter-gatherer humans, as feral wolves evolved into various sub-species of canid. That hangdog puppy look is now innate in all dogs, but as a survival strategy, it was, and remains, brilliant. And the damn dogs are still at it, aren't they, wheedling and whining their way into pretty much one treat, walkie, play date, or belly rub after another? But never once, if you love them, will they hold a grudge if these don't materialize. Never. Treat them well, and dogs are the epitome of pure faithfulness, protectiveness, and love, dignified and dogified. Joy and I both agree Otter made our marriage stronger by half. Lacking children as we do, he became an anchor of attention and affection that filled all gaps. He seemed so utterly without affect, selfishness, or judgment. Mary Oliver once wrote: "A dog can never tell you what [he] knows from the smells of the world, but you know, watching [him], that you know almost nothing." How little I knew of true love, without strings, expectations, and wants until Otter came into my life.

In time, our lives just turned naturally on the dog leash of Otter. All our travels became long car trips so he could be with us. All camping trips were thought through to maximize the things he loved, such as swimming in lakes or the sea, cool mountain trails, off-leash woodlands. Because of Otter, I came to explore every inch of the Sierra Nevada Mountains within a half-day radius of Fresno: beaten tracks, faint forest service roads, bush-whacked hikes over the burnt summer stubble of dry foothill grasses. I took him everywhere. And when in the evening the moon rose up above the icy peaks in the west where we camped by a still lake, after dinner I would gaze in perfect silence at Selene in her white raiment, Otter would lean against me and gaze into my face, his moon I guess, his wonderful dad. Was it adoration? I like to think so. Later, when I reluctantly got out of my sleeping bag to pee in the cold midnight of the mountainside, there would be Otter curled on his mat beside me. While I wandered out into the mystical night, gazing at the heavens, I'd relieve myself, only to find upon my return that a spot stealer was curled inside my warm and comfy down bag. There was nothing for it; once the warmth was stolen, he wouldn't budge an inch. Somehow, we both managed to squeeze in and sleep till dawn. Thanks for the fleas. Whatever my manifest failings, Otter always had the decency to forget, to forgive, and to find that sweet spot in his devotion to love me all the same. He was our beloved for ten straight years.

A few days before Christmas, 2018, I again took him to the upper Kings River, miles above the reservoir and dam, far beyond the last cattle grate, deep into the gorge country of the upper torrent. The waters are gin clear there and run fast and cold. Here by the river was our favorite spot, a sandy shoreline where a gnarled sycamore, shorn of leaves at mid-winter, embraced the air above land and water at river's edge with out-stretched branches. We had a lovely day together, tossing his ball, though I noticed he seemed tired. When we returned in the evening, he struggled out to the back yard and collapsed. I lay down with him until dark, worried sick. Finally, my alarm grew too great and I took him to a nearby 24/7 veterinary hospital. He could barely walk. The sleepy employees and the kind vet took him swiftly away on a gurney. I sat like a pillar of salt in the waiting room. At last, the vet returned. She had a worried look. She'd taken X-rays but was no expert in reading them, though she said there were similar-sized masses on each lung. She also had him on an IV to hydrate his body; she was worried his kidney function might be failing. How forlorn and scared the poor boy looked wrapped in his blanket on the gurney, needles in his pained leg. He looked at me with uncomprehending eyes. Joy and I were stunned to disbelief at his rapid decline, for just a few days before he seemed his old boisterous self. On Christmas Eve, about midday, the vet came into our little waiting room and said that none of Otter's vital signs had improved through the night. We asked about taking him home. She demurred, saying that would probably more painful for him. Do we then put him down? The sad look on her face said it all.

For the next half hour we tried, probably with scant success, to give our beloved Otter all the love we could muster in our despondent emptiness. Gloom was ours, which we nevertheless withheld from him since he too suffered, giving him glum smiles of wan comfort instead. He licked both our hands, his big brown eyes looking up with pained lack of understanding. Then it was time. I could not fathom the thought of his cremation in some sterile officious pet crematorium so I wrapped dear Otter in a blanket and took his stiffening body back up to the sandy bar that very day, there beneath the lovely sycamore, and buried him with his bowl, balls, collar, and dog biscuits for his journey into the earthen underworld. I spent hours gathering a few perfectly mossy rocks, those that in their beauty spoke to me of some childhood memory, and built for him a small cairn for a headstone. I also threw several packets of wildflower seed upon the moist soft soil and gave my blessing. With no shame, I wept the entire time.

When I returned a few days after Christmas to visit him, the Forest Service had tossed aside my gravestone cairn. I didn't mind. It's illegal to bury pretty much anything on federal lands. A few seeds, though, had already sprouted with the rain, rising on frail little stems in the moist earth—soft green shoots of yearning, each a slow mounting marvel of new life. Since that time, I have gone to sit under the beautiful sycamore tree pretty much every few weeks. I have found there my solace at the ruin of the world, there beneath the shading tree of old life, with its rootedness and patient dignity, where the murmuring river carries its secrets down into the far valley below, and my sorrows with it. I watch the redheaded mergansers (*Mergus serrator*) feed in the back eddies, and follow the bobcat paw prints until they vanish in the undergrowth. A lovely little water ouzel often comes to be my companion, hopping from rock to rock. Occasionally, a coyote trots by. A black phoebe, a favorite little bird, is always there to be my steadfast companion; he flicks out and back, picking off mayfly spinners coming off the flowing current. I am alone here, with not a soul for miles. And I am at peace. I always give thanks to Gaia while here for all the bounty that she has bestowed upon me, sometimes with my turtle rattle in hand. I am her vessel of gratitude; she is my sacred palimpsest. This is my true benediction to the end.

Spinner Fall on the Kings River

In the remaining light that is left
let us walk the leafy path
to the trout pool and watch
the spinners fall, the evening
glow in late December revealing
the dimpled ring of a rainbow
rising slowly from the gravel
where the currents sweep
the boulders round, then eddy back
in lazy circles, widdershins,

yellow foam bobbing under
gorgon roots, tendrils of a gnarled tree
old as Methuselah, older than
the night is wise, and wiser
in its bony silence than
all the wonder we onlookers
can muster in our starry minds.
Nearby, my departed dog slumbers
beneath the tree of light,
his eternal rest like my own
waiting for the far rains to fetch
us home, where I too will find
my bed in the shimmering, here
in the clear sunlight to come.

Index

Abbey, Edward, 335-7, 409
Adam (dog), 137-42, 144
army ants, 265-6
Arthur (May, friend), 199-200, 208, 211
Austin Cary Forest (Florida), 341-3

Bahamas (club), 217-9, 221-2
Baker, John, 294-7
Baptiste (club owner), 218-23
Basquiat, Jean-Michel *see* SAMO
Bioneers conference, 403-4
Black Flag, 209, 218-20, 222
Blackouts (band), 209, 225, 233, 309
Brahms, Johannes, 3, 43, 51
Brown, James, 226-9
Buckley, William F., 75, 109-10
Bukowski, Charles, 383

California State University System, *see also* Fresno State 369, 385-6, 388, 422
Campbell, Joseph, 418

Cardigan Mountain School (New Hampshire), 48, 50-3
Carruth, Hayden, 375-6
CBGB (club), 187, 204-5, 301
Chavez, Cesar, 382-3
Chelsea Hotel, 201-3, 206, 213
Churchill, Ward, 329-30, 339
Clapton, Eric, 2, 65, 84-5, 98, 107, 226, 261
Cohen, Leonard, 177-8
Colin (groundskeeper), 83-5, 94, 98, 261
Columbia University, 97, 204, 242, 296, 303, 312, 353
    Rare Book School, 288-9, 291
Copper Canyon Press, 372-3
Core Agricultural Literature Project (CALP), 322, 324-5
cormorant, 256-8
Cornell University, 195, 197, 322-4, 326-9, 331-2, 353, 370, 378-9
Counter-Quincentennial, 329-32
Crowley, Aleister, 38, 248

Drake, Francis, 194-5
Durland Alternatives Library (DAL), 327-8
Eco-Village Project, 424
Eisenhower, Dwight D., 14-6
El Salvador, 270-2
Emerson, Ralph Waldo, 280
Emilio (club owner), 220-1, 223
Eric (friend), 81-2, 94, 111

FALN (Las Fuerzas Armadas de Liberación Nacional), 39-45
Ferlinghetti, Lawrence, 374-5
Fleming, Ian, 34-5
Frankie (friend), 306-9
Fresno, CA, 379-84, 392, 413, 421-4, 431-2
Fresno State *see also* California State University System, 34, 365, 370, 378, 380, 384-88, 421-2
   Henry Madden Library, 384-6, 388-9
Friends of Jesse Morrow Mountain (Wa-ha-lish), 393-6

Gaia, 172, 256, 263, 344, 346, 397-8, 407, 409, 418-9, 425, 437
Galbraith, John Kenneth, 108-10
Gary (hitchhiker), 128-32
Gates, Bill, 401
gay(s) see homosexual(s)
golden toad, 263-4
Goldman, Emma, 149, 391
Gould, Stephen Jay, 197-8

Graham, Peter, 363, 368-9
Green New Deal, 402, 406
Greene, Graham, 292-3
Grolier Club, 292
Guevara, Ernesto "Che", 40-1
Gypsy (Prince Gypsy Lee), 86-94, 100

Hamill, Sam, 371-3
Harry, Debbie, 225
Hecate (cat), 251, 255
Hecate (goddess), 336-7
Henry Madden Library (CSU, Fresno) *see* Fresno State
homosexual(s), *see also* Papplewick, 202, 207, 230, 240, 301, 321
Huerta, Delores, 382-3
Hurrah (club), 207-8
Huxley, Aldous, 60, 64, 71, 159-60

Ithaca Gun Company Factory, 332-5

jays (birds), 165-6, 267
Jones, Grace, 230
Joris (friend), 99-102, 179-84, 187-9
Joy (Quigley, wife), 3, 379-80, 399, 421, 426, 431-6
Jung, Carl, 2, 252, 254

Kagan, Al, 312-3, 353
Kate (girlfriend), 201, 319-21
Kent School (Connecticut), 48, 60-4, 70, 75, 78, 97, 187
Kensho, 242-6, 254, 280-2
Kerouac, Jack, 60, 202, 281-2

Kingsnorth, Paul, 22, 400, 411
Kligman, Ruth, 209-10

Lanza, Robert, 242-3
Laughlin, James, 376-8
Laurie (girlfriend), 246-7, 250, 259-60
Lawrence, D.H., 9, 72-4, 139, 158, 274, 399
Leary, Timothy, 60-3
Levertov, Denise, 328-9, 376, 378
Liliana (girlfriend), 323-4, 332
Lilly, John C., 195
Linda (girlfriend), 78, 80-1, 85, 87, 94, 107, 110-16
Lipton, James, 299-300
Lopez, Barry, 284
LSD, 2, 60-1, 64-5, 83-4, 99, 112-5, 195

Mailer, Norman, 160, 297
manakins (birds), 264-5, 268
marijuana *see* pot
Martin, Tony (friend), 143-50
Matthiessen, Peter, 331, 383
Max's Kansas City, 204-6, 208
McDonald, Carey (sister), 3, 6, 8, 11-12, 15, 30, 34-5, 48, 55, 61, 274, 430
McDonald, David (brother), 3, 6, 8, 11-12, 22, 25, 30, 55, 61, 125, 159, 170, 217
  in Alaska, 127-8, 132-4, 152-5, 186, 189, 198
  boarding school, 16, 19, 34, 48, 60, 71, 97
  in Costa Rica, 260-4, 269
  in Florida, 339-41
  in Mexico, 119-22
McDonald, Edward D., Jr. (father), 9-10, 14, 16, 30-31, 4, 38, 44, 47, 69, 80, 91, 102-3, 106-10, 153, 257, 274
  concern for son's career, 1, 31, 77-8, 261
  death of, 426-30
  in England, 13-14, 102
  in Mexico, 53, 56-7, 59, 66, 111
  and music, 51, 318-19
  in South America, 33
McDonald, Edward D., Sr. (grandfather), 9, 18, 71-3, 139
McDonald, Ellen *nee* Robertson (mother), 5, 8-10, 12, 30-1, 34, 43-5, 51-2, 80, 102-3, 106-8, 204, 309, 426-7
  death of, 429-30
  early life, 9-10, 273-4, 431
  friends and acquaintances of, 43, 110, 178
  travels with, 12, 25-6, 122-3
McDonald, John (uncle), 261, 277
McGill University, 152-3, 173, 175-9
McKenna, Terrance, 257-8
McKibben, Bill, 391, 400, 403-4
Merwin, W.S., 279, 376, 378
mescalin, 64-5
Metropolitan Museum of Art, 285-7
Mexico City, 10, 53-6, 63-4, 66-69, 122
Michael (Nilluka, shaman), 240-2, 248, 278, 345
Miller, Henry, 60, 160, 272, 351

Modern Productions, 224-5, 229, 231, 305
Monk, Thelonious, 3, 178
Monteverde, Costa Rica, 260-3, 265, 270, 272
Montreal, ON, 152, 175-9, 184-6
Mort (barber), 302-3
Mount Toluca, 120-2
mushrooms, hallucinogenic, 191, 234, 236, 255, 257-8, 267, 268-9
Myrth, (Robin, friend), 246-51, 254-8, 278

Nanook (dog), 137, 139-41, 144
National Museum of the American Indian, 314-5, 330
New Directions Press, 351, 376-7
New York, NY, 10, 53-4, 173, 186, 198 205, 225, 285-7, 294-6, 310-1, 318-22, 329, 331
New York Public Library (NYPL), 74, 294-7, 303-4, 309-11, 313-4
Newton, Isaac, 245
Nirvana (band), 217, 224, 233, 389-90
Novoselic, Krist, 389-90
nuthatch(es) (bird), 340-1, 343, 346-7

Olsen, Jan, 323-5
Olsen, Wally, 325
Olympics
　Mexico City, 54, 56, 66, 71, 221
　Montreal, 178-80, 185-7
Order of the Dolphin, 194-5
Ormsby-Gore, Alice, 98

Ormsby-Gore, Francis, 98-100, 107, 261
Orwell, George, 60, 365, 404
O'Toole, Peter, 27-8
Otter (dog), 34, 432-7
owl(s), 167, 290, 336-7

Pancho's (club), 220-3
Panic Productions, 185-6
Papplewick (boarding school), 16-18, 27, 47, 274
　corporal punishment, 19-20
　food, 20-1
　homosexuality, 22-5
　loneliness, 30, 274
　teachers, 18-20
Patrick (friend), 137-42, 144
Penrose (friend), 81, 86-8, 92-3, 110
Pollan, Michael, 255, 258
Pop, Iggy, 1, 3, 205, 226, 231-2
porcupine(s), 235-6, 263, 268-9
pornography
　movie theater, 305-9
　Times Square, 302-5, 309
pot, 53, 55, 60-1, 76, 119, 123, 374, 386
Potawatomi, 314-5, 344-5
Pound, Ezra, 71-2, 125, 175, 377-8
Powell, Colin, 356, 364
Powell, John, 403-4
precognition, 35-37
Progressive Librarians Guild (PLG), 312-3, 328, 353, 355-6, 363, 396

Quakers, 262, 267

Random (Greene, friend), 246-51, 254-8, 278
Rezak, David, 366-8
Rollins, Henry, 218-9
Ryan, Christopher, 196, 253, 255

Sagan, Carl, 195, 197, 332, 334
SAMO, 200-4, 319
satori, 242, 281-3
Shakespeare, 27, 105, 429
Sharon (friend), 314-7
shire(s), 400, 412-7, 419
Showbox (club), 224-7, 229, 231, 302
Simon, Paul, 51, 54, 318-9
Society of Friends *see* Quakers
Solnit, Rebecca, 330
Somoza family, 75
spearpoint, pre-historic, 167-71, 256, 283
Spungen, Nancy, 205-6
Steinbeck, John, 160, 170, 382, 392
strangler fig, 263, 267-9
Studio 54, 207
Sugar Grove, 190-4
Sulzberger Sr., Arthur Ochs, 295-6
Syracuse University, 353, 363-5, 369 70, 375, 378-9

Taylor (friend), 179-85, 199-201, 203-5, 207-11

Tom (housemate), 254, 279-81
Tuchman, Barbara, 298-9
Tucker, Officer, 99-106
turtle(s), 315-6, 348
  rattle, 315, 345, 348-9, 437
  shell, 315-6, 343-6

University of Connecticut, Torrington, 123-6, 239
University of Florida, 339, 341
University of Washington, 170, 217, 277-8, 329

Vicious, Sid, 2, 202, 204-7, 302
Vietnam War, 38, 53, 61, 79, 124, 131, 148, 177, 284
Vogue (club), 1, 231-2
Volcán de Parícutin, 58-60
Vonnegut, Kurt, 124

Washington, DC, 187-9
Watson, Lyall, 36, 168-9, 249
Watts, Alan, 239
weed *see* pot
Weller, Francis, 241, 351, 419
Werner, Eric, 233-5, 309
Whitman, Walt, 83, 375, 409-10, 419
WolfBob (spirit), 250-5
Wright, Ronald, 197, 406
Wroxton College, 97-102, 107

www.ingramcontent.com/pod-product-compliance
Lightning Source LLC
Chambersburg PA
CBHW071355300426
44114CB00016B/2075